The Art-Work of the Future and Other Works

THE ART-WORK OF THE FUTURE

AND OTHER WORKS

By Richard Wagner

TRANSLATED BY
William Ashton Ellis

University of Nebraska Press
Lincoln and London

Manufactured in the United States of America

First Bison Book printing: 1993
Most recent printing indicated by the last digit below:
10   9   8   7   6   5   4   3   2   1

Library of Congress Cataloging-in-Publication Data
Wagner, Richard, 1813–1883.
[Literary works. English. Selections]
The art-work of the future, and other works / by Richard Wagner;
translated by William Ashton Ellis.
p.   cm.
Originally published as vol. 1 of: Richard Wagner's prose works.
London: K. Paul, Trench, Trübner, 1895.
Includes index.
Contents: Autobiographic sketch—Art and revolution, with intro-
duction—The art-work of the future—Wieland the smith—Art
and climate—A communication to my friends.
ISBN 0-8032-9752-1 (pa)
1. Wagner, Richard, 1813–1883.   2. Art—Philosophy.
3. Music—Philosophy and aesthetics.   4. Opera.   I. Title.
ML410.W1A1434   1994
700'.1—dc20
93-25288
CIP
MN

Reprinted from Volume 1 of *Richard Wagner's Prose Works*, published in 1895 by Kegan Paul, Trench, Trübner & Co., Ltd.

∞

CONTENTS

———

                                                                    PAGE

TRANSLATOR'S PREFACE vi

AUTHOR'S INTRODUCTION TO THE COLLECTED WORKS xv

NOTE TO SECOND EDITION xxi

———

AUTOBIOGRAPHIC SKETCH 1

ART AND REVOLUTION, WITH INTRODUCTION 21

THE ART-WORK OF THE FUTURE 69

WIELAND THE SMITH 215

ART AND CLIMATE 249

A COMMUNICATION TO MY FRIENDS 267

———

APPENDIX 393

SUMMARY 397

INDEX 409

TRANSLATOR'S PREFACE

IN view of the curious range of theories erroneously attributed to the Bayreuth master, the need of a complete English version of Wagner's Prose is obvious. A passage here and there has often been dragged from its context, maltreated, and made to point a moral with which, in the original, it had nothing whatever to do; while, on the other hand, the most valuable commentaries upon his own artistic works lie buried in the native German of Wagner's writings, because folk have been scared away from reading them by the report that his style is 'impossible.' To the latter subject I shall presently return; meanwhile as an example of the phantom theories, I may adduce the following from an exhaustive article on *Poetry* in the last edition of the *Encyclopædia Britannica* (1885): "We must be cautious how we follow the canons of Wagner and the more enthusiastic of his disciples, who almost seem to think that inarticulate tone can not only suggest ideas but express them—can give voice to the *Verstand*, in short, as well as to the *Vernunft* of man." In this instance, the learned author 'would seem' to have covered his flank by his "almost seem"; but he uncovers it again by proceeding: "If it is indeed possible to establish the identity of musical and metrical laws, it can only be done by a purely scientific investigation; it can only be done by a most searching inquiry into the subtle relations that we know must exist throughout the universe between all the laws of undulation"; and, having thus introduced a new factor, he deduces the conclusion: "But when we find that Shelley seems to have been without the real passion for music, that Rossetti disliked it, and that Coleridge's apprehension of musical effects was of the ordinary nebulous kind, we must hesitate before accepting the theory of Wagner." To *which* "theory" Mr Theodore Watts refers, is somewhat unclear; but neither that of music's "giving voice to the *Verstand*," nor that of the "*identity* of musical and metrical laws"—if the latter term applies to poetry—has ever been advanced by Richard Wagner; nor does it seem likely that the "laws of undulation" will throw much light upon the question.

I have adduced this author as an example of what havoc even an unprejudiced critic may innocently play, with the views of a man whose theoretic works are but little known. If, however, I had chosen to cite from the articles of those to whom the name of Wagner is *anathema maranatha*, I might have brought forward quite a startling collection of the products of ignorance. This, however, would be a little too much waste of precious time. I therefore hasten on to a few remarks on the Prose-works themselves, and the order I have chosen for their appearance.

Something like 10 years ago, when Richard Wagner died, the world suddenly awoke to the fact that he had been the greatest composer of dramatic *music* ever born. During the past decad, it has gradually been opening its eyes to the genius displayed in his dramatic *poems*. Now, in Germany at least, there is beginning to arise a conviction—I mean, outside the circle of Wagnerians— that as a philosopher and æsthetician he is a thinker to be taken seriously, and whose opinions, whether they be eventually accepted or not, are pregnant with deep meaning. An attempt has even been made—in an earnest and impartial work by Dr Hugo Dinger, entitled *Richard Wagner's geistige Entwickelung*—to trace the mental evolution of the man by the light of his writings, and to ascertain his standing toward philosophers such as Hegel, Feuerbach and Schopenhauer. The second volume, which is to deal in detail with the latter question, has not as yet appeared ; so that I am unable to say, as yet, with what success the task has been accomplished. But the phenomenon is in itself significant, and I trust will prove an incentive to English thinkers to take up so interesting a problem.

In the accompanying volume most weighty material for such an inquiry will be found, for it embraces two of the chief contributions of Richard Wagner to the store of art-literature, namely *The Art-work of the Future* and *A Communication to my Friends*, and by the juxtaposition of the *Autobiographic Sketch* and the *Introduction to Art and Revolution* affords a glimpse into periods of development separated by a whole generation. The style of Wagner's prose—at least, so much thereof as I have been able to distil into the English—will also be seen in its progress from terse and almost journalistic phrases, in the *Sketch*, through the somewhat involved, but epigrammatic sentences of the *Art-work* to the calmly-flowing periods of the two *Introductions*. The same earnestness of thought, however, may be traced throughout the whole volume, mingled with an occasional dash of that quiet, half-serious humour which one would expect from the author of *Die Meistersinger.*

To touch upon the individual contents of this book, I will begin with the *Autobiography.* As will be seen on page 2, this was originally written for a German journal (1843) and was intended as a mere collection of notes which the editor, Heinrich Laube, was to expand into a more connected history; in the editorial notice that accompanied the *Sketch,* Laube referred to the surprise it would probably give Wagner, to find his notes produced without elaboration. This will account for the touch of jerkiness in what is otherwise a lifelike picture.—For my own part, I have chosen this work, and the *Introduction to the Collected Edition,* from Vol. I. of the Ges. Schr., as forming the best opening for a series of writings which the author collected in order to give a portrait of his Life and thinkings. As prefigured on page xvi, there is still a much longer Autobiography to come; but as that is not likely to be issued by the Wagner-heirs for some years yet, the present *Sketch* and its supplement, the *Communication,* must satisfy our desire to know what Richard Wagner thought of himself. In order to keep such information together, I have also departed from the order of the Ges. Schr. in printing the latter work before its actual predecessor, *Opera and Drama.* These two, however, were really stable-mates, and, as is evident from page 396, it was a mere accident that the one left its stall before the other. Another reason for my including the *Communication* in the present volume, was furnished by the inconvenience of cutting *Opera and Drama* into two separate portions, as in Vols. III. and IV. of the Ges. Schr. While on the topic of arrangement, perhaps it will be as well to justify my action in leaping over the works that appeared between the *Autobiography* and *Art and Revolution.* In acting thus, I was governed by the desire to lose no time in bringing out the real substance of Wagner's art-theories, which found their first unfaltering voice in the work last-named. To have included the prose of Vols. I. and II. of the Ges. Schr. in this opening volume would have involved a delay of two years, for they occupy a space as large as itself. I therefore deemed it best to reserve them for the last—probably the sixth—volume of this series, as " Wagner's Earlier Works "; i.e. to delay their publication, at least in the present form, for some ten years or so. The chronological order shall not be broken again, excepting for the omission of the poems, as indicated by the title chosen: "Richard Wagner's *Prose* Works."

Art and Revolution and *The Art-work of the Future*, which form the bulk of the following book, mark a distinct epoch in Richard Wagner's thought, and, with *Opera and Drama*, stand almost apart from any of the prose writings before or since. They were written under the immediate influence of the events of 1849 in Germany, Wagner's own share in which I have already attempted to outline in a little book called "1849. A VINDICATION." The disastrous outcome of the Dresden revolt had driven Wagner from his native country, and sent him to Zurich, thence to Paris, and back again to Zurich, within the space of a couple of months. What with his own revolutionary ideas and what he must have heard in Paris, his mind was in a state of ferment, the only direct *artistic* product whereof was the dramatic sketch, *Wieland the Smith*. But the poetry that could not find an immediate outlet in drama, has overflowed into these two remarkable essays; of which the first is purely a poem, in everything but form. Scarcely was *Art and Revolution* published, when Wagner seems to have settled down to a 'good think' about the artistic problems that there had sprung into life; the results of his thought were embodied in *The Art-work of the Future*, conceived and executed within the incredibly short period of two months.

With regard to *The Art-work of the Future*, and perhaps *Art and Revolution*, there is another factor that must not be lost sight of, namely the influence of Ludwig Feuerbach. I say, perhaps *Art and Revolution*, for there is no proof that Feuerbach had dawned upon Wagner's horizon before the writing of the *Art-work*. The latter work was originally dedicated to the Bruckberg philosopher (see Appendix), but Art and Revolution was *not*. Again, the first appearance of Feuerbach's name, in Wagner's letters, occurs in one to Uhlig of January 1850, *after* both these works were published. The next mention of Feuerbach is in June '50, when Wagner asks Uhlig to get Wigand to send him the complete works of that philosopher; Wigand being their publisher, as also of Wagner's own two latest works. Now the third edition of Feuerbach's *Wesen des Christenthums* appeared in 1849 as the last volume of a series of his complete works, and it, and it *alone*, bore

an advertisement announcing the contents of the earlier six, which
had been in process of reprinting since 1846.   It would therefore
seem most likely, that Wigand, being at work on the printing of
Art and Revolution, brought the *Wesen des Christenthums* under
Wagner's notice—we all know those nice little circulars one gets
from one's publisher every now and then—and that it was the
advertisement on its fly-leaf that led Wagner, as soon as he had
digested the book, to ask for more.   It certainly is significant,
that it was not until the autumn of '49, i.e. *after* the writing of
Art and Revolution, that the Feuerbachian phraseology crept into
his letters to Liszt, and that on Sep. 16, '49, in the same letter
to Uhlig in which he talks of writing the *Art-work*, he uses words
which are almost literally those I have quoted on page xi from
an *early* chapter—the third—of the *Wesen des Christenthums*.

In any case, there is everything to disprove the theory of any
personal intercourse between Wagner and the philosopher of
Bruckberg ; in fact, it was only on the suggestion of Wigand that
he wrote to Feuerbach at all, even after dedicating the *Art-work*
to him.   This letter was written about the end of August 1850,
and elicited an answer, as to which Wagner tells Uhlig on Sep.
20, '50 : "Within the past few days, I have had a great joy.
Feuerbach has written to me, and once again I have had the good
fortune to experience what it is to have to do with a *thorough*
fellow.   There is no 'yet' and 'but' about him ; he says straight
out what he had already written to Wigand at Leipzig—who, however, told me nothing about it—namely 'that he failed to understand how there could be *two* opinions about my book ; that he
had read it with enthusiasm, with delight, and must assure me of
his fullest sympathy and warmest thanks.'"

It is pretty clear, then, that Wagner's acquaintance with Feuerbach's views must have been somewhat slight, even at the time
when he wrote the *Art-work ;* and a comparison with the *Essence of
Christianity* will show any one, who wishes to pursue this inquiry
farther, how few of Wagner's tenets were derived therefrom.   The
chief signs of any borrowing of ideas are exhibited by the plentiful
use of the terms to which the Bayreuth master has referred on
pages 25-27, and of a few others such as "Necessity," and the
"Species" (see my Footnotes to pages 260 and 276-7), together
with the materialistic thread that forms so strange a contrast with
the general texture of the work.   To this, or a kindred temporary

influence we must also ascribe the mistrustful tone (altogether absent from *Jesus of Nazareth*) employed toward Christianity, a tone which was the fashion with Feuerbach and his young-Hegelian colleagues. Partly from this source, and partly from his disgust at the general social system, Wagner seems at that time to have been a little inclined to sacrifice the ideal substance of the Christian religion, in consequence of a revolt against the hypocrisy of many observers of its forms. But that it was merely a sacrifice prepared by the reason, and not offered by the soul, is evident from the high place that he gives to Love in his philosophy.

Herein again, we have a hint as to the point of time when the writings of Feuerbach brought their troubling influence to bear upon Wagner's mind, for both in his *Jesus of Nazareth* and in *Art and Revolution* (notably page 38, line 2) he makes Jesus Christ the teacher of Love, or to use a wellnigh lost expression, Lovingkindness, thus distinguishing the founder's Christianity from that of his later followers; whereas Feuerbach says, "Love is only the *exoteric*, Faith the esoteric doctrine of Christianity." Now in the *Art-work*, though Love is still upheld as the ideal governor of the world, we hear little of the precepts of Jesus, but much of the selfish Faith of the Christian. The same conclusion, as to the date of this first contact, may be drawn even more forcibly from Wagner's use of the Feuerbachian terms "necessity" (*Nothwendigkeit*) and "need" (*Bedürfniss*). The latter does not appear at all in *Art and Revolution*, and the former is there only used three times, in the sense of the Greek Fate; but on the very first page of the *Art-work* we have these terms employed in a sense which, though its substance foreshadows the 'Will-to-live' of Schopenhauer, yet takes its form from Feuerbach's "Whence, then, is the world? From *Want* (Noth) is it, from *Need*, from *Necessity*. But not from a necessity which lies in *another essence* (Wesen) *cut off from itself*—which is a sheer contradiction—but from its *most own, most inner necessity, from the necessity of Necessity;* since without the world there is no Necessity, without Necessity no reason and no understanding."

Having thus derived two abstract terms from an author who professed to abhor abstractions, Wagner has developed them at length, in *The Art-work of the Future*, in a fashion that puts their originator (?) quite in the shade; as he says on page 25: "I had borrowed various terms of abstract nomenclature," which were "prejudicial to my clearness of expression." But the truth is, that he had sought for a hand-hold in the system of a philosopher who betrays an utter lack of system; for Feuerbach's works are brilliant chiefly by their paradox : detached sentences of his read extremely well—in fact, he is at his best in his collection of scattered aphorisms—but if one thinks back a little, after reading one of his books, one can only resent the having been treated to an exhibition of syllogistic somersaults. The brilliance of display was just the kind to temporarily attract Wagner, in the dearth of more solid entertainment; but its glitter seems to have soon faded for him, and there is little wonder that he should later have regretted that one of his most important works was larded here and there with terms which, however thoughtful in their use, could only prove a stumbling-block. Not that the *Art-work* depends at all upon this "intercalation" for its real structure : for Feuerbach was almost solely occupied with contra-theology, and Wagner with art ; but Wagner has laid among the courses of his bricks an occasional string of wooden ' binders,' and these, decaying in the lapse of time, have almost imperilled the building. Yet it would be easy to remove these layers gently, and leave the edifice quite unimpaired. The Bayreuth master, however, has rightly chosen to perpetuate them as they stand.

Had space permitted, I should have liked to point out the deep spirit of true religion and warm humanity that breathes through all these works of Wagner, despite their occasional wrestlings with formalistic dogma ; but this, after all, is only a Preface, and I have still a word to say on the *Communication*.

If this *Communication to my Friends* had been penned as a fiction, it would probably have long ago been greeted as one of the most notable psychological studies ever written, and have found a place in every library. But it is only—a true account by an artist of the stages which his own mind passed through in his creations ! Perhaps some day this fact will make it the more valuable in the eyes of the reading world. The most remarkable of the features of this work, is the boldness that prompted an artist to stop short in the middle of his career, and tell the world that was scoffing at him, what he felt, and how he worked. Men before him have done this at the finish of their course, but—I think—no one else in its midst. And this it is, that makes it so important; for we here have an auto-photograph, taken at the 'psychological moment' of a man's life; we see him in the weighing-room, just before getting into the saddle for the race of the *Ring des Nibelungen*. From such a work the word 'self' is inseparable; but the extraordinary thing about it, is that the author has had the daring to write of himself from an 'objective' standpoint, to record his weaknesses, and his faculties too, as though he were another man. No other eyes have ever seen Wagner, the man and artist, so clearly as he has seen himself in this *Communication*.

I now must say a word upon my own share in the present volume. It would be affectation, to pretend that the translation has not been an arduous task; but I can honestly say that it was not such by reason of the unwonted difficulties often alleged to exist in the original. Any one who has a moderate knowledge of German, and is accustomed to thinking a little deeper than the ordinary light literature of the day, can read Wagner's prose in the original, and profit by it. No, the same difficulty exists in every attempt to render faithfully and readably into English any of the more serious products of German literature. However rich our own language may be, we have to depend, for philosophic and æsthetic terms, too much upon words of Greek or Latin derivation; whereas the German classic has at his disposal words that have sprung from the spirit of the language, words that, however philosophically used, have still a direct relation with what may be called concrete—as opposed to abstract—modes of thought. The difficulty, therefore, is to translate these expressions into terms that shall not be so conventional as to rob them of their vital play of meaning. I need only instance the words *Stoff, Gestalten, Trieb, Drang, Stimmung, Empfindung, Wesen,* and *Erscheinung,* to give to any German scholar an idea of the hindrances to which I allude.—Again, we English are impatient of delay in getting to the end of a sentence; we object to waiting for the qualifications of a thought before we reach the thought itself. And thus it is, that we lend ourselves so often to misquotation: the one sentence of the German is split by us into two or three, whilst the conscience of the quoter is generally satisfied by 'a full stop.' To give a homely example: an English mother might tell her child "You may go into the garden," and off runs the child without waiting to hear the finish—"after dinner"; whereas the German mother would be more cautious, and say "After dinner into the garden mayst thou go"—the child is disappointed, but learns to restrain its impulse. Thus, in translation from German into English, one has always to be on the look out for the saving efficacy of a *comma*. I may say that that comma is the most difficult of all to translate; it is used in another fashion to ours, and often represents our semicolon. So one has to stand over one's rough transcript with a pepper-box of commas, semicolons, colons and full stops, ready to spice it up for the English table.

As to the *matter* of the translations, I have omitted nothing of the original, excepting one little clause of a sentence in the "Art of Sculpture." On the other hand, I have given in the Appendix the *variants* between the Ges. Schr. and the original editions of those works contained in this volume—omitting, of course, such as were mere changes of punctuation, spelling, or absolutely synonymous words. For the discovery of these variations I have chiefly to thank the book of Dr Hugo Dinger already referred to, though I had previously unearthed a few, notably the Dedication to Feuerbach (which led to my investigation of his intellectual relationship to Wagner, before Dr Dinger's book was printed), and the additional footnotes from the original editions which I have inserted under the text in their proper places. In order further to assist the reader, I have drawn up a Summary and an Index, neither of which aids exists in the German; though Glasenapp's *Wagner - Lexicon* and *Wagner - Encyclopædia* afford a splendid assistance to a general survey of the whole domain of Wagner's prose.

I have only in conclusion to thank for their encouraging words those members of the Press who have already welcomed the appearance of these translations, and to state that the next volume will consist of *Opera and Drama*, to be brought out in the same serial form, and therefore to be completed, if all goes well, by the end of 1894.

WILLIAM ASHTON ELLIS.

LONDON, *December* 1892.

AUTHOR'S INTRODUCTION TO THE COLLECTED EDITION OF HIS WRITINGS (*Gesammelte Schriften*).

SEEING that the literary remains of noted musicians have repeatedly been collected and published after their death, I suppose that the first thing I ought to do, in the collected edition of the products of my authorship, is to justify myself in face of the reproach, that I still live. What in their case has been welcomed as an act of piety, might easily, in mine, be reckoned to my vanity. Whereas those happy dead cared nothing, what might be thought of their literary jottings: it seems that I am busied for the earnest consideration of my own. It would be hard for me, to contradict this. Whosoever thinks necessary to read into this confession the avowal of a weakness of my artistic works, is welcome to follow such need to his heart's content; for, in the long run, if my works do not speak out clearly for themselves—those of my art, by correct performances, and those of my literary labour, by being properly understood—it does not really make much difference whether folk think necessary to lay my weakness in the one direction or in the other.

Whether the most unusual efforts will succeed in helping my artistic works to a true life in the nation's midst, by the constant guarantee of correct representations, I leave to the decrees of Fate; yet I believe that I shall supplement these efforts, if, on the other side, I take care that at least the labours of my pen shall share in an advantage common to all literary products, that of lying clearly and comprehensively before the public. This care has naturally come to me since I have observed around me a growing earnestness of interest in my art-writings, while at like time I could not but see the disadvantages inseparable from the fact, that in these writings I have not stepped before the public in well-calculated continuity, but at very diverse times and under the most various of promptings to their composition. Since, however, even the most heterogeneous promptings have always woken in me the *one* motif, which lies at the bottom of my whole, howsoever scattered literary exertions, I here felt the need of a carefully-ordered and complete reproduction of my addresses (*Mittheilungen*), whereof many have stayed altogether unknown, and the most have been only regarded in that fugitive light which attaches to every "Brochure."

The wish to arrive at such completeness provided me, again, with a sort of psychological method of arrangement, by help of which the sympathetic reader might come to see how it was that I lit, at all, upon the path of penmanship. Although, eventually, a correct account of my life itself would be the only thing that could give full information hereon, yet for the present I have seized on the advantage of a chronological arrangement, in accordance wherewith my essays will be laid before the reader in the order of their origin. By this plan I have also won two other privileges, in virtue of which I hope to gain a gentle handling at the judgment-seat both of our art-philosophers and of our poets by profession. To wit, I have escaped the temptation to cobble together my piecemeal art-writings in such a fashion that they should assume the appearance of an actual scientific system—a course that might easily have been treated by our professional æsthetes as unblushing impudence ; while on the other hand, seeing that I was making up a kind of day-book of all my labours, I could thus strew-in my poems in their proper biographic place, instead, maybe, of binding them up in a separate volume—a proceeding that would certainly have roused the contemptuous wrath of our professional poets, and drawn down on me the charge of placing my "opera-texts" on *a level* with poesies in which the music (as in that provincial performance of the *Dame Blanche*) is replaced by a "lively dialogue and a choice diction."

What circle of readers it is, that I now shall have to stand amidst with this collection, cannot but be of the greatest moment to me, not only for the verdict on my own exertions, but also for that on the elements which are coming to the front in the present stage of our German cultural evolution. People have begun to take me seriously, in a sphere where nothing is really taken seriously : namely in that of our scientific-posing *Belles lettres*, in which philosophy, natural science, philology, and especially poetry are handled with a flippant wit, excepting when an incomprehensible reason exists for some measure of unconditional recognition. I have noticed that this system of valiant calumny bases itself on the assumption that the writings and books reviewed are not read by the critic's readers. On the other hand, those persons on whom stage performances of my dramatic compositions had worked with a stimulating effect, felt prompted to an earnest reading of my writings. Many of these hearers, however, have not been able to conceive why I should write essays on an art which I did best to practise as an artist. Only in quite recent times have I met several persons, and especially among the younger generation, who have understood this thing too: why I wrote about my art; for they consider that they have found in my writings a better explanation of the problems started by my artistic creations, than in the emissions of such who themselves can make nothing in the way of Art. Here one or two have come to the belief, that he who understands a thing, can also speak best about it; as, for instance, that he who himself knows how to conduct, is also the best man to show others how to conduct.

Now it would be interesting, if the verdict upon Art should fall back into the hands of those who understand Art: whereas the peculiarity of our present course of education has brought round the view, that the judgment on a thing must come from a quite different domain to that of the thing itself; forsooth, from the "*absolute Vernunft*," or mayhap from the "self-thinking Thought." The analogy has been derived from our modern State, whose political evolution has brought this curiosity with it, that a states-man has to justify his success in the eyes of those who before had never dreamt of its possibility, and to submit his measures to the judgment of those to whom it must be made clear for the first time, on such occasions, what the whole matter is about. As in our case, it is a matter of Music, about which every one has his own impression, often the most trivial—the writer Gutzkow, indeed (since the time when the art-historian Lübke appears to have thoroughly ruined his phantasy) for the most part a quite unseemly—one must perceive at once that there can be really no question of a *judgment* on the part of those who do not under-stand Art; and one must either strike Music completely off the list of arts, or admit that it first becomes an *art* by the very fact of its being dealt with in artistic fashion by those alone who understand music.

Often was it painful to myself, and often bitterness, to have to write about my art, when I would so gladly have listened to others on it. When finally I accustomed myself to this necessity, because I learnt to comprehend why others could not say the thing that was given to just me to say, neither could it but in time grow ever clearer to me, that in the insights which had been opened up to me by my own art-doings there dwelt a wider meaning than is to be ascribed to a merely problematic-seeming artistic individuality. Upon this path I have come to the view that the real question concerns an entire re-birth of Art, which we now know only as a shadow of its genuine self; since it has quite deserted actual Life, and is only to be discovered in a scanty stock of popular remains.

Whoever will permit himself to be led by the hand of one who has become clear upon this point—not on the path of abstract speculation, but guided by the impulse of direct artistic Need,— to be led to a hopeful outlook upon the possibilities reserved for the German spirit, I trust will not be vexed to wander with me over the path on which I reached that outlook. For his assistance, I have placed my writings of every kind so together that he can follow me on every side of my development. He will thus perceive that he has not to do with the collected-works of a Scribe, but with a record of the life-activity of an Artist who, disregarding *schema*, sought in his art itself for Life.

But this Life is naught else than the essence of *true Music*, in which I recognise the only real art of the Present, as of the Future; for it alone will give us back again the laws for a genuine wider Art. So is it; and every one must recognise this fact with me, so soon as ever he compares the effect upon the souls of all, of the only living power among us, Music, with that of our literature-poesy of nowadays, or of any of the plastic arts, which now can only borrow foreign *schemata*, for parleying with our so deeply sunken modern life. But in Drama glorified by Music, the Folk will one day find itself and every art ennobled and embellished.

This as greeting to the friendly reader!

TRIBSCHEN, near Lucerne, July 1871.

RICHARD WAGNER.

NOTE TO SECOND EDITION.

THE first edition of this first volume of Richard Wagner's Prose Works, as rendered into English, was issued to Members of the Wagner Society (London Branch) and to Subscribers, in serial parts of 32 pages each, during the years 1891 and 1892. Its issue in book-form to the public, however, did not take place until the end of January 1893, and the stock is already exhausted; so that Wagnerians may congratulate themselves upon the existence of a far more active interest in the master's philosophic and artistic thought than his opponents had foretold, or than we ourselves had dared to hope. In a like regard I may record the fact that, owing to a widely expressed desire on the part of the Press, the publication of the remaining volumes has been hastened, with the result that volumes ii and iii are already in the public's hands, and present indications warrant me in trusting that *their* second edition, also, will be necessary at no distant date.

As to the matter of the present edition, it has been reprinted from the 'stereos' taken from the first, and therefore differs in no material respect. Beyond the correction of the errata notified on page 396 of that first edition, the only alteration is that of the page now directly under the reader's eye. In the original edition it was occupied by the following Dedication, which I now have the honour to repeat :—

"To Frau Cosima Wagner this English rendering of Richard Wagner's Prose Works, construed under the shelter of the London Branch of the Wagner Society, is respectfully dedicated by the translator, in the hope that the outcome of his labours may in some small measure help to further that great Work of Bayreuth which She has inherited from her husband and is so devotedly carrying forward."

WILLIAM ASHTON ELLIS.

LONDON, *February* 1895.

AUTOBIOGRAPHIC SKETCH.

"AUTOBIOGRAPHISCHE SKIZZE"

(Bis 1842).

This sketch of his life, down to the year 1842, *was drawn up by Wagner, at the request of his friend Heinrich Laube, for publication* (1843) *in a journal edited by the latter, and called the* "Zeitung für die Elegante Welt." *The editor then prefaced it by the following remark :—*

"*The storm and stress of Paris have rapidly developed the Musician into a Writer. I should only spoil the life-sketch, did I attempt to alter a word of it.*"

TRANSLATOR'S NOTE.

AUTOBIOGRAPHIC SKETCH.

Y name is *Wilhelm Richard Wagner*, and I was born at Leipzig on May the 22nd, 1813. My father was a police-actuary, and died six months after I was born. My step-father, Ludwig Geyer, was a comedian and painter; he was also the author of a few stage plays, of which one, "*Der Bethlehemitische Kindermord*" (The Slaughter of the Innocents), had a certain success. My whole family migrated with him to Dresden. He wished me to become a painter, but I showed a very poor talent for drawing.

My step-father also died ere long,—I was only seven years old. Shortly before his death I had learnt to play "*Üb' immer Treu und Redlichkeit*" and the then newly published "*Jungfernkranz*" upon the pianoforte; the day before his death, I was bid to play him both these pieces in the adjoining room; I heard him then, with feeble voice, say to my mother: "Has he perchance a talent for music?" On the early morrow, as he lay dead, my mother came into the children's sleeping-room, and said to each of us some loving word. To me she said: "He hoped to make *something* of thee." I remember, too, that for a long time I imagined that something indeed would come of me.

In my ninth year I went to the Dresden *Kreuzschule*: I wished to study, and music was not thought of. Two of my sisters learnt to play the piano passably; I listened to them, but had no piano lessons myself. Nothing pleased me so much as *Der Freischütz*; I often saw *Weber* pass before our house, as he came from rehearsals; I always watched him with a reverent awe. A tutor who explained to me

Cornelius Nepos, was at last engaged to give me pianoforte instructions; hardly had I got past the earliest finger-exercises, when I furtively practised, at first by ear, the Overture to *Der Freischütz;* my teacher heard this once, and said nothing would come of me.—He was right; in my whole life I have never learnt to play the piano properly.—Thenceforward I only played for my own amusement, nothing but overtures, and with the most fearful 'fingering.' It was impossible for me to play a passage clearly, and I therefore conceived a just dread of all scales and runs. Of Mozart, I only cared for the *Magic Flute;* *Don Juan* was distasteful to me, on account of the Italian text beneath it : it seemed to me such rubbish.

But this music-strumming was quite a secondary matter : Greek, Latin, Mythology, and Ancient History were my principal studies. I wrote verses too. Once there died one of my schoolfellows, and our teacher set us the task of writing a poem upon his death ; the best lines were then to be printed :—my own were printed, but only after I had cleared them of a heap of bombast. I was then eleven years old. I promptly determined to become a poet; and sketched out tragedies on the model of the Greeks, urged by my acquaintance with Apel's works : *Polyidos, Die Ätolier*, &c., &c. Moreover, I passed in my school for a good head "*in litteris;*" even in the 'Third form' I had translated the first twelve books of the Odyssey. For a while I learnt English also, merely so as to gain an accurate knowledge of Shakespeare ; and I made a metrical translation of Romeo's monologue. Though I soon left English on one side, yet Shakespeare remained my exemplar, and I projected a great tragedy which was almost nothing but a medley of *Hamlet* and *King Lear*. The plan was gigantic in the extreme ; two-and-forty human beings died in the course of this piece, and I saw myself compelled, in its working-out, to call the greater number back as ghosts, since otherwise I should have been short of characters for my last Acts. This play occupied my leisure for two whole years.

Meanwhile, I left Dresden and its *Kreuzschule*, and went to Leipzig. In the *Nikolaischule* of that city I was relegated to the 'Third form,' after having already attained to the 'Second' in Dresden. This circumstance embittered me so much, that thenceforward I lost all liking for philological study. I became lazy and slovenly, and my grand tragedy was the only thing left me to care about. Whilst I was finishing this I made my first acquaintance with Beethoven's music, in the Leipzig *Gewandhaus* concerts; its impression upon me was overpowering. I also became intimate with Mozart's works, chiefly through his *Requiem*. Beethoven's music to *Egmont* so much inspired me, that I determined—for all the world—not to allow my now completed tragedy to leave the stocks until provided with suchlike music. Without the slightest diffidence, I believed that I could myself write this needful music, but thought it better to first clear up a few of the general principles of thorough-bass. To get through this as swiftly as possible, I borrowed for a week Logier's " *Method of Thorough-bass*," and studied it in hot haste. But this study did not bear such rapid fruit as I had expected: its difficulties both provoked and fascinated me; I resolved to become a musician.

During this time my great tragedy was unearthed by my family: they were much disturbed thereat, for it was clear as day that I had woefully neglected my school lessons in favour of it, and I was forthwith admonished to continue them more diligently. Under such circumstances, I breathed no word of my secret discovery of a calling for music; but, notwithstanding, I composed in silence a Sonata, a Quartet, and an Aria. When I felt myself sufficiently matured in my private musical studies, I ventured forth at last with their announcement. Naturally, I now had many a hard battle to wage, for my relations could only consider my penchant for music as a fleeting passion—all the more as it was unsupported by any proofs of preliminary study, and especially by any already won dexterity in handling a musical instrument.

I was then in my sixteenth year, and, chiefly from a perusal of E. A. Hoffmann's works, on fire with the maddest mysticism : I had visions by day in semi-slumber, in which the 'Keynote,' 'Third,' and 'Dominant' seemed to take on living form and reveal to me their mighty meaning : the notes that I wrote down were stark with folly.—At last a capable musician was engaged to instruct me : the poor man had a sorry office in explaining to me that what I took for wondrous shapes and powers were really chords and intervals. What could be more disturbing to my family than to find that I proved myself negligent and refractory in this study also ? My teacher shook his head, and it appeared that here too no good thing could be brought from me. My liking for study dwindled more and more, and I chose instead to write Overtures for full orchestra—one of which was once performed in the Leipzig theatre. This Overture was the culminating point of my foolishness. For its better understanding by such as might care to study the score, I elected to employ for its notation three separate tints of ink : red for the 'strings,' green for the 'wood-wind,' and black for the 'brass.' Beethoven's Ninth Symphony was a mere Pleyel Sonata by the side of this marvellously concocted Overture. Its performance was mainly prejudiced by a *fortissimo* thud on the big drum, that recurred throughout the whole overture at regular intervals of four bars ; with the result, that the audience gradually passed from its initial amazement at the obstinacy of the drum-beater to undisguised displeasure, and finally to a mirthful mood that much disquieted me. This first performance of a composition of mine left on me a deep impression.

But now the July Revolution took place ; with one bound I became a revolutionist, and acquired the conviction that every decently active being ought to occupy himself with politics exclusively. I was only happy in the company of political writers, and I commenced an Overture upon a political theme. Thus was I minded, when I left school and went to the university : not, indeed, to devote myself to studying for any profession—for my musical career was now resolved on—but to attend lectures on philosophy and æsthetics. By this opportunity of improving my mind I profited as good as nothing, but gave myself up to all the excesses of student life; and that with such reckless levity, that they very soon revolted me. My relations were now sorely troubled about me, for I had almost entirely abandoned my music. Yet I speedily came to my senses; I felt the need of a completely new beginning of strict and methodical study of music, and Providence led me to the very man best qualified to inspire me with fresh love for the thing, and to purge my notions by the thoroughest of instruction. This man was *Theodor Weinlig*, the Cantor of the Leipzig *Thomasschule.* Although I had previously made my own attempts at Fugue, it was with him that I first commenced a thorough study of Counterpoint, which he possessed the happy knack of teaching his pupils while playing.

At this epoch I first acquired an intimate love and knowledge of Mozart. I composed a Sonata, in which I freed myself from all buckram, and strove for a natural unforced style of composition. This extremely simple and modest work was published by Breitkopf und Härtel. My studies under Weinlig were ended in less than half a year, and he dismissed me himself from his tuition as soon as he had brought me so far forward that I was in a position to solve with ease the hardest problems of Counterpoint. "What you have made your own by this dry study," he said, "we call Self-dependence." In that same half year I also composed an Overture on the model of Beethoven; a model which I now understood somewhat better. This Overture was played in one of the Leipzig Gewandhaus concerts, to most encouraging applause. After several other works, I then engaged in a Symphony: to my head exemplar, Beethoven, I allied Mozart, especially as shewn in his great C major Symphony. Lucidity and force— albeit with many a strange aberration—were my end and aim.

My Symphony completed, I set out in the summer of
1832 on a journey to Vienna, with no other object than to
get a hasty glimpse of this renowned music-city.   What I
saw and heard there edified me little; wherever I went, I
heard *Zampa* and Straussian pot pourris on *Zampa*.   Both
—and especially at that time—were to me an abomination.
On my homeward journey I tarried a while in Prague,
where I made the acquaintance of Dionys Weber and
Tomaschek; the former had several of my compositions
performed in the conservatoire, and among them my
Symphony.   In that city I also composed an opera-book
of tragic contents: "*Die Hochzeit.*"   I know not whence
I had come by the mediæval subject-matter:—a frantic
lover climbs to the window of the sleeping chamber of his
friend's bride, wherein she is awaiting the advent of the
bridegroom ; the bride struggles with the madman and
hurls him into the courtyard below, where his mangled
body gives up the ghost.   During the funeral ceremony,
the bride, uttering one cry, sinks lifeless on the corpse.

Returned to Leipzig, I set to work at once on the
composition of this opera's first 'number,' which contained
a grand Sextet that much pleased Weinlig.   The text-
book found no favour with my sister; I destroyed its every
trace.

In January of 1833 my Symphony was performed at a
Gewandhaus concert, and met with highly inspiriting
applause.   At about this time I came to know Heinrich
Laube.

To visit one of my brothers, I travelled to Wurzburg in
the spring of the same year, and remained there till its
close; my brother's intimacy was of great importance to
me, for he was an accomplished singer.   During my stay
in Wurzburg I composed a romantic opera in three Acts:
"*Die Feen,*" for which I wrote my own text, after Gozzi's :
"*Die Frau als Schlange.*"   Beethoven and Weber were my
models; in the *ensembles* of this opera there was much
that fell out very well, and the Finale of the Second Act,
especially, promised a good effect.   The 'numbers' from

this work which I brought to a hearing at concerts in Wurzburg, were favourably received. Full of hopes for my now finished opera, I returned to Leipzig at the beginning of 1834, and offered it for performance to the Director of that theatre. However, in spite of his at first declared readiness to comply with my wish, I was soon forced to the same experience that every German opera-composer has nowadays to win: we are discredited upon our own native stage by the success of Frenchmen and Italians, and the production of our operas is a favour to be cringed for. The performance of my *Feen* was set upon the shelf.

Meanwhile I heard the *Devrient* sing in Bellini's *Romeo and Juliet*. I was astounded to witness so extraordinary a rendering of such utterly meaningless music. I grew doubtful as to the choice of the proper means to bring about a great success; far though I was from attaching to Bellini a signal merit, yet the subject to which his music was set seemed to me to be more propitious and better calculated to spread the warm glow of life, than the pains-taking pedantry with which we Germans, as a rule, brought naught but laborious make-believe to market. The flabby lack of character of our modern Italians, equally with the frivolous levity of the latest Frenchmen, appeared to me to challenge the earnest, conscientious German to master the happily chosen and happily exploited means of his rivals, in order then to outstrip them in the production of genuine works of art.

I was then twenty-one years of age, inclined to take life and the world on their pleasant side. *"Ardinghello"* (by Heinse) and *"Das Junge Europa"* (by H. Laube) tingled through my every limb; while Germany appeared in my eyes a very tiny portion of the earth. I had emerged from abstract Mysticism, and I learnt a love for Matter. Beauty of material and brilliancy of wit were lordly things to me: as regards my beloved music, I found them both among the Frenchmen and Italians. I forswore my model, Beethoven; his last Symphony I deemed the key-

stone of a whole great epoch of art, beyond whose limits
no man could hope to press, and within which no man
could attain to independence.   Mendelssohn also seemed
to have felt with me, when he stepped forth with his smaller
orchestral compositions, leaving untouched the great and
fenced-off form of the Symphony of Beethoven ; it seemed
to me that, beginning with a lesser, completely unshackled
form, he fain would create for himself therefrom a greater.

Everything around me appeared fermenting : to abandon
myself to the general fermentation, I deemed the most
natural course.   Upon a lovely summer's journey among
the Bohemian watering-places, I sketched the plan of a
new opera, " *Das Liebesverbot,*" taking my subject from
Shakespeare's *Measure for Measure*—only with this difference, that I robbed it of its prevailing earnestness, and thus
re-moulded it after the pattern of *Das Junge Europa ;* free
and frank physicalism (*Sinnlichkeit*) gained, of its own
sheer strength, the victory over Puritanical hypocrisy.

In the summer of this same year, 1834, I further took
the post of Music-Director at the Magdeburg theatre.
The practical application of my musical knowledge to the
functions of a conductor bore early fruit; for the vicissitudes
of intercourse with singers and singeresses, behind the
scenes and in front of the footlights, completely matched
my bent toward many-hued distraction.   The composition
of my *Liebesverbot* was now begun.   I produced the Overture to *Die Feen* at a concert ; it had a marked success.
This notwithstanding, I lost all liking for this opera, and,
since I was no longer able to personally attend to my
affairs at Leipzig, I soon resolved to trouble myself no
more about this work, which is as much as to say that I
gave it up.

For a festival play for New Year's day, 1835, I hastily
threw together some music, which aroused a general interest.
Such lightly won success much fortified my views that in
order to please, one must not too scrupulously choose one's
means.   In this sense I continued the composition of my
Liebesverbot, and took no care whatever to avoid the echoes

of the French and Italian stages. Interrupted in this work for a while, I resumed it in the winter of 1835-6, and completed it shortly before the dispersal of the Magdeburg opera troupe. I had now only twelve days before the departure of the principal singers; therefore my opera must be rehearsed in this short space of time, if I still wished them to perform it. With greater levity than deliberation, I permitted this opera—which contained some arduous rôles—to be set on the stage after a ten days' study. I placed my trust in the prompter and in my conductor's baton. But, spite of all my efforts, I could not remove the obstacle, that the singers scarcely half knew their parts. The representation was like a dream to us all : no human being could possibly get so much as an idea what it was all about; yet there was some consolation in the fact that applause was plentiful. From various reasons, a second performance could not be given.

In the midst of all this, the 'earnestness of life' had knocked at my door; my outward independence, so rashly grasped at, had led me into follies of every kind, and on all sides I was plagued by penury and debts. It occurred to me to venture upon something out of the ordinary, in order not to slide into the common rut of need. Without any sort of prospect, I went to Berlin and offered the Director to produce my *Liebesverbot* at the theatre of that capital. I was received at first with the fairest promises ; but, after long suspense, I had to learn that not one of them was sincerely meant. In the sorriest plight I left Berlin, and applied for the post of Musical Director at the Königsberg theatre, in Prussia—a post which I subsequently obtained. In that city I got married in the autumn of 1836, amid the most dubious outward circumstances. The year which I spent in Königsberg was completely lost to my art, by reason of the pressure of petty cares. I wrote one solitary Overture : "*Rule Britannia.*"

In the summer of 1837 I visited Dresden for a short time. There I was led back by the reading of Bulwer's "*Rienzi*"

to an already cherished idea, viz., of turning the last of
Rome's tribunes into the hero of a grand tragic opera.
Hindered by outward discomforts, however, I busied
myself no further with dramatic sketches. In the
autumn of this year I went to Riga, to take up the
position of first Musical Director at the theatre recently
opened there by Holtei. I found there an assemblage of
excellent material for opera, and went to its employment
with the greatest liking. Many interpolated passages for
individual singers in various operas, were composed by me
during this period. I also wrote the libretto for a comic
opera in two Acts : " *Die Glückliche Bärenfamilie*," the
matter for which I took from one of the stories in the
" Thousand and One Nights." I had only composed two
' numbers ' for this, when I was disgusted to find that I was
again on the high road to music-making *à la Adam*. My
spirit, my deeper feelings, were wounded by this discovery,
and I laid aside the work in horror. The daily studying
and conducting of Auber's, Adam's, and Bellini's music
contributed its share to a speedy undoing of my frivolous
delight in such an enterprise.

The utter childishness of our provincial public's verdict
upon any art-manifestation that may chance to make its
first appearance in their own theatre—for they are only
accustomed to witness performances of works already
judged and accredited by the greater world outside—
brought me to the decision, at no price to produce for
the first time a largish work at a minor theatre. When,
therefore, I felt again the instinctive need of undertaking
a major work, I renounced all idea of obtaining a speedy
representation of it in my immediate neighbourhood : I
fixed my mind upon some theatre of first rank, that would
some day produce it, and troubled myself but little as to
where and when that theatre would be found. In this wise
did I conceive the sketch of a grand tragic opera in five
Acts : " Rienzi, the last of the Tribunes ; " and I laid my
plans on so important a scale, that it would be impossible
to produce this opera—at any rate for the first time—at

any lesser theatre. Moreover, the wealth and force of the material left me no other course, and my procedure was governed more by necessity than set purpose. In the summer of 1838 I completed the poem; at the same time, I was engaged in rehearsing our opera troupe, with much enthusiasm and affection, in Méhul's "*Jacob and his Sons.*"

When, in the autumn, I began the composition of my *Rienzi*, I allowed naught to influence me except the single purpose to answer to my subject. I set myself no model, but gave myself entirely to the feeling which now consumed me, the feeling that I had already so far progressed that I might claim something significant from the development of my artistic powers, and expect some not insignificant result. The very notion of being consciously weak or trivial—even in a single bar—was appalling to me.

During the winter I was in the full swing of composition, so that by the spring of 1839 I had finished the long first two Acts. About this time my contract with the Director of the theatre terminated, and various circumstances made it inconvenient to me to stay longer at Riga. For two years I had nursed the plan of going to Paris, and with this in view, I had, even while at Königsberg, sent to Scribe the sketch of an opera plot, with the proposal that he should elaborate it for his own benefit and procure me, in reward, the commission to compose the opera for Paris. Scribe naturally left this suggestion as good as unregarded. Nevertheless, I did not give up my scheme; on the contrary, I returned to it with renewed keenness in the summer of 1839; and the long and the short of it was, that I induced my wife to embark with me upon a sailing vessel bound for London.

This voyage I never shall forget as long as I live; it lasted three and a half weeks, and was rich in mishaps. Thrice did we endure the most violent of storms, and once the captain found himself compelled to put into a Norwegian haven. The passage among the crags of Norway made a wonderful impression on my fancy; the legends of

the Flying Dutchman, as I heard them from the seamen's
mouths, were clothed for me in a distinct and individual
colour, borrowed from the adventures of the ocean through
which I then was passing.

Resting from the severe exhaustion of the transit, we
remained a week in London ; nothing interested me so
much as the city itself and the Houses of Parliament,—of
the theatres, I visited not one. At Boulogne-sur-mer I
stayed four weeks, and there made the acquaintance of
Meyerbeer. I brought under his notice the two finished
Acts of my *Rienzi;* he promised me, in the friendliest
fashion, his support in Paris. With very little money, but
the best of hopes, I now set foot in Paris. Entirely without
any personal references, I could rely on no one but Meyerbeer. He seemed prepared, with the most signal attentive-
ness, to set in train whatever might further my aims ; and
it certainly seemed to me that I should soon attain a
wished-for goal—had it not unfortunately so turned out that,
during the very period of my stay in Paris, Meyerbeer was
generally, nay almost the whole time, absent from that
city. It is true that he wished to serve me even from a
distance ; but, according to his own announcement, epis-
tolary efforts could avail nothing where only the most
assiduous personal mediation is of any efficacy.

First of all, I entered upon negotiations with the
Théâtre de la Renaissance, where both comedy and opera
were then being given. The score of my *Liebesverbot*
seemed best fitted for this theatre, and the somewhat
frivolous subject appeared easily adaptable to the French
stage. I was so warmly recommended by Meyerbeer to
the Director of the theatre, that he could not help receiving
me with the best of promises. Thereupon, one of the
most prolific of Parisian dramatists, *Dumersan,* offered to
undertake the poetical setting of the subject. He translated three 'numbers,' destined for a trial hearing, with so
great felicity that my music looked much better in its new
French dress than in its original German ; in fact, it was
music such as Frenchmen most readily comprehend, and

everything promised me the best success—when the *Théâtre de la Renaissance* immediately became bankrupt.   All my labours, all my hopes, were thus in vain.

In the same winter, 1839-40, I composed—besides an Overture to the first part of Goethe's *Faust*—several French Ballads; among others, a French translation made for me of H. Heine's *The Two Grenadiers*. I never dreamt of any possibility of getting my *Rienzi* produced in Paris, for I clearly foresaw that I should have had to wait five or six years, even under the most favourable conditions, before such a plan could be carried out; moreover, the translation of the text of the already half-finished composition would have thrown insuperable obstacles in the way.

Thus I began the summer of 1840, completely bereft of immediate prospects. My acquaintance with Habeneck, Halévy, Berlioz, &c., led to no closer relations with these men: in Paris no artist has time to form a friendship with another, for each is in a red hot hurry for his own advantage.   Halévy, like all the composers of our day, was aflame with enthusiasm for his art only so long as it was a question of winning a great success: so soon as he had carried off this prize, and was enthroned among the privileged ranks of artistic 'lions,' he had no thought for anything but making operas and pocketing their pay. Renown is everything in Paris: the happiness and ruin of the artist.   Despite his stand-off manners, Berlioz attracted me in a far higher degree.   He differs by the whole breadth of heaven from his Parisian colleagues, for he makes no music for gold.   But he cannot write for the sake of purest art; he lacks all sense of beauty.   He stands, completely isolated, upon his own position; by his side he has nothing but a troup of devotees who, shallow and without the smallest spark of judgment, greet in him the creator of a brand new musical system and completely turn his head;—the rest of the world avoids him as a madman.

My earlier easy-going views of the means and ends of

music received their final shock—from the Italians.   These idolised heroes of song, with Rubini at their head, finished by utterly disgusting me with their music.   The public to whom they sang, added their quota to this effect upon me. The Paris Grand Opera left me entirely unsatisfied, by the want of all genius in its representations : I found the whole thing commonplace and middling.   I openly confess that the *mise en scène* and the decorations are the most to my liking of anything at the *Académie Royale de Musique.* The *Opéra Comique* would have had much more chance of pleasing me—it possesses the best talents, and its performances offer an *ensemble* and an individuality such as we know nothing of in Germany—but the stuff that is nowadays written for this theatre belongs to the very worst productions of a period of degraded art.   Whither has flown the grace of Méhul, Isouard, Boieldieu, and the *young* Auber, scared by the contemptible quadrille rhythms which rattle through this theatre to-day?   The only thing worthy the regard of a musician that Paris now contains, is the *Conservatoire* with its orchestral concerts. The renderings of German instrumental compositions at these concerts produced on me a deep impression, and inducted me afresh into the mysteries of noble art.   He who would fully learn the Ninth Symphony of Beethoven, must hear it executed by the orchestra of the Paris Conservatoire.   But these concerts stand alone in utter solitude ; there is naught that answers to them.

I hardly mixed at all with musicians : scholars, painters, &c., formed my *entourage,* and I gained many a rare experience of friendship in Paris.—Since I was so completely bare of present Paris prospects, I took up once more the composition of my *Rienzi.*   I now destined it for Dresden : in the first place, because I knew that this theatre possessed the very best material—Devrient, Tichatschek, &c ; secondly, because I could more reasonably hope for an *entrée* there, relying upon the support of my earliest acquaintances.   My *Liebesverbot* I now gave up almost completely ; I felt that I could no longer regard myself as its composer. With all the greater freedom, I followed now my true artistic creed, in the prosecution of the music to my *Rienzi*. Manifold worries and bitter need besieged my life. On a sudden, Meyerbeer appeared again for a short space in Paris. With the most amiable sympathy he ascertained the position of my affairs, and desired to help. He therefore placed me in communication with Léon Pillet, the Director of the Grand Opera, with a view to my being entrusted with the composition of a two- or three-act opera for that stage. I had already provided myself for this emergency with an outline plot. The "Flying Dutchman," whose intimate acquaintance I had made upon the ocean, had never ceased to fascinate my phantasy; I had also made the acquaintance of H. Heine's remarkable version of this legend, in a number of his '*Salon*'; and it was especially his treatment of the redemption of this Ahasuerus of the seas—borrowed from a Dutch play under the same title—that placed within my hands all the material for turning the legend into an opera-subject. I obtained the consent of Heine himself; I wrote my sketch, and handed it to M. Léon Pillet, with the proposal that he should get me a French text-book made after my model. Thus far was everything set on foot when Meyerbeer again left Paris, and the fulfilment of my wish had to be relinquished to destiny. I was very soon astounded by hearing from Pillet that the sketch I had tendered him pleased him so much that he should be glad if I would cede it to him. He explained : that he was pledged by a previous promise to supply another composer with a-libretto as soon as possible ; that my sketch appeared to be the very thing for such a purpose, and I should probably not regret consenting to the surrender he begged, when I reflected that I could not possibly hope to obtain a direct commission for an opera before the lapse of four years, seeing that he had in the interval to keep faith with several candidates for grand opera; that such a period would naturally be too long for myself to be brooding over this subject; and that I should certainly discover a

B

fresh one, and console myself for the sacrifice. I struggled
obstinately against this suggestion, without being able, however, to effect anything further than a provisional postpone-
ment of the question.   I counted upon the speedy return
of Meyerbeer, and held my peace.

During this time I was prompted by Schlesinger to
write for his " *Gazette Musicale.*" I contributed several
longish articles on "German Music," &c., &c., among which
the one which found the liveliest welcome was a little
romance entitled, "A Pilgrimage to Beethoven."   These
works assisted not a little to make me known and noticed
in Paris.   In November of this year I put the last touches
to my score of *Rienzi,* and sent it post-haste to Dresden.
This period was the culminating point of the utter misery
of my existence.   I wrote for the *Gazette Musicale* a short
story : " The Life's End of a German Musician in Paris,"
wherein I made the wretched hero die with these words
upon his lips : " I believe in God, Mozart, and Beethoven."

It was well that my opera was finished, for I saw myself
now compelled to bid a long farewell to any practice of my
art. I was forced to undertake, for Schlesinger, arrangements of airs for all the instruments under heaven, even
the *cornet à piston ;* thus only was a slight amelioration of
my lot to be found.   In this way did I pass the winter of
1840-1, in the most inglorious fashion.   In the spring I
went into the country, to Meudon ; and with the warm
approach of summer I began to long again for brain-work.
The stimulus thereto was to touch me quicker than I had
thought for ; I learnt, forsooth, that my sketch of the text
of the *Flying Dutchman* had already been handed to a
poet, Paul Fouché, and that if I did not declare my willingness to part therewith, I should be clean robbed of it on
some pretext or other.   I therefore consented at last to
make over my sketch for a moderate sum.*   I had now to

* Herr C. F. Glasenapp, in his "*Richard Wagner's Leben und Wirken,*"
tells us that the name of the composer for whom Fouché adapted Wagner's
sketch was Dietsch ; that his opera was called "*Le Vaisseau Fantôme,*" was

work post-haste to clothe my own subject with German verses. In order to set about its composition, I required to hire a pianoforte; for, after nine months' interruption of all musical production, I had to try to surround myself with the needful preliminary of a musical atmosphere. As soon as the piano had arrived, my heart beat fast for very fear; I dreaded to discover that I had ceased to be a musician. I began first with the "Sailors' Chorus" and the "Spinning-song"; everything sped along as though on wings, and I shouted for joy as I felt within me that I still was a musician. In seven weeks the whole opera was composed; but at the end of that period I was over-whelmed again by the commonest cares of life, and two full months elapsed before I could get to writing the overture to the already finished opera—although I bore it almost full-fledged in my brain. Naturally nothing now lay so much at my heart as the desire to bring it to a speedy production in Germany; from Munich and Leipzig I had the disheartening answer: the opera was not at all fitted for Germany. Fool that I was! I had fancied it was fitted for Germany alone, since it struck on chords that can only vibrate in the German breast.

At last I sent my new work to Meyerbeer, in Berlin, with the petition that he would get it taken up for the theatre of that city. This was effected with tolerable rapidity. As my *Rienzi* had already been accepted for the Dresden Court theatre, I therefore now looked forward to the production of two of my works upon the foremost German stages; and involuntarily I reflected on the strangeness of the fact, that Paris had been to me of the greatest service for Germany. As regards Paris itself, I was completely without prospects for several years: I therefore left it in the spring of 1842. For the first time I saw the Rhine—with hot tears in my eyes, I, poor artist, swore eternal fidelity to my German fatherland.

produced a few years later at the Paris Grand Opera, and was so overloaded with minor personages that it had no more dramatic than musical success.—A righteous nemesis !—TR.

ART AND REVOLUTION.

"DIE KUNST UND DIE REVOLUTION."

(Written in Paris, 1849.)

The INTRODUCTION *translated on the opposite and follow-ing pages was written by Richard Wagner as the Preface to Volumes III. and IV. of his* "Gesammelte Schriften," *or Collected Writings, for the Edition of* 1872 ; *and applies not only to* "Art and Revolution," *but also to* "The Art-Work of the Future" *and* "Opera and Drama," *&c.*

TRANSLATOR'S NOTE.

INTRODUCTION TO ART AND REVOLUTION.

THOMAS CARLYLE, in his *History of Frederick the Great*,* characterises the outbreak of the French Revolution as the First Act of the "Spontaneous Combustion" of a nation "sunk into torpor, abeyance, and dry-rot," and admonishes his readers in the following words :—

"There is the next mile-stone for you, in the History "of Mankind ! That universal Burning-up, as in hell- "fire, of Human Shams. The oath of Twenty-five "Million men, which has since become that of all men "whatsoever, ' Rather than live longer under lies, we "will die ! '—that is the New Act in World-History. "New Act,—or, we may call it New *Part;* Drama of "World-History, Part Third. If Part *Second* was "1800 years ago, this I reckon will be Part *Third.* "This is the truly celestial-infernal Event : the strang- "est we have seen for a thousand years. Celestial in "the one part ; in the other, infernal. For it is withal "the breaking-out of universal mankind into Anarchy, "into the faith and practice of *No*-Government,— "that is to say (if you will be candid), into unappeas- "able revolt against Sham-Governors and Sham- "Teachers,—which I do charitably define to be a "Search, most unconscious, yet in deadly earnest, for "true Governors and Teachers. . . . . When the "Spontaneous Combustion breaks out ; and, many- "coloured, with loud noises, envelopes the whole "world in anarchic flame for long hundreds of years : "then has the Event come ; there is the thing for all

* Book XXI. chap i.—Tʀ.

"men to mark, and to study and scrutinise as the
"strangest thing they ever saw. Centuries of it yet
"lying ahead of us; several sad Centuries, sordidly
"tumultuous, and good for little! Say Two Centuries
"yet,—say even Ten of such a process : before the Old
"is completely burnt out, and the New in any state of
"sightliness? Millennium of Anarchies ;—*abridge it,*
"*spend your heart's-blood upon abridging it, ye Heroic*
"*Wise that are to come !*"

When, in the feverish excitement of the year 1849, I
gave vent to an appeal such as that contained in the
immediately succeeding essay : "*Art and Revolution,*" I
believe that I was in complete accord with the last words
of this summons of the grey-headed historian. I believed
in the Revolution, and in its unrestrainable necessity, with
certainly no greater immoderation than Carlyle : only, I
also felt that I was called to point out to it the way of
rescue. Far though it was from my intent to define the
New, which should grow from the ruins of a sham-filled
world, as a fresh *political* ordering :* I felt the rather
animated to draw the outlines of the *Art-work* which
should rise from the ruins of a sham-bred *Art.* To hold
this Art-work up to Life itself, as the prophetic mirror of
its Future, appeared to me a weightiest contribution toward the work of damming the flood of Revolution within
the channel of the peaceful-flowing stream of Manhood.
I was bold enough to prefix the following motto to the
little pamphlet : "When Art erst held her peace, State-
wisdom and Philosophy began : when now both Statesman
and Philosopher have breathed their last, let the Artist's
voice again be heard."

It is needless to recall the scorn which my presumption
brought upon me ; since in the course of my succeeding
literary labours, whose connected products I here append,

---

* Even Carlyle can only betoken this as the "Death of the Anarchies : or
a world once more built wholly on Fact better or worse ; and the lying
jargoning professor of Sham-Fact . . . become a species extinct, and well
known to be gone down to Tophet ! "—R. WAGNER.

I had occasion enough to defend myself against the grossest of these attacks.   I have also exhaustively treated this whole matter, both with regard to the inception of these works and the characteristic incitement thereto, not only in the "Communication to my Friends," * which brings this whole period to a close, but also in a later treatise, entitled : " The Music of the Future " (" *Zukunftsmusik* "). I will only say here that the principal cause which brought down the ridicule of our art-critics upon my seemingly paradoxical ideas, is to be found in the fervid enthusiasm which pervaded my style and gave to my remarks more of a poetic than a scientific character.   Moreover, the effect of an indiscriminate intercalation of philosophical maxims was prejudicial to my clearness of expression, especially in the eyes of those who could not or would not follow my line of thought and general principles.   Actively aroused by the perusal of some of *Ludwig Feuerbach's* essays, I had borrowed various terms of abstract nomenclature and applied them to artistic ideas with which they could not always closely harmonise.   In thus doing, I gave myself up without critical deliberation to the guidance of a brilliant writer, who approached most nearly to my reigning frame of mind, in that he bade farewell to Philosophy (in which he fancied he detected naught but masked Theology) and took refuge in a conception of man's nature in which I thought I clearly recognised my own ideal of artistic manhood.   From this arose a kind of impassioned tangle of ideas, which manifested itself as precipitance and indistinctness in my attempts at philosophical system.

While on this subject, I deem it needful to make special mention of two chief 'terms,' my misunderstanding of which has since been strikingly borne in upon me.

I refer in the first place to the concept *Willkür* and *Unwillkür*,† in the use of which a great confusion had

* " *Eine Mittheilung an meine Freunde ;* "—see end of the present volume. —TR.

† We have no English equivalents of these words, except in the adjectival form : *voluntary* and *involuntary*, in which there lies the same confusion of

long preceded my own offending; for an adjectival term,
unwillkürlich, had been promoted to the rank of a substan-
tive. Only those who have learnt from *Schopenhauer* the
true meaning and significance of the *Will*, can thoroughly
appreciate the abuse that had resulted from this mixing up
of words; he who has enjoyed this unspeakable benefit,
however, knows well that that misused " *Unwillkür* " should
really be named " *Der Wille* " (the Will); whilst the term
Willkür (Choice or Caprice) is here employed to signify
the so-called Intellectual or Brain Will, influenced by the
guidance of reflection. Since the latter is more concerned
with the properties of Knowledge,—which may easily be
led astray by the purely individual aim,—it is attainted
with the evil qualities with which it is charged in the
following pages, under the name of *Willkür* · whereas the
pure *Will*, as the " *Thing-in-itself* " that comes to consciousness in man, is credited with those true productive
qualities which are here—apparently the result of a confusion sprung from the popular misuse of the term—
assigned to the negative expression, " *Unwillkür.*" Therefore, since a thorough revision in this sense would lead too
far and prove a most fatiguing task, the reader is begged,
when doubtful of the meaning of any of such passages, to
bear graciously in mind the present explanation.

Further, I have to fear that my continual employment
of the term " *Sinnlichkeit*," * in a sense prompted by the
same authority, may give origin, if not to positively harmful misunderstanding, at least to much perplexity. Since
the idea conveyed by this term can only have the meaning,

ideas as that for which Wagner here upbraids himself; and even now, when
Schopenhauer's definition of the " Will " is pretty generally accepted, it would
seem better, for clearness' sake, to delimit the term by some such prefix as the
" *Inner*," or " *Instinctive* " Will, in order to distinguish it from the " Outer "
or " Intellectual " Choice.   In this series of translations I shall endeavour to
render such expressions in the sense the author here indicates.—W. A. E.

* *Sinnlichkeit*= Qualities appealing to the senses ; or again, the bent to an
objective method of viewing things.   Hence it may at times be best rendered
by *Physicalism* or *Materialism ;* at others, by *Physical perception, Physical
contemplation*, or even—borrowing from Carlyle—*Five-sense-philosophy.*—Tʀ

in my argument, of the direct antithesis to "*Gedanken*" (Thought), or—which will make my purport clearer—to "*Gedanklichkeit*" (Ideation): its absolute misunderstanding would certainly be difficult, seeing that the two opposite factors, Art and Learning, must readily be recognised herein. But since, in ordinary parlance, this word is employed in the evil sense of "Sensualism," or even of abandonment to Sensual Lust, it would be better to re-place it by a term of less ambiguous meaning, in theoretical expositions of so warm a declamatory tone as these of mine, however wide a currency it has obtained in philo-sophical speech. Obviously, the question here is of the contrast between intuitive and abstract knowledge, both in themselves and their results ; but above all, of the sub-jective predisposition to these diverse modes. The term "*Anschauungsvermögen*" (Perceptive Faculty) would suf-ficiently denote the former ; were it not that for the specific *artistic* perception, a distinctive emphasis seems necessary, for which it might well appear indispensable to retain the expression "*Sinnliches Anschauungsvermögen*" (Physical perceptive faculty), and briefly "*Sinnlichkeit*" (Physicality), alike for the faculty, for the object of its exercise, and for the force which sets the two in rapport with each other.

But the greatest peril of all, is that which the author would incur by his frequent use of the word *Communism*, should he venture into the Paris of to-day with these art-essays in his hand ; for he openly proclaims his adherence to this severely scouted category, in contradistinction to *Egoism.** I certainly believe that the friendly German reader, to whom the meaning of this antithesis will be obvious, will have no special trouble in overcoming the doubt as to whether he must rank me among the partisans of the newest Parisian "*Commune*." Still, I cannot deny that I should not have embarked with the same energy upon the use of this word "Communism" (employing it in

---

* To use the now more customary antithesis : *Socialism* v. *Individualism*. —Tr.

a sense borrowed from the said writings of Feuerbach) as the opposite of Egoism : had I not also seen in this idea a socio-political ideal which I conceived as embodied in a "*Volk*" (People) that should represent the incomparable productivity of antique brotherhood, while I looked forward to the perfect evolution of this principle as the very essence of the associate Manhood of the Future.—It is significant of my experiences on the practical side, that in the first of these writings, *Art and Revolution*, which I had originally intended for a certain political journal* then appearing in Paris (where I stayed for a few weeks in the summer of 1849), I avoided this word "Communism,"—as it now seems to me, from fear of gross misunderstanding on the part of our French brethren, materialistic ("*sinnlich*") as they are in their interpretation of so many an abstract idea, —whereas I forthwith used it without scruple in my next art-writings, designed expressly for Germany ; a fact I now regard as a token of my implicit trust in the attributes of the German mind.   In pursuance of this observation, I attach considerable importance also to the experience, that my essay met with absolutely no whit of understanding in Paris, and that no one at the time could understand why I should single out a political journal for my mouthpiece ; in consequence whereof, my article did not after all attain to publication there.

But it was not only from the effects of these and similar experiences, that the quick of my ideas drew gradually back from contact with the political excitement of the day, and soon developed more and more exclusively as an *artistic* ideal.   Hereof the sequence of the writings collected in these two volumes † gives sufficient indication ; and this the reader will best recognise from the insertion, in their midst, of a dramatic sketch : *Wieland der Schmied,* executed by me in the same chronological order as that in

---

* "In the *National* you will shortly see an important article of mine : *Art and Revolution,* which I believe will also appear in German at Wigand's in Leipzig."—From Wagner's letter to Uhlig, of 9th August 1849.—TR.

† Volumes III. and IV. of the *Gesammelte Schriften,* or "Collected Writings."—TR.

which it now stands.　If that artistic ideal, which I have ever since held fast to as my inmost acquisition, under whatsoever form of its manifestment,—if that ideal remained the only actual outcome of a labour which taxed the whole energy of my nature ; and finally, if only as a creative artist could I live up to this ideal without disquietude: then my belief in the German spirit, and the trust in its predestined place amid the Council of the Nations that took an ever mightier hold upon me as time rolled on, could alone inspire me with the hopeful equanimity so indispensable to the artist—even from the outer aspect of the human lot, however much the care for the latter had forced its passionate disturbance upon my views of life. Already I have been enabled to preface the second edition of *Opera and Drama* by a dedication to a friend * I had won in the interval,—and to whose instructive suggestions I have had to thank the most comforting solutions of the last named problem,—in order to reach to him the hand of the artist as well as of the man, in token of the hopes that cheer us both.

I have now only to conclude these comments by pointing back once more to their opening sentences, wherein I cited the dictum of Carlyle upon the import of the great world epoch that dawned upon us with the French Revolution. According to the high opinion which this great thinker has proclaimed, of the destiny of the German nation and its spirit of veracity, it must be deemed no vain presumption that we recognise in this German people—whose own completed *Reformation* would seem to have spared it from the need of any share in Revolution—the pre-ordained "Heroic Wise" on whom he calls to abridge the period of horrible World-Anarchy.　For myself, I feel assured that just the same relation which my ideal of Art bears to the reality of our general conditions of existence, that relation is allotted to the German race in its destiny amid a whole political world in the throes of "Spontaneous Combustion."

* 1868 ; Constantin Frantz.—Tr.

ART AND REVOLUTION.

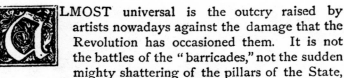LMOST universal is the outcry raised by artists nowadays against the damage that the Revolution has occasioned them. It is not the battles of the "barricades," not the sudden mighty shattering of the pillars of the State, not the hasty change of Governments,—that is bewailed; for the impression left behind by such capital events as these, is for the most part disproportionately fleeting, and short-lived in its violence. But it is the protracted character of the latest convulsions, that is so mortally affecting the artistic efforts of the day. The hitherto-recognised foundations of industry, of commerce, and of wealth, are now threatened; and though tranquillity has been outwardly restored, and the general physiognomy of social life completely re-established, yet there gnaws at the entrails of this life a carking care, an agonising distress. Reluctance to embark in fresh undertakings, is maiming credit; he who wishes to preserve what he has, declines the prospect of uncertain gain; industry is at a standstill, and—Art has no longer the wherewithal to live.

It were cruel to refuse human sympathy to the thousands who are smarting from this blow. Where, a little while ago, a popular artist was accustomed to receive, at the hands of the care-free portion of our well-to-do society, the reward of his appreciated services in sterling payment, and a like prospect of comfort and contentment in his life,—it is hard for him now to see himself rejected by tight-closed hands, and abandoned to lack of occupation. In this he shares the fate of the mechanic, who must lay the cunning fingers with which he was wont to create a thousand dainty trifles for the rich, in idleness upon his breast above a hungering stomach. He has the right then to bewail his lot ; for to him who feels the smart of pain, has Nature given the gift of tears. But whether he has a right to confound his own personality with that of Art, to decry his ills as the ills of Art, to scold the Revolution as the arch-enemy of Art, because it interferes with the easy ministry to his own wants : this were grave matter for question. Before a decision could be arrived at on this point, at least those artists might be interrogated who have shown by word and deed that they loved and laboured for Art for its own pure sake ; and from these we should soon learn, that they suffered also in the former times when others were rejoicing.

The question must be therefore put to Art itself and its true essence ; nor must we in this matter concern ourselves with mere abstract definitions ; for our object will naturally be, to discover the meaning of Art as a factor in the life of the State, and to make ourselves acquainted with it as a social product. A hasty review of the salient points of the history of European art will be of welcome service to us in this, and assist us to a solution of the above-named problem—a problem which is surely not of slight importance.

N any serious investigation of the essence of our art of to-day, we cannot make one step forward without being brought face to face with its intimate connection with the *Art of ancient Greece.* For, in point of fact, our modern art is but one link in the artistic development of the whole of Europe; and this development found its starting-point with the Greeks.

After it had overcome the raw religion of its Asiatic birth-place, built upon the nature-forces of the earth, and had set the *fair, strong manhood of freedom* upon the pinnacle of its religious convictions,—the Grecian spirit, at the flowering-time of its art and polity, found its fullest expression in the god Apollo, the head and national deity of the Hellenic race.

It was Apollo,—he who had slain the Python, the dragon of Chaos; who had smitten down the vain sons of boastful Niobe by his death-dealing darts; who, through his priestess at Delphi, had proclaimed to questioning man the fundamental laws of the Grecian race and nation, thus holding up to those involved in passionate action, the peaceful, undisturbed mirror of their inmost, unchangeable Grecian nature, —it was this Apollo who was the fulfiller of the will of Zeus upon the Grecian earth; who was, in fact, the Grecian people.

Not as the soft companion of the Muses,—as the later and more luxurious art of sculpture has alone preserved his likeness,—must we conceive the Apollo of the spring-time of the Greeks; but it was with all the traits of energetic earnestness, beautiful but strong, that the great tragedian *Æschylus* knew him. Thus, too, the Spartan youths learnt the nature of the god, when by dance and joust they had developed their supple bodies to grace and strength; when the boy was taken from those he loved, and sent on horse to farthest lands in search of perilous adventure; when the young man was led into the circle of fellowship, his only password that of his beauty and his native worth, in which alone lay all his might and all his riches. With such eyes also the Athenian saw the god, when all the impulses of his fair body, and of his restless soul, urged him to the new birth of his own being through the ideal expression of art ; when the voices, ringing full, sounded forth the choral song, singing the deeds of the god, the while they gave to the dancers the mastering measure that meted out the rhythm of the dance,—which dance itself, in graceful movements, told the story of those deeds ; and when above the harmony of well-ordered columns he wove the noble roof, heaped one upon the other the broad crescents of the amphitheatre, and planned the scenic trappings of the stage. Thus, too, inspired by Dionysus, the tragic poet saw this glorious god : when, to all the rich elements of spontaneous art, the harvest of the fairest and most human life, he joined the bond of speech, and concentrating them all into one focus, brought forth the highest conceivable form of art—the DRAMA.

The deeds of gods and men, their sufferings, their delights, as they,—in all solemnity and glee, as eternal rhythm, as everlasting harmony of every motion and of all creation, —lay disclosed in the nature of Apollo himself; here they became actual and true. For all that in them moved and lived, as it moved and lived in the beholders, here found its perfected expression; where ear and eye, as soul and heart, lifelike and actual, seized and perceived all, and saw all in spirit and in body revealed; so that the imagination need no longer vex itself with the attempt to conjure up the image. Such a tragedy-day was a Feast of the God; for here the god spoke clearly and intelligibly forth, and the poet, as his high-priest, stood real and embodied in his art-work, led the measures of the dance, raised the voices to a choir, and in ringing words proclaimed the utterances of godlike wisdom.

Such was the Grecian work of art ; such their god Apollo, incarnated in actual, living art; such was the Grecian people in its highest truth and beauty.

This race, in every branch, in every unit, was rich in indi-

C

viduality, restless in its energy, in the goal of one undertaking seeing but the starting-point of a fresh one; in
constant mutual intercourse, in daily-changing alliances,
in daily-varying strifes; to-day in luck, to-morrow in mischance; to-day in peril of the utmost danger, to-morrow
absolutely exterminating its foes ; in all its relations, both
internal and external, breathing the life of the freest and
most unceasing development.   This people, streaming in
its thousands from the State-assembly, from the Agora, from
land, from sea, from camps, from distant parts,—filled with
its thirty thousand heads the amphitheatre.   To see the
most pregnant of all tragedies, the " Prometheus," came
they; in this Titanic masterpiece to see the image of
themselves, to read the riddle of their own actions, to fuse
their own being and their own communion with that of
their god ; and thus in noblest, stillest peace to live again
the life which a brief space of time before, they had lived
in restless activity and accentuated individuality.

Ever jealous of his personal independence, and hunting
down the "Tyrannos" who, howsoever wise and lofty,
might imperil from any quarter the freedom of his own
strong will: the Greek despised the soft complacence
which, under the convenient shelter of another's care, can
lay itself down to passive egoistic rest.   Constantly on his
guard, untiring in warding off all outside influence : he gave
not even to the hoariest tradition the right over his own
free mundane life, his actions, or his thoughts.   Yet, at the
summons of the choir his voice was hushed, he yielded
himself a· willing slave to the deep significance of the
scenic show, and hearkened to the great story of Necessity
told by the tragic poet through the mouths of his gods
and heroes on the stage.   For in the tragedy he found
himself again,—nay, found the noblest part of his own
nature united with the noblest characteristics of the whole
nation ; and from his inmost soul, as it there unfolded itself
to him, proclaimed the Pythian oracle.   At once both God
and Priest, glorious godlike man, one with the Universal,
the Universal summed up in him : like one of those

thousand fibres which form the plant's united life, his slender form sprang from the soil into the upper air ; there to bring forth the one lovely flower which shed its fragrant breath upon eternity. This flower was the highest work of Art, its scent the spirit of Greece ; and still it intoxicates our senses and forces from us the avowal, that it were better to be for half a day a Greek in presence of this tragic Art-work, than to all eternity an—un-Greek *God!*

Hand-in-hand with the dissolution of the Athenian State, marched the downfall of Tragedy. As the spirit of *Community* split itself along a thousand lines of egoistic cleavage, so was the great united work of Tragedy disintegrated into its individual factors. Above the ruins of tragic art was heard the cry of the mad laughter of Aristophanes, the maker of comedies ; and, at the bitter end, every impulse of Art stood still before Philosophy, who read with gloomy mien her homilies upon the fleeting stay of human strength and beauty.

To *Philosophy* and not to Art, belong the two thousand years which, since the decadence of Grecian Tragedy, have passed till our own day. In vain did Art send hither and thither her dazzling beams into the night of discontented thought, of mankind grovelling in its madness ; they were but the cries, of pain or joy, of the units who had escaped from the 'desert of the multitude, and, like fortunate wanderers from distant lands, had reached the hidden, bubbling spring of pure Castalian waters, at which they slaked their thirsty lips but dared not reach the quickening draught unto the world. Or else it was, that Art entered on the service of one or other of those abstract ideas or even conventions which, now lighter and now more heavily, weighed down a suffering humanity and cast in fetters the freedom both of individuals and communities. But never more was she the free expression of a free community. Yet true Art is highest freedom, and only the highest freedom can bring her forth from out itself; no commandment, no ordinance, in short, no aim apart from Art, can call her to arise.

The Romans,—whose national art had early vanished before the influence of an indoctrinated Grecian art,— procured the services of Greek architects, sculptors and painters; and their own *savants* trained themselves to Grecian rhetoric and versification. Their giant theatres, however, they opened not to the gods and heroes of the ancient myths, nor to the free dancers and singers of the sacred choirs! No! Wild beasts, lions, panthers and elephants, must tear themselves to pieces in their amphitheatres, to glut the Roman eye; and gladiators, slaves trained up to the due pitch of strength and agility, must satiate the Roman ear with the hoarse gulp of death.

These brutal conquerors of the world were pleased to wallow in the most absolute realism; their imaginationcould find its only solace in the most material of presentments. Their philosophers they gladly left to flee shuddering from public life to abstract speculations; but, for themselves, they loved to revel in concrete and open bloodthirstiness, beholding human suffering set before them in absolute physical reality.

These gladiators and fighters with wild beasts, were sprung from every European nation; and the kings, nobles, and serfs of these nations were all slaves alike of the Roman Emperor, who showed them, in this most practical of ways, that all men were equals; just as, on the other hand, he himself was often shown most palpably by his own Pretorian Guard, that he also was no more than a mere slave.

This mutual and general slavery—so clear, that no one could gainsay it—yearned, as every universal feeling of the world must yearn, for an adequate expression of itself. But the manifest degradation and dishonour of all men; the consciousness of the complete corruption of all manly worth; the inevitably ensuing loathing of the material pleasures that now alone were left; the deep contempt for their own acts and deeds, from which all spirit of Genius and impulse of Art had long since joined with Freedom in her flight; this sorrowful existence, without actual aimful life,—could find but one expression; which, though certainly universal as the condition that called it forth, must yet be the direct antithesis of Art. For Art is pleasure in itself, in existence, in community; but the condition of that period, at the close of the Roman mastery of the world, was self-contempt, disgust with existence, horror of community. Thus *Art* could never be the true expression of this condition: its only possible expression was *Christianity*.

Christianity adjusts the ills of an honourless, useless, and sorrowful existence of mankind on earth, by the miraculous love of God; who had not — as the noble Greek supposed—created man for a happy and self-conscious life upon this earth, but had here imprisoned him in a loathsome dungeon: so as, in reward for the self-contempt that poisoned him therein, to prepare him for a posthumous state of endless comfort and inactive ecstasy. Man was therefore bound to remain in this deepest and unmanliest degradation, and no activity of this present life should he exercise; for this accursed life was, in truth, the world of the devil, *i.e.*, of the senses; and by every action in it, he played into the devil's hands. Therefore the poor wretch who, in the enjoyment of his natural powers, made this life his own possession, must suffer after death the eternal torments of hell! Naught was required of mankind but *Faith*—that is to say, the confession of its miserable plight, and the giving up of all spontaneous attempt to escape from out this misery; for the *undeserved Grace* of God was alone to set it free.

The historian knows not surely that this was the view of the humble son of the Galilean carpenter; who, looking on the misery of his fellow-men, proclaimed that he had not come to bring peace, but a sword into the world; whom we must love for the anger with which he thundered forth against the hypocritical Pharisees who fawned upon the power of Rome, so as the better to bind and heartlessly

enslave the people; and finally, who preached the reign of
universal human love—a love he could never have enjoined
on men whose duty it should be to despise their fellows
and themselves.   The inquirer more clearly discerns the
hand of the miraculously converted Pharisee, Paul, and
the zeal with which, in his conversion of the heathen, he
followed so successfully the monition: "Be ye wise as
serpents . . . ;" he may also estimate the deep and universal degradation of civilised mankind, and see in this the
historical soil from which the full-grown tree of finally
developed Christian dogma drew forth the sap that fed its
fruit.   But thus much the candid *artist* perceives at the
first glance: that neither was Christianity Art, nor could
it ever bring forth from itself the true and living Art.

The free Greek, who set himself upon the pinnacle of
Nature, could procreate Art from very joy in manhood: the
Christian, who impartially cast aside both Nature and himself, could only sacrifice to his God on the altar of renunciation; he durst not bring his actions or his work as offering, but believed that he must seek His favour by abstinence from all self-prompted venture.   Art is the highest
expression of activity of a race that has developed its
physical beauty in unison with itself and Nature; and
man must reap the highest joy from the world of sense,
before he can mould therefrom the implements of his art;
for from the world of sense alone, can he derive so much as
the impulse to artistic creation.   The Christian, on the
contrary, if he fain would create an art-work that should
correspond to his belief, must derive his impulse from the
essence of abstract spirit (*Geist*), from the grace of God,
and therein find his tools.—What, then, could he take for
aim?   Surely not physical beauty,—mirrored in his eyes
as an incarnation of the devil?   And how could pure
spirit, at any time, give birth to a something that could be
cognised by the senses?

All pondering of this problem is fruitless; the course of
history shows too unmistakeably the results of these two
opposite methods.   Where the Greeks, for their edification,

gathered in the amphitheatre for the space of a few short
hours full of the deepest meaning : the Christian shut himself away in the life-long imprisonment of a cloister. In
the one case, the Popular Assembly was the judge: in the
other, the Inquisition ; here the State developed to an
honourable Democracy: there, to a hypocritical Despotism.

Hypocrisy is the salient feature, the peculiar characteristic,
of every century of our Christian era, right down to our
own day ; and indeed this vice has always stalked abroad
with more crying shamelessness, in direct proportion as
mankind, in spite of Christendom, has refreshed its vigour
from its own unquenchable and inner well-spring, and
ripened toward the fulfilment of its true purpose. Nature
is so strong, so inexhaustible in its regenerative resources,
that no conceivable violence could weaken its creative force.
Into the ebbing veins of the Roman world, there poured
the healthy blood of the fresh Germanic nations. Despite
the adoption of Christianity, a ceaseless thirst of doing,
delight in bold adventure, and unbounded self-reliance,
remained the native element of the new masters of the
world. But, as in the whole history of the Middle Ages
we always light upon one prominent factor, the warfare
between worldly might and the despotism of the Roman
Church : so, when this new world sought for a form of
utterance, it could only find it in opposition to, and strife
against, the spirit of Christendom. The Art of Christian
Europe could never proclaim itself, like that of ancient
Greece, as the expression of a world attuned to harmony ;
for reason that its inmost being was incurably and irrecon-
cilably split up between the force of conscience and the
instinct of life, between the ideal and the reality. Like
the order of Chivalry itself, the chivalric poetry of the
Middle Ages, in attempting to heal this severance, could,
even amid its loftiest imagery, but bring to light the false-
hood of the reconciliation ; the higher and the more
proudly it soared on high, so the more visibly gaped the
abyss between the actual life and the idealised existence,

between the raw, passionate bearing of these knights in
physical life and their too delicate, etherealised behaviour
in romance. For the same reason did actual life, leaving
the pristine, noble, and certainly not ungraceful customs of
the People, become corrupt and vicious ; for it durst not
draw the nourishment for its art-impulse from out of its
own being, its joy in itself, and its own physical demeanour ;
but was sent for all its spiritual sustenance to Christianity,
which warned it off from the first taste of life's delight, as
from a thing accursed.—The poetry of Chivalry was thus
the honourable hypocrisy of fanaticism, the parody of
heroism : in place of Nature, it offered a convention.

Only when the enthusiasm of belief had smouldered
down, when the Church openly proclaimed herself as
naught but a worldly despotism appreciable by the senses,
in alliance with the no less material worldly absolutism of
the temporal rule which she had sanctified : only then,
commenced the so-called Renaissance of Art. That
wherewith man had racked his brains so long, he would
fain now see before him clad in body, like the Church
itself in all its worldly pomp. But this was only possible
on condition that he opened his eyes once more, and
restored his senses to their rights. Yet when man took
the objects of belief and the revelations of phantasy and
set them before his eyes in physical beauty, and with the
artist's delight in that physical beauty,—this was a complete denial of the very essence of the Christian religion ;
and it was the deepest humiliation to Christendom that
the guidance to these art-creations must be sought from
the pagan art of Greece. Nevertheless, the Church appropriated to herself this newly-roused art-impulse, and did
not blush to deck herself with the borrowed plumes of
paganism ; thus trumpeting her own hypocrisy.

Worldly dominion, however, had its share also in the
revival of art. After centuries of combat, their power
armed against all danger from below, the security of riches
awoke in the ruling classes the desire for more refined
enjoyment of this wealth : they took into their pay the

arts whose lessons Greece had taught. *"Free"* Art now
served as handmaid to these exalted masters, and, looking
into the matter more closely, it is difficult to decide who
was the greater hypocrite :—Louis XIV., when he sat and
heard the Grecian hate of Tyrants, declaimed in polished
verses from the boards of his Court-theatre; or Corneille
and Racine, when, to win the favour of their lord, they set
in the mouths of their stage-heroes the warm words of
freedom and political virtue, of ancient Greece and Rome.

Could Art be present there in very deed, where it
blossomed not forth as the living utterance of a free,
self-conscious community, but was taken into the service
of the very powers which hindered the self-development of
that community, and was thus capriciously transplanted
from foreign climes? No, surely! Yet we shall see that
Art, instead of enfranchising herself from eminently respectable masters, such as were the Holy Church and witty
Princes, preferred to sell her soul and body to a far worse
mistress—*Commerce.*

The Crecian Zeus, the father of all life, sent a messenger
from Olympus to the gods upon their wanderings through
the world—the fair young *Hermes.* The busy thought of
Zeus was he; winged he clove from the heights above to
the depths below, to proclaim the omnipresence of the
sovereign god. He presided, too, at the death of men, and
led their shades into the still realm of Night; for wherever
the stern necessity of Nature's ordering showed clearly
forth, the god Hermes was visible in action, as the
embodied thought of Zeus.

The Romans had a god, *Mercury,* whom they likened to
the Grecian Hermes. But with them his winged mission
gained a more practical intent. For them it was the restless diligence of their chaffering and usurious merchants,
who streamed from all the ends of the earth into the heart
of the Roman world; to bring its luxurious masters, in

barter for solid gain, all those delights of sense which their own immediately surrounding Nature could not afford them. To the Roman, surveying its essence and its methods, Commerce seemed no more nor less than trickery; and though, by reason of his ever-growing luxury, this world of trade appeared a necessary evil, he cherished a deep contempt for all its doings. Thus Mercury, the god of merchants, became for him the god withal of cheats and sharpers.

This slighted god, however, revenged himself upon the arrogant Romans, and usurped their mastery of the world. For, crown his head with the halo of Christian hypocrisy, decorate his breast with the soulless tokens of dead feudal orders: and ye have in him the god of the modern world, the holy-noble god of 'five per cent,' the ruler and the master of the ceremonies of our modern—'art.' Ye may see him embodied in a strait-laced English banker, whose daughter perchance has been given in marriage to a ruined peer. Ye may see him in this gentleman, when he engages the chief singers of the Italian Opera to sing before him in his own drawing-room rather than in the theatre, because he will have the glory of paying higher for them here than there; but on no account, even here, on the sacred Sunday. Behold *Mercury* and his docile hand-maid, *Modern Art!*

This is Art, as it now fills the entire civilised world! Its true essence is Industry; its ethical aim, the gaining of gold; its æsthetic purpose, the entertainment of those whose time hangs heavily on their hands. From the heart of our modern society, from the golden calf of wholesale Speculation, stalled at the meeting of its cross-roads, our art sucks forth its life-juice, borrows a hollow grace from the lifeless relics of the chivalric conventions of mediæval times, and—blushing not to fleece the poor, for all its professions of Christianity—descends to the depths of the proletariate, enervating, demoralising, and dehu-manising everything on which it sheds its venom.

Its pleasaunce it has set up in the Theatre, as did the art

of Greece in its maturity; and, indeed, it has a claim upon
the theatre : for is it not the expression of our current
views of present life ?   Our modern stage materialises the
ruling spirit of our social life, and publishes its daily record
in a way that no other branch of art can hope to rival ; for
it prepares its feasts, night in night out, in almost every
town of Europe.   Thus, as the broad-strewn art of drama,
it denotes, to all appearance, the flower of our culture ; just
as the Grecian tragedy denoted the culminating point of
the Grecian spirit ; but ours is the efflorescence of corruption, of a hollow, soulless and unnatural condition of human
affairs and human relations.

This condition of things we need not further characterise
here ; we need but honestly search the contents and the
workings of our public art, especially that of the stage, in
order to see the spirit of the times reflected therein as in
a faithful mirror ; for such a mirror public Art has ever
been.*

Thus we can by no means recognise in our theatrical
art the genuine Drama; that one, indivisible, supreme
creation of the mind of man.   Our theatre merely offers
the convenient *locale* for the tempting exhibition of the
heterogeneous wares of art-manufacture.   How incapable
is our stage to gather up each branch of Art in its highest
and most perfect expression—the Drama—it shows at
once in its division into the two opposing classes, Play and
Opera ; whereby the idealising influence of music is forbidden to the Play, and the Opera is forestalled of the
living heart and lofty purpose of actual drama.   Thus on
the one hand, the spoken Play can never, with but few

* In the original text of both the present treatise and *The Art-work of the
Future*, the expression "*öffentlich*" is frequently made use of.   In English
the only available equivalent is that which I have here employed, viz. :
"public"; but our word "public" must be stretched a little in its significance,
to answer to Richard Wagner's purpose.   When he speaks of "public art" or
"public life," it must be borne in mind that the idea of officialdom or State-
endowment is not necessarily included ; but rather the word is employed in the
sense in which we use it when talking of a "public appearance"; thus "public
art" will mean such an art as is not merely designed for private or home
consumption.—TR.

exceptions, lift itself up to the ideal flight of poetry ; but, for very reason of the poverty of its means of utterance,— to say nothing of the demoralising influence of our public life,—must fall from height to depth, from the warm atmosphere of passion into the cold element of intrigue. On the other hand, the Opera becomes a chaos of sensuous impressions jostling one another without rhyme or reason, from which each one may choose at will what pleases best his fancy ; here the alluring movements of a dancer, there the *bravura* passage of a singer ; here the dazzling effect of a triumph of the scene-painter, there the astounding efforts of a Vulcan of the orchestra. Do we not read from day to day, that this or that new opera is a masterpiece because it contains a goodly number of fine *arias* and duets, the instrumentation is extremely brilliant, &c., &c. ? The aim which alone can justify the employment of such complex means,—the great dramatic aim,—folk never give so much as a thought.

Such verdicts as these are shallow, but honest ; they show exactly what is the position of the audience. There are even many of our most popular artists who do not in the least conceal the fact, that they have no other ambition than to satisfy this shallow audience. They are wise in their generation ; for when the prince leaves a heavy dinner, the banker a fatiguing financial operation, the working man a weary day of toil, and go to the theatre : they ask for rest, distraction, and amusement, and are in no mood for renewed effort and fresh expenditure of force. This argument is so convincing, that we can only reply by saying : it would be more decorous to employ for this purpose any other thing in the wide world, but not the body and soul of Art. We shall then be told, however, that if we do not employ Art in this manner, it must perish from out our public life : *i.e.,*—that the artist will lose the means of living.

On this side everything is lamentable, indeed, but candid, genuine, and honest ; civilised corruption, and modern Christian dulness !

But, affairs having undeniably come to such a pass, what shall we say to the hypocritical pretence of many an art-hero of our times, whose fame is now the order of the day?—when he dons the melancholy counterfeit of true artistic inspiration; when he racks his brains for thoughts of deep intent, and ever seeks fresh food for awe, setting heaven and hell in motion : in short, when he behaves just like those honest journeymen of art who avowed that one must *not* be too particular if one wish to get rid of one's goods. What shall we say, when these heroes not only seek to entertain, but expose themselves to all the peril of fatiguing, in order to be thought profound ; when, too, they renounce all hope of substantial profit, and even—though only a rich man, born and bred, can afford that !—spend their own money upon their productions, thus offering up the highest modern sacrifice? To what purpose, this enormous waste? Alas ! there yet remains one other thing than gold, a thing that nowadays a man may buy for gold like any other pleasure : that thing is *Fame !*—Yet what sort of fame is there to reach in our public art ? Only the fame of the same publicity for which this art is planned, and which the fame-lusting man can never obtain but by submission to its most trivial claims. Thus he deludes both himself and the public, in giving it his piebald art-work; while the public deludes both itself and him, in bestowing on him its applause. But this mutual lie is worthy of the lying nature of modern Fame itself; for we are adepts in the art of decking out our own self-seeking passions with the monstrous lies of such sweet-sounding names as " Patriotism," " Honour," " Law and Order," &c., &c.

Yet, why do we deem it necessary so publicly to cheat each one the other ?—Because, mid all the ruling evils, these notions and these virtues are present still within our conscience ; though truly in our *guilty* conscience. For it is sure, that where honour and truth are really present, there also is true Art at hand. The greatest and most noble minds—whom Æschylus and Sophocles would have

greeted with the kiss of brotherhood—for centuries have
raised their voices in the wilderness.   We have heard their
cry, and it lingers still within our ears ; but from our base
and frivolous hearts we have washed away its living echo.
We tremble at their fame, but mock their art.   We admit
their rank as artists of lofty aim, but rob them of the realisation of their art-work ; for the one great, genuine work of
Art they cannot bring to life unaided : we, too, must help
them in its birth.   The tragedies of Æschylus and Sophocles were the work of Athens !

What boots, then, the fame of these Masters ?   What
serves it us, that *Shakespeare*, like a second Creator, has
opened for us the endless realm of human nature ?   What
serves it, that *Beethoven* has lent to Music the manly, independent strength of Poetry ?   Ask the threadbare
caricatures of your theatres, ask the street-minstrel commonplaces of your operas : and ye have your answer !   But do
ye need to ask ? Alas, no ! Ye know it right well ; indeed,
ye would not have it otherwise ; ye only give yourselves
the air as though ye knew it not!

What then is your Art, and what your Drama ?

The Revolution of February deprived the Paris theatres
of public support ; many of them were on the brink of
bankruptcy.   After the events of June, Cavaignac, busied
with the maintenance of the existing order of society, came
to their aid and demanded a subvention for their continuance.   Why?—Because the Breadless Classes, the *Prolé-
tariat*, would be augmented by the closing of the theatres.
—So ; this interest alone has the State in the Stage !   It
sees in it an industrial workshop, and, to boot, an influence
that may calm the passions, absorb the excitement, and
divert the threatening agitation of the heated public mind ;
which broods in deepest discontent, seeking for the way
by which dishonoured human nature may return to its
true self, even though it be at cost of the continuance of
our—so appropriate theatrical institutions !

Well ! the avowal is candid ; and on all fours with
the frankness of this admission, stands the complaint

of our modern artists and their hatred for the Revolution. Yet what has *Art* in common with these cares and these complaints ?

Let us now compare the chief features of the public art of modern Europe with those of the public art of Greece, in order to set clearly before our eyes their characteristic points of difference.

The public art of the Greeks, which reached its zenith in their Tragedy, was the expression of the deepest and the noblest principles of the people's consciousness : with *us* the deepest and noblest of man's consciousness is the direct opposite of this, namely the denunciation of our public art. To the Greeks the production of a tragedy was a religious festival, where the gods bestirred themselves upon the stage and bestowed on men their wisdom : *our* evil conscience has so lowered the theatre in public estimation, that it is the duty of the police to prevent the stage from meddling in the slightest with religion ; * a circumstance as characteristic of our religion as of our art. Within the ample boundaries of the Grecian amphitheatre, the whole populace was wont to witness the performances : in our superior theatres, loll only the affluent classes. The Greeks sought the instruments of their art in the products of the highest associate culture : we seek ours in the deepest social barbarism. The education of the Greek, from his earliest youth, made himself the subject of his own artistic treatment and artistic enjoyment, in body as in spirit : our foolish education, fashioned for the most part to fit us merely for future industrial gain, gives us a ridiculous, and withal arrogant satisfaction with our own unfitness for art, and forces us to seek the subjects of any kind of artistic

---

* R. Wagner to F. Heine, March 18, '41 :—" This showed me still more decidedly that the religious-catholic part of my *Rienzi* libretto was a chief stumbling-block. . . . If in my *Rienzi* the word ' Church ' is not allowed to stand," &c.—To W. Fischer, Dec. 8, '41 :—" Sixteen singers must remain for the Priests, or on account of the censorship, aged Citizens."—TR.

amusement outside ourselves,—like the rake who goes for
the fleeting joys of love to the arms of a prostitute.
Thus the Greek was his own actor, singer, and dancer ;
his share in the performance of a tragedy was to him the
highest pleasure in the work of Art itself, and he rightly
held it an honour to be entitled by his beauty and his
culture to be called to this beloved task : we, on the other
hand, permit a certain portion of our proletariate, which is
to be found in every social stratum, to be instructed for
our entertainment ; thus prurient vanity, claptrap, and at
times unseemly haste for fortune-making, fill up the ranks
of our dramatic companies.   Where the Grecian artist
found his only reward in his own delight in the masterpiece, in its success, and the public approbation : we have
the modern artist boarded, lodged, and—*paid*.   And thus
we reach the essential distinction between the two : with
the Greeks their public art was very *Art*, with us it is
artistic—*Handicraft*.

The *true artist* finds delight not only in the aim of his
creation, but also in the very process of creation, in the
handling and moulding of his material.   The very act of
production is to him a gladsome, satisfying activity : no
toil.   The *journeyman* reckons only the goal of his labour,
the profit which his toil shall bring him ; the energy which
he expends, gives him no pleasure ; it is but a fatigue, an
inevitable task, a burden which he would gladly give over
to a machine ; his toil is but a fettering chain.   For this
reason he is never present with his work in spirit, but
always looking beyond it to its goal, which he fain would
reach as quickly as he may.   Yet, if the immediate aim of
the journeyman is the satisfaction of an impulse of his own,
such as the preparing of his own dwelling, his chattels, his
raiment, &c. : then, together with his prospective pleasure
in the lasting value of these objects, there also enters by
degrees a bent to such a fashioning of the material as shall
agree with his individual tastes.   After he has fulfilled the
demands of bare necessity, the creation of that which answers to less pressing needs will elevate itself to the rank

of artistic production. But if he bargains away the product of his toil, all that remains to him is its mere money-worth; and thus his energy can never rise above the character of the busy strokes of a machine; in his eyes it is but weariness, and bitter, sorrowful toil. The latter is the lot of the Slave of Industry; and our modern factories afford us the sad picture of the deepest degradation of man,—constant labour, killing both body and soul, without joy or love, often almost without aim.

It is impossible to mistake the lamentable effects of Christian dogma, in this also. As this dogma set man's goal entirely outside his earthly being, and that goal was centred in an absolute and superhuman God: so only from the aspect of its most inevitable needs, could life remain an object of man's care; for, having once received the gift of life, it was his bounden duty to maintain it until that day when God alone should please relieve him of its burden. But in no wise should his needs awake a lust to treat with loving hand the matter given him for their satisfaction; only the abstract aim of life's bare maintenance could justify the operation of his senses. And thus we see with horror the spirit of modern Christianity embodied in a cotton-mill: to speed the rich, God has become our Industry, which only holds the wretched Christian labourer to life until the heavenly courses of the stars of commerce bring round the gracious dispensation that sends him to a better world.

The Greek knew no handicraft, rightly so described. The so-called necessaries of life,—which, strictly speaking, make up the whole concernment of our private and our public life,—he deemed unworthy to rank as objects of special and engrossing attention. His soul lived only in publicity, in the great fellowship of his nation; the needs of this public life made up the total of his care; whereas these needs were satisfied by the patriot, the statesman, and the artist, but not the handicraftsman. The Greek went forth to the delights of this publicity from a simple, unassuming home. It would have seemed to him disgrace-

D

ful and degrading to revel, within the costly walls of a
private palace, in the refinements of luxury and extravagance which to-day fill out the life of a hero of the Bourse;
for this was the distinction that he drew between himself
and the egoistic "Barbärians" of the East. He sought
the culture of his body in the general public baths and
gymnasia; his simple, noble clothing was for the most
part the artistic care of the women; and whenever he fell
upon the necessity of manual toil, it was of his very nature
that he should find out its artistic side, and straightway
raise it to an art. But the drudgery of household labour
he thrust away—to *Slaves*.

This Slave thus became the fateful hinge of the whole
destiny of the world. The Slave, by sheer reason of the
assumed necessity of his slavery, has exposed the null and
fleeting nature of all the strength and beauty of exclusive
Grecian manhood, and has shown to all time that *Beauty and
Strength, as attributes of public life, can then alone prove lasting blessings, when they are the common gifts of all mankind.*

Unhappily, things have not as yet advanced beyond the
mere demonstration. In fact, the Revolution of the human
race, that has lasted now two thousand years, has been
almost exclusively in the spirit of Reaction. It has
dragged down the fair, free man to itself, to slavery; the
slave has not become a freeman, but the freeman a slave.

To the Greek the fair, strong man alone was free, and
this man was none other than *himself;* whatever lay outside the circle of Grecian manhood and Apollonian priest-
hood, was to him *barbarian,* and if he employed it,—*slave.*
True that the man who was not Greek, was actually
barbarian and slave; but he was still a *man,* and his
barbarianism and his slavery were not his nature but his
fate : the sin of history against his nature, just as to-day it
is the sin of our social system, that the healthiest nations
in the healthiest climates have brought forth cripples and
outcasts. This historical sin, however, was destined soon
to be avenged upon the free Greek himself. Where there
lived among the nations no feeling of *absolute human-love,*

the Barbarian needed only to subjugate the Greek : and all
was over with Grecian freedom, strength, and beauty.
Thus, in deep humiliation, two hundred million men,
huddled in helpless confusion in the Roman empire, too
soon found out that—when *all* men cannot be *free alike*
and *happy*—all men must *suffer alike* as *slaves.*

Thus we are slaves until this very day, with but the sorry
consolation of knowing that we are all slaves together.
Slaves, to whom once the Christian Apostles and the
Emperor Constantine gave counsel, to patiently submit to
a suffering life below, for sake of a better world above ;
slaves, whom bankers and manufacturers teach nowadays
to seek the goal of Being in manual toil for daily bread.
Free from this slavery, in his time, felt the Emperor Constantine alone ; when he enthroned himself, a pleasure-
seeking heathen despot, above this life which he had
taught his believing subjects to deem so useless. And
free alone, to-day,—at least in the sense of freedom from
open slavery,—feels he who has money ; for he is thus
able to employ his life to some other end than that of
winning the bare means of subsistence. Thus, as the
struggle for freedom from the general slavery proclaimed
itself in Roman and Medieval times as the reaching after
absolute dominion : so it comes to light to-day as the
greed for gold. And we must not be astonished, if even
Art grasps after gold ; for everything strives to its freedom,
towards its god,—and our god is Gold, our religion the
Pursuit of Wealth.

Yet Art remains in its essence what it ever was ; we
have only to say, that it is not present in our modern
public system. It lives, however, and has ever lived in
the individual conscience, as the one, fair, indivisible Art.
Thus the only difference is this : with the Greeks it lived
in the public conscience, whereas to-day it lives alone in
the conscience of private persons, the public *un*-conscience
recking nothing of it. Therefore in its flowering time the
Grecian Art was *conservative*, because it was a worthy and
adequate expression of the public conscience : with us,

true Art is *revolutionary*, because its very existence is
opposed to the ruling spirit of the community.

With the Greeks the perfect work of art, the Drama,
was the abstract and epitome of all that was expressible
in the Grecian nature.   It was the nation itself—in intimate connection with its own history—that stood mirrored in its art-work, that communed with itself and,
within the span of a few hours, feasted its eyes with its
own noblest essence.   All division of this enjoyment, all
scattering of the forces concentred on *one* point, all
diversion of the elements into separate channels, must
needs have been as hurtful to this *unique* and noble Art-
work as to the like-formed State itself ; and thus it could
only mature, but never change its nature.   Thus Art was
conservative, just as the noblest sons of this epoch of the
Grecian State were themselves conservative.   *Æschylus* is
the very type of this conservatism, and his loftiest work of
conservative art is the " *Oresteia*," with which he stands
alike opposed as poet to the youthful *Sophocles*, as statesman
to the revolutionary *Pericles*.   The victory of Sophocles,
like that of Pericles, was fully in the spirit of the advancing
development of mankind ; but the deposition of Æschylus
was the first downward step from the height of Grecian
Tragedy, the first beginning of the dissolution of Athenian
Polity.

With the subsequent downfall of Tragedy, Art became
less and less the expression of the public conscience.
The Drama separated into its component parts ; rhetoric,
sculpture, painting, music, &c., forsook the ranks in which
they had moved in unison before ; each one to take its
own way, and in lonely self-sufficiency to pursue its own
development.   And thus it was that at the Renaissance of
Art we lit first upon these isolated Grecian arts, which had
sprung from the wreck of Tragedy.   The great unitarian
Art-work of Greece could not at once reveal itself to our
bewildered, wandering, piecemeal minds in all its fulness ;
for how could we have understood it ?   But we knew how
to appropriate those dissevered handiworks of Art ; for as

goodly handiwork, to which category they had already sunk in the Romo-Greek world, they lay not so far from our own nature and our minds. The guild and handicraft spirit of the new citizenship rose quick and lively in the towns ; princes and notabilities were well pleased that their castles should be more becomingly built and decorated, their walls bedecked with more attractive paintings, than had been possible to the raw art of the Middle Ages ; the priests laid hands on rhetoric for their pulpits and music for their choirs ; and the new world of handicraft worked valiantly among the separate arts of Greece, so far at least as it understood them or thought them fitted to its purpose.

Each one of these dissevered arts, nursed and luxuriously tended for the entertainment of the rich, has filled the world to overflowing with its products ; in each, great minds have brought forth marvels ; but the one true Art has not been born again, either in or since the Renaissance. The perfect Art-work, the great united utterance of a free and lovely public life, the *Drama, Tragedy,*—howsoever great the poets who have here and there indited tragedies, —is not yet born again : for reason that it cannot be *re-born*, but must be *born anew.*

Only the great *Revolution of Mankind*, whose beginnings erstwhile shattered Grecian Tragedy, can win for us this Art-work. For only this Revolution can bring forth from its hidden depths, in the new beauty of a nobler Universalism, *that* which it once tore from the conservative spirit of a time of beautiful but narrow-meted culture—and tearing it, engulphed.

But only *Revolution*, not slavish *Restoration*, can give us back that highest Art-work. The task we have before us is immeasurably greater than that already accomplished in days of old. If the Grecian Art-work embraced the spirit of a fair and noble nation, the Art-work of the Future must embrace the spirit of a free mankind, delivered from every shackle of hampering nationality ; its racial imprint must be no more than an embellishment, the individual charm of manifold diversity, and not a cramping barrier.   We have thus quite other work to do, than to tinker at the resuscitation of old Greece.   Indeed, the foolish restoration of a sham Greek mode of art has been attempted already,—for what will our artists not attempt, to order ? But nothing better than an inane patchwork could ever come of it—the offspring of the same juggling endeavour which we find evinced by the whole history of our official civilisation, seized as it is with a constant wish to avoid the only lawful endeavour, the striving after Nature.

No, we do not wish to revert to Greekdom ; for what the Greeks knew not, and, knowing not, came by their downfall : that know *we*.   It is their very fall, whose cause we now perceive after years of misery and deepest universal suffering, that shows us clearly what we should become ; it shows us that we must love all men before we can rightly love ourselves, before we can regain true joy in our own personality.   From the dishonouring slave-yoke of universal journeymanhood, with its sickly Money-soul, we wish to soar to the free manhood of Art, with the star-rays of its World-soul ; from the weary, overburdened day-labourers of Commerce, we desire to grow to fair strong men, to whom the world belongs as an eternal, inexhaustible source of the highest delights of Art.

To this end we need the mightiest force of Revolution ; for only *that* revolutionary force can boot us, which presses forward to the goal—to that goal whose attainment alone can justify its earliest exercise upon the disintegration of Greek Tragedy and the dissolution of the Athenian State.

But whence shall we derive this force, in our present state of utmost weakness ?   Whence the manly strength against the crushing pressure of a civilisation which disowns all manhood, against the arrogance of a culture which employs the human mind as naught but steam-power for its machinery ?   Whence the light with which to illumine the gruesome ruling heresy, that this civilisation and this culture are of more value in themselves than the true living Man ?—that Man has worth and value only as a tool of these despotic abstract powers, and not by virtue of his manhood ?

When the learned physician is at the end of his resources, in despair we turn at last to—*Nature*. Nature, then, and only Nature, can unravel the skein of this great world-fate. If Culture, starting from the Christian dogma of the worthlessness of human nature, disown humanity : she has created for herself a foe who one day must inevitably destroy her, in so far as she no longer has place for manhood ; for this foe is the eternal, and only living Nature. Nature, Human Nature, will proclaim this law to the twin sisters Culture and Civilisation : " So far as I am contained in you, shall ye live and flourish ; so far as I am not in you, shall ye rot and die ! "

In the man-destroying march of Culture, however, there looms before us this happy result : the heavy load with which she presses Nature down, will one day grow so ponderous that it lends at last to down-trod, never-dying Nature the necessary impetus to hurl the whole cramping burden from her, with one sole thrust ; and this heaping up of Culture will thus have *taught* to Nature her own gigantic force. The releasing of this force is—*Revolution*.

In what way, then, does this revolutionary force exhibit itself in the present social crisis ? Is it not in the mechanic's pride in the moral consciousness of his labour, as opposed to the criminal passivity or immoral activity of the rich ? Does he not wish, as in revenge, to elevate the principle of labour to the rank of the one and orthodox religion of society ? To force the rich like him to work,— like him, by the sweat of their brow to gain their daily bread ? Must we not fear that the exercise of this compulsion, the recognition of this principle, would raise at last the man-degrading journeymanhood to an absolute and universal might, and—to keep to our chief theme— would straightway make of Art an impossibility for all time ?

In truth, this is the fear of many an honest friend of Art and many an upright friend of men, whose only wish is to preserve the nobler core of our present civilisation. But they mistake the true nature of the great social agitation. They are led astray by the windy theories of our socialistic doctrinaires, who would fain patch up an impossible compact with the present conditions of society. They are deceived by the immediate utterance of the indignation of the most suffering portion of our social system, behind which lies a deeper, nobler, natural instinct : the instinct which demands a worthy taste of the joys of life, whose material sustenance shall no longer absorb man's whole life-forces in weary service, but in which he shall rejoice as Man. Viewed closer, it is thus the straining from journeymanhood to artistic manhood, to the free dignity of Man.

It is for Art therefore, and Art above all else, to teach this social impulse its noblest meaning, and guide it toward its true direction. Only on the shoulders of this great social movement can true Art lift itself from its present state of civilised barbarianism, and take its post of honour. Each has a common goal, and the twain can only reach it when they recognise it jointly. This goal is *the strong fair Man,* to whom *Revolution* shall give his *Strength,* and *Art* his *Beauty !*

Neither is it our present purpose to indicate more closely the march of this social development and the records it will stamp on history, nor could dogmatic calculation foretell the historical demeanour of man's social nature, so little dependent upon preconceived ideas. In the history of man nothing is *made,* but everything evolves by its own inner necessity. Yet it is impossible that the final state which this movement shall attain one day, should be other than the direct opposite of the present ; else were the whole history of the world a restless zig-zag of cross purposes, and not the ordered movement of a mighty stream ; which with all its bends, its deviations, and its floods, yet flows for ever in one steadfast course.

Let us glance, then, for a moment at this future state of Man, when he shall have freed himself from his last heresy, the denial of Nature,—that heresy which has taught him hitherto to look upon himself as a mere instrument to an end which lay outside himself. When Mankind knows, at last, that itself is the one and only object of its existence, and that only in the community of all men can this purpose be fulfilled : then will its mutual creed be couched in an actual fulfilment of Christ's injunction, " Take no *care* for your life, what ye shall eat, or what ye shall drink ; nor yet for your body, what ye shall put on, for your Heavenly Father knoweth that ye have need of all these things." This Heavenly Father will then be no other than the social wisdom of mankind, taking Nature and her fulness for the common weal of all. The crime and the curse of our social intercourse have lain in this : that the mere physical maintenance of life has been till now the one object of our *care*,—a real *care* that has devoured our souls and bodies and well nigh lamed each spiritual impulse. This *Care* has made man weak and slavish, dull and wretched ; a creature that can neither love nor hate ; a thrall of commerce, ever ready to give up the last vestige of the freedom of his Will, so only that this *Care* might be a little lightened.

When the Brotherhood of Man has cast this care for ever from it, and, as the Greeks upon their slaves, has lain it on machines,—the artificial slaves of free creative man, whom he has served till now as the Fetish-votary serves the idol his own hands have made,—then will man's whole enfranchised energy proclaim itself as naught but pure *artistic* impulse. Thus shall we regain, in vastly higher measure, the Grecian element of life ; what with the Greek was the result of natural development, will be with us the product of ages of endeavour ; what was to him a half-unconscious gift, will remain with us a conquered knowledge ; for what mankind in its wide communion doth truly *know*, can never more be lost to it.

Only the *Strong* know *Love;* only Love can fathom *Beauty;* only Beauty can fashion *Art.* The love of weaklings for each other can only manifest as the goad of lust ; the love of the weak for the strong is abasement and fear ; the love of the strong for the weak is pity and forbearance ; but the love of the strong for the strong is *Love*, for it is the free surrender to one who cannot compel us.   Under every fold of heaven's canopy, in every race, shall men by real freedom grow up to equal strength ; by strength to truest love ; and by true love to beauty.   But Art is Beauty energised.

Whatsoever we deem the goal of life, to that we train our selves and children.   The Goth was bred to battle and to chase, the genuine Christian to abstinence and humility : while the liegeman of the modern State is bred to seek industrial gain, be it even in the exercise of art and science. But when life's maintenance is no longer the exclusive aim of life, and the Freemen of the Future—inspired by a new and deed-begetting faith, or better, Knowledge—find the means of life assured by payment of a natural and reasonable energy ; in short, when Industry no longer is our mistress but our handmaid : then shall we set the goal of life in joy of life, and strive to rear our children to be fit and worthy partners in this joy.   This training, starting from the exercise of strength and nurture of corporeal beauty, will soon take on a pure artistic shape, by reason of our undisturbed affection for our children and our gladness at the ripening of their beauty ; and each man will, in one domain or other, become in truth an artist.   The diversity of natural inclination will build up arts in manifold variety and countless forms of each variety, in fulness hitherto undreamed.   And as the Knowledge of all men will find at last its religious utterance in the one effective Knowledge of free united manhood : so will all these rich developments of Art find their profoundest focus in the Drama, in the glorious Tragedy of Man.   The Tragedy will be the feast of all mankind ; in it,—set free from each conventional etiquette,—free, strong, and beauteous man will celebrate the dolour and delight of all his love, and consecrate in lofty worth the great Love-offering of his Death.

This Art will be *conservative* afresh. Yet truly of its own immortal force, will it maintain itself and blossom forth : not merely cry for maintenance, on pretext of some outward-lying aim. For mark ye well, *this* Art seeks not for *Gain!*

" Utopia ! Utopia !" I hear the mealy-mouthed wise-acres of our modern State-and-Art-barbarianism cry ; the so-called practical men, who in the manipulation of their daily practice can help themselves alone with lies and violence, or—if they be sincere and honest — with ignorance at best.

" Beautiful ideal ! but, alas ! like all ideals, one that can only float before us, beyond the reach of man condemned to imperfection." Thus sighs the smug adorer of the heavenly kingdom in which—at least as far as himself is concerned—God will make good the inexplicable short-comings of this earth and its human brood.

They live and lie, they sin and suffer, in the loathliest of actual conditions, in the filthy dregs of an artificial, and therefore never realised Utopia ; they toil and over-bid each other in every hypocritical art, to maintain the cheat of this Utopia ; from which they daily tumble headlong down to the dull, prosaic level of nakedest reality,—the mutilated cripples of the meanest and most frivolous of passions. Yet they cry down the only natural release from their bewitchment, as " Chimeras " or " Utopias ; " just as the poor sufferers in a madhouse take their insane imaginings for truth, and truth itself for madness.

If history knows an actual Utopia, a truly unattainable ideal, it is that of Christendom ; for it has clearly and plainly shown, and shows it still from day to day, that its dogmas are *not* realisable. How could those dogmas become really living, and pass over into actual life : when they were directed against life itself, and denied and cursed the principle of living? Christianity is of purely spiritual, and super-spiritual contents; it preaches humility,

renunciation, contempt of every earthly thing; and amid
this contempt—Brotherly Love! How does the fulfilment
work out in the modern world, which calls itself, forsooth,
a Christian world, and clutches to the Christian religion as
its inexpugnable basis? As the arrogance of hypocrisy, as
usury, as robbery of Nature's goods, and egoistic scorn of
suffering fellow-men. Whence comes this shocking contradiction between the ideal and the fulfilment? Even hence:
that the ideal was morbid, engendered of the momentary
relaxing and enfeeblement of human nature, and sinned
against its inbred robust qualities. Yet how strong this
nature is, how unquenchable its ever fresh, productive fulness—it has shown all the more plainly under the universal
incubus of that ideal; which, if its logical consequences
had been fulfilled, would have completely swept the human
race from off the earth; since even abstinence from sexual
love was included in it as the height of virtue. But still ye
see that, in spite of that all-powerful Church, the human
race is so abundant that your Christian-economic State-
wisdom knows not what to do with this abundance, and ye
are looking round for means of social murder, for its uprootal; yea, and would be right glad, were mankind slain
by Christianity, so only that the solitary abstract god of
your own beloved *Me* might gain sufficient elbow-room
upon this earth!

These are the men who cry " Utopia," when the healthy
human understanding (*Menschenverstand*) appeals from
their insane experiments to the actuality of visible and tan-
gible Nature ; when it demands no more from man's godlike
reason (*Vernunft*) than that it should make good to us the
instinct of dumb animals, and give us the means of finding
for ourselves the sustenance of our life, set free from care
though not from labour! And, truly, we ask from it no
higher result for the community of mankind, in order that
we may build upon this one foundation the noblest, fairest
temple of the true Art of the Future!

The true artist who has already grasped the proper standpoint, may labour even now—for this standpoint is ever

present with us—upon the Art-work of the Future! Each
of the sister Arts, in truth, has ever, and therefore also now,
proclaimed in manifold creations the conscience of her own
high purpose. Whereby, then, have the inspired creators
of these noble works from all time suffered, and above all
in our present pass? Was it not by their contact with the
outer world, with the very world for whom their works
were destined? What has revolted the architect, when he
must shatter his creative force on bespoken plans for bar-
racks and lodging-houses? What has aggrieved the painter,
when he must immortalise the repugnant visage of a million-
aire? What the musician, when he must compose his music
for the banquet-table? And what the poet, when he must
write romances for the lending-library? What then has
been the sting of suffering to each? That he must squander
his creative powers for gain, and make his art a handicraft!—
And finally, what suffering has the dramatist to bear, who
would fain assemble every art within Art's master-work,
the Drama? The sufferings of all other artists combined
in one!

What *he* creates, becomes an Art-work only when it enters
into open life; and a work of dramatic art can only enter
life upon the stage. But what are our theatrical institutions
of to-day, with their disposal of the ample aid of every
branch of art?—Industrial undertakings: yes, even when
supported by a special subsidy from Prince or State. Their
direction is mostly handed over to the same men who have
yesterday conducted a speculation in grain, and to-morrow
devote their well-learned knowledge to a 'corner' in sugar;
or mayhap, have educated their taste for stage proprieties
in the mysteries of back-stairs intrigue, or such like functions.* So long as—in accordance with the prevailing
character of public life, and the necessity it lays upon the
theatrical director to deal with the public in the manner of
a clever commercial speculator—so long as we look upon a

---

* It is impossible to realise the full sting of this allusion, without having read
in "*Wagner's Letters to Uhlig*" (H. Grevel & Co.) the account of the author's
own experience at Dresden of the conduct of these gentry.—TR.

theatrical institution as a mere means for the circulation of money and the production of interest upon capital, it is only logical that we should hand over its direction, *i.e.*, its exploitation, to those who are well-skilled in such transactions ; for a really artistic management, and thus such an one as should fulfil the original purpose of the Theatre, would certainly be but poorly fitted to carry out the modern aim.   For this reason it must be clear to all who have the slightest insight, that if the Theatre is at all to answer to its natural lofty mission, it must be completely freed from the necessity of industrial speculation.

How were this possible ?   Shall this solitary institution be released from a service to which all men, and every associate enterprise of man, are yoked to-day ?   Yes : it is precisely the Theatre, that should take precedence of every other institution in this emancipation ; for the Theatre is the widest-reaching of Art's institutes, and the richest in its influence ; and till man can exercise in freedom his noblest, his artistic powers, how shall he hope to become free and self-dependent in lower walks of life ?   Since already the service of the State, the military service, is at least no longer an industrial pursuit, let us begin with the enfranchisement of public art ; for, as I have pointed out above, it is to *it* that we must assign an unspeakably lofty mission, an immeasurably weighty influence on our present social upheaval.   More and better than a decrepit religion to which the spirit of public intercourse gives the lie direct ; more effectually and impressively than an incapable statesmanship which has long since lost its compass : shall the ever-youthful Art, renewing its freshness from its own well-springs and the noblest spirit of the times, give to the passionate stream of social tumult—now dashing against rugged precipices, now lost in shallow swamps—a fair and lofty goal, the goal of noble Manhood.

If ye friends of Art are truly concerned to know it saved from the threatening storms : then hear me, when I tell you that it is no mere question of preserving Art, but of first allowing it to reach its own true fill of life !

Is it your real object, ye *honourable* Statesmen, confronted
with a dreaded social overthrow,—against which, mayhap,
ye strive because your shattered faith in human nature's
purity prevents your understanding how this overthrow can
help but make a bad condition infinitely worse,—is it, I say,
your object to graft upon this mighty change a strong and
living pledge of future nobler customs? Then lend us all
your strength, to give back Art unto itself and to its lofty
mission!

Ye suffering brethren, in every social grade, who brood
in hot displeasure how to flee this slavery to money and
become free men: fathom ye our purpose, and help us to
lift up Art to its due dignity; that so we may show you
how ye raise mechanical toil therewith to Art, and the serf
of industry to the fair, self-knowing man who cries, with
smiles begotten of intelligence, to sun and stars, to death
and to eternity: "Ye, too, are mine, and I your lord!"

Ye to whom I call, were ye at one with us in heart and
mind, how easy were it to your Will to set the simple rules
to work, whose following must infallibly ensure the flourishing of that mightiest of all art-establishments,—the Theatre!
In the first place it would be the business of the State and
the Community to adjust their means to this end: that the
Theatre be placed in a position to obey alone its higher
and true calling. This end will be attained when the
Theatre is so far supported that its management need only
be a purely artistic one; and no one will be better situated
to carry this out than the general body of the artists themselves, who unite their forces in the art-work and assure the
success of their mutual efforts by a fit conception of their
task. Only the fullest freedom can bind them to the endeavour to fulfil the object for sake of which they are freed
from the fetters of commercial speculation; and this object
is Art, which the free man alone can grasp, and not the
slave of wages.

The judge of their performance, will be the free public.
Yet, to make this public fully free and independent
when face to face with Art, one further step must be taken

along this road : the public must have *unbought* admission
to the theatrical representations. So long as money is
indispensable for all the needs of life, so long as without
pay there remains naught to man but air, and scarcely
water : the measures to be taken can only provide that the
actual stage-performances, to witness which the populace
assembles, shall not take on the semblance of *work paid by
the piece*,—a mode of regarding them which confessedly
leads to the most humiliating misconception of the
character of art-productions,—but it must be the duty of
the State, or rather of the particular Community, to form a
common purse from which to recompense the artists for
their performance as a whole, and not in parts.

Where means should not suffice for this, it were better,
both now and always, to allow a theatre which could only
be maintained as a commercial undertaking, to close its
doors for ever ; or at least, for so long as the community's
demand had not proved strong enough to bring about the
necessary sacrifice for its supply.

When human fellowship has once developed its manly
beauty and nobility,—in such a way as we shall not attain,
however, by the influence of our Art alone, but as we must
hope and strive for by union with the great and inevitably
approaching social revolution,—then will theatrical performances be the first associate undertaking from which
the idea of wage or gain shall disappear entirely. For
when, under the above conditions, our education more and
more becomes an artistic one, then shall we be ourselves
all thus far artists : that we can join together in free and
common service for the one great cause of Art, in its
special manifestment, abandoning each sidelong glance at
gain.

Art and its institutes, whose desired organisation could
here be only briefly touched on, would thus become the
herald and the standard of all future communal institutions.
The spirit that urges a body of artists to the attainment of
its own true goal, would be found again in every other
social union which set before itself a definite and honour-

able aim; for if we reach the right, then all our future social bearing cannot but be of pure artistic nature, such as alone befits the noble faculties of man.

Thus would *Jesus* have shown us that we all alike are men and brothers; while *Apollo* would have stamped this mighty bond of brotherhood with the seal of strength and beauty, and led mankind from doubt of its own worth to consciousness of its highest godlike might. Let us therefore erect the altar of the future, in Life as in the living Art, to the two sublimest teachers of mankind :—*Jesus, who suffered for all men; and Apollo, who raised them to their joyous dignity !*

E

THE

ART-WORK OF THE FUTURE

"DAS

KUNSTWERK DER ZUKUNFT."

" *For the last fortnight,* i.e. *since I have settled down quietly in my new home, I have been seized with an ungovernable desire to undertake a fresh literary labour,* 'The Art-work of the Future' . . ." (R. Wagner's Letters to Uhlig ; Zurich, October 26, 1849.) " *I thought you would like to look through my new work before it came with due ceremony before the world.* . . . *This will be my last literary work. If I have been understood, and if I have convinced others —even if few in number—others must and will fulfil that portion of the task which is the work of many, not of one.*" (Ibidem, Nov. 1849.) "Das Kunstwerk der Zukunft" *was originally published by Wigand of Leipzig at the end of the year* 1849.

TRANSLATOR'S NOTE.

I.

MAN AND ART, IN GENERAL.

1.

Nature, Man, and Art.

S Man stands to Nature, so stands Art to Man. When Nature had developed in herself those attributes which included the conditions for the existence of Man, then Man spontaneously evolved.   In like manner, as soon as human life had engendered from itself the conditions for the manifestment of Art-work, this too stepped self-begotten into life.

Nature engenders her myriad forms without caprice or arbitrary aim (*"absichtlos und unwillkürlich"*), according to her need (*"Bedürfniss"*), and therefore of Necessity (*"Nothwendigkeit"*).   This same Necessity is the generative and formative force of human life.   Only that which is un-capricious and un-arbitrary can spring from a real need ; but on Need alone is based the very principle of Life.*

---

* The above sentences, whose peculiar epigrammatic force it is welnigh impossible to convey in a translation, are of the highest significance as bearing upon the much debated question whether Wagner's philosophy was self-originated or derived from that of Schopenhauer.   In our opinion, they and the following sections of this chapter give most positive answer in the former sense.   Except that Wagner does not employ the term "Will," but rather "Necessity," the whole scheme is Schopenhauerian from beginning to end, and the gradual evolution of the "Will's" manifestation, from elementary force to Intellect and Spirit, might have been written by that greatest philosopher of the century.   It is unnecessary to draw special attention to individual sentences ; but an attentive perusal of this pregnant chapter cannot fail to bring home to those conversant with Schopenhauer's "*Wille und Vorstellung*" the remarkable fact that two cognate minds have developed an almost identical

Man only recognises Nature's *Necessity* by observing the harmonious connection of all her phenomena; so long as he does not grasp the latter, she seems to him Caprice.

From the moment when Man perceived the difference between himself and Nature, and thus commenced his own development as *man*, by breaking loose from the unconsciousness of natural animal life and passing over into conscious life,—when he thus looked Nature in the face and from the first feelings of his dependence on her, thereby aroused, evolved the faculty of Thought,—from that moment did Error begin, as the earliest utterance of consciousness. But Error is the mother of Knowledge ; and the history of the birth of Knowledge out of Error is the history of the human race, from the myths of primal ages down to the present day.

Man erred, from the time when he set the cause of Nature's workings outside the bounds of Nature's self, and for the physical phenomena subsumed a super-physical, anthropomorphic, and arbitrary cause ; when he took the endless harmony of her unconscious, instinctive energy for the arbitrary demeanour of disconnected finite forces. Knowledge consists in the laying of this error, in fathoming the Necessity of phenomena whose underlying basis had appeared to us Caprice.

Through this knowledge does Nature grow conscious of herself ; and verily by Man himself, who only through discriminating between himself and Nature has attained that point where he can apprehend her, by making her his 'object.' But this distinction is merged once more, when Man recognises the essence of Nature as his very own, and perceives the same Necessity in all the elements and lives around him, and therefore in his own existence no less

system of philosophy. For it must not be forgotten that R. Wagner was at the period of writing this essay, and long after, completely ignorant—as indeed was almost the whole world—of even the existence of the sage of Frankfort (*vide* Wagner's letters to Liszt). Another curious reflection aroused by this chapter is, that it should have been written when the Darwinian theory of the influence of environment upon evolution was as yet unpublished, if even formed.—Tr.

than in Nature's being ; thus not only recognising the mutual bond of union between all natural phenomena, but also his own community with Nature.

If Nature then, by her solidarity with Man, attains *in* Man her consciousness, and if Man's life is the very activation of this consciousness—as it were, the portraiture in brief of Nature,—so does man's Life itself gain understanding by means of Science, which makes this human life in turn an object of experience. But the activation of the consciousness attained by Science, the portrayal of the Life that it has learnt to know, the impress of this life's Necessity and Truth, is—*Art.**

Man will never be that which he can and should be, until his Life is a true mirror of Nature, a conscious following of the only real Necessity, the *inner natural necessity*, and is no longer held in subjugation to an *outer* artificial counterfeit,—which is thus no necessary, but an *arbitrary* power. Then first will Man become a living man ; whereas till now he carries on a mere existence, dictated by the maxims of this or that Religion, Nationality, or State.—In like manner will Art not be the thing she can and should be, until she is or can be the true, conscious image and exponent of the real Man, and of man's genuine, nature-bidden life ; until she therefore need no longer borrow the conditions of her being from the errors, perversities, and unnatural distortions of our modern life.

The real Man will therefore never be forthcoming, until true Human Nature, and not the arbitrary statutes of the State, shall model and ordain his Life ; while real Art will never live, until its embodiments need be subject only to the laws of Nature, and not to the despotic whims of Mode. For as Man only then becomes free, when he gains the glad consciousness of his oneness with Nature ; so does Art only then gain freedom, when she has no more to blush for her affinity with actual Life. But only in the joyous conscious-

---

* I.e. Art in general, or the Art of the Future in particular.—R. WAGNER.— The word 'Science' (*Wissenschaft*), also, must be understood in the broad sense in which it is employed in the next section (2).—TR.

ness of his oneness with Nature does Man subdue his dependence on her ; while Art can only overcome her
dependence upon Life through her oneness with the life
of free and genuine Men.

2.

Life, Science, and Art.

Whilst Man involuntarily moulds his Life according to the
notions he has gathered from his arbitrary views of Nature,
and embalms their intuitive expression in Religion : these
notions become for him in Science the subject of conscious,
intentional review and scrutiny.

The path of Science lies from error to knowledge, from
fancy (" *Vorstellung* ") to reality, from Religion to Nature.
In the beginning of Science, therefore, Man stands toward
Life in the same relation as he stood towards the phenomena of Nature when he first commenced to part his life
from hers.   Science takes over the arbitrary concepts
of the human brain, in their totality ; while, by her side,
Life follows in its totality the instinctive evolution of
Necessity.   Science thus bears the burden of the sins of
Life, and expiates them by her own self-abrogation ; she
ends in her direct antithesis, in the knowledge of Nature,
in the recognition of the unconscious, instinctive, and
therefore real, inevitable, and physical.   The character of
Science is therefore finite : that of Life, unending ; just as
Error is of time, but Truth eternal.   But that alone is true
and living which is sentient, and hearkens to the terms of
physicality (*Sinnlichkeit*).   Error's crowning folly is the
arrogance of Science in renouncing and contemning the
world of sense (*Sinnlichkeit*) ; whereas the highest victory
of Science is her self-accomplished crushing of this arrogance, in the acknowledgment of the teaching of the senses.

The end of Science is the justifying of the Unconscious,
the giving of self-consciousness to Life, the re-instatement
of the Senses in their perceptive rights, the sinking of

Caprice in the world-Will (" *Wollen*") of Necessity. Science is therefore the vehicle of Knowledge, her procedure mediate, her goal an intermediation ; but Life is the great Ultimate, a law unto itself. As Science melts away into the recognition of the ultimate and self-determinate reality, of actual Life itself : so does this avowal win its frankest, most direct expression in Art, or rather in the *Work of Art.*

True that the artist does not at first proceed directly ; he certainly sets about his work in an arbitrary, selective, and mediating mood. But while he plays the go-between and picks and chooses, the product of his energy is not as yet the Work of Art ; nay, his procedure is the rather that of Science, who seeks and probes, and therefore errs in her caprice. Only when his choice is made, when this choice was born from pure Necessity,—when thus the artist has found himself again in the subject of his choice, as perfected Man finds his true self in Nature,—then steps the Art-work into life, then first is it a real thing, a self-conditioned and immediate entity.

The actual Art-work, i.e. *its immediate physical portrayal, in the moment of its liveliest embodiment,* is therefore the only true redemption of the artist ; the uprootal of the final trace of busy, purposed choice ; the confident determination of what was hitherto a mere imagining ; the enfranchisement of thought in sense ; the assuagement of the life-need in Life itself.

The Art-work, thus conceived as an immediate vital act, is therewith the perfect reconcilement of Science with Life, the laurel-wreath which the vanquished, redeemed by her defeat, reaches in joyous homage to her acknowledged victor.

3.

The Folk and Art.

The redemption of Thought and Science and their trans-mutation into Art-work would be impossible, could Life itself be made dependent upon scientific speculation. Could conscious autocratic Thought completely govern Life, could it usurp the vital impulse and divert it to some other purpose than the great Necessity of absolute life-needs : then were Life itself dethroned, and swallowed up in Science. And truly Science, in her overweening arrogance, has dreamed of such a triumph ; as witness our tight-reined State and modern Art, the sexless, barren children of this dream.

The great instinctive errors of the People—which found their earliest utterance in Religion, and then became the starting-points of arbitrary speculation and system-making, in Theology and Philosophy—-have reared themselves, in these Sciences and their coadjutrix and adopted sister, Statecraft, to powers which make no less a claim than to govern and ordain the world and life by virtue of their innate and divine infallibility. Irrevocably, then, would Error reign in destructive triumph throughout eternity : did not the same life-force which blindly bore it, once more effectually annihilate it, by virtue of its innate, natural Necessity ; and that so decisively and palpably, that Intellect, with all its arrogant divorce from Life, can see at last no other refuge from actual insanity, than in the unconditional acknowledgment of this only definite and visible force. And this vital force is—The Folk (*das Volk*).—

Who is then the Folk ?—It is absolutely necessary that, before proceeding further, we should agree upon the answer to this weightiest of questions.

" The Folk," was from of old the inclusive term for *all the units* which made up the total of a *commonality*. In the beginning, it was the family and the tribe ; next, the tribes united by like speech into a nation. Practically, by the Roman world-dominion which engulfed the nations, and theoretically, by the Christian religion which admitted of naught but men, *i.e.* no racial, but only *Christian* men— the idea of " the People " has so far broadened out, or even evaporated, that we may either include in it mankind in general, or, upon the arbitrary political hypothesis, a

certain, and generally the propertyless portion of the
Commonwealth. But beyond a frivolous, this term has
also acquired an ineradicable *moral* meaning ; and on
account of this it is, that in times of stir and trouble all
men are eager to number themselves among the People ;
each one gives out that he is careful for the People's weal,
and no one will permit himself to be excluded from it.
Therefore in these latter days also has the question frequently been broached, in the most diverse of senses : Who
then is the People ? In the sum total of the body politic,
can a separate party, a particular fraction of the said body
claim this name for itself alone ? Rather, are we not all·
alike " the People," from the beggar to the prince ?

This question must therefore be answered according to
the conclusive and world-historical sense that now lies at
its root, as follows :—

The " Folk " is the epitome of all those men *who feel a
common and collective Want* (" *gemeinschaftliche Noth* "). To
it belong, then, all of those who recognise their individual
want as a collective want, or find it based thereon ; ergo, all
those who can hope for the stilling of their want in nothing
but the stilling of a common want, and therefore spend
their whole life's strength upon the stilling of their thus
acknowledged common want. For only that want
which urges to the uttermost, is genuine Want ; but this
Want alone is the force of true Need (" *Bedürfniss* ") ; but
a common and collective need is the only true Need ; but
only he who feels within him a true Need, has a right to its
assuagement ; but only the assuagement of a genuine Need
is Necessity ; and it is *the Folk alone that acts according to
Necessity's behests*, and therefore irresistibly, victoriously,
and right as none besides.

Who now are they who belong *not* to this People, and
who are its sworn foes ?

All those *who feel no Want ;* whose life-spring therefore
consists in a need which rises not to the potence of a Want,
and thus is artificial, untrue, and egoistic ; and not only is
not embraced within a common Need, but as the empty need

of preserving superfluity—as which alone can one conceive of need without the force of want—is diametrically opposed to the collective Need.

Where there is no Want, there is no true Need; where no true Need, no necessary action. But where there is no *necessary* action, there reigns Caprice; and where Caprice is king, there blossoms every vice, and every criminal assault on Nature. For only by forcing back, by barring and refusing the assuagement of true Need, can the false and artificial need endeavour to assuage itself.

But the satisfaction of an artificial need is *Luxury;* which can only be bred and supported in opposition to, and at the cost of, the necessities of others.

Luxury is as heartless, inhuman, insatiable, and egoistic as the ' need' which called it forth, but which, with all its heaping-up and over-reaching, it never more can still. For this need itself is no natural and therefore satisfiable one; by very reason that, being false, it has no true, essential antithesis in which it may be spent, consumed, and satisfied. Actual physical hunger has its natural antithesis, satiety, in which —by feeding—it is spent: but unwanting need, the need that craves for luxury, is in itself already luxury and superfluity. The error of it, therefore, can never go over into truth; it racks, devours, torments and burns, without an instant's stilling; it leaves brain, heart and sense for ever vainly yearning, and swallows up all gladness, mirth, and joy of life. For sake of one sole, and yet unreachable moment of refreshment, it squanders the toil and life-sweat of a thousand needy wanters; it lives upon the unstilled hunger of a thousand thousand poor, though impotent to satiate its own for but the twinkling of an eye; it holds a whole world within the iron chains of despotism, without the power to momentarily break the golden chains of that arch-tyrant which it is unto itself.

And this fiend, this crack-brained need-without-a-need, this need of Need,—this *need of Luxury*, which is *Luxury itself* withal,—is sovereign of the world. It is the soul of that Industry which deadens men, to turn them to machines; the soul of our State which swears away men's honour, the better then to take them back as lieges of its grace; the soul of our deistic Science, which hurls men down before an immaterial God, the product of the sum of intellectual luxury, for his consumption.   It is—alas!—the soul, the stipulation, of our—*Art !*

Who then will bring to pass the rescue from this baleful state?—

Want,—which shall teach the world to recognise its own *true need;* that need which *by its very nature admits of satisfaction.*

Want will cut short the hell of Luxury; it will teach the tortured, Need-lacking spirits whom this hell embraces in its bounds the simple, homely need of sheer human, physical hunger and thirst; but in fellowship will it point us to the health-giving bread, the clear sweet springs of Nature; in fellowship shall we taste their genuine joys, and grow up in communion to veritable men.   In common, too, shall we close the last link in the bond of holy Necessity; and the brother-kiss that seals this bond, will be the *mutual Art-work of the Future.*   But in this, also, our great redeemer and well-doer, Necessity's vicegerent in the flesh,—*the Folk,* will no longer be a severed and peculiar class; for in this Art-work we shall all be *one,*— heralds and supporters of Necessity, knowers of the unconscious, willers of the unwilful, betokeners of Nature,— *blissful men.*

4.

The Folk as the Force conditioning the Art-work.

All that subsists, depends on the conditions by which it subsists; nothing, either in Nature or Life, stands shut-off and alone.   Everything is rooted in one unending and harmonious whole; and therewith likewise the capricious, unnecessary, and harmful.   The harmful practises its might in hindering the necessary; nay, it owes its being and its

force to this hindrance and naught else ; and thus, in truth,
it is nothing but the powerlessness of the necessary.   Were
this powerlessness to last forever, then must the natural
ordering of the world be other than it really is ; Caprice
would be Necessity, and the necessary would lack its need.
But this weakness is but transient, and therefore only seeming ; for the force of Necessity shows its living rule even as
the sole and ground condition of the continuance of the
arbitrary.   Thus the luxury of the rich is built upon the
penury of the poor ; and it is the very want of the poorer
classes that hurls unceasingly fresh fodder to the luxury of
the rich ; while the poor man, from very need of food for
his life-forces, thus offers up his own life-strength unto the
rich.

Thus did the life-force, the life-need, of telluric Nature
nurture once those baleful forces—or rather the potentiality
of those alliances and offspring of the elements — which
blocked her way in giving true and fitting utterance to the
fulness of her vital energy.   The reason hereof lay in the
great abundance, the swelling overfill of generative force
and life-stuff, the inexhaustible supply of matter.—The
need of Nature was therefore utmost multiple variety, and
she reached the satisfaction of this need herewith : that—so
to say—she drew off all her life-force from Exclusiveness,
from the monumental singleness that she herself had
hitherto fed so full, and resolved it into Multiplicity.—The
exclusive, sole, and egoistic, can only take and never give :
it can only let itself be born, but cannot bear ; for bearing
there is need of I and Thou, the passing over of Egoism
into Communism.   The richest procreative force lies therefore in the utmost multiplicity ; and when Earth-nature
had emanated to the most manifold variety, she attained
therewith the state of saturation, of self-contentment, of
self-delight, which she manifests amid her present harmony.
She works no longer by titanic, total transformations, for
her period of revolutions is foreby ; she now is all that she
can be, and thus that she ever could have been, and ever
must become.   She no longer has to lavish life-force on

barren impotence ; throughout her endless-stretching realm she has summoned multiformity, the Manly and the Womanly, the ever self-renewing and engendering, the ever self-completing and assuaging, into life,—and in this eternal harmony of parts, she has become forevermore her stable self.

It is in the reproduction of this great evolutionary process of Nature *in Man himself*, that the human race, from the time of its self-severance from Nature, is thus involved. The same necessity is the mainspring of the great revolution of mankind; the same assuagement will bring this revolution to its close.

But that impelling force, the plain and innate force of Life which vindicates itself in life-needs, is unconscious and instinctive by its very nature ; and where it is this—in the Folk—it also is the only true, conclusive might. Great, then, is the error of our folk-instructors when they fancy that the Folk must *know* first what it wills—*i.e.* in *their* eyes *should* will—ere it be justified, or even able, to will at all. From this chief error all the wretched makeshifts, all the impotent devices, and all the shameful weakness of the latest world-commotions take their rise.

The truly known is nothing other than the actual physical phenomenon, become by thought the vivid presentation of an object. Thought is arbitrary so long as it cannot picture to itself the physical present and that which has passed away from sense, with the completest unconditional perception of their necessary coherence (" *Zusammenhang*"); for the consciousness of this conception (" *Vorstellung*") is the essence of all reasonable Knowledge (" *vernünftiges Wissen*"). Therefore the more truthful is Knowledge, the more frankly must it recognise that its whole existence hangs upon its own coherence with that which has come to actual, finished, and fulfilled manifestation to the senses, and thus admit its own possibility of existence as *a priori* conditioned by actuality. But so soon as Thought abstracts from actuality, and would fain construct the concrete future, it can no longer bring forth *Knowledge ;* but utters itself as *Fancy* ("*Wähnen*"), which forcibly dissevers itself from *the Unconscious.* Only when it can fathom physicality, and unflinchingly plunge its sympathetic gaze into the depths of an actual physical need, can it take its share in the energy of the Unconscious; and only that which is brought to light of day by an instinctive, necessary *Need,* to wit the actual physical Deed, can again become the satisfying object of thought and knowledge. For the march of human evolution is the rational and natural progress from the unconscious to the conscious, from un-knowledge to knowledge, from need to satisfying; and not from satisfaction back to need,—at least not to that selfsame need whose end lay in that satisfying.

Not ye wise men, therefore, are the true inventors, but the Folk; for Want it was, that drove it to invention. All great inventions are the People's deed; whereas the devisings of the intellect are but the exploitations, the derivatives, nay, the splinterings and disfigurements of the great inventions of the Folk. Not ye, invented *Speech,* but the Folk; ye could but spoil its physical beauty, break its force, mislay its inner understanding, and painfully explore the loss. Not ye, were the inventors of *Religion,* but the Folk; ye could but mutilate its inner meaning, turn the heaven that lay within it to a hell, and its out-breathing truth to lies. Not ye are the inventors of the *State ;* ye have but made from out the natural alliance of like-needing men a natureless and forced allegiance of unlike-needing; from the beneficent defensive league of all a maleficent bulwark for the privileged few; from the soft and yielding raiment upon man's blithely moving body a stiff, encumbering iron harness, the gaud of some historic armoury. It is not ye that give the Folk the wherewithal to live, but it gives you; not ye who give the Folk to think, but it gives you. Therefore it is not ye that should presume to teach the Folk, but ye should take your lessons from it; and thus it is to you that I address myself, *not to the Folk,* —for to *it* there are but scant words to say, and e'en the exhortation: "Do as thou must!" to it is quite superfluous, for of itself it does that which it must.   But to you I turn,—in the same sense as the Folk, albeit of necessity in your own mode of utterance,—to you, ye prudent men and intellectual, to offer you, with all the People's open-heartedness, the redemption from your egoistic incantations in the limpid spring of Nature, in the loving arm-caresses of the Folk—there where I found it; where it became for me my art-instructor; where, after many a battle between the hope within and the blank despair without, I won a dauntless faith in the assurance of the Future.

The *Folk* will thus fulfil its mission of redemption, the while it satisfies itself and at like time rescues its own foes. Its procedure will be governed by the instinctive laws of Nature; with the Necessity of elemental forces, will it destroy the *bad coherence* that alone makes out the conditions of Un-nature's rule.   So long as these conditions last, so long as they suck out their life-sap from the squandered powers of the People, so long as they—themselves unable to create—bootlessly consume the productive faculties of the Folk for their own egoistic maintenance,—so long too will all showing, doing, changing, bettering, and reforming,* be naught but wilful, aimless, and unfruitful. But the Folk has only to deny by deeds *that* thing which in very deed is *no-thing*—to wit, is needless, superfluous, and null ; it requires thus to merely know what thing it wills *not*,—and this its own instinctive life-bent teaches it ; it needs but to turn this *Willed-not* to a *Non-existing*, and by the force of its own Want to annihilate what is fit for nothing but annihilation ; and then the *Some-thing* of the fathomed Future will stand before it of itself.

Are the conditions heaved away, which sanction Super-fluity to feed upon the marrow of Necessity : then of themselves arise the conditions which call the necessary, the true, the imperishable, to life.   Are the conditions heaved away, which permit the continuance of the need of Luxury : then

---

* For who can nurse less hopes of the success of his reforming efforts, than he who acts therein with greatest *honesty ?*—R. WAGNER.

F

of themselves are given the conditions which allow the stilling of the *necessary* need of man in the teeming overflow of Nature and of his own productive human faculties, in unimaginably rich but ever fitting measure.   And yet once more,—are the conditions of the tyranny of *Fashion* heaved away : then of themselves are the conditions of *True Art* at hand ; and with one waive of the enchanter's wand, will holy, glorious Art, the daughter of the noblest Manhood, blossom in like fulness and perfection with Mother Nature, the conditions of whose now completed harmony of form have issued from the birth-pangs of the elements.   Like to this blissful harmony of Nature, will she endure and ever show her fruitfulness, as the purest and most perfect satisfaction of the truest, noblest need of perfected mankind ; *i.e.* of men who *are* all that which of their essence they *can* be, and therefore *should* and shall be.

5.

The Art-antagonistic shape of Present Life, under the sway of Abstract Thought and Fashion.

The first beginning and foundation of all that exists and all that is conceivable, is actual physical being.   The inner recognition of his life-need as the *common* life-need of his *Species*, in contradistinction to Nature and all her countless living species that lie apart from Man,—is the beginning and foundation of man's Thinking.   Thought is therefore the faculty possessed by Man, not merely to sense the actual and physical from its external aspect, but to distinguish all its parts according to their essence, and finally to grasp and picture to himself their intimate connection. The idea (" *Begriff* ") of a thing is the image formed in Thought of its actual substance ; the portrayal of the images of all discernible substances in one joint-image, in which the faculty of Thought presents to itself the picture of the essence of all realities in their connected sequence, is the work of the highest energy of the human soul,—the *Spirit*

("*Geist*"). If in this joint-image man must necessarily have included the image, the idea, of his own being also,— nay, if this his own prefigured being must be, before all else, the artistic force that pictures forth the whole conceptual art-work: then does this force, with all its joint portrayal of each reality, proceed alone from the real, physical man; and thus, at bottom, from his life-need, and finally from that which summoned forth this life-need, the physical reality of Nature. But where Thought casts aside this linking cable; where, after doubled and again redoubled presentment of itself, it fain would look upon itself as its original cause; where Mind ("*Geist*") instead of as the last and most conditioned, would conceive itself as the first and least conditioned energy ("*Thätigkeit*"), and therefore as the ground and cause of Nature,—there also is the fly-wheel of Necessity upheaved, and blind Caprice runs headlong— free, boundless, and unfettered, as our metaphysicians fancy —through the workshops of the brain, and hurls herself, a raging stream of madness, upon the world of actuality.

If Mind has manufactured Nature, if Thought has made the Actual, if the Philosopher comes before the Man: then Nature, Actuality and Man are no more necessary, and their existence is not only superfluous but even harmful; for the greatest superfluity of all is the lagging of the In- complete *when once the Complete has come to being.* In this wise Nature, Actuality and Man would only then have any meaning, or any pretext for their presence, when Mind— the unconditioned Spirit, the only cause and reason, and thus the only law unto itself—employed them for its absolute and sovereign pleasure. If Mind is *in itself* Necessity, then Life is mere caprice, a fantastic masquerade, an idle pastime, a frivolous whim, a "*car tel est notre plaisir*" of the mind; then is all purely human virtue, and Love before all else, a thing to be approved or disallowed according to occasion; then is all purely human Need a luxury, and Luxury the only current need; then is the wealth of Nature a thing to be dispensed with, and the parasitic growth of Culture the only indispensable; then is the happiness of man a secondary matter, and the abstract State the main

consideration ; the Folk the accidental stuff, and the prince
and savant the necessary consumers of this stuff.

If we take the end for the beginning, the assuagement
for the need, satiety for hunger ; then is all movement, all
advance, not even conceivable except in line with a concocted need, a hunger brought about by stimulation ; and
this, in very truth, is the lifespring of our whole Culture of
to-day, and its utterance is—*Fashion.*

Fashion is the artificial stimulus that rouses an unnatural
need where the natural is not to hand ; but whatsoever does
not originate in a real need, is arbitrary, uncalled-for, and
tyrannical. Fashion is therefore the maddest, most unheard-of tyranny that has ever issued from man's per-
versity ; it demands from Nature an absolute obedience ; it
dictates to real need a thorough self-disownment in favour
of an artificial ; it compels man's natural sense of beauty to
worship at the shrine of what is hateful ; it kills his health,
to bring him to delight in sickness ; it breaks his strength
and all his force, to let him find content in weakness.
Where the absurdest Fashion reigns, there must Nature be
regarded as the height of absurdity ; where the most criminal un-Nature reigns, there must the utterance of Nature
appear the fellest crime ; where craziness usurps the place
of truth, there must Truth herself be prisoned under lock
and bar, as crazy.

The soul of Fashion is the most absolute uniformity,
and its god an egoistic, sexless, barren god. Its motive
force is therefore arbitrary alteration, unnecessary change,
confused and restless striving after the opposite of its
essential uniformity. Its might is the might of habit.
But *Habit* is the invincible despot that rules all weaklings,
cowards, and those bereft of veritable need. Habit is the
communism of egoism, the tough, unyielding swathe of
mutual, free-from-want self-interest ; its artificial life-pulse
is even that of Fashion.

Fashion is therefore no artistic begetting from herself,
but a mere artificial deriving from her opposite, Nature ;
from whom alone she must at bottom draw her nourish-

ment, just as the luxury of the upper classes feeds only on the straining of the lower, labouring classes towards assuagement of their natural life-needs. The caprice of Fashion, therefore, can only draw upon the stores of actual Nature ; all her reshapings, flourishes, and gewgaws have at the last their archetype in Nature. Like all our abstract thinking, in its farthest aberrations, she finally can think out and invent naught else than what already is at hand in Nature and in Man, in substance and in form. But her procedure is an arrogant one, capriciously cut loose from Nature ; she orders and commands, where everything in truth is bound to hearken and obey. Thus with all her figurings she can but disfigure Nature, and not portray her ; she can but *derive*, and not *invent* ; for invention, in effect, is naught but *finding out*, the finding and discerning of Nature.

Fashion's invention is therefore mechanical. But the mechanical is herein distinguished from the artistic : that it fares from derivative to derivative, from means to means, to finally bring forth but one more mean, the *Machine*. Whereas the artistic strikes the very opposite path : throws means on means behind it, pierces through derivative after derivative, to arrive at last at the source of every derivation, of every mean, in *Nature's* self, and there to slake its need in understanding.

Thus the *Machine* is the cold and heartless ally of luxury-craving men. Through the machine have they at last made even human reason their liege subject; for, led astray from Art's discovery, dishonoured and disowned, it consumes itself at last in mechanical refinements, in absorption into the Machine, instead of in absorption into Nature in the Art-work.

The need of *Fashion* is thus the diametrical antithesis of the need of *Art;* for the artistic need cannot possibly be present where Fashion is the lawgiver of Life. In truth, the endeavour of many an enthusiastic artist of our times could only be directed to rousing first that necessary Need, from the standpoint and by the means of Art; yet we must look on all such efforts as vain and fruitless. The one impossibility for Mind is, to awaken a real need :—to answer to an actual present need, man always has the speedy means to hand, but never to evoke it where Nature has withheld it, where its conditionments are not contained in her economy. But if the craving for art-work does not exist, then art-work is itself impossible and only the Future can call it forth for us, and that by the natural begettal of its conditionments from out of Life.

Only from *Life*, from which alone can even the need for her grow up, can Art obtain her *matter* and her *form;* but where Life is modelled upon Fashion, Art can never fashion aught from Life. Straying far away from the necessity of Nature, Mind wilfully—and even in the so-called 'common' life, involuntarily—exercises its disfiguring influence upon the matter and the form of Life; in such a manner that Mind, at last unhappy in its separation, and longing for its healthy sustenance by Nature and its complete re-union with her, can no more find the matter and the form for its assuagement in actual present life. If, in its striving for redemption, it yearns for unreserved acknowledgment of Nature, and if it can only reconcile itself with her in her faithfulest portrayal, in the physical actuality of the Art-work: yet it sees that this reconciliation can nevermore be gained by acknowledgment and portrayal of its actual surroundings, of this Fashion-governed parody of life. Involuntarily, therefore, must it pursue an arbitrary course in its struggle for redemption by Art; it must seek for Nature—which in sound and wholesome life would rush to meet it—amid times and places where it can recognise her in less, and finally in least, distortion. Yet everywhere and everywhen has natural man thrown on the garment, if not of Fashion, still of *Custom* ("*Sitte*") The simplest and most natural, the fairest and the noblest Custom is certainly the least disfigurement of Nature,— nay, her most fitting human garb. But the copying and reproduction of this Custom,—without which the modern artist can never manage to effect his portraiture of Nature,

—is still, in face of modern Life, an irreclaimably arbitrary and purpose-governed dealing; and whatsoever has been thus formed and fashioned by even the honestest striving after Nature, appears, so soon as e'er it steps before our present public life, either a thing incomprehensible, or else another freshly fangled Fashion.

In truth we have nothing for which to thank this mode of striving after nature, within the bounds of modern life and yet in contrast to it, but *Mannerism* and its ceaseless, restless change. The character of Fashion has once more unwittingly betrayed itself in Mannerism; without a shred of consequent coherence with actual life, it trips up to Art with just the same despotic orders as Fashion wields on Life; it bands itself with Fashion, and rules with equal might each separate branch of art. Beneath its serious mien it shows itself—almost as inevitably as does its colleague—in utmost ridicule. Not only the Antique, the Renaissance and Middle Ages, but the customs and the garb of savage races in new-discovered lands, the primal fashions of Japan and China, from time to time usurp as "Mannerisms," in greater or in less degree, each several department of our modern art. Nay, with no other effect than that of an insufficient stimulus, our lightly veering 'manner of the day' sets before the least religiously disposed and most genteel of theatre-goers the fanaticism of religious sects;* before the luxurious un-nature of our fashionable world the naïvety of Swabian peasants; before the pampered gods of commerce the want of the hungering rabble.

Here, then, does the artist whose spirit strives to be re-knit with Nature see all his hopes thrust forward to the Future, or else his soul thrust back upon the mournful exercise of resignation. He recognises that his thought can only gain redemption in a physically present art-work, thus only in a truly art-demanding, *i.e.* an art-conditioning Present that shall bring forth Art from its own native truth and beauty; he therefore sets his hopes upon the Future,

* The slap at Meyerbeer's *Huguenots, Prophète,* etc, is obvious.—TR.

his trust upon the power of Necessity, for which this Work of the Future is reserved. But in face of the actual Present, he renounces all appearing of the Art-work upon the surface of this present, *i.e.* in public show ; and consequently he quits publicity itself, so far as it is ruled by fashion. The great United Art-work, which must gather up each branch of art to use it as a mean, and in some sense to undo it for the common aim of *all*, for the unconditioned, absolute portrayal of perfected human nature,—this great United Art-work he cannot picture as depending on the arbitrary purpose of some human unit, but can only conceive it as the instinctive and associate product of the Manhood of the Future. The instinct that recognises itself as one that can only be satisfied in fellowship, abandons modern fellowship—that conglomerate of self-seeking caprice—and turns to find its satisfaction in solitary fellowship with itself and with the manhood of the Future,—so well as the lonely unit can.

6.

Standard for the Art-work of the Future.

It is not the lonely spirit, striving by Art for redemption into Nature, that can frame the Art-work of the Future ; only the spirit of Fellowship, fulfilled by Life, can bring this work to pass. But yet the lonely one can prefigure it to himself ; and the thing that saves his preconception from becoming a mere idle fancy, is the very character of his striving,—his striving after *Nature*. The mind that casts back longing eyes to Nature, and therefore goes a-hungering in the modern Present, sees not alone in Nature's great sum-total, but also in the *human nature* that history lays before it, the types by whose observing it may reconcile itself with life in general. It recognises in this nature a type for all the Future, already shown in narrower bounds ; to widen out these bounds to broadest compass, rests on the imaginative faculty of its nature-craving instinct.

Two *cardinal moments* of his development lie clear before us in the history of Man : the *generic national*, and the *un-national universal*.   If we still look forward to the Future for the completion of the second evolutionary step, yet in the Past we have the rounded-off conclusion of the first set clear as day before our eyes.   To what a pitch man once— so far as, governed by generic ancestry, by community of mother-tongue, by similarity of climate, and the natural surroundings of a common fatherland, he yielded himself unconsciously to the influence of Nature—to what a pitch man once was able to unfold himself beneath these welnigh directly moulding influences, we have certainly full reason to acknowledge with most heartfelt thanks.   It is in the natural customs of all peoples, so far as they embrace the normal man, and even of those decried as most uncultured, that we first learn the truth of human nature in its full nobility, and in its real beauty.   Not *one* true virtue has any Religion soever taken into itself as its god's command, but it was already self-included in these natural customs ; not *one* genuine idea of human right has the later civilised State developed—though, alas, to the point of complete distortion !—but it already found its sure expression in them ; not *one* veritable discovery for the common weal has later Culture made her own—with arrogant ingratitude !—but she derived it from the fruits of the homely understanding of the stewards of those customs.

But that *Art* is not an *artificial* product,—that the need of Art is not an arbitrary issue, but an inbred craving of the natural, genuine, and uncorrupted man,—who proves this in more striking manner than just these Peoples ? Nay, whence shall our uneasy " spirit " derive its proofs of Art's necessity, if not from the testimony of this artistic instinct and its glorious fruits afforded by these nature-fostered peoples, by the great *Folk* itself ?   Before what phenomenon do we stand with more humiliating sense of the impotence of our frivolous culture, than before the art of the *Hellenes ?*   To this, to the art of the darlings of all-loving Nature, of those fairest children whom the great glad Mother holds up to us before the darksome cloud of modern modish culture, as the triumphant tokens of what she can bring forth,—let us look far hence to glorious Grecian Art, and gather from its inner understanding the outlines for the Art-work of the Future! Nature has done all that she could do,—she has given birth to the Hellenic people, has fed it at her breast and formed it by her mother-wisdom ; she sets it now before our gaze with all a mother's pride, and cries to wide mankind with mother-love : " This have I done for you ; now, of your love for one another, do ye that which ye can ! "

Thus have we then to turn *Hellenic* art to *Human* art ; to loose from it the stipulations by which it was but an *Hellenic* and not a *Universal* art. The *garment of Religion,* in which alone it was the common Art of Greece, and after whose removal it could only, as an egoistic, isolated art-species, fulfil the needs of Luxury—however fair—but no longer those of Fellowship,—this specific garb of the *Hellenic Religion,* we have to stretch it out until its folds embrace the Religion of the Future, the Religion of *Universal Manhood,* and thus to gain already a presage of the Art-work of the Future. But this bond of union, this *Religion of the Future,* we wretched ones shall never clasp the while we still are *lonely units,* howe'er so many be our numbers who feel the spur towards the Art-work of the Future. The Art-work is the living presentation of Religion ;—but religions spring not from the artist's brain ; their only origin is from the *Folk.*—

Let us then—without a spark of egoistic vanity, without attempting to console ourselves with any kind of self-derived illusion, but honestly and lovingly and hopefully devoted to the Art-work of the Future—content ourselves to-day by testing first the nature of the art-*species* which, in their shattered segregation, make up the general substance of our modern art ; let us sharpen our gaze for this examination by glancing at Hellenic art ; and thereafter let us draw a bold and confident conclusion anent the *great and universal Art-work of the Future !*

II.

ARTISTIC MAN, AND ART AS DERIVED DIRECTLY FROM HIM.

I.

Man as his own Artistic Subject and Material.

AN'S nature is twofold, an *outer* and an *inner*. The senses to which he offers himself as a subject for Art, are those of *Vision* and of *Hearing*: to the eye appeals the outer man, the inner to the ear.

The eye apprehends the *bodily form of man*, compares it with surrounding objects, and discriminates between it and them. The corporeal man and the spontaneous expression of his sensations of physical anguish or physical well-being, called up by outward contact, appeal directly to the eye; while indirectly he imparts to it, by means of facial play and gesture, those emotions of the inner man which are not directly cognisable by the eye. Again, through the expression of the eye itself, which directly meets the eye of the beholder, man is able to impart to the latter not only the feelings of the heart, but even the characteristic activity of the brain; and the more distinctly can the outer man express the inner, the higher does he show his rank as an artistic being.

But the inner man can only find *direct* communication through the ear, and that by means of *his voice's* Tone. Tone is the immediate utterance of feeling and has its physical seat within the heart, whence start and whither flow the waves of life-blood. Through the sense of hearing, tone urges forth from the feeling of one heart to the feeling of its fellow: the grief and joy of the emotional-man impart themselves directly to his counterpart through the manifold expression of vocal tone; and where the outer corporeal-man finds his limits of expressing to the eye the qualities of those inner feelings of the heart he fain would utter and convey, there steps in to his aid the sought-for envoy, and takes his message through the voice to hearing, through hearing to the feelings of the heart.

Yet where, again, the direct expression of vocal tone finds its limits of conveying the separate feelings of the heart in clear and sharply outlined definition to the sympathies of the recipient inner man, there enters on the scene, through the vehicle of vocal tone, the determinative utterance of *Speech*. *Speech* is the condensation * of the element of Voice, and the Word is the crystallised measure of Tone. In Speech, feeling conveys itself by ear to feeling, but to that likewise to be condensed and crystallised feeling to which it seeks to bring itself in sure and unmistakable understanding. It is thus the organ of that special feeling which reasons with itself and yearns for others' understanding,—the Intellect.—For the more vague and general feeling the immediate attributes of Tone sufficed. This general feeling therefore abode by Tone, as its adequate and materially contenting utterance; in the *quantitative* value of its compass it found the means of, so to say, accenting its own peculiar *qualities* in their universal bearings. But the *definite* need which seeks by Speech to gain an understanding is more decided and more pressing; it abides not in contentment with its physical expression, for it has to differentiate its own subjective feeling from a general feeling, and therefore to depict and to describe what Tone gave forth directly as the expression of this general feeling. The speaker has therefore to take his images from correlative but diverse objects, and to weld them with each other. In this mediate and complex

---

* " *Verdichtete* " = " condensed "; but the mere English equivalent will not convey the hidden allusion—worked out later on—to " *Dichtkunst* " (Poetry), which is thus shown to be the condensation into spoken words of the nebulous ideas of fancy.—TR.

process he has to take a wider field ; and, under pressure
of his quest for comprehension, he accelerates this process
by the utmost brevity of his lingering over Tone, and by
complete abandonment of its general powers of expression.
Through this enforced renunciation, through this giving up
of all delight in the physical element of his own utterance
—at least of that degree of pleasure which the corporeal-
and the emotional-man experience in their method of
expression,—the intellectual-man attains the faculty of
giving by means of his speech-organ that certain utterance
in seeking which the former found their bounds, each in
his own degree.   His capability is unlimited : he collects
and sifts the universal, parts and unites according to his
need and pleasure the images which all his senses bear him
from the outer world ; he binds and looses the particular
and general even as he judges best, in order to appease his
own desire for a sure and intelligible utterance of his
feelings, his reflections, or his will.   Yet he finds once more
his limit where, in the agitation of his feelings, in the living
pulse of joy or the violence of grief,—there, where the
particular and arbitrary draw back before the generality
and spontaneity of the feeling that usurps his heart ; where
from out the egoism of his narrowed and conditioned personal sensations he finds himself again amid the wide communion of all-embracing world-emotions, a partaker in the
unconditioned truth of universal feeling and emotion; where,
finally, he has to subordinate his individual selfwill to the
dictates of Necessity, be it of grief or joy, and to hearken
in place of commanding,—he craves for the only adequate
and direct expression of his endlessly enhanced emotion.
Here must he reach back once more to the universal mode
of utterance ; and, in exact proportion as he has pressed
forward to his special standpoint, has he now to retrace his
steps and borrow from the emotional man the physical
tones of feeling, from the corporeal man the physical
gestures of the body.   For where it is a question of giving
utterance, immediate and yet most certain, to the highest
and the truest that man can ever utter, there above all

must man display himself in his entirety ; and this whole man is the man of understanding united with the man of heart and man of body,—but neither of these parts for self alone.—

The progress of the man of understanding, from the bodily man and through the man of feeling, is that of an ever increasing accommodation, just as his organ of expression, Speech, is the most mediate and dependent ; for all the attributes that lie beneath him must be normally developed, before the conditions of *his* normal attributes can be at hand.   But the most conditioned faculty is at like time the most exalted ; and the joy in his own self, engendered by the knowledge of his higher, unsurpassable attributes, betrays the intellectual-man into the arrogant imagining that he may use those attributes which are really his foundation-props as the handmaids of his own caprice. The sovereign might of physical sensation and heart-emotion, however, breaks down his pride of intellect, as soon as these proclaim their sway as one which all men must obey in common, as that of feelings and emotions of the race.   The isolated feeling, the separate emotion, which show themselves in the individual, aroused by this or that particular and personal contact with this or that particular phenomenon, he is able to suppress or subjugate in favour of a richer combination of manifold phenomena conceived by him ; but the richest combination of all the phenomena that he can cognise leads him at last to *Man as a species and an integral factor in the totality of Nature ;* and, in presence of this great, all-mastering phenomenon, his pride breaks down.   He now can only will the universal, true, and unconditional ; he yields himself, not to a love for this or that particular object, but to wide *Love* itself.   Thus does the egoist become a communist, the unit all, the man God, the art-variety Art.

2.

The Three Varieties of Humanistic Art, in their original Union.*

The three chief artistic faculties of the entire man have once, and of their own spontaneous impulse, evolved to a trinitarian utterance of human Art; and this was in the primal, earliest manifested art-work, the *Lyric,* and its later, more conscious, loftiest completion, the *Drama.*

The arts of *Dance,*† of *Tone,* and *Poetry :* thus call themselves the three primeval sisters whom we see at once entwine their measures wherever the conditions necessary for artistic manifestment have arisen. By their nature they are inseparable without disbanding the stately minuet of Art ; for in this dance, which is the very cadence of Art itself, they are so wondrous closely interlaced with one another, of fairest love and inclination, so mutually bound up in each other's life, of body and of spirit : that each of the three partners, unlinked from the united chain and bereft thus of her own life and motion, can only carry on an artificially inbreathed and borrowed life ;—not giving forth her sacred ordinances, as in their trinity, but now receiving despotic rules for mechanical movement.

As we gaze on this entrancing measure of the truest and most high-born Muses of artistic man, we see the three first stepping forward, each with her loving arm entwined around her sister's neck ; then, now this one and now that, as though to show the others her beauteous form in full and individual symmetry, loosing herself from their embrace, and merely brushing with her utmost finger-tips the others' hands. Again the one, rapt by the spectacle of the twin-beauty of her close-locked sisters, bending herself before them ; next the two, transported by her unique charm,

---

* " *Reinmenschliche,*" lit. " purely human."—TR.

† It must be distinctly understood that by " Dance " Wagner does not refer to the Ballet, or anything approaching it ; it is the grace of gesture and of motion which he sums up in this terse and comprehensive term.—TR.

greeting the one with tender homage; until at last, all three, tight-clasped, breast on breast, and limb to limb, melt with the fervour of love-kisses into one only, living shape of beauty.—Such is the love and life, the wooing and the winning of Art; its separate units, ever themselves and ever for each other, severing in richest contrast and re-uniting in most blissful harmony.

This is Art the free. The sweet and forceful impulse in that dance of sisters, is the *impulse of Freedom ;* the love-kiss of their enlocked embraces, the *transport of a freedom won.*

The solitary unit is unfree, because confined and fettered in un-Love; the *associate is free,* because unfettered and unconfined through Love.—

In every creature that exists the mightiest impulse is that of its *Life ;* this is the resistless force of the correlation of those conditions which have first called into being that which here exists,—thus, of those things or life-forces which, in that which has arisen through them, are *that* which they will to be—and, willing, can be—in this their point of common union. Man appeases his Life-need by *taking* from Nature: this is no theft, but a receiving, an adoptment, an absorption of that which, as a condition of man's life, wills to be adopted into and absorbed in him. For these conditions of man's Life, *themselves* his Life-needs, are not forsooth upheaved by birth,—rather do they endure and feed themselves within him and by him so long as e'er he lives; and the dissolution of their bond, itself is—Death.

But the Life-need of man's life-needs is the *need of Love.* As the conditions of natural human life are contained in the love-bond of subordinated nature-forces, which craved for their agreement, their redemption, their adoption into the higher principle, Man ; so does man find his agreement, his redemption, his appeasement, likewise in something higher; and this higher thing is the *human race, the fellowship of man,* for there is but one thing higher than *man's* self, and that is—*Men.* But man can only gain the stilling

of his life-need through *Giving*, through *Giving of himself*
to other men, and in its highest climax, to *all the world of
human beings*.   The monstrous sin of the absolute egoist is
that he sees in (fellow) Men also nothing but the natural
conditionments of his own existence, and—albeit in a quite
particular, barbaric-cultivated manner—*consumes* them like
the fruits and beasts of nature ; thus will not *give*, but only
take.

Now as Man is not free except through Love, neither is
anything that proceeds, or is derived, from him.   Freedom
is the satisfaction of an imperative Need, and the highest
freedom is the satisfaction of the highest need : but the
highest human need is *Love*.

No living thing can issue from the true and undistorted
nature of mankind or be derived from it, unless it fully
answers to the characteristic essence of that nature : but
the most characteristic token of this essence is the need of
Love.

Each separate faculty of man is limited by bounds ; but
his united, agreed, and reciprocally helping faculties—and
thus his faculties in *mutual love* of one another—combine
to form the self-completing, unbounded, universal faculty
of men.   Thus too has every *artistic* faculty of man its
natural bounds, since man has not *one only Sense* but
separate *Senses ;* while every faculty springs from its
special sense, and therefore each single faculty must find its
bounds in the confines of its correlated sense.   But the
boundaries of the separate senses are also their joint meet-
ing-points, those points at which they melt in one another
and each agrees with each : and exactly so do the faculties
that are derived from them touch one another and agree.
Their confines, therefore, are removed by this agreement ;
but only those that love each other can agree, and 'to
love' means : to acknowledge the other, and at like time to
know one's self.   Thus Knowledge through Love is Freedom ; and the freedom of man's faculties is—*All-faculty*.

Only the Art which answers to this 'all-faculty' of man
is, therefore, *free ;* and not the Art-*variety*, which only

G

issues from a single human faculty. The Arts of Dance, of Tone, of Poetry, are each confined within their several bounds; in contact with these bounds each feels herself unfree, be it not that, across their common boundary, she reaches out her hand to her neighbouring art in unrestrained acknowledgment of love. The very grasping of this hand lifts her above the barrier; her full embrace, her full absorption in her sister—*i.e.* her own complete ascension beyond the set-up barrier—casts down the fence itself. And when every barrier has thus fallen, then are there no more *arts* and no more boundaries, but only *Art*, the universal, undivided.

It is a sorry misconception of Freedom—that of the being who would fain be free in loneliness. The impulse to loose one's self from commonalty, to be free and independent for individual self alone, can only lead to the direct antithesis of the state so arbitrarily striven after: namely to utmost lack of self-dependence.—Nothing in Nature is self-dependent excepting that which has the conditionments of its self-standing not merely in itself, but also outside of itself: for the inner are first possible by virtue of the outer. That which would separate * itself must, necessarily, first have that from which to separate. He who would fain be nothing but himself, must first know what he is; but this he only learns by distinguishing from what he is not: were he able to lop off entirely that which differs from him, then were he himself no differentiated entity, and thus no longer cognisable by himself. In order to will to be the whole thing which of and in himself he is, the individual must learn to be absolutely not the thing he is not; but the thing that is absolutely what *he* is not, is that thing which lies apart from him; and only in the fullest of communion

---

* The verb "*unterscheiden*" is here used in so many different shades of its meaning that it is impossible to do justice in a translation to the philosophical play of words. Literally it means: "to cleave asunder," and hence, "to separate, to distinguish, to discern, to discriminate, to differentiate." There being no one English word that will embrace the varying sense in which the term is here employed, I have been forced to replace it by varying expressions. —TR.

with that which is apart from him, in the completest absorption into the commonalty of those who differ from him, can he ever be completely *what* he is by nature, what he must be, and as a reasonable being, can but will to be. Thus only in Communism does Egoism find its perfect satisfaction.

That Egoism, however, which has brought such immeasurable woe into the world and so lamentable a mutilation and insincerity into Art, is of another breed to the natural and rational egoism which finds its perfect satisfaction in the community of all. In pious indignation it wards off the name of " Egoism " from it, and dubs itself " Brotherly-" and " Christian- " " Art-" and " Artist-Love " ; founds temples to God and Art ; builds hospitals, to make ailing old-age young and sound,—and schools to make youth old and ailing ; establishes " faculties," courts of justice, governments, states, and what not else ?—merely to prove that it is not Egoism. And this is just the most irredeemable feature of it, and that which makes it utterly pernicious both to itself and to the general commonalty. This is the isolation of the single, in which each severed nullity shall rank as somewhat, but the great commonalty as naught; in which each unit struts as something special and " original," while the whole, forsooth, can then be nothing in particular and for ever a mere imitation. This is the self-dependence of the individual, where every unit lives upon the charges of his fellows, in order to be " free by help of God ; " pretends to be what others *are;* and, briefly, follows the inversion of the teaching of Jesus Christ : " To *take* is more blessed than to give."

This is the genuine Egoism, in which each *isolated art-variety* would give itself the airs of universal Art ; while, in truth, it only thereby loses its own peculiar attributes. Let us pry a little closer into what, under such conditions, has befallen those three most sweet Hellenic sisters !—

3.

The Art of Dance.

The most realistic of all arts is that of Dance. Its artistic 'stuff' is the actual living Man; and in troth no single portion of him, but the whole man from heel to crown, such as he shows himself unto the eye. It therefore includes within itself the conditions for the enunciation of all remaining arts: the singing and speaking man must necessarily be a bodily man; through his outer form, through the posture of his limbs, the inner, singing and speaking man comes forth to view. The arts of Tone and Poetry become first understandable in that of Dance, the Mimetic art, by the entire art-receptive man, *i.e.* by him who not only hears but also sees.

The Art-work cannot gain its freedom until it proclaims itself directly to the answering sense, until in addressing this sense the artist is conscious of the certain understanding of his message. The highest subject for Art's message is Man himself; and, for his own complete and conscious calming, man can at bottom only parley through his bodily form with the corresponding sense, the eye. Without addressing the eye, all art remains unsatisfying, and thus itself unsatisfied, unfree. Be its utterance to the Ear, or merely to the combining and mediately compensating faculty of Thought, as perfect as it may—until it makes intelligible appeal likewise unto the Eye, it remains a thing that merely *wills*, yet never completely *can ;* but Art must '*can*,'* and from "*können*" it is that Art in our tongue has fittingly gotten itself its name "*Die Kunst.*"—

The corporeal-man proclaims his sensations of weal and woe directly in and by those members of his body which feel the hurt or pleasure; his whole body's sense of weal or woe he expresses by means of correlated and complement-

---

* Compare Carlyle *On Heroes :*—"King, *Könning*, which means *Can*-ning, Able-man. . . . Find me the true *Könning*, King, or Able-man, and he *has* a divine right over me."—Tʀ.

ary movements of all, or of the most expression-able of these members. From their relation with each other, then from the play of complementary and accenting motions, and finally from the manifold interchange of these motions— as they are dictated by the progressive change of feelings passing, now by slow degrees and now in violent haste, from soft repose to passionate turmoil—from these arise the very laws of endless-changing motion by the which man rules his artistic presentation of himself. The savage, governed by the rawest passions, knows in his dance almost no other change than that from monotonous tumult to monotonous and apathetic rest. In the wealth and multiform variety of his transitions speaks out the nobler, civilised man; the richer and more manifold are these transitions, the more composed and stable is the ordering of their mutual inter- change. But the law of this ordering is *Rhythm.*

Rhythm is in no wise an arbitrary canon, according to which the artistic-man forsooth *shall* move his body's limbs; but it is the conscious soul of those necessitated (?—" reflex "—TR.) movements by which he strives in- stinctively to impart to others his own emotions. If the motion and the gestures are themselves the feeling *Tone* of his emotion, then is their Rhythm its articulate *Speech.* The swifter the play of emotion: the more passionately embarrassed and unclear is the man himself, and therefore the less capable is he of imparting his emotion in a clear and intelligible fashion. On the other hand, the more restful the change: so much the plainer will the emotion show its nature. Rest is continuance; but continuance of motion is repetition of motion: that which repeats itself allows of reckoning, and the law of this reckoning is *Rhythm.*

By means of Rhythm does Dance become an art. It is the *Measure* of the movements by which emotion mirrors forth itself,—the measure by which it first attains that perspicuity which renders understanding possible. But the 'stuff' by means of which this Rhythm makes itself outwardly discernible and measure-giving, as the self-dictated Law of motion, is necessarily taken from another element than that of bodily motion ;—only through a thing apart from myself, can I first know myself; but this thing which lies apart from bodily motion is that which appeals to a sense that lies apart from the sense to which the body's motion is addressed ; and this fresh sense is *Hearing*. Rhythm—which sprang from the inner Necessity which spurred corporeal motion on to gain an understanding— imparts itself to the dancer, as the outward manifestment of this Necessity, the Law of Measure, chiefly through the medium of that which is perceptible by the ear alone, namely *Sound ;*—just as in music the abstract measure of rhythm, the 'Bar,' is imparted by a motion cognisable only by the eye.   This equal-meted repetition, springing as it does from Motion's innermost Necessity, invites alike and guides the dancer's movements by its exposition through the rhythmic beat of Sound, such as is at first evoked by simple clapping of the hands, and then from wooden, metal, or other sonorous objects.

However, the mere definition of the points of Time at which a movement shall repeat itself, does not suffice completely for the dancer who submits the ordering of his movements to an outwardly perceptible law.   Just as the Motion, beside its swift change from time-point to time-point, is maintained abidingly, and thus becomes a continuous performance : so does the dancer require that the Sound, which had hitherto vanished as suddenly as it had appeared, shall be compelled to an abiding continuance, to an extension in regard of Time.   He demands, in short, that the emotion which forms the living Soul of his movements shall be equally expressed in the continuance of the Sound ; for only so does the self-dictated rhythmic Measure become one that corresponds completely with the Dance, inasmuch as it embraces not merely *one* of the essential conditions of the latter but, as far as possible, *all*.   This *Measure* must therefore be the embodiment of the essence of Dance in a separate, but allied, branch of art.

This other branch of art into which Dance yearns instinctively to pass, therein to find again and know her own true nature, is the art of *Tone ;* which, in its turn, receives the solid scaffold of its vertebration from Dance's rhythm.

Rhythm is the natural, unbreakable bond of union between the arts of Dance and Tone; without it, no art of Dance, and none of Tone. If Rhythm, as her regulating and unifying law, is the very *Mind* of Dance—to wit, the abstract summary of corporeal motion,—so is it, on the other hand, the moving, self-progressive *Skeleton* of Tone. The more this skeleton invests itself with tonal flesh, the more does the law of Dance lose its own features in the special attributes of Tone ; so much the more, however, does Dance at like time raise herself to the capability of that expression of the deeper feelings of the heart by which alone she can keep abreast of the essential nature of Tone. But Tone's most living flesh is the *human voice ;* and *the Word*, again, is as it were the bone-and-muscle rhythm of this human voice. And thus, at last, the movement-urging emotion, which overflowed from art of Dance to art of Tone, finds in the definite decision of the Word the sure, unerring utterance by means of which it can both seize itself as 'object' and clearly speak forth what it is. Thus, through tone become Speech, it wins at once its highest satisfaction and its most satisfying heightening in the tonal art become the art of Poesy ; for it mounts aloft from Dance to *Mimicry*, from the broadest delineation of general bodily sensations to the subtlest and most compact* utterance of definite mental phases of emotion and of will-force.—

From this frank and mutual permeation, generation, and completion of each several art from out itself and through its fellow—which, as regards Music and Poetry, we have so far merely hinted at—is born the united *Lyric Art-work*. In it each art is what its nature accords to it ; that which lies beyond its power of being, it does not egoistically borrow from

* The German equivalent for "compact" is "*dicht*" ; the term seems to have been purposely chosen by the author, in order to bring out the true meaning of "*Dichtkunst*," "The art of Poetry," as a crystallisation—so to say—of ideas and emotions only vaguely felt before.—TR.

its fellow, but its fellow *is that* in its place.   But in *Drama*, the perfected form of Lyric, each several art unfolds its highest faculty ; and notably that of Dance.   In Drama, Man is at once his own artistic ' subject ' and his ' stuff,' to his very fullest worth.   Now as therein the art of Dance has to set directly forth the separate or joint expressive movements which are to tell us of the feelings both of units and of masses ; and as the law of Rhythm, begotten from her, is the standard whereby the whole dramatic semblance is brought into agreement (" *Verständigung* "), — so does Dance withal exalt herself in Drama to her most spiritual ex- pression, that of *Mimicry*.   As Mimetic art, she becomes the direct and all-embracing utterance of the inner man ; and it is now no longer the raw material rhythm of Sound, but the spiritual rhythm of Speech, that shows itself to her as law,—a law, however, which took its earliest rise from her dictation.   What Speech endeavours to convey (" *ver- ständlichen* "), the whole wide range of feelings and emotions, ideas and thoughts, which mount from softest tenderness to indomitable energy, and finally proclaim themselves as naked Will—all this becomes an uncondi- tionally intelligible, unquestioned truth through Mimic art alone ; nay, Speech itself cannot become a true and quite convincing physical utterance without the immediate aid of Mimicry.   From this, the Drama's pinnacle, Dance broadens gradually down again to her original domain : where Speech now only hints and pictures ; where Tone, as Rhythm's soul, restricts herself to homage of her sister ; and where the beauty of the Body and its movements alone can give direct and needful utterance to an all- dominating, all-rejoicing feeling.

Thus Dance reaches in Drama her topmost height, entrancing where she orders, affecting where she sub- ordinates herself; ever and throughout—herself : because ever spontaneous and, therefore, of indispensable Necessity. For only where an art is indispensable, is it alike the whole thing *that it is* and can and should be.——

Just as in the building of the Tower of Babel, when

THE ART-WORK OF THE FUTURE.

their speech was confounded and mutual understanding
made impossible, the nations severed from each other,
each one to go its several way: so, when all national
solidarity had split into a thousand egoistic severalities,
did the separate art-branches cut-off themselves from the
proud and heaven-soaring tree of Drama, which had lost the
inspiring soul of mutual understanding.

Let us consider for a moment what fate befell the art of
Dance, when she left the graceful chain of sisters, to seek
her fortune in the world's great wilderness.—

Though Dance now ceased to offer to the mawkish and
sentimental schoolmaster-poetry of Euripides the hand of
fellowship which the latter cast away in sullen arrogance,
only to take it later when humbly proffered for an '*occasional*'
service ("*Zweckleistung*") ; though she parted from her
philosophical sister who, with sour-faced frivolity, could
only *envy* and no longer love her youthful charms : yet she
could not wholly dispense with the help of her bosom-
comrade, Tone. By an indisruptible band was she linked to
her, for the art of Tone held fast within her hands the *key*
to her very soul. But, as after the death of a father in
whose love his children have all been knit together, and have
held their life-goods as one common store, the heirs in
selfish strife compute the several stock of each,—so did
Dance contend that this key was wrought by *her*, and
claimed it back as the first condition of her now separate
life. Willingly did she forego the feeling tones of her
sister's Voice; for by this voice, whose marrow was the
Word of *Poetry*, she must forsooth have felt herself inextricably chained to that proud leader ! But this *instrument*, of
wood or metal, the musical *tool* which her sister, in sweet
urgence to inspire with her soulful breath even the dead
stuff of Nature, had fashioned for the buttress and enhancement of her voice,—this tool, which verily was fit enough
to mete for her the needful guiding measure of rhythm and
of beat, nay even to wellnigh imitate the tonal beauty of
her sister's voice,—the Musical Instrument she took with
her. Not caring for aught else, she left her sister Tone to

float adown the shoreless stream of Christian harmony, tied to her faith in Words, the while she cast herself in easy-going self-sufficience upon the pleasure-craving places of the world.

We know too well this tricked-out figure : who is it that has not come across her ? Wherever fatuous modern ease girds itself up to seek for entertainment, she sets herself with utmost complaisance upon the scene, and plays, for gold, whatever pranks one wills. Her highest faculty, the use of which she can no longer see, the faculty of ransoming by her mien and gestures the Thought of Poetry in its yearning for actual human birth, she has lost or made away in thoughtless foolishness, and minds her not—to whom. With all the features of her face, with all the gestures of her limbs, she has nothing now to bring to light but unconfined complaisance. Her solitary care is lest she should seem capable of making a refusal ; and of this care she unburdens herself by the only mimetic expression of which she still is mistress, by the most unruffled smile of unconditional surrender to each and all. With her features set in this unchangeable and fixed expression, she answers the demand for change and motion by her lower limbs alone ; all her artistic capability has sunk down from her vertex, through her body, to her feet. Head, neck, trunk and thighs are only present as unbidden guests ; whereas her feet have undertaken to show alone what she can do, and merely for the sake of needful balance call on her arms and hands for sisterly support. What in private life—when our modern citizens, in accordance with tradition and the time-killing habits of society, indulge themselves in dance, in our so-called 'Balls'—it is only allowable to timidly suggest with all the woodenness of civilised vapidity : *that* is permitted to the kindly *ballerina* to tell aloud upon the public stage with frankest candour ; for—her gestures, forsooth, are merely art and not reality, and now that she has been declared *beyond* the law, she stands *above* the law. In effect, we may let ourselves be incited by her, without, for all that, following in our moral life her incitations,—just as, on the other hand, Religion also offers us its incitations, to goodness and to virtue, and yet we are not in the smallest bound to yield to them in everyday existence. Art is *free*,—and the art of Dance draws her profit from this freedom. And she does right in this: else what were Freedom made for?—

How comes it that this noble art has fallen so low that, in our public art-life, she can only find her passport and her lease of life as the hasp of all the banded arts of harlotry? That she must give herself beyond all ransom into the most dishonouring chains of nethermost dependence?— Because everything torn from its connexions, every egoistic unit, must needs become in truth *unfree, i.e.* dependent on an alien master. The mere corporeal man, the mere emotional, the mere intellectual man, are each incapable of any self-sufficience of the genuine Man. The exclusiveness of their nature leads them into every excess of immoderation ; for the salutary Measure arises only—and of itself—from the community of natures like and yet unlike. But immoderation is the absolute un-freedom of any being ; and this unfreedom must of necessity evince itself as dependence upon sheer externals.—

In her separation from true Music, and especially from Poetry, Dance not only gave up her highest attributes, but she also lost a portion of her *individuality*. Only that is individual, which can beget from out itself: Dance was a completely individual art for just so long as she could bring forth from her inmost nature, and her Need, the laws in accordance with which she came to an intelligible manifestment. To-day the *only* remaining individual dance is the *national* dance of the *Folk ;* for, as it steps into the world of show, it proclaims its own peculiar nature in inimitable fashion by gestures, rhythm, and beat, whose laws itself had made instinctively; while these laws only become cognisable and communicable when they have really issued from the art-work of the People as the abstract of its essence. Further evolution of the folk-dance towards the richer capabilities of Art is only possible by union with the arts of Tone and Poetry, no longer tyrannised by Dance, but bearing themselves as free agents ; for only amid the correlated faculties, and under the stimulation, of these arts can she unfold and broaden out her individual faculties to their fullest compass.

The Grecian Lyric art-work shows us how the laws of Rhythm, the individual mark of Dance, were developed in the arts of Tone and, above all, of Poetry to endless breadth and manifold richness of characterisation by the individuality of these very arts, and thus gave back to Dance an inexhaustible store of novel stimulus to the finding of fresh movements peculiar to herself ; and how, in lively joy of fecund interaction, the individuality of each several art was able thus to lift itself to its most perfect fill. The modern folk-dance could never bring to bearing the fruits of such an interaction : for as all folk-art of the modern nations was nipped in the bud by Christianity and Christian-political civilisation, neither could *it*, a solitary shrub, bush out in rich and manifold development. Yet the only individual phenomena in the domain of Dance known to our world of today are the sheer products of the Folk, such as they have budded, or even now still bud, from the character of this or that nationality. All our actual civilised Dance is but a compilation from these dances of the Folk : the folk-styles of every nationality are taken up by her, employed, and mutilated,—but not developed farther ; because, as an art, she only feeds herself on foreign food. Her procedure, therefore, is ever a mere intentional and artificial copying, patching together, and dovetailing ; in no wise a bringing forth and new-creating. Her nature is that of Mode, which, of sheer craving for vicissitude, gives today to this style, tomorrow to that, the preference. She is therefore forced to found her arbitrary systems, to set her purpose down in rules, and to proclaim her will in needless axioms and assumptions, in order to enable her disciples to comprehend and execute it. But these rules and systems wholly *isolate* her as an art, and fence her off from any healthy union with another branch of art for mutual collaboration. Un-nature, held to artificial life by laws and arbitrary formulæ, is from top to bottom egoistic ; and as it is incapable of bringing forth from out itself, so also is any wedding of it a thing impossible.

This art has therefore no love-need; she can only *take*, but not *give*. She draws all foreign life-stuff into herself, disintegrates and devours it, assimilating it with her own unfruitful being ; but cannot blend herself with any element whose life is based on grounds outside her, because she cannot give herself.

Thus does our modern Dance attempt in *Pantomime* the task of Drama. Like every isolated, egoistic branch of art, she fain would be all things unto herself, and reign in lonely all-sufficiency. She would picture men and human haps, conditions, conflicts, characters and motives, without employing that faculty by which man first attains completion, —*Speech*. She would poetise, without the faintest comradeship with Poetry. And what does she breed, in this demure exclusiveness and "independence"? The most utterly dependent and cripple-like monstrosity : men who cannot talk ; and not forsooth since some mischance has robbed them of the gift of speech, but since their stubborn choice forbids their speaking ; actors whose release from some unholy spell we look for every moment, if only they could gain the courage to end the painful stammering of their Gestures by a wholesome spoken Word, but whom the rules and prescripts of pantomimic art forbid to dishallow by one natural syllable the unflecked sense of Dance's self-dependence.

And yet so lamentably dependent is this absolute dumb *Spectacle*, that in its happiest moments it only ventures to concern itself with dramatic stuffs that require to enter on no relations with the human reason,—nay, even in the most favourable of such cases, still sees itself compelled to the ignominious expedient of acquainting the spectators with its particular intention by means of an *explanatory programme !*

Yet herewith is undeniably manifested the remnant of
Dance's noblest effort ; she would still at least be somewhat, and soars upward to the yearning for the highest
work of Art, the Drama ; she seeks to withdraw from the
wanton gaze of frivolity, and clutches after some artistic
veil wherewith to cloak her shameful nakedness.   But into
what a dishonouring dependence must she cast herself,
in the very manifestment of this effort!   With what piti-
able distortion must she expiate the vain desire for unnatural self-dependence !   She, without whose highest and
most individual help the highest, noblest Art-work cannot
attain to show, must—severed from the union of her sisters
—take refuge from prostitution in absurdity, from absurdity
in prostitution !—

O glorious Dance ! O shameful Dance !—

4.

The Art of Tone.

The ocean binds and separates the land : so does Music
bind and separate the two opposite poles of human Art,
the arts of Dance and Poetry.

She is the *heart* of man ; the blood, which takes this
heart for starting-point, gives to the outward-facing flesh
its warm and lively tint, — while it feeds the inward-
coursing brain-nerves with its welling pulse.   Without the
heart's activity, the action of the brain would be no more
than of a mere automaton ; the action of the body's outer
members, a mechanical and senseless motion.   Through
the heart the understanding feels itself allied with the
whole body, and the man of mere ' five-senses ' mounts
upwards to the energy of Reason.

But the organ of the heart is *tone ;* its conscious speech,
the *art of Tone.*   She is the full and flowing heart-love, that
ennobles the material sense of pleasure, and humanises
immaterial thought.   Through Tone are Dance and

Poetry brought to mutual understanding : in her are intercrossed in loving blend the laws by which they each proclaim their own true nature ; in her, the wilfulness of each becomes instinctive ' Will ' (" *Unwillkürlichen* "), the Measure of Poetry and the Beat of Dance become the undictated Rhythm of the Heart-throb.)

Does she receive from her sisters the conditions under which she manifests herself, so does she give them back to them in infinite embellishment, as the conditions of their own enunciation.   If Dance conveys to Tone her own peculiar law of motion, so does Tone bring it back to her with soul and sense embodied in her Rhythm, for the measure of more noble, more intelligible motion.   If Tone obtains from Poetry her pregnant coil of sharp-cut Words, entwined by meaning and by measure, and takes it as a solid mesh of thought wherewith to gird her boundless fluid mass of sound : so does she hand her sister back this ideal coil of yearning syllables, that indirectly shadow forth in images, but cannot yet express their thought with all the truth and cogence of necessity,—and hands it as the direct utterance of Feeling, the unerring vindicator and redeemer, *Melody*.

In *Rhythm* and in *Melody*, ensouled by Tone, both Dance and Poetry regain their own true essence, materialised and endlessly enhanced and beautified ; and thus they learn to know and love themselves.   But melody and rhythm are the *arms* of Tone, with which she locks her sisters in the close embrace of triple growth ; they are the *shores* through which *the sea*, herself, unites two continents. If this sea draws backward from the shores, and broadens out the waste of an abyss between itself and each of them, then can no light-winged ship bear aught from either continent unto the other ; forever must they rest dissundered,—until some outcome of machinery, perchance a railroad, shall bridge the waste !   Then men shall start therefrom, forsooth upon their steamboats, to cross the open sea ; the breath of all-enlivening breezes replaced by sickening fumes from the machine.   Blow the winds of

heaven eastward : what matters it ?—the machine shall
clatter westward, or wherever else men choose to go. Even
as the dance-wright fetches from the continent of Poetry,
across the steam-tamed ocean crests of Music, the programme for his novel ballet ; while the play-concoctor im-
ports from the far-off continent of Dance just so much
leg-gymnastics as he deems expedient for filling up a
halting situation.—

Let us see, then, what has come to sister Tone, since the
death of all-loving father, *Drama !*—

We cannot yet give up our simile of the *Ocean*, for picturing Tone's nature. If *Melody* and *Rhythm* are the shores
through which the art of Tone lays fruitful hands upon
twain continents of art, allied to her of yore : so is Sound
itself her fluent, native element, and its immeasurable
expanse of waters make out the sea of *Harmony*. The
eye knows but the surface of this sea ; its depth the depth
of Heart alone can fathom. Upwards from its lightless
bottom it expands into a sun-bright mirror ; the ever-
widening rings of Rhythm cross over on it from one shore ;
from the shady valleys of the other arise the yearning
zephyrs that rouse this restful surface to the grace of
swelling, sinking waves of Melody.

Man dives into this sea ; only to give himself once more,
refreshed and radiant, to the light of day. His heart feels
widened wondrously, when he peers down into this depth,
pregnant with unimaginable possibilities whose bottom his
eye shall never plumb, whose seeming bottomlessness thus
fills him with the sense of marvel and the presage of
Infinity. It is the depth and infinity of Nature herself,
who veils from the prying eye of Man the unfathomable
womb of her eternal Seed-time, her Begetting, and her
Yearning ; even because man's eye can only grasp the
already manifested, the Blossom, the Begotten, the Fulfilled. This Nature is, however, none other than *the nature
of the human heart itself*, which holds within its shrine the
feelings of desire and love in their most infinite capacity ;
which is *itself* Desire and Love, and—as in its insatiable

longing it yet wills nothing but itself—can only grasp and comprehend itself.

If this sea stir up its waters of itself, if it beget the ground of its commotion from the depths of its own element: then is this agitation an endless one and never pacified; for ever returning on itself unstilled, and ever roused afresh by its eternal longing. But if the vast reach of this Desire be kindled by an outward object; if this measure-giving object step toward it from the sure and sharply outlined world of manifestment; if sun-girt, slender, blithely-moving Man incend the flame of this desire by the lightning of his glancing eye,—if he ruffle with his swelling breath the elastic crystal of the sea, — then let the fire crackle as it may, let the ocean's bosom heave with ne'er so violent a storm : yet the flame at last, when its wild glow has smouldered down, will shine with mild serenity of light,—the sea-rind, the last foam-wreath of its giant crests dissolved, will crisp itself at last to the soft play of rippling waves ; and Man, rejoicing in the sweet harmony of his whole being, will entrust himself to the beloved element in some frail coracle, and steer his steadfast course towards the beacon of that kindly light.—

The *Greek*, when he took ship upon his sea, ne'er let the coast line fade from sight : for him it was the trusty stream that bore him from one haven to the next, the stream on which he passed between the friendly strands amidst the music of his rhythmic oars,—here lending glances to the wood-nymphs' dance, there bending ear to sacred hymns whose melodious string of meaning words was wafted by the breezes from the temple on the mountain-top. On the surface of the water were truly mirrored back to him the jutting coasts, with all their peaks and valleys, trees and flowres and men, deep-set within the æther's blue; and this undulating mirror-picture, softly swayed by the fresh fan of gentle gusts, he deemed was *Harmony*.—

The *Christian* left the shores of Life.—Farther afield, beyond all confines, he sought the sea,—to find himself at last upon the Ocean, twixt sea and heaven, boundlessly

H

alone. The *Word*, the word of *Faith* was his only compass;
and it pointed him unswervingly toward Heaven. This
heaven brooded far above him, it sank down on every side
in the horizon, and fenced his sea around. But the sailor
never reached that confine; from century to century he
floated on without redemption, towards this ever imminent,
but never reached, new home; until he fell a-doubting of the
virtue of his compass, and cast it, as the last remaining
human bauble, grimly overboard. And now, denuded of
all ties, he gave himself without a rudder to the never-
ending turmoil of the waves' caprice. In unstilled, ireful
love-rage, he stirred the waters of the sea against the
unattainable and distant heaven : he urged the insatiate
greed of that desire and love which, reft of an external
object, must ever only crave and love itself,—that deepest,
unredeemable hell of restless Egoism, which stretches out
without an end, and wills and wishes, yet ever and forever
can only wish and will itself,—he urged it 'gainst the
abstract universalism of heaven's blue, that universal longing without the shadow of an 'object'—against the very
vault of absolute un-objectivity. (Bliss, unconditioned
bliss,—to gain in widest, most unbounded measure the
height of bliss, and yet to stay completely *wrapt in self*:
this was the unallayable desire of Christian passion.) So
reared the sea from out its deepest depth to heaven, so sank
it ever back again to its own depths ; ever its unmixed
self, and therefore ever unappeased,—like the all-usurping,
measureless desire of the heart that ne'er will give itself
and dare to be consumed in an external object, but
damns itself to everlasting *selfish solitude.*

Yet in Nature each immensity strives after Measure ;
the unconfined draws bounds around itself ; the elements
condense at last to definite show ; and even the boundless
sea of Christian yearning found the new shore on which its
turbid waves might break. Where on the farthest horizon
we thought to find the ever made-for, never happed-on
gateway into the realms of Heaven unlimited, there did the
boldest of all seafarers discover *land* at last,—man-tenanted,

real, and blissful land. Through his discovery the wide
ocean is now not only meted out, but made for men an inland sea, round which the coasts are merely broadened out
in unimaginably ampler circle.   Did Columbus teach us to
take ship across the ocean, and thus to bind in one each
continent of Earth ; did his world-historical discovery
convert the narrow-seeing national-man into a universal
and all-seeing *Man :* so, by the hero who explored the
broad and seeming shoreless sea of absolute Music unto its
very bounds, are won the new and never dreamt-of coasts
which this sea no longer now divorces from the old and
primal continent of man, but *binds together* with it for the
new-born, happy art-life of the Manhood of the Future.
And this hero is none other than—*Beethoven.*—

When Tone unloosed her from the chain of sisters, she
took as her unrelinquishable, her foremost life's-condition
—just as light-minded sister Dance had filched from *her*
her rhythmic measure—from thoughtful sister Poetry her
Word ; yet not the human-breathing spirit of the musing
("*dichtende*") word, but only its bare corporeal condensation ("*verdichtete*") into tones.   As she had abandoned
her rhythmic beat to parting Dance's use and pleasure,
she thenceforth built upon the Word alone ; the word
of Christian Creed, that toneless, fluid, scattering word
which, un-withstanding and right gladly, soon gave to her
complete dominion over it.   But the more this word
evaporated into the mere stammer of humility, the mere
babbling of implicit, childlike love, so much the more
imperatively did Tone see herself impelled to shape herself from out the exhaustless depths of her own liquid
nature.   The struggle for such shaping is the building up
of *Harmony.*

Harmony grows from below upwards as a perpendicular
pillar, by the joining-together and overlaying of correlated
tone-stuffs.   Unceasing alternation of such columns, each
freshly risen member taking rank beside its fellows, constitutes the only possibility of absolute harmonic movement 'in breadth.'   The feeling of needful care for the

beauty of this motion 'in breadth' is foreign to the nature of absolute Harmony; she knows but the beauty of her columns' changing play of colour, but not the grace of their marshalling in point of 'time,'—for that is the work of Rhythm.   On the other hand, the inexhaustible variety of this play of colours is the ever-fruitful source on which she draws, with immoderate self-satisfaction, to show herself in constant change of garb; while the life-breath which en-souls and sets in motion this restless, capricious, and self-conditioning change, is the essence of elemental tone itself, the outbreathing of an unfathomable, all-dominating heart's-desire.   In the kingdom of Harmony there is therefore no beginning and no end; just as the objectless and self-devouring fervour of the soul, all ignorant of its source, is nothing but itself, nothing but longing, yearning, tossing, pining—and *dying out, i.e.* dying without having assuaged itself in any 'object'; thus dying without death,* and therefore everlasting falling back upon itself.

So long as the Word was in power, it commanded both beginning and ending; but when it was engulfed in the bottomless depths of Harmony, when it became naught but "groanings and sighings of the soul,"†—as on the ardent summit of the music of the Catholic Church,—then was the word capriciously hoisted to the capitals of those harmonic columns, of that unrhythmic melody, and cast as though from wave to wave; while the measureless harmonic possibilities must draw from out themselves the laws for their own finite manifestment.   There is no other artistic faculty of man that answers to the character of Harmony : it cannot find its mirror in the physical precision of the

---

* Compare *Tristan u. Isolde*, Act 3, "Sehnen ! Sehnen—im Sterben mich zu sehnen, vor Sehnsucht nicht zu sterben ! "—a passage which has more than any other been ascribed to Schopenhauer's influence, but which is almost a literal reproduction of the words used in the present instance.—TR.

† See Wagner's *Letters to Uhlig* (Letter 67,—July, 1852).   "*E. D. defends music against me.*   Is not that delicious?   He appeals to 'harmonies of the spheres,' and 'groanings and sighings of the soul !'   Well, I have got a pretty millstone hung about my neck ! "—TR.

movements of the body, nor in the logical induction of the thinking brain,—it cannot set up for itself its standard in the recognised necessity of the material world of show, like Thought, nor like corporeal Motion in the periodic calculation of its instinctive, physically governed properties : it is like a nature-force which men perceive but cannot comprehend.   Summoned by outer—not by inner—necessity to resolve on surer and more finite manifestment, Harmony must mould from out its own immensurate depths the laws for its own following.   These laws of harmonic sequence, based on the nature of Affinity,—just as those harmonic columns, the chords, were formed by the affinity of tone-stuffs,—unite themselves into one standard, which sets up salutary bounds around the giant playground of capricious possibilities.   They allow the most varied choice from amid the kingdom of harmonic families, and extend the possibility of union by elective-affinity ("*Wahlverwand-schaftliche Verbindungen*") with the members of neighbouring families, almost to free liking ; they demand, however, before all a strict observance of the house-laws of affinity of the family once chosen, and a faithful tarrying with it, for sake of a happy end.   But this end itself, and thus the measure of the composition's extension *in time*, the countless laws of harmonic decorum can neither give nor govern.   As the scientifically teachable or learnable department of the art of Tone, they can cleave the fluid tonal masses of Harmony asunder, and part them into fenced-off bodies ; but they cannot assign the periodic measure of these fenced-off masses.

When the limit-setting might of Speech was swallowed up, and yet the art of Tone, now turned to Harmony, could never find her time-assigning law within herself : then was she forced to face towards the remnant of the rhythmic beat that Dance had left for her to garner. Rhythmic figures must now enliven harmony ; their change, their recurrence, their parting and uniting, must condense the fluid breadths of Harmony—as Word had earlier done with Tone—and bring their periods to more sure conclusion.

But no inner necessity, striving after purely human exposition, lay at the bottom of this rhythmic livening; not the feeling, thinking, will-ing Man, such as proclaims himself by speech and bodily motion, was its motive power; nothing but an *outer* necessity, which Harmony, in struggle for her selfish close, had taken up into herself. This rhythmic interchange and shaping, which moved not of its inner, own necessity, could therefore only borrow life from arbitrary laws and canons. These laws and canons are those of *Counterpoint*.

Counterpoint, with its multiple births and offshoots, is Art's artificial playing-with-itself, the mathematics of Feeling, the mechanical rhythm of egoistic Harmony. In its invention, abstract Tone indulged her whim to pass as the sole and only self-supporting Art;—as that art which owes its being, its absolute and godlike nature, to no human Need soever, but purely to *itself*. The wilful quite naturally believes itself the absolute and right monopolist; and it is certain that to her own caprice alone could Music thank her self-sufficient airs, for that mechanical, contrapunctal artifice was quite incapable of answering any *soul-need*. Music therefore, in her pride, had become her own direct antithesis: from a *heart's* concern, a matter of the *intellect;* from the utterance of unshackled Christian soul's-desire, the cashbook of a modern market-speculation.

The living breath of fair, immortal, nobly-feeling Human Voice, streaming ever fresh and young from the bosom of the Folk, blew this contrapunctal house of cards, too, of a heap. The *Folk-tune*, that had rested faithful to its own untarnished grace; the simple, surely outlined *Song*, close-woven with the poem, soared-up on its elastic pinions to the regions of the beauty-lacking, scientifically-musical artworld, with news of joyous ransom. This world was longing to paint *men* again, to set men to sing—not pipes; so it seized the folk-tune for its purpose, and constructed out of it the *opera-air*. But just as Dance had seized the folk-dance, to freshen herself therewith when needed, and to convert it to an artificial compost according to the

dictates of her modish taste,—so did this genteel Operatic
tone-art behave to the folk-tune. She had not grasped
the *entire* man, to show him in his whole artistic stature
and nature-bidden necessity, but only the *singing* man ; and
in his song she had not seized the Ballad of the Folk, with
all its innate generative force, but merely the melodic Tune,
abstracted from the poem, to which she set conventional
and purposely insipid sentences, according to her pleasure ;
it was not the beating heart of the nightingale, but only
its warbling throat that men could fathom, and practised
themselves to imitate. Just as the art-dancer had set his
legs, with their manifold but still monotonous bendings,
flingings, and gyrations, to *vary* the natural folk-dance
which he could not of himself develop further,—so did the
art-singer set his throat to paraphrase with countless orna-
ments, to alter by a host of flourishes, those tunes which
he had stolen from the People's mouth, but whose nature
he could never fertilise afresh ; and thus another species
of mechanical dexterity filled up the place which contrapunctal ingenuity had left forlorn. We need not further
characterise the repugnant, ineffably repulsive disfigurement and rending of the folk-tune, such as cries out from
the modern operatic *Aria*—for truly it is nothing but a
mutilated folk-tune, and in no wise a specific fresh invention — such as, in entire contempt of Nature and all
human feeling, and severed from all basis of poetic speech,
now tickles the imbecile ears of our opera-frequenters with
its lifeless, soul-less toy of fashion. We must content ourselves with candidly, though mournfully, avowing that our
modern public sums up in *it* its whole idea of Music's
essence.—

But apart from this public and its subservient fashion-
mongers and mode-purveyors, the inmost individual essence of Tone was yet to soar up from its plumbless
depths, in all the unlost plenitude of its unmeasured
faculties, to redemption in the sunlight of the universal,
one Art of the Future. And this spring it was to take
from off *that* ground which is the ground of all sheer

human art: the *plastic motion of the body*, portrayed in musical *Rhythm*.

Though in the Christian lisping of the stereotyped Word, eternally repeated until it lost itself in utter dearth of Thought, the human *voice* had shrunk at last to a mere physical and flexile implement of Tone: yet, by its side, those tone-implements which mechanism had devised for Dance's ample escort had been elaborated to ever more enhanced expressive faculty. As bearers of the dance-tune, the *rhythmic Melody* had been consigned to their exclusive care; and, by reason of the ease with which their blended forces took up the element of Christian Harmony, to them now fell the call for all further evolution of the art of Tone from out itself. *The harmonised dance* is the basis of the richest art-work of the modern *Symphony*.—Even this 'harmonised dance' fell as a savoury prey into the hands of counterpoint-concocting mechanism; which loosed it from obedient devotion to its mistress, body-swaying Dance, and made it now to take its turns and capers from *its* rules. Yet it needed but the warm lifebreath of the natural folk-tune to beat upon the leathern harness of this schooled and contrapunctal dance,—and lo! it stretched at once to the elastic flesh of fairest human artwork. This artwork, in its highest culmination, is *the Symphony of Haydn, of Mozart, and Beethoven*.

In the Symphony of Haydn the rhythmic dance-melody moves with all the blithesome freshness of youth: its entwinements, disseverings, and re-unitings, though carried out with highest contrapunctal ingenuity, yet hardly show a trace of the results of such ingenious treatment; but rather take the character peculiar to a dance ordained by laws of freest Phantasy,—so redolent are they of the warm and actual breath of joyous human Life. To the more tempered motion of the middle section of the symphony we see assigned by Haydn a broad expansion of the simple song-tune of the Folk; in this it spreads by laws of *melos* peculiar to the character of Song, through soaring graduations and 'repeats' enlivened by most manifold expression.

This form of melody became the very element of the Symphony of song-abundant, and song-glad *Mozart.* He breathed into his instruments the passionate breath of *Human Voice,* that voice toward which his genius bent with overmastering love. He led the stanchless stream of teeming Harmony into the very heart of Melody ; as though in restless care to give it, only mouthed by Instruments, in recompense the depth of feeling and of fervour that forms the exhaustless source of human utterance within the inmost chambers of the heart. Whilst, in his Symphonies, Mozart to some extent but made short work of everything that lay apart from this his individual impulse and, with all his remarkable dexterity in counterpoint, departed little from those traditional canons which he himself helped forward to stability : he lifted up the 'singing' power of instrumental music to such a height that it was now enabled, not only to embrace the mirth and inward still content which it had learnt from Haydn, but the whole depth of endless heart's-desire.

It was *Beethoven* who opened up the boundless faculty of Instrumental Music for expressing elemental storm and stress. His power it was, that took the basic essence of the Christian's Harmony, that bottomless sea of unhedged fulness and unceasing motion, and clove in twain the fetters of its freedom. *Harmonic Melody*—for so must we designate this melody divorced from speech, in distinction from the Rhythmic Melody of dance—was capable, though merely borne by instruments, of the most limitless expression together with the most unfettered treatment. In long, connected tracts of sound, as in larger, smaller, or even smallest fragments, it turned beneath the Master's poet hand to vowels, syllables, and words and phrases of a speech in which a message hitherto unheard, and never spoken yet, could promulgate itself. Each letter of this speech was an infinitely soul-full element ; and the measure of the joinery of these elements was utmost free commensuration, such as could be exercised by none but a tone-poet who longed for the unmeasured utterance of this unfathomed yearning.

Glad in this unspeakably expressive language, but suffering beneath the weight of longing of his artist soul—a longing which, in its infinity, could only be an 'object' to itself, not satisfy itself outside—the happy-wretched, sea-glad and sea-weary mariner sought for a surer haven wherein to anchor from the blissful storms of passionate tumult. Was his faculty of speech unending—so also was the yearning which inspired that speech with its eternal breath. How then proclaim the end, the satisfaction, of this yearning, in the selfsame tongue that was naught but its expression? If the utterance of immeasurable heart-yearning be vented in this elemental speech of absolute tone, then the *endlessness* of such utterance, like that of the yearning itself, is its only true Necessity; the yearning cannot find contentment in any finite *shutting-off* of sound, —for that could only be Caprice. Now by the definite expression which it borrows from the rhythmic dance-melody, Instrumental Music may well portray and bring to close a placid and self-bounded mood; for reason that it takes its measure from an originally outward-lying object, namely the motion of the body. If a tone-piece yield itself *ab initio* to this expression, which must always be conceived as that of mirth, in greater or in less degree, —then, even mid the richest, most luxuriant unfolding of the faculty of tonal speech, it holds within itself the necessary grounds of every phase of 'satisfaction'; while equally inevitably must this 'satisfaction' be a matter of caprice, and therefore in truth unsatisfying, when that sure and sharp-cut mode of utterance endeavours merely *thus* to terminate the storms of endless yearning. The transition from the endless agitation of desire to a mood of joyous satisfaction, can necessarily take place no otherwise than by the ascension of desire into an *object*. But, in keeping with the character of infinite yearning, this 'object' can be none other than such an one as shows itself with finite, physical and ethical exactitude. Absolute Music, however, finds well-marked bounds dividing her from such an object; without indulging in the most arbitrary of assumptions, she can now and never, of her own unaided powers, bring the physical and ethical Man to distinct and plainly recognisable presentment.   Even in her most infinite enhancement, she still is but *emotion ;* she enters *in the train* of the ethical deed, but not as that *Deed itself ;* she can set moods and feelings side by side, but not evolve one mood from out another by any dictate of her own Necessity ;—she lacks the *Moral Will.*

What inimitable art did Beethoven employ in his "C-minor Symphony," in order to steer his ship from the ocean of infinite yearning to the haven of fulfilment ! He was able to raise the utterance of his music *almost* to a moral resolve, but not to speak aloud that final word ; and after every onset of the Will, without a moral hand-hold, we feel tormented by the equal possibility of falling back again to suffering, as of being led to lasting victory. Nay, this falling-back must almost seem to us more 'necessary' than the morally ungrounded triumph, which therefore—not being a necessary consummation, but a mere arbitrary gift of grace—has not the power to lift us up and yield to us that *ethical* satisfaction which we demand as outcome of the yearning of the heart.

Who felt more uncontented with this victory than Beethoven himself ? Was he lief to win a second of the sort ? 'Twas well enough for the brainless herd of imi-tators, who from glorious ' major '-jubilation, after van-quished ' minor '-tribulation, prepared themselves unceas-ing triumphs,—but not for the Master, who was called to write upon his works the *world-history of Music.*

With reverent awe, he shunned to cast himself afresh into that sea of boundless and insatiate yearning. He turned his steps towards the blithesome, life-glad Men he spied encamped on breezy meads, along the outskirt of some fragrant wood beneath the sunny heaven ; kissing, dancing, frolicking. There in shadow of the trees, amid the rustling of the leaves, beside the tender gossip of the brook, he made a happy pact with Nature; there he felt that he was Man, felt all his yearning thrust back deep into his breast before the sovereignty of sweet and blissful *manifestment*. So thankful was he toward this manifestment that, faithfully and in frank humility, he superscribed the separate portions of the tone-work, which he built from this idyllic mood, with the names of those life-pictures whose contemplation had aroused it in him :—" Reminiscences of Country Life " he called the whole.

But in very deed they were only " Reminiscences "— pictures, and not the direct and physical actuality. Towards this actuality he was impelled with all the force of the artist's inexpugnable (" *nothwendig* ") yearning. To give his tone-shapes that same compactness, that directly cognisable and physically sure stability, which he had witnessed with such blessed solace in Nature's own phenomena,—this was the soul of the joyous impulse which created for us that glorious work the " Symphony in A major." All tumult, all yearning and storming of the heart become here the blissful insolence of joy, which snatches us away with bacchanalian might and bears us through the roomy space of Nature, through all the streams and seas of Life, shouting in glad self-consciousness as we tread throughout the Universe the daring measures of this human sphere-dance. This symphony is the *Apotheosis of Dance* herself : it is Dance in her highest aspect, as it were the loftiest Deed of bodily motion incorporated in an ideal mould of tone. Melody and Harmony unite around the sturdy bones of Rhythm to firm and fleshy human shapes, which now with giant limbs' agility, and now with soft, elastic pliance, *almost before our very eyes*, close up the supple, teeming ranks ; the while now gently, now with daring, now serious,* now wanton, now pensive, and again

---

* Amid the solemn-striding rhythm of the second section, a secondary theme uplifts its wailing, yearning song ; to that rhythm, which shows its firm-set tread throughout the entire piece, without a pause, this longing melody clings like the ivy to the oak, which without its clasping of the mighty bole would trail its crumpled, straggling wreaths upon the soil, in forlorn rankness ; but now, while weaving a rich trapping for the rough oak-rind, it gains for itself a sure and undishevelled outline from the stalwart figure of the tree. How brainlessly has this deeply significant device of Beethoven been exploited by

exulting, the deathless strain sounds forth and forth ; until, in the last whirl of delight, a kiss of triumph seals the last embrace.

And yet these happy dancers were merely shadowed forth in tones, mere sounds that imitated men ! Like a second Prometheus who fashioned men of clay (" *Thon* ") Beethoven had sought to fashion them of *tone*. Yet not from ' *Thon* ' or Tone, but from both substances together, must Man, the image of live-giving Zeus, be made. Were Prometheus' mouldings only offered to the *eye*, so were those of Beethoven only offered to the *ear*. But only *where eye and ear confirm each other's sentience of him, is the whole artistic Man at hand.*

But where could Beethoven find *those* men, to whom to stretch out hands across the element of his music ? Those men with hearts so broad that he could pour into them the mighty torrent of his harmonic tones? With frames so stoutly fair that his melodic rhythms should *bear* them and not *crush* them ?—Alas, from nowhere came to him the brotherly Prometheus who could show to him these men ! He needs must gird his loins about, and start *to find out for himself the country of the Manhood of the Future.*

From the shore of Dance he cast himself once more upon that endless sea, from which he had erstwhile found a refuge on this shore ; the sea of unallayable heart-yearning. But 'twas in a stoutly-built and giant-bolted ship that he embarked upon the stormy voyage ; with firm-clenched fist he grasped the mighty helm : he *knew* the journey's goal, and was determined to attain it. No imaginary triumphs would he prepare himself, nor after boldly overcome privations tack back once more to the lazy haven of his home ; for he desired to measure out the ocean's bounds, and find the land which needs must lie beyond the waste of waters.

Thus did the Master urge his course through unheard-of

our modern instrumental-composers, with their eternal " subsidiary themes *!* —R. WAGNER.

possibilities of absolute tone-speech—not by fleetly slipping
past them, but by speaking out their utmost syllable from
the deepest chambers of his heart—forward to where the
mariner begins to sound the sea-depth with his plumb;
where, above the broadly stretched-forth shingles of the
new continent, he touches on the heightening crests of
solid ground; where he has now to decide him whether he
shall face about towards the bottomless ocean, or cast his
anchor on the new-found shore.   But it was no madcap
love of sea-adventure, that had spurred the Master to so
far a journey; with might and main he willed to land
on this new world, for toward *it* alone had he set sail.
Staunchly he threw his anchor out; and this anchor was
the Word.   Yet this Word was not that arbitrary and
senseless cud which the modish singer chews from side to
side, as the gristle of his vocal tone; but the necessary, all-
powerful, and all-uniting word into which the full torrent
of the heart's emotions may pour its stream; the steadfast
haven for the restless wanderer; the light that lightens up
the night of endless yearning : the word that the redeemed
world-man cries out aloud from the fulness of the world-
heart.   This was the word which Beethoven set as crown
upon the forehead of his tone-creation; and this word was:
—" *Freude !*" (" Rejoice !") With this word he cries to men :
" *Breast to breast, ye mortal millions !   This one kiss to all
the world !*"—And *this Word* will be the language of the
Art-work of the Future.—

The Last Symphony of Beethoven is the redemption of
Music from out her own peculiar element into the realm
of *universal Art.*   It is the human Evangel of the art of
the Future.   Beyond it no forward step is possible; for
upon it the perfect Art-work of the Future alone can
follow, the *universal Drama* to which Beethoven has forged
for us the key.

*Thus has Music of herself fulfilled what neither of the
other severed arts had skill to do.*   Each of these arts but
eked out her own self-centred emptiness by *taking*, and
egoistic borrowing; neither, therefore, had the skill to *be*

herself, and of herself to weave the girdle wherewith to link the whole. But Tone, in that she *was herself* completely, and moved amid her own unsullied element, attained the force of the most heroic, most loveworthy self-sacrifice,—of mastering, nay of renouncing 'her own self, to reach out to her sisters the hand of rescue. She thus has kept herself as *heart* that binds both head and limbs in one; and it is not without significance, that it is precisely the art of Tone which has gained so wide extension through all the branches of our modern public life.

To get a clearer insight into the *contradictory* spirit of this public life, however, we must first bear in mind that it was *by no means a mutual coöperation between art-hood and publicity, nay, not even a mutual coöperation of tone-artists themselves*, that carried through the titanic process we have here reviewed: but *simply a richly-gifted individual*, who took up into his solitary self the spirit of community that was absent from our public life; nay, from the fulness of his being, united with the fulness of musical resource, evolved within himself this spirit of community which his artist soul had been the first to yearn for. We see this wonderful creative process, which breathes the fashioning breath of Life through all the symphonies of Beethoven, not only completed by the Master in the most secluded loneliness, but not so much as *comprehended* by his artistic fellows; the rather, shamefully *misunderstood* by them. The forms in which the Master brought to light his world-historical wrestling after Art, remained but *forms* in the eyes of contemporaneous and succeeding music-makers, and passed through Mannerism across to Mode; and despite the fact that no other instrumental composer could, even within these forms, divulge the smallest shred of original inventiveness, yet none lost courage to write symphonies and suchlike pieces by the ream, without a moment happening on the thought that the *last* symphony had *already been written.** Thus have we lived to see

* Whosoever may undertake to write the special history of instrumental music since Beethoven, will undoubtedly have to take account of isolated

Beethoven's great world-voyage of discovery—that unique and throughly unrepeatable feat whose consummation we have witnessed in his "*Freude*"-symphony, as the last and boldest venture of his genius—once more superfluously attempted in foolishest simplicity, and happily got over without one hardship. A new *genre*, a "Symphony with Choruses"—was all the dullards saw therein ! Why should not X or Y be also able to write a "Symphony with Choruses"? Why should not "God the Lord" be praised from swelling throat in the Finale, after three preceding instrumental sections had paved the way as featly as might be ? * Thus has Columbus only discovered America for the sugary hucksters of our times !

The ground of this repugnant phenomenon, however, lies deep within the very nature of our modern music. The art of Tone, set free from those of Dance and Poetry, is no longer an art instinctively necessary to man. It has been forced to construct itself by laws which, taken from its own peculiar nature, find no affinity and no elucidation in any purely human manifestment. Each of the other arts held fast by the measure of the outer human figure, of the outward human life, or of Nature itself,—howsoever capriciously it might disfigure this unconditional first principle. Tone, —which found alone in timid Hearing, susceptible to every

phenomena which are of such a nature as to merit a particular and close attention. He who regards the history of Art, however, from so wide-reaching a point of view as here was necessary, can only keep to its decisive moments ; he must leave unconsidered whatever lies aside from these 'moments,' or is merely their derivative. But the more undeniably is great ability evinced by such detached phenomena, so much the more strikingly do *they themselves* prove, by the barrenness of all their art-endeavour, that in their peculiar art-province somewhat may have yet been left to discover in respect of technical treatment, but nothing in respect of the living spirit, now that *that* has once been spoken which Beethoven spoke through Music. In the great universal Art-work of the Future there will ever be fresh regions to discover ; but not in the separate branch of art, when once the latter—as Music, by Beethoven— has already been led to universalism but yet would linger in her solitary round. —R. WAGNER.

* The original sentence is somewhat too forcible for English notions :— "nachdem er geholfen hat, drei vorangehende Instrumentalsätze so geschickt wie möglich zu Stande zu bringen." The reference is, of course, to Mendels sohn's "*Lobgesang.*" —TR.

cheat and fancy, her outward, human measure,—must frame herself more abstract laws, perforce, and bind these laws into a compact scientific system. This system has been the basis of all modern music: founded on this system, tower was heaped on tower; and the higher soared the edifice, the more inalienable grew the fixed foundation,—this founding which was nowise that of Nature. To the sculptor, the painter, and the poet, their laws of Art explain the course of *Nature;* without an inner understanding of Nature they can make no thing of beauty. To the musician are explained the laws of Harmony, of Counterpoint; his learning, without which he can build no musical structure, is an abstract, scientific system. By attained dexterity in its application, he becomes a craftsman; and from this craftsmanlike standpoint he looks out upon the outer world, which must needs appear to *him* a different thing from what it does to the unadmitted worldling,—the *layman.* The uninitiate layman thus stands abashed before this artificial product of art-music, and very rightly can grasp no whit of it but what appeals directly to the heart; from all the built-up prodigy, however, this only meets him in the unconditioned ear-delight of Melody. All else but leaves him cold, or baffles him with its disquiet; for the simple reason that he does not, and cannot, understand it. Our modern concert-public, which feigns a warmth and satisfaction in presence of the art-symphony, merely lies and plays the hypocrite; and the proof of this hypocrisy is evident enough so soon as, after such a symphony, a modern and melodious operatic 'number' is performed,—as often happens even in our most renowned concert-institutes,—when we may hear the genuine musical pulse of the audience beat high at once in unfeigned joy.

A vital coherence between our art-music and our public taste, must be emphatically denied: where it would fain proclaim its existence, it is affected and untrue; or, with a certain section of our Folk which may from time to time be unaffectedly moved by the drastic power of a Beethovenian symphony, it is—to say the least—unclear, and

I

the impression produced by these tone-works is at bottom
but imperfect and fragmentary.   But where this coherence
is not to hand, the guild-like federation of our art-professors
can only be an outward one ; while the growth and fashioning of art from within outwards cannot depend upon a fellowship which is nothing but an artificial system,—but only in
the separate unit, from the individuality of its specific
nature, can a natural formative and evolutionary impulse
take operation by its own instinctive inner laws.   Only on
the fulness of the special gifts of an individual artist-nature,
can that art-creative impulse feed itself which nowhere
finds its nourishment in outer Nature ; for this individuality
alone can find in its particularity, in its personal intuition,
in its distinctive longing, craving, and willing, the stuff
wherewith to give the art-mass form, the stuff for which it
looks in vain in outer Nature.   In the individuality of this
one and separate human being does Music first become a
purely human art ; she devours up this individuality,—
from the dissolution of its elements to gain her own con-
densement, her own individualisation.

Thus we see in Music as in the other arts, though from
totally different causes, mannerisms and so-called 'schools'
proceeding for the most part from the individuality of a
particular artist.   These 'schools' were the guilds that
gathered—in imitation, nay in repetition—round some great
master in whom the soul of Music had individualised itself.
So long as Music had not fulfilled her world-historical task :
so long might the widely spreading branches of these
schools grow up into fresh stems, under this or that con-
genial fertiliser.   But so soon as that task had been accomplished by the greatest of all musical individualities, so
soon as Tone had used the force of that individuality to
clothe her deepest secrets with the broadest form in which
she still might stay an egoistic, self-sufficient art,—so soon,
in one word, as *Beethoven* had written his Last Symphony,
—then all the musical guilds might patch and cobble as
they would, to bring an absolute music-man to market :
only a patched and cobbled harlequin, no sinewy, robust

son of Nature, could issue now from out their workshops.
After Haydn and Mozart, a Beethoven not only could, but
must come ; the genie of Music claimed him of Necessity,
and without a moment's lingering—he was there.   Who
now will be to Beethoven what *he* was to Mozart and Haydn,
in the realm of absolute music ?   The greatest genius would
not here avail, since the genie of Music no longer needs him.

Ye give yourselves a bootless labour, when, as an opiate
for your egoistic tingling for 'production', ye fain would
deny the cataclysmic significance of Beethoven's Last
Symphony ; and even your obtuseness will not save you,
by which ye make it possible not once to understand this
work !   Do what ye will ; look right away from Beethoven,
fumble after Mozart, gird you round with Sebastian Bach ;
write Symphonies with or without choruses, write Masses,
Oratorios,—the sexless embryos of Opera !—make songs
without words, and operas without texts—: ye still bring
naught to light that has a breath of true life in it.   For
look ye,—ye lack *Belief !* the great belief in the necessity
of what ye do !   Ye have but the belief of simpletons, the
false belief in the possible necessity of your own selfish
caprice !—

In gazing across the busy wilderness of our musical art-
world ; in witnessing the hopeless sterility of this art-chaos,
for all its everlasting ogling ; in presence of this formless
brew, whose lees are mouldering pedantic shamelessness,
and from which, with all its solemn arrogance of musical
'old-master'-hood, at last but dissolute Italian opera-airs
or wanton French *cancan*-tunes can rise as artificial distillate
to the glare of modern public life ;—in short, in pondering
on this utter creative incapacity, we look, without an
instant's blenching, towards the great catastrophe which
shall make an end of the whole unwieldy musical
monstrosity, to clear free space for the Art-work of the
Future ; in which true Music will truly have no minor rôle
to play, but to which both breath and breathing space are
utterly forbidden on such a musical soil as ours.*

* However lengthily I have here expressed myself upon the nature of
Music, in comparison with what I have said upon the other branches of Art

5.

The Poetic Art.

If wont or fashion permitted us to take up again the old and genuine style of speech, and write instead of "*Dichten*" "*Tichten*"; then should we gain in the group of names for the three primeval human arts, "*Tanz-, Ton- und Tichtkunst*" (Dance, Tone, and Poetry), a beautiful word-picture of the nature of this trinity of sisters, namely a perfect *Stabreim*,* such as is native to the spirit of our language.

(my reasons lying in both the highly individual character of Music and its special and eventful evolutionary course, proceeding from this individuality), yet I am well aware of the countless gaps in my recital. But it would need not one book but an entire library, to lay bare the whole unseemliness, the flabbiness and ignominy of the bonds uniting our modern music with our modern life ; to penetrate the piteous, over-sentimental idiosyncracy of our art of Tone, which makes her the object of the speculation of our educational " Folk-improvers," who would trickle drops of Music's honey upon the acid sweat of ill-used factory-hands as the only possible alleviation of their sufferings (very much as our sages of the State and Bourse are all agog to stuff their pliant patches of religion between the gaping rents of the police-officials' tender care of men); and finally to explain the mournful psychological phenomenon, that a man may be not only base and bad, but also *dull*—without these qualities hindering him from being a quite respectable musician.—R. WAGNER.

  * *Stabreim* and Alliteration.—A fuller explanation of this form of ' rhyme' will be found in " *Opera and Drama* " (Part II., chap. vi. and Part III., chap. ii.), which work will form the second volume of this series of translations.   Meanwhile a few words of elucidation may not be found amiss.—The English equivalent, "Alliteration," does not convey the full force of this method of versification, as may be seen at once by the oft-quoted specimen from Churchill, "with apt alliteration's artful aid," for therein one of the fundamental rules is violated in such a manner as to show how little the true principle of this ' rhyme' is now understood in England ; the rule in question being, that if vowels are employed for this artifice, they must be of different sound ; as in Wagner's own lines " *U*nheilig | *a*cht' ich den Eid " (the *stabreim* being here reduplicated in the immediately following line : "der *U*nliebende *ei*nt "). The simple rule, as given in the *Encyclopædia Britannica*, is that this rhyme is "indifferent as to the *number of syllables* in a couplet ; but imperative as to the number of *accented*. syllables, of which there must be four (two in each half), the *first three* beginning with the *same* letter" (in the case of consonants), the writer adducing the lines from *Piers the Ploughman :* " I was *w*eary of *w*andering | and *w*ent me to rest" &c. In Brockhaus' *Conversations-lexikon*, however, it is stated that the original rule was : that in a couplet the first half

This *Stabreim,* moreover, would be especially appropriate by reason of the position which it gives to " *Tichtkunst*" (Poetry): as the last member of the 'rhyme,' this word would first decide that rhyme; since two alliterative words are only raised to a perfect *Stabreim* by the advent or begettal of the third; so that without this third member the earlier pair are merely accidental, being first shown as necessary factors by the presence of the third,—as man and wife are first shown in their true and necessary interdependence by the child which they beget. *

But just as the effective operation of this rhyme works backward from the close to the commencement, so does it also press onward with no less necessity in the reverse direction : the beginning members, truly, gain their first significance as rhyme by the advent of the closing member,

should contain *one* or *two* rhyming initials, the second only *one*—in each case the rhyme being borne by the strongly accented syllable ; but that this rule was extended to allow of the use of *two* rhymes also in the second half, but r.*ver more.   This authority cites a couplet from the 9th Century Saxon poem " *Hêliand,*" which runs thus : " so *l*erda he tho thea *L*iudi | *l*iot hon wordon "; and adds that the word " Stabreim " is an abbreviation from " Buchstabenreim " (lit. = " spelling-rhyme "); that the first verse-half of the couplet ("*Langzeile*" or " *Liedstäbe*") was called " Stollen," the second : " Hauptstab," or principal rhyme,—a circumstance emphasised by Wagner above.   In his great tetralogy, the *Ring des Nibelungen,* the poet-composer has made almost exclusive use of this form of versification, amplifying its rules much in the same way as he amplified those of Music, from that plastic power of genius which melts all rules into new moulds.   But the great characteristic of the *Stabreim* proper, he has almost invariably preserved, viz. :—the marking thereby of the accented, *i.e.* the *root* word, and the commencing of the line by a strong (or 'long') syllable.   As a perfect specimen may be instanced : " *L*achend muss ich dich *l*ieben ; | *l*achend will ich erblinden " (*Siegfried,*—last Scene) ; while a rich example of doubled and re-doubled *Stabreim* is found at the end of the *Götterdämmerung*: " *N*icht *G*ut, *n*icht *G*old, | *n*och *G*öttliche *P*racht; | *n*icht *H*aus, *n*icht *H*of, | *n*och *h*errischer *P*runk : "—These specimens, taken at ramdom from the *Ring,* must suffice for the present purpose.—TR.

* Compare *Die Meistersinger,* Act 3.—" *Ob euch gelang ein rechtes Paar zu finden, das zeigt sich jetzt an den Kinden,*" " If you've had wit to match your pair, *that* we shall see in their son and heir,"—where Hans Sachs is instructing Walther in the mysteries of the old Meistersingers' ' After-song.'—It is curious also that Wagner should have again hit upon the same thought as Schopenhauer, who explains the love of man to woman as governed by the ' Will-to-live ' of their future progeny.—TR.

but the closing member is not so much as conceivable without the earlier pair. Thus the Poetic art can absolutely not create the genuine art-work—and this is only such an one as is brought to direct physical manifestment—without those arts to which the physical show belongs directly. Thought, that mere phantom of reality, is formless by itself ; and only when it retraces the road on which it rose to birth, can it attain artistic perceptibility. In the Poetic art, the purpose of all Art comes first to consciousness : but the other arts contain within themselves the unconscious Necessity that forms this purpose. The art of Poetry is the creative process by which the Art-work steps into life : but out of Nothing, only the god of the Israelites can make some-thing,—the Poet must have that Something ; and that something is the whole artistic man, who proclaims in the arts of Dance and Tone the physical longing become a longing of the soul, which through its force first generates the poetic purpose and finds in that its absolution, in its attainment its own appeasing.

Wheresoever *the Folk* made poetry,—and only by the Folk, or in the footsteps of the Folk, can poetry be really made,—there did the Poetic purpose rise to life alone upon the shoulders of the arts of Dance and Tone, as the *head* of the full-fledged human being. The Lyrics of Orpheus would .never have been able to turn the savage beasts to silent, placid adoration, if the singer had but given them forsooth some dumb and printed verse to read : their ears must be enthralled by the sonorous notes that came straight from the heart, their carrion-spying eyes be tamed by the proud and graceful movements of the body,—*in such a way* that they should recognise instinctively in this whole man no longer a mere object for their maw, no mere objective for their feeding-, but for their hearing- and their seeing-powers,—before they could be attuned to duly listen to his moral sentences.

Neither was the true *Folk-epic* by any means a mere recited poem : the songs of Homer, such as we now possess them, have issued from the critical siftings and compilings

of a time in which the genuine Epos had long since ceased
to live.   When Solon made his laws and Pisistratus introduced his political regime, men searched among the ruins
of the already fallen Epos of the Folk and pieced the
gathered heap together for reading service,—much as in
the Hohenstaufen times they did with the fragments of the
lost *Nibelungen-lieder.*   But before these epic songs became
the object of such literary care, they had flourished mid the
Folk, eked out by voice and gesture, as a bodily enacted
Art-work ; as it were, a fixed and crystallised blend of
lyric song and dance, with predominant lingering on portrayal of the action and reproduction of the heroic dialogue.
These epic-lyrical performances form the unmistakable
middle stage between the genuine older Lyric and Tragedy,
the normal point of transition from the one to the other.

Tragedy was therefore the entry of the Art-work of the
Folk upon the public arena of political life ; and we may
take its appearance as an excellent touchstone for the
difference in procedure between the Art-*creating* of the
Folk and the mere literary-historical *Making* of the so-
called cultured art-world.   At the very time when live-born
Epos became the object of the critical dilettantism of the
court of Pisistratus, it had already shed its blossoms in the
People's life—yet not because the Folk had lost its true
afflatus, but since it was already able to surpass the old,
and from unstanchable artistic sources to build the less
perfect art-work up, until it became the more perfect.   For
while those pedants and professors in the Prince's castle
were labouring at the construction of a *literary Homer,*
pampering their own unproductivity with their marvel at
their wisdom, by aid of which they yet could only understand the thing that long had passed from life,—*Thespis*
had already slid his car to Athens, had set it up beside the
palace walls, dressed out his *stage* and, stepping from the
chorus of the Folk, had *trodden* its planks ; *no longer did
he shadow forth* the deeds of heroes, as in the Epos, but *in
these heroes' guise enacted them.*

With the Folk, all is reality and deed ; it *does*, and then

rejoices in the thought of its own doing. Thus the blithe
Folk of Athens, enflamed by persecution, hunted out from
court and city the melancholy sons of Pisistratus; and then
bethought it how, by this its deed, it had become a free and
independent people. Thus it raised the platform of its
stage, and decked itself with tragic masks and raiment of
some god or hero, in order itself to be a god or hero: and
Tragedy was born ; whose fruits it tasted with the blissful
sense of its own creative force, but whose metaphysical
basis it handed, all regardless, to the brain-racking speculation of the dramaturgists of our modern court-theatres.

Tragedy flourished for just so long as it was inspired
by the spirit of the Folk, and as this spirit was a veritably
popular, *i.e.* a *communal* one. When the national brotherhood of the Folk was shivered into fragments, when the
common bond of its Religion and primeval Customs was
pierced and severed by the sophist needles of the egoistic
spirit of Athenian self-dissection,—then the Folk's art-work
also ceased : then did the professors and the doctors of the
literary guilds take heritage of the ruins of the fallen
edifice, and delved among its beams and stones ; to
pry, to ponder, and to re-arrange its members. With
Aristophanian laughter, the Folk relinquished to these
learned insects the refuse of its meal, threw Art upon
one side for two millennia, and fashioned of its innermost necessity the history of the world ; the while those
scholars cobbled up their tiresome history of Literature,
by order of the supreme court of Alexander.

The career of Poetry, since the breaking-up of Tragedy,
and since her own departure from community with mimetic Dance and Tone, can be easily enough surveyed,—
despite the monstrous claims which she has raised. The
lonely art of Poetry—prophesied no more* ; she no longer

---

* " Die einsame Dichtkunst—*dichtete* nicht mehr."—Again it is impossible
to translate " *dichten*," for lack of an English *verb ;* our " poetise " has a
derogatory strain in it ; ' compose ' and ' indite ' will neither of them here take
the place of the German original ; and we are forced upon a paraphrase, which
may perhaps find justification from the analogous term for him who ' pro-
phesies,' namely, ' Seer,'—which Carlyle has so often applied to the true
Poet.—TR.

showed, but only *described;* she merely played the go-between, but gave naught from herself ; she pieced together what true seers had uttered, but without the living bond of unity ; she suggested, without satisfying her own suggestions ; she urged to life, without herself attaining life ; she gave the catalogue of a picture-gallery, but not the paintings. The wintry stem of Speech, stripped of its summer wreath of sounding leaves, shrank to the withered, toneless signs of *Writing :* instead of to the Ear, it dumbly now addressed the *Eye ;* the poet's strain became a *written dialect,*— the poet's breath the *penman's scrawl.*

There sate she then, the lonely, sullen sister, behind her reeking lamp in the gloom of her silent chamber,—a female *Faust,* who, across the dust and mildew of her books, from out the uncontenting warp and woof of Thought, from off the everlasting rack of fancies and of theories, yearned to step forth into actual life ; with flesh and bone, and spick and span, to stand and go mid real men, a genuine human being. Alas ! the poor sister had cast away her flesh and bone in over-pensive thoughtlessness ; a disembodied soul, she could only now *describe* that which she lacked, as she watched it from her gloomy chamber, through the shut lattice of her thought, living and stirring its limbs amid the dear but distant world of Sense ; she could only picture, ever picture, the beloved of her youth : " so looked his face, so swayed his limbs, so glanced his eye, so rang the music of his voice." But all this picturing and describing, however deftly she attempted to raise it to a special art, how ingeniously soever she laboured to fashion it by forms of speech and writing, for Art's consoling recompense,—it still was but a vain, superfluous labour, the stilling of a need which only sprang from a failing that her own caprice had bred ; it was nothing but the indigent wealth of alphabetical signs, distasteful in themselves, of some poor mute.

The sound and sturdy man, who stands before us clad in panoply of actual body, describes not what he wills and whom he loves ; but *wills* and *loves,* and imparts to us by

his artistic organs the joy of his own willing and his loving.
This he does with highest measure of directness in the enacted Drama.   But it is only to the straining for a shadowy
substitute, an artificially objective method of description,—
on which the art of Poetry, now loosed from all substant-
iality, must exercise her utmost powers of detail,—that we
have to thank this million-membered mass of ponderous
tomes, by which she still, at bottom, can only trumpet forth
her utter helplessness.   This whole impassable waste of
stored-up literature—despite its million phrases and centuries of verse and prose, without once coming to the
living Word—is nothing but the toilsome stammering of
aphasia-smitten Thought, in its struggle for transmutation
into natural articulate utterance.

     This Thought, the highest and most conditioned faculty
of artistic man, had cut itself adrift from fair warm Life,
whose yearning had begotten and sustained it, as from a
hemming, fettering bond that clogged its own unbounded
freedom :—so deemed the Christian yearning, and believed
that it must break away from physical man, to spread in
heaven's boundless æther to freest waywardness.   But this
very severance was to teach that thought and this desire
how inseparable they were from human nature's being:
how high soever they might soar into the air, they still
could do this in the form of bodily man alone.   In sooth,
they could not take the carcase with them, bound as it
was, by laws of gravitation ; but they managed to abstract
a vapoury emanation, which instinctively took on again
the form and bearing of the human body.   Thus hovered
in the air the poet's Thought, like a human-outlined cloud
that spread its shadow over actual, bodily earth-life, to
which it evermore looked down ; and into which it needs
must long to shed itself, just as from earth alone it sucked
its steaming vapours.   The natural cloud dissolves itself,
in giving back to earth the conditions of its being: as
fruitful rain it sinks upon the meadows, thrusts deep into
the thirsty soil, and steeps the panting seeds of plants,
which open then their rich luxuriance to the sunlight,—to

that light which had erstwhile drawn the lowering cloud
from out the fields. So should the Poet's thought once
more impregnate Life ; no longer spread its idle canopy of
cloud twixt Life and Light.

What Poetry perceived from that high seat, was after all
but Life : the higher did she raise herself, the more pano-
ramic became her view ; but the wider the connection in
which she was now enabled to grasp the parts, the livelier
arose in her the longing to fathom the depths of this great
whole. Thus Poetry turned to *Science*, to *Philosophy*. To
the struggle for a deeper knowledge of Nature and of
Man, we stand indebted for that copious store of literature
whose kernel is the poetic musing (*gedankenhaftes Dichten*)
which speaks to us in Human- and in Natural- History,
and in Philosophy. The livelier do these sciences evince
the longing for a genuine portrayal of the known, so much
the nearer do they approach once more the artist's poetry;
and the highest skill in picturing to the senses the phenomena of the universe, must be ascribed to the noble works
of this department of literature. But the deepest and
most universal science can, at the last, know nothing else
but Life itself ; and the substance and the sense of Life
are naught but Man and Nature. Science, therefore, can
only gain her perfect confirmation in the work of Art ; in
that work which takes both Man and Nature—in so far as
the latter attains her consciousness in Man—and shows
them forth directly. Thus the consummation of Knowledge is its redemption into Poetry ; into that poetic art,
however, which marches hand in hand with her sister arts
towards the perfect Artwork ;—and this artwork is none
other than the *Drama*.

Drama is only conceivable as the fullest expression of a
joint artistic longing to impart; while this longing, again,
can only parley with a common receptivity. Where either
of these factors lacks, the drama is no necessary, but
merely an arbitrary art-product. Without these factors
being at hand in actual Life, the poet, in his striving for
immediate presentation of the life that he had apprehended,

sought to create the drama for himself alone; his creation therefore fell, perforce, a victim to all the faults of arbitrary dealing. Only in exact measure as his own proceeded from a common impulse, and could address itself to a common interest, do we find the necessary conditions of Drama fulfilled—since the time of its recall to life— and the desire to answer those conditions rewarded with success.

A common impulse toward dramatic art-work can only be at hand in those who actually enact the work of art in common; these, as we take it, are the *fellowships of players*. At the end of the Middle Ages, we see such fellowships arising directly from the Folk; while those who later over-mastered them and laid down their laws from the stand-point of absolute poetic art, have earned themselves the fame of destroying root-and-branch *that* which the man who sprang directly from such a fellowship, and made his poems for and with it, had created for the wonder of all time. From out the inmost, truest nature of the Folk, *Shakespeare* created (*dichtete*) for his fellow-players that Drama which seems to us the more astounding as we see it rise by might of naked speech alone, without all help of kindred arts. *One* only help it had, the *Phantasy* of his audience, which turned with active sympathy to greet the *inspiration* of the poet's comrades. A genius the like of which was never heard, and a group of favouring chances ne'er repeated, in common made amends for what they lacked in common. Their joint creative force, however, was—*Need;* and where this shows its nature-bidden might, there man can compass even the impossible to satisfy it: from poverty grows plenty, from want an overflow; the boorish figure of the homely Folk's-comedian takes on the bearing of a hero, the raucous clang of daily speech be-comes the sounding music of the soul, the rude scaffolding of carpet-hung boards becomes a world-stage with all its wealth of scene. But if we take away this art-work from its frame of fortunate conditions, if we set it down outside the realm of fertile force which bore it from the need of

this one definite epoch, then do we see with sorrow that
the poverty was still but poverty, the want but want; that
Shakespeare was indeed the mightiest Poet of all time, but
his Artwork was not yet the work for every age ; that not
his genius, but the incomplete and merely will-ing, not yet
can-ning, spirit of his age's art had made him but the
Thespis of the Tragedy of the Future. In the same relation
as stood the car of Thespis, in the brief time-span of the
flowering of Athenian art, to the stage of Æschylus and
Sophocles : so stands the stage of Shakespeare, in the unmeasured spaces of the flowering time of universal human
art, to the Theatre of the Future. The deed of the one and
only Shakespeare, which made of him a universal Man,
a very god, is yet but the kindred deed of the solitary
Beethoven, who found the language of the Artist-manhood
of the Future : only where these twain Prometheus'—
Shakespeare and Beethoven—shall reach out hands to one
another; where the marble creations of Phidias shall bestir
themselves in flesh and blood ; where the painted counterfeit of Nature shall quit its cribbing frame on the chamber-
walls of the egoist, and stretch its ample breadths on the
warm-life-blown framework of the Future Stage,—there
first, in the communion of all his fellow-artists, will the
Poet also find redemption.

It was on the long journey from Shakespeare's stage to
the art-work of the future, that the poet was first to gain
full consciousness of his unhappy loneliness. Out of the
fellowship of actors, had the *Dramatic poet* evolved by
natural law; but, in his foolish arrogance, he fain would
now exalt himself above his comrades, and *without* their
love, without their impulse, dictate the drama from behind
his pedant desk to *those* from whose free gift of personation
it could gain alone a natural growth, and to whose joint
will he had only power to point the informing aim. Thus
the organs of dramatic art, reduced to slavish drudgery,
grew dumb before the poet, who desired not merely now
to *utter*, but to *dominate* the artistic impulse. As the
virtuoso presses or releases at his will the pianoforte's

keys, so would the poet play upon the automaton troupe of
actors ; as on an instrument of wood and steel erected to
display his own particular dexterity, and from which men
should expect to hear no other thing but *him* the playing
marvel.   But the keys of the instrument made *their own*
rejoinder to the ambitious egoist : the harder he hammered,
in his gymnastic frenzy, the more they stuck and clattered.

Goethe once reckoned up but four weeks of pure happiness in all his well-filled life : his most unhappy years he
made no special count of ; but we know them :—they were
those in which he sought to tune that jangling instrument
for his use.   This man of might was longing to take refuge
from the soundless desert of art-literature in the living,
sonorous art-work.   Whose eye was surer, and wider-
ranging in its knowledge of life than his ?   What he had
seen, described, and pictured, he now would bring to ear
upon that instrument.   Great heavens ! how deformed and
past all recognition did his views of life confront him, when
forced into this metric music ! *   How must he wrench his
tuning-key, how tug and stretch the strings, until at last
they snapped with one great whine !—He was forced to
see that everything is possible in this world, excepting that
abstract spirit should govern men : where this spirit is not

---

* "O himmel ! wie entstellt, wie unkennbar klangen ihm seine, in dichterische Musik gebrachten, Anschauungen entgegen !"   Probably Wagner
here refers to the opera-texts, such as *Proserpina*, written by Goethe for the
Weimar Court-theatre, the direction of which was entrusted to him by the
Duke ; for in his article, "Zukunftsmusik" (The "Music of the Future,"
vol. vii. of the *Ges. Schriften*) our author writes as follows : "Goethe himself
indited several opera-texts (libretti), and, in order to place himself on the level
of that *genre*, he thought right to keep both his invention and his working-out
as trivial as possible ; so that it is only with regret, that we can see these
extremely mawkish pieces numbered in the ranks of his poems."—As to the
allusion to the "poodle" at the end of the present paragraph, it is an absolute
statement of fact.   In 1817 Goethe, who had long felt the growing impossibility of maintaining the high standard of the Weimar theatrical performances,
in face of the favour shown to Kotzebue and his claptrap, finally laid down the
reins of direction in consequence of the production, against his express desire,
of a piece called the "*Hund des Aubry.*"   We cannot discover whether
Kotzebue had a hand in this piece or not, for it is merely described in
Schaefer's "Life of Goethe" as imported from France ; the biographer adds,
that in it a *rôle was assigned to a trained Poodle !*—TR.

seeded in the whole sound man and blossomed out of him,
it can never be poured into him from above.   The egoistic
poet can make mechanical puppets move according to his
wish, but never turn machines to actual living men.   From
the stage where Goethe wished to make his *men*, he was
chased at last by a performing *poodle :*—as an exemplary
warning to all unnatural government from on high !

Where Goethe shipwrecked, it could but become " good
tone " to look upon oneself as shipwrecked in advance : the
poets still wrote plays, but not for the unpolished stage ;
simply for their cream-laid paper.   Only the second- or
third- rate poetasters, who here and there adapted their
conceits to local exigence, still busied their brains with
the players ; but not the eminent poet, who wrote "out
of his own head " and, of all the many hues of life, found
only abstract, Prussian-territorial, black-on-white respectable.   Thus happened the unheard-of : *Dramas written for
dumb reading !*

Did Shakespeare, in his stress for unadulterated Life,
take shelter in the uncouth scaffold of his People's-stage :
so did the egoistic resignation of the modern dramatist
content itself with the bookseller's counter ; on which he
laid him out for market half-dead and half-alive.   Had the
physically embodied drama cast itself upon the bosom of
the Folk : so did the " published " incarnation of the play
lie down beneath the feet of the art-critic's good pleasure.
Accommodating herself to one servile yoke after the other,
Dramatic Poetry swung herself aloft—in her own idle
fancy—to unbound freedom.   Those burdensome conditions under which alone a drama can step into life, she
might now forsooth cast overboard without ado ; for only
that which wills to *live*, must hearken to necessity,—but
that which wills to do much *more* than live, namely to
lead a *dead* existence, can make of itself what it pleases :
the most arbitrary is to it the most necessary ; and the
more her independence of the terms of physical show, the
more freely could Poetry abandon herself to her own
self-will and absolute self-admiration.

Thus by the taking up of Drama into literature, a mere new form was found in which the art of Poetry might indite herself afresh ; only borrowing from Life the accidental stuff which she might twist and turn to suit her solitary need, her own self-glorification. All matter and each form were only there to help her introduce to the best graces of the reader one abstract thought, the poet's idealised, beloved ' I.' How faithlessly she forgot, the while, that she had first to thank them all—even the most complex of her forms — to just this haughtily-despised material Life ! From the Lyric through all the forms of poetry down to this literary Drama, there is not one which has not blossomed in *far purer and more noble* shape from the bodily directness of the People's life. What are all the products of the seeming spontaneous action of abstract poetic art, exhibited in language, verse, and expression, compared with the ever fresh-born beauty, variety, and perfection of the *Folk's-lyric*, whose teeming riches the *spirit of research* is toiling now at last to drag from under the rubbish-heap of ages ?

But these Folk-ballads are not so much as thinkable without their twin-bred melodies : and what was not only said but also *sung*, was part and parcel of Life's immediate utterance. Who speaks and sings, at the same time expresses his feelings by *gestures* and by *motion*—at least whoever does this from sheer instinct, like the *Folk*,— though not the tutored foundling of our song-professors.— Where such an art still flourishes, it finds of itself a constant train of fresh turns of expression, fresh forms of composition ("*Dichtung*") ; and the Athenians teach us unmistakably, how, in the progress of this self-unfolding, the highest artwork, Tragedy, could come to birth.—Opposed to this, the art of Poetry must ever stay unfruitful when she turns her back on Life ; all her shaping then can never be aught else but that of Fashion, that of wilful combination,— not invention. Unfortunate in her every rub with Matter, she therefore turns for ever back to *thought :* that restless mill-wheel of the Wish, the ever craving, ever unstilled

Wish which—thrusting off its only possible assuagement, in the *world of sense*—must only wish *itself* eternally, eternally consume *itself*.

The Literary Drama can only redeem itself from this state of misery by becoming the actual *living* Drama. The path of that redemption has been repeatedly entered, and even in our latter days,—by many an one from honest yearning, but alas! by the majority for no other reason than that the Theatre had imperceptibly become a more remunerative market than the counter of the Publisher.

The judgment [1] of the *public*, in howsoever great a social disfigurement it may show itself, holds ever by the direct and physical reality; nay, the mutual give-and-take of the world of sense (*die Wechselwirkung des Sinnlichen*) makes up, at bottom, what we call "publicity." [2] Had the impotent conceit of Poetry withdrawn her from this immediate interaction: so, as regards the Drama, had the *players* seized it for their own advantage. Most rightly does the public aspect [3] of the stage belong *de facto* to the performing fellowship alone; but where everything was selfishly dissundering,—like the poet from this fellowship, to which in the natural order of affairs he immediately belonged,—there did the fellowship itself cut through the common band which alone had made it an *artistic* one. Would the poet unconditionally see *himself* alone upon the stage,—did he thus dispute in advance the artistic value of the fellowship,—so, with far more natural excuse, did the individual actor break his bonds in order to unconditionally stamp *himself* as the only current coin; and herein he was supported by the encouraging plaudits of the Public, which ever holds by instinct to the sheer and absolute show.

The art of Comedy became through this the art of *the Comedian*, a personal virtuosity: *i.e.* that egoistic form of

[1], [2], [3]—The same word, "Öffentlichkeit," is used in these three instances; it has seemed, however, impossible to translate this half abstract, half concrete term, excepting by the use of three different expressions, in order to keep touch with the meaning.—Tr.

K

art which exists for its exclusive *self*, and wills but the glory of the absolute personality. The common aim, through which alone the Drama becomes a work of Art, lay quite beyond the ken of the individual virtuoso ; and that which should generate the art of comedy from out itself, as a common outcome of the spirit of communion,—to wit the dramatic Art-work,—*that* is entirely neglected by this virtuoso or this guild of virtuosi, who only seek the special thing that answers to their personal dexterity, the thing that alone can pay its tribute to their vanity. Yet hundreds of the *best-skilled* egoists, though all collected on one spot of earth, cannot fulfil *that* task which can only be the work of communism (*Gemeinsamkeit*) ; at least until they cease to be mere egoists. But so long as they are this, their ground of common action—only attainable under *external* pressure —is that of mutual hate and envy; and our theatre, therefore, often resembles the battlefield of the two lions, on which we can discover nothing but their tails, the sole remainder of their mutual meal off one another.

Nevertheless, where this very *virtuosity of the performer* makes up the total of the public's notion of theatric art, as in the generality of the French theatres and even in the opera-world of Italy, we have at hand a more natural expression of the bent to artistic exhibition, than where the 'abstract' poet would fain usurp this bent for his own self-glorification. Experience has often proved that from out that world of virtuosi, given a true *heart* to beat in unison with the *artistic* talent, there may come forth a dramatic performer who by one solitary impersonation* shall disclose to us the inmost essence of dramatic art far more distinctly than a hundred art-dramas *per se*. Where, on the other hand, dramatic art-poetry would experiment with living actors, she can only manage in the end to quite confuse both virtuosi and public ; or else, for all her self-

---

* From all that Wagner has written about Wilhelmine Schröder-Devrient, it cannot be doubted that it is to her that he here refers. Compare page 9 of the "*Autobiographic Sketch*," also "*A Pilgrimage to Beethoven*," the "*Communication to my Friends*," and "*On Actors and Singers*."—TR.

inflation, to betake herself to shamefullest subservience. She either brings but stillborn children into the world,—and that is the best result of her activity, for then she does no harm,—or else she inoculates her constitutional disease, of *will*ing without *can*-ning, like a devastating plague into the still half-healthy members of the art of comedy. In any case she needs must follow the coercive laws of the most dependent lack of self-dependence : in order to attain some semblance of a form, she must look around for any form that may have sometime emanated from the life of genuine comedy.   This then she almost always borrows, in our latest times, from the disciples of *Molière* alone.

With the lively, abstraction-hating people of France, the art of Comedy—in so far as it was not governed by the influence of the Court—lived for the most part its own indigenous life : amid the overpowering hostility to Art of our general social condition, whatever healthy thing has been able to evolve from Comedy, since the dying out of the Shakespearian drama, we owe to the French alone. But even among them—under pressure of the ruling world-*geist* that kills all common weal, whose soul is Luxury and Fashion—the true, complete, Dramatic Art-work could not so much as distantly appear : the only universal factor of our modern world, the spirit of *usury and speculation*, has with them also held each germ of true dramatic art in egoistic severance from its fellow.   Art-forms to answer to this sordid spirit, however, the French dramatic school has found, without a doubt : with all the unseemliness of their contents, they evince uncommon skill in making these contents as palatable as may be ; and these forms have this distinctive merit, that they have actually emanated from the inborn spirit of the *French* comedian's art, and thus from life itself.

Our German dramatists, in their longing for some seeming-necessary form wherewith to clothe the arbitrary contents of their poetic thought, and since they lacked the inborn plastic gift, set up this needful form in pure caprice ; for they seized upon the Frenchman's 'scheme,' without reflecting that this scheme had sprung from quite another, and a *genuine* Need.   But he who does not act from sheer necessity, may choose where'er he pleases. Thus our dramatists were not quite satisfied with their adoption of French forms : the stew still lacked of this or that, — a pinch of Shakespearian audacity, a spice of Spanish pathos, and, for a sauce, a remanet of Schiller's ideality or Iffland's burgher bonhomie.   All this is now dished up with unheard archness, according to the French recipe, and served with journalistic reminiscences of the latest scandal ; the favourite actor—since the real poet had not learnt how to play his comedies—provided with the rôle of some fictitious poet, wherever possible ;—with a further slice from here or there thrown in to suit the special circumstance—: and so we have the modernest dramatic art-work, the poet who in sooth *writes down himself, i.e., his palpable poetic incapacity.*

Enough ! of the unexampled squalor of our *theatric* poetry ! with which indeed we here have alone to do ; since we need not draw the special subdivision of *literary poesy* within our closer ken.   For, with our eyes directed toward the Artwork of the Future, we are seeking out Poetic art where she is struggling to become a living and immediate art, and this is in the *Drama ;* not where she renounces every claim to this life-issue, and yet—for all her fill of thought —but takes the terms of her peculiar manufacture from the hopeless artistic unfitness of our modern public life.   This Literature-poesy (*die litteraturpoesie*) supplies the only solace—however sad and impotent !—of the lonely human being of the Present who longs to taste poetic food.   Yet the solace that she gives is truly but an access of the *longing after Life,* the longing for the living Artwork ; for the urgence of this longing is her very soul,—where *this* does not speak out, does not proclaim itself with might and main, there has the last trace of verity departed from this poesy too.   The more honestly and tumultuously, however, does it throb within her, so much the more veraciously does she admit her own unsolaceable plight, and confess the only possible assuagement of her longing, to be *her own self-abrogation, her dissolution into Life, into the living Art-work of the Future.*

Let us ponder how this fervent, noble longing of Literary Poesy must one day be responded to ; and meanwhile let us leave our modern Dramatic Poetry to the pompous triumphs of her own ridiculous vanity !

6.

Whilom attempts at re-uniting the three humanistic Arts.

In our general survey of the demeanour of each of the three humanistic (*rein menschlich*) arts after its severance from their initial communion, we could not but plainly see that exactly where the one variety touched on the province of the next, where the faculty of the second stepped-in to replace the faculty of the first, there did the first one also find its natural bounds. Beyond these bounds, it might stretch over from the second art-variety to the third ; and through this third, again, back to itself, back to its own especial individuality,—but only in accordance with the natural laws of *Love,* of *self-offering* for the common good impelled by Love. As Man by love sinks his whole nature in that of Woman, in order to pass over through her into a third being, the Child,—and yet finds but himself again in all the loving trinity, though in this self a widened, filled, and finished whole : so may each of these individual arts find its own self again in the perfect, throughly liberated Artwork—nay, look upon itself as broadened to this Artwork—so soon as, on the path of genuine love and by sinking of itself within the kindred arts, it returns upon itself and finds the guerdon of its love in the perfect work of Art to which it knows itself expanded. Only that art-variety, however, which wills the common art-work, reaches therewith the highest fill of its own particular nature ; whereas that art which merely wills *itself,* its own exclusive fill of self, stays empty and unfree—for all the luxury that it may heap upon its solitary semblance. But the *Will* to form the common artwork arises in each branch of art by instinct and unconsciously, so soon as e'er it touches on its own confines and *gives* itself to the answering art, not merely strives to take from it. It only stays *throughout itself*, when it *throughly gives itself away :* whereas it must fall to its very opposite, if it at last must only feed upon the other :—" whose bread I eat, his song I'll sing." But when it gives itself *entirely* to the second, and stays *entirely* enwrapt therein, it then may pass from that *entirely* into the third ; and thus become once more *entirely itself*, in highest fulness, in the associate Art-work.

(Of all these arts not one so sorely needed an espousal with another, as that of *Tone ;* for her peculiar character is that of a fluid nature-element poured out betwixt the more defined and individualised substances of the two other arts) Only through the Rhythm of Dance, or as bearer of the Word, could she brace her deliquescent being to definite and characteristic corporeality. But neither of the other arts could bring herself to plunge, in love without reserve, into the element of Tone : each drew from it so many bucketsful as seemed expedient for her own precise and egoistic aims ; each took from Tone, but gave not in return ; so that poor Tone, who of her life-need stretched out her hands in all directions, was forced at last herself to *take* for very means of maintenance. Thus she engulfed the Word at first, to make of it what suited best her pleasure : but while she disposed of this word as her wilful feeling listed, in Catholic music, she lost its bony framework—so to say—of which, in her desire to become a human being, she stood in need to bear the liquid volume of her blood, and round which she might have crystallised a sinewy flesh. A new and energetic handling of the Word, in order to gain shape therefrom, was shown by *Protestant* church-music ; which, in the " *Passion-music*," pressed on towards an ecclesiastical drama, wherein the word was no longer a mere shifting vehicle for the expression of feeling, but girt

itself to thoughts depicting Action. In this church-drama,
Music, while still retaining her predominance and building
everything else into her own pedestal, almost compelled
Poetry to behave in earnest and like a man towards her.
But coward Poetry appeared to dread this challenge; she
deemed it as well to cast a few neglected morsels to swell
the meal of this mightily waxing monster, Music, and thus
to pacify it; only, however, to regain the liberty of staying
undisturbed within her own peculiar province, the egoistic
sphere of Literature. It is to this selfish, cowardly bearing
of Poetry toward Tone that we stand indebted for that unnatural abortion the *Oratorio*, which finally transplanted
itself from the church into the concert-hall. The Oratorio
would give itself the airs of Drama; but only precisely in
so far as it might still preserve to *Music* the unquestioned
right of being the chief concern, the only leader of the
drama's ' tone.'

Where Poetry fain would reign in solitude, as in the
spoken Play, she took Music into her menial service, for
her own convenience; as, for instance, for the entertainment of the audience·between the acts, or even for the enhancement of the effect of certain dumb transactions, such
as the irruption of a cautious burglar, and matters of that
sort! Dance did the selfsame thing, when she leapt proudly
on to saddle, and graciously condescended to allow Music
to hold the stirrup.   Exactly so did Tone behave to
Poetry in the Oratorio : she merely let her pile the heap
of stones, from which she might erect her building as she
fancied.

But Music at last capped all this ever-swelling arrogance,
by her shameless insolence in the *Opera*. Here she claimed
tribute of the art of Poetry down to its utmost farthing:
it was no longer to merely make her verses, no longer to
merely suggest dramatic characters and sequences, as in the
Oratorio, in order to give her a handle for her own disten-
tion,—but it was to lay down its whole being and all its
powers at her feet, to offer up complete dramatic characters and complex situations, in short the entire ingredients

of Drama; in order that she might take this gift of homage
and make of it whatever her fancy listed.

The *Opera*, as the seeming point of reunion of all the
three related arts, has become the meeting-place of these
sisters' most self-seeking efforts. Undoubtedly Tone claims
for herself the supreme right of legislation therein; nay, it
is solely to her struggle—though led by egoism—towards
the genuine artwork of the Drama, that we owe the
Opera at all. But in degree as Poetry and Dance were
bid to be her simple slaves, there rose amid *their* egoistic
ranks a growing spirit of rebellion against their domineer-
ing sister. The arts of Dance and Poetry had taken a
personal lease of Drama *in their own way:* the spectacular
Play and the pantomimic Ballet were the two territories
between which Opera now deployed her troops, taking
from each whatever she deemed indispensable for the self-
glorification of Music. Play and Ballet, however, were
well aware of her aggressive self-sufficiency: they only lent
themselves to their sister against their will, and in any
case with the mental reservation that on the first favourable opportunity they each would clear themselves an
exclusive field. So Poetry leaves behind her feeling and
her pathos, the only fitting wear for Opera, and throws
her net of modern Intrigue around her sister Music; who,
without being able to get a proper hold of it, must willy-
nilly twist and turn the empty cobweb, which none but
the nimble play-sempstress herself can plait into a tissue:
and there she chirps and twitters, as in the French con-
fectionary-operas, until at last her peevish breath gives
out, and sister Prose steps in to fill the stage. Dance, on
the other hand, has only to espy some breach in the
breath-taking of the tyrannising songstress, some chilling
of the lava-stream of musical emotion,—and in an instant
she flings her legs astride the boards; trounces sister
Music off the scene, down to the solitary confinement of
the orchestra; and spins, and whirls, and runs around,
until the public can no longer see the wood for wealth of
leaves, *i.e.* the opera for the crowd of legs.

Thus Opera becomes the mutual compact of the egoism of the three related arts. To rescue her supremacy, Tone contracts with Dance for so many quarters-of-an-hour which shall belong to the latter *alone:* during this period the chalk upon the shoe-soles shall trace the regulations of the stage, and music shall be made according to the system of the *leg-*, and not the *tone-*, vibrations ; item, that the singers shall be expressly forbidden to indulge in any sort of graceful bodily motion,—this is to be the exclusive property of the dancer, whereas the singer is to be pledged to complete abstention from any fancy for mimetic gestures, a restriction which will have the additional advantage of conserving his voice. With Poetry Tone settles, to the former's highest satisfaction, that she will not employ her in the slightest on the stage ; nay, will as far as possible not even articulate her words and verses, and will relegate her instead to the printed text-book, necessarily to be read *after* the performance, in Literature's decorous garb of black and white. Thus, then, is the noble bond concluded, each art again itself; and between the dancing legs and written book, Music once more floats gaily on through all the length and breadth of her desire.—*This is modern Freedom in the faithful counterfeit of Art !*

Yet after such a shameful compact the art of Tone, however brilliantly she seem to reign in Opera, must needs be deeply conscious of her humiliating *dependence*. Her life-breath is the heart's affection ; and if this also be centred on itself and its own contentment, then not only is it as much in need of the wherewithal of this contentment as are the yearnings of the senses and the understanding, but it feels its need of that object far more piercingly and vividly than they. The keenness of this need gives to the heart its courage of self-sacrifice ; and just as Beethoven has spoken out this courage in a valiant deed, so have tone-poets like *Gluck* and *Mozart* expressed by glorious deeds of love the joy with which the lover sinks himself within his object ; ceasing to be himself, but becoming in reward an infinitely greater thing. Wherever the edifice

of Opera—though originally erected for the egoistic mani-
festoes of segregated arts—betrayed within itself the trace
of a condition for the full absorption of Music into Poetry,
these masters have accomplished the redemption of their
art into the conjoint artwork.   But the baleful influence of
the ruling evil plight explains to us the utter isolation of
such radiant deeds, together with the isolation of the very
tone-poets who fulfilled them.   That which was possible
to the unit under certain fortunate, but almost purely
accidental circumstances, is very far indeed from forming
a law for the great mass of phenomena ; and in the latter
we can only recognise the distracted, egoistic oscillations of
Caprice; whose methods indeed are those of all mere copying, since it cannot originate anything of itself.   Gluck
and Mozart, together with the scanty handful of kindred
tone-poets,* serve us only as load-stars on the midnight
sea of operatic music, to point the way to the pure artistic
possibility of the ascension of the richest music into a still
richer dramatic poetry, namely into *that* Poetic art which
by this free surrender of Music to her shall first become an
all-effectual Dramatic art.   How impossible is the perfect
artwork amid the ruling state of things, is proved by the
very fact that, after Gluck and Mozart had disclosed the
highest capabilities of Music, these deeds have yet remained
without the smallest influence on our actual modern art's
demeanour,—that the sparks which flew from their genius
have only hovered before our art-world like sputtering fire-
works, but have been absolutely unable to incend the fire
which must have caught its flame from them, had the fuel
for it been to hand.

But even the deeds of Gluck and Mozart were but onesided deeds, *i.e.* they revealed the capability and the
instinctive will of Music without their being understood by
her sister arts, without the latter contributing towards
those deeds from a like-felt genuine impulse to be absorbed

---

* Among these, the masters of the French-school of the beginning of this
century should be specially noted.—R. Wagner.—See also p. 16, "*Autobiographic Sketch.*"—TR.

in one another, and in fact without any response from their side. Only, however, from a like and common impulse of all three sister arts, can their redemption into the true Art-work, and thus this artwork itself, become a possibility. When at last the pride of all three arts in their own self-sufficiency shall break to pieces, and pass over into love for one another; when at last each art can only love itself when mirrored in the others; when at last they cease to be dissevered arts,—then will they all have power to create the perfect artwork; aye, and their own desistence, in this sense, is already of itself this Art-work, their death immediately its life.

Thus will the Drama of the Future rise up of itself, when nor Comedy, nor Opera, nor Pantomime, can any longer live; when the conditions which allowed their origin and sustained their unnatural life, shall have been entirely upheaved. These conditions can only be up-heaved by the advent of those fresh conditions which breed from out themselves the Art-work of the Future. The latter, however, cannot arise alone, but only in the fullest harmony with the conditions of our whole Life. Only when the ruling religion of Egoism, which has split the entire domain of Art into crippled, self-seeking art-tendencies and art-varieties, shall have been mercilessly dislodged and torn up root and branch from every moment of the life of man, can the *new religion* step forth of itself to life; the religion which includes within itself the conditions of the Artwork of the Future.

Before we turn with straining eyes to the prefigurement of this Artwork—such as we have to win for ourselves from the utter disowning of our present art-surroundings—it is necessary, however, to cast a glance upon the nature of the so-called *plastic arts.*

III.

MAN SHAPING ART FROM NATURE'S STUFFS.*

I.

Architectural Art.

S Man becomes the subject and the matter of his own artistic treatment, in the first and highest reference, so does he extend his longing for artistic portrayal to the objects of surrounding, allied, ministering *Nature.* Exactly in proportion as Man knows how to grasp the reference of Nature to *himself,* in his portrayal of her, and to set himself in the centre of his survey of the world as the conscience-woken and the conscience-wakener,† is he able to picture Nature to himself *artistically;* and thereafter to *impart* her to the only beings for whom this portrait can be destined—to wit, to Men. In this he proceeds from a like, though not an equally imperative, impulse to that which urged the art-work whose subject and whose stuff he was himself. But only the man who has already brought forth from and in himself the directly human artwork, and can thus both comprehend and impart himself artistically, is also able to represent *Nature* to

* The title of this chapter, " *Der Mensch als künstlerischer Bildner aus natürlichen Stoffen,*" presents many difficulties to the translator. If we possessed a good equivalent for " Bildner " (from " *bilden,*" to fashion, shape or form, *e.g.* a picture) that would cover the three different varieties of ' plastic ' artist, we should still be short of a generally accepted substitute for " *Stoff.*" The idea of the original is : to include in the term "stuff" not only the *raw material,* as in Architecture or Sculpture, but also the *subject-matter,* as in Landscape-painting. This being thus, perhaps we may be permitted to employ the word in the sense in which Shakespeare uses it, in the line " We are such stuff as dreams are made on."—TR.

† Compare *Götterdämmerung,* Act 3, " Der Wecker kam ; er küsst dich wach . . . . da lacht ihm Brünnhilde's Lust ! "—TR.

himself artistically; not the unawakened thrall of Nature. The *Asiatic* peoples, and even the *Egyptians*—to whom Nature only showed herself as a self-willed, elementary, or brutish force, to which Man stood in the relation either of un-conditioned suffering or of grovelling self-debasement—set Nature up *above* them as the object of their adoration, the graven symbol of their worship; without, for that very reason, being able to exalt themselves to free, artistic con-sciousness. Here, then, Man could never form the subject of his own artistic exposition; but seeing that, whether he willed or no, he could only conceive all personality—such as the personal nature-force—according to a human standard, he made over his own image, in sooth in horrible distortion, to those objects of Nature which he fain would portray.

It was reserved for the *Hellenes* to first evolve the humanistic (*rein menschliche*) art-work in their own person, and from that to expand it to the exposition of Nature. But they could not be ripe for this human art-work itself until they had conquered Nature, in the sense in which she presented herself to the Asiatic peoples, and had so far set Man on Nature's pinnacle that they conceived those personal nature-forces as clothed with the perfect shape of human beauty, as Gods that bore themselves as men. First when Zeus breathed life throughout the world from his Olympian height, when Aphrodite rose from out the sea-foam, and Apollo proclaimed the spirit and the form of his own being as the law of beauteous human life, did the uncouth nature-deities of Asia vanish with their idols, and fair artistic Man, awakening to self-consciousness, apply the laws of human beauty to his conception and his portraiture of Nature.

Before the *God's-oak* at Dodona the Pelasgian ("*Ur-hellene*") bowed himself, in waiting for the oracle; beneath the shady thatch of leaves, and circled by the verdant pillars of the *God's-grove*, the *Orpheist* raised his voice; but under the fair-ceiled roof, and amid the symmetry of marble columns of the *God's-temple*, the art-glad *Lyrist* led the mazes of his dance, to strains of sounding hymns,—and in the *Theatre*, which reared itself around the God's-altar—as its central point—on the one hand to the message-giving stage, on the other to the ample rows where sat the message-craving audience, the *Tragedian* brought to birth the living work of consummated Art.

Thus did *artistic* Man, of his longing for *artistic commune with himself*, rule Nature to his own *artistic* needs and bid her serve his highest purpose.   Thus did the Lyrist and Tragedian command the *Architect* to build the artistic edifice which should answer to their art in worthy manner.

The foremost, natural need urged men to build them homes and strongholds: but in that land and mid that folk from which our whole Art originates, it was not this purely physical need, but the need of men engaged in artistic presentation of themselves, that was destined to convert the Handicraft of building into a genuine Art. Not the royal dwellings of Theseus and Agamemnon, not the rude rock-built walls of Pelasgian citadels, have reached our physical or even our mental field of vision,—but the *Temples* of the Gods, the *Tragic theatres* of the Folk.   Every relic that has come to us of architectural art applied to objects outside *these*, dates after the decline of Tragedy, *i.e.* of the completed Grecian Art, and is essentially of Asiatic origin.

As the Asiatic, that perpetual thrall of Nature, could only show the majesty of man in the *one* and absolute ruling despot, so did he heap all pomp of circumstance around this "God on earth" alone: and all this heaping-up was merely reckoned for the satisfaction of that egoistic sensuous longing which, even to the pitch of brutish fury, but wills *itself*, but loves *itself* to madness, and in such never-sated appetite piles object upon object, mass on mass, in order to attain a final satisfaction of its prodigiously developed physicality. *Luxury*, therefore, is the root of all the Asiatic architecture: its monstrous, soulless sense-confounding outcrop we witness in the city-seeming palaces of Asiatic despots.

Sweet repose and noble charm breathe on us, on the

other hand, from the radiant aspect of Hellenic temples; in which we recognise the form of Nature, but spiritualised by human Art. The broadening of the temple of the Gods to the assembled People's show-place of the highest human art, was *the Theatre*. Herein Art, and verily that common-nurtured art which communed with a commonwealth, was a law and standard to herself; proceeding by her own Necessity and answering that necessity to the fullest,—nay, bringing forth *therefrom* the boldest and most marvellous creations.

Meanwhile the dwellings of the individual units but answered to the need from which they sprang. Originally carpentered of wooden logs, and fitted—like the pavilion of Achilles—in accordance with the simplest laws of useful-ness: in the heyday of Hellenic culture they were indeed adorned with walls of polished stone, and duly broadened out to give free space for hospitality; but they never stretched themselves beyond the natural needs of private persons, and neither in nor by them did the individual seek to satisfy a longing which he found appeased in noblest fashion in the common polity; from which alone, at bottom, it can spring.

The attitude of Architecture was entirely reversed, when the common bonds of public life dissolved, and the self-indulgence of the unit laid down her laws. When the private person no longer sacrificed to gods in common, to *Zeus* and to *Apollo*, but solely to the lonely bliss-purveyor *Plutus*, the God of Riches,—when each would be for his particular self what he had erstwhile only been amid the general community,—then did he take the architect also into his pay, and bade him build a temple for his idol, Egoism. But the slender temple of chaste Athene sufficed not the rich egoist for his private pleasures: his household goddess was Voluptuousness, with her all-devouring, never sated maw. To her must Asiatic piles be reared, for her consumption; and only bizarre curves and flourishes could seek to stanch her whim. Thus we see the despotism of Asia stretching out its beauty-crushing arms into the very heart of Europe—as though in vengeance for Alexander's conquest—and exercising its might to such effect beneath the imperial rule of Rome, that Beauty, having fled completely from the living conscience of mankind, could now be only conned from memory of the past.

The most prosperous centuries of the Roman era present us, therefore, with the repugnant spectacle of pomp swelled up to a monstrosity in the palaces of the Emperors and richer classes, and *Utilitarianism*—however colossal in its proportions — stalking naked through the public buildings.

Public life, having sunk to a mere general expression of the universal egoism, had no longer any care for the beautiful; it now knew naught but *practical utility*. The beautiful had withdrawn in favour of the absolutely useful; for the delight in *man* had contracted to the exclusive lust of the belly. To speak plainly, it is to the satisfaction of the belly that all this public utilitarianism * leads back, especially in our modern time with its boasted practical inventions, this time which—characteristically enough !— the more it invents, in this sense, the less is able to really fill the stomachs of the hungering classes. But where men had forgotten that the truly beautiful is likewise the highest expression of the useful, in so much as it can only manifest itself in life when the needs of life are secured a natural satisfaction, and not made harder, or interdicted, by useless prescripts of utility,—where the public care was concentrated on the catering for food and drink, and the utmost stilling of this care proclaimed itself as the vital condition of the rule of Cæsars and of plutocrats alike ; and that in such gigantic measure as during the Roman mastery of the world :—there arose those astounding causeways and aque-

---

* Certainly the provision of the useful, is the first and greatest necessity : but an epoch which can never soar beyond this care nor cast it behind it in order to attain the beautiful, but makes this care the sole prescriptor of every branch of public life and drags it even into Art,—that epoch is in truth *barbarian.* Yet it is only the most unnatural *civilisation*, that can produce such absolute barbarism : it is for ever heaping up obstructions to the useful, to give itself the air of for ever taking thought for utility alone.—R. WAGNER.

ducts which we seek to-day to rival by our railway-tracks; there did Nature become a *milch-cow*, and Architecture a *milking-pail;* the wanton splendour of the rich lived on the skilful skimming of the cream from off the gathered milk, which then was taken, blue and watery, along those aqueducts to the beloved rabble.

Yet with the Romans this utilitarian toil and moil, this ostentation, put on imposing forms : the radiant world of Greece lay not so far from them but that, for all their practical stolidity and all their Asiatic gaudiness, they still could cast an ogling glance towards her ; so that our eyes discern, and rightly, outspread o'er all the buildings of the Roman world a majestic charm which almost seems to us a beauty. But whatever has accrued to *us* from that same world, across the steeples of the Middle Ages, lacks both the charm of beauty and of majesty ; for where we still may trace a gloomy shade of undelighting *majesty*, as in the colossal domes of our cathedrals, we see alas! no longer any drop of *beauty*. The genuine temples of our modern religion, the buildings of the Bourse, are certainly most ingenuously propped by *Grecian columns ;* Greek tympana invite us to our railroad journeys; and from under the Athenian Parthenon the military guard is marched towards us, on its ' relief,'—but however elevating these exceptions may be, they are still but mere exceptions, and the rule of our utilitarian architecture is desperately vile and trivial. Let the modern Art of Building bring forth the gracefullest and most imposing edifice she can, she still can never keep from sight her shameful want of independence : for our public, as our private, needs are of such a kind that, in order to supply them, Architecture can never produce, but forever merely copy, merely piece together. Only a real *need* makes man inventive : whilst the real need of our present era asserts itself in the language of the rankest utilitarianism ; therefore it can only get its answer from mechanical contrivances, and not from Art's creations. That which lies beyond this actual need, however, is with us the need of *Luxury*, of the

un-needful; and it is only by the superfluous and un-needful that Architecture can serve it—*i.e.* she *reproduces* the
buildings which earlier epochs had produced from their
felt need of beauty; she pieces together the individual
details of these works, according to her wanton fancy;
out of a restless longing for alteration, she stitches every
national style of building throughout the world into
her motley, disconnected botches; in short—she follows the
caprice of Fashion, whose frivolous laws she needs must
make her own because she nowhere hears the call of inner,
beautiful Necessity.

Architecture has thus to share in all the humbling destiny of the divided humanistic arts; insomuch as she
can only be incited to a true formative process by the
need of men who manifest, or long to manifest, their inborn
beauty.   In step with the withering of Grecian Tragedy,
her fall began; that is, her own peculiar productive power
commenced to weaken.   The most lavish of the monuments which she was forced to rear to the glory of the
colossal egoism of later times—aye, even of that of the
Christian faith—seem, when set beside the lofty simplicity
and pregnant meaning of Grecian buildings at the flowering-time of Tragedy, like the rank, luxuriant parasites of
some midnight dream, against the radiant progeny of the
cleansing, all-enlivening light of day.

Only together with the redemption of the egoistically
severed humanistic arts into the collective Art-work of the
Future, with the redemption of *utilitarian man* himself into
the *artistic manhood* of the Future, will Architecture also
be redeemed from the bond of serfdom, from the curse of
barrenness, into the freest, inexhaustible fertility of art-
resource.

The Art of Sculpture.

Asiatics and Egyptians, in their representation of the
nature-forces that governed them, had passed from the

delineation of the forms of beasts to that of the *human* figure itself; under which, although in immoderate proportions and disfigured by repugnant symbolism, they now sought to picture to themselves those forces. They had no wish to copy *man ;* but since man, at bottom, can only conceive the highest in his own generic form, they involuntarily transferred the human stature—distorted for this very reason—to the objects of their nature-worship.

In this sense, and from a similar impulse, we also see the oldest Hellenic races portraying their gods, *i.e.*, their deified embodiments of nature-forces, under the human shapes they hewed from wood or stone for objects of their worship. The religious need for objectification of invisible, adored or dreaded godlike powers, was answered by the oldest Sculptural art through the shaping of natural substances to imitate the *human form ;* just as Architecture answered an immediate human need by the fitting and framing of natural 'stuffs' into what we may call a condensation of *Nature's* features to suit the special aim : as, for instance, we may recognise in the *God's - temple* the condensed presentment of the *God's-grove.* Now we have seen that if the man whose purpose informed the builder's art had no thought for aught but the immediate practical use, then this art could only stay a handiwork, or return thereto ; while if, on the contrary, he were an *artist* and set himself in the forefront of this purpose, as the man who had already become the subject and the matter of his own artistic treatment, he also raised the building-handicraft to Art. In like manner, so long as Man felt bound in brutish slavery to Nature, he might indeed conceive the objects of his nature-worship under the guise of a human form, but could only shape their plastic images according to the standard by which he measured *himself,* namely in the garb and with the attributes of that Nature on whom he felt so brutishly dependent. But in measure as he raised *himself,* his own uncrippled body, and his inborn human faculties, to the stuff and purport of his artistic handling, he gained the power to also show his

Gods in the image of a free, uncrippled human form ; until at last he frankly set before himself, in highest glee, this beauteous human shape itself as nothing but the likeness of a man.

Here we touch the fatal ridge on which the living Human Artwork splintered, and left its fragments to linger through an artificial life of petrefaction in the monumental fixity of Plastic art. The discussion of this vital question we have been forced to reserve for our present exposition of the art of Sculpture.—

The first and earliest association of men was the work of Nature. The purely tribal fellowship, *i.e.*, the circle of all those who claimed descent from a common ancestor and the lineal seed of his loins, is the original bond of union of every race of people that we meet in history. This tribal stem preserves in its traditional Sagas, as in an ever lively memory, the instinctive knowledge of its common ancestry : while the impressions derived from the particular natural features of its surroundings exalt these legendary recollections to the rank of religious ideas. Now, in however manifold accretion these ideas and reminiscences may have heaped themselves together and crowded into novel forms, among the quickest-witted historical nations, owing to racial admixture on the one hand, and on the other to change of natural surroundings as the result of tribal migration, — however broadly, in their Sagas and religions, these peoples may have stretched the narrowing bands of nationality, so that the idea of their own particular origin was expanded to the theory of a universal descent and derivation of men in general from their Gods, as from the Gods in general,—yet in every epoch and every land where Myth and Religion have flourished in the lively faith of any racial stem, the peculiar bond of union of this particular stem has always lain in its specific myth and its particular religion. The Hellenic races solemnised the joint memorial celebration of their common descent in their religious feasts, *i.e.*, in the glorification and adoration of the God or Hero in whose being they felt themselves included as one common whole. Finally and with the greatest truth to life—as though from a felt need to fix with utmost definition their recollection of what was ever dropping farther back into the past—they materialised their national traditions in their Art, and most directly in that full-fledged work of art, the Tragedy. The lyric and the dramatic art-works were each a *religious act :* but there was already evinced in this act, when compared with the simple primiitve religious rite, a taint of artificial effort ; the effort, namely, to bring forward of set purpose that common memory which had already lost its immediate living impress on the life of every day. Thus Tragedy was the religious rite become a *work of Art,* by side of which the traditional observance of the genuine religious temple-rite was necessarily docked of so much of its inwardness and truth that it became indeed a mere conventional and soulless ceremony, whereas its kernel lived on in the Art-work.

In the highly important matter of the *externals* of the religious act, the tribal fellowship shows its communal character by certain ancestral usages, by certain forms and garments. The *garb* of Religion is, so to speak, the *costume* of the Race by which it mutually recognises itself, and that at the first glance. This garment, hallowed by the use of ages, this—in a manner—religio-social convention, had shifted from the religious to the artistic rite, the Tragedy ; in it and by it the Tragic actor embodied the familiar, reverenced figure of the People's fellowship. It was by no means the mere vastness of the theatre and the distance of the audience, that prescribed the heightening of the human stature by the *cothurnus,* or, precisely, that admitted the employment of the immobile tragic mask ;—but the cothurnus and the mask were necessary, religiously significant attributes which, accompanied by other symbolical tokens, first gave to the performer his weighty character of Priest. Now where a religion, commencing to fade from daily life and wholly withdrawing from its political aspect, is discernible by its outer garb alone, but this garment, as with the Athenians, can only now take on the folds of actual Life when it forms the in-

vestiture of Art : there must this actual life at last confess
itself the core of that religion, by frankly throwing off its
last disguise.   But the core of the Hellenic religion, the
centre round which its whole system revolved, and which
instinctively asserted its exclusive rule in actual life, was :
Man.   It was for Art to formulate aloud this plain confession : she did it, when she cast aside the last concealing
garment of Religion, and showed its core in simple nakedness, the *actual* bodily man.

Yet this unveiling was alike the final annihilation of the
collective Artwork : for its bond of union had been that
very garment of Religion.   While the contents of the common mythical religion, the traditional subject of Dramatic art, were employed to point the poet's moral, developed
to fit his purpose, and finally disfigured by his selfwilled
fancy, the religious belief had already disappeared completely from the life of the Folk-fellowship, now only linked
by political interests.   This belief however, the honour
paid to national Gods, the sure assumption of the truth of
primal race-traditions, had formed the bond of all community.   Was this now rent and hooted as a heresy, at
least the core of that religion had come to light as unconditioned, actual, naked *Man ;* but this Man was no longer
the associate man, united by the bond of racial fellowship :
only the *absolute, egoistic, solitary unit,* — man beautiful
and naked, but loosed from the beauteous bond of brotherhood.

From here on, from the shattering of the Greek religion,
from the wreck of the Grecian Nature-State, and its resolution into the Political State,—from the splintering of the
common Tragic Artwork,—the manhood of world-history
begins with measured tread its new gigantic march of
evolution, from the fallen *natural kinsmanship of national
community* to the *universal fellowship of all mankind.*   The
band which the full-fledged Man, coming to consciousness
in the national Hellenian, disrupted as a cramping fetter—
with this awakened consciousness—must now expand into
a universal girdle embracing *all* mankind.   The period from

that point of time down to our own to-day is, therefore, the history of *absolute Egoism ;* and the end of this period will be its redemption into *Communism.**

The art which has taken this solitary, egoistic, naked Man, the point of departure of the said world-historical period, and set him up before us as a beauteous monument of admonition—is the *art of Sculpture,* which reached its height exactly at the time when the conjoint human art-work of Tragedy declined from its meridian.—

The beauty of the human body was the foundation ot all Hellenic Art, nay even of the natural State. We know that with the noblest of Hellenic stems, the Doric Spartans, the healthiness and unmarred beauty of the newborn child made out the terms on which alone it was allowed to live, while puling deformity was denied the right of life. This beauteous naked man is the kernel of all Spartanhood : from genuine delight in the beauty of the most perfect human body, that of the male, arose that spirit of comrade-ship which pervades and shapes the whole economy of the Spartan State. This love of man to man, in its primitive purity, proclaims itself as the noblest and least selfish utter-ance of man's sense of beauty, for it teaches man to sink and merge his entire self in the object of his affection. And exactly in degree as woman, in perfected womanhood, through love to man and sinking of herself within his being, has developed the manly element of that womanhood and brought it to a thorough balance with the purely womanly, and thus in measure as she is no longer merely man's *beloved* but his *friend*—can man find fullest satisfaction in the love of woman.†

* It is a political crime to use this word : however, there is none which will better describe the direct antithesis of *Egoism.* Whosoever is ashamed to-day to pass current as an Egoist—and indeed no one will openly confess himself as such—must allow us to take the liberty of calling him a Communist.—R. WAGNER.

† The redemption of woman into participation in the nature of man is the outcome of Christian-Germanic evolution. The Greek remained in ignorance of the psychic process of the ennobling of woman to the rank of man. To him everything appeared under its direct, unmediated aspect,—woman to him was woman, and man was man ; and thus at the point where his love to

The higher element of that love of man to man consisted even in this : that it excluded the motive of egoistic physicalism.   Nevertheless it not only included a purely spiritual bond of friendship, but this spiritual friendship was the blossom and the crown of the physical friendship. The latter sprang directly from delight in the beauty, aye, in the material, bodily beauty of the beloved comrade ; yet this delight was no egoistic yearning, but a thorough stepping out of self into unreserved sympathy with the comrade's joy in himself, involuntarily betrayed by his life-glad, beauty-prompted bearing.   This love, which had its basis in the noblest pleasures of both eye and soul—not like our modern postal correspondence of sober friendship, half businesslike, half sentimental—was the Spartan's only tutoress of youth, the never aging instructress alike of boy and man, the ordainer of the common feasts and valiant enterprises ; nay, the inspiring helpmeet on the battlefield.   For this it was that knit the fellowships of love into battalions of war and forewrote the tactics of death-daring, in rescue of the imperilled or vengeance for the slaughtered comrade, by the infrangible laws of the soul's most natural necessity.—

The Spartan who thus directly carried out in Life his purely human, communistic artwork, instinctively portrayed it also in his *Lyric;* that most direct expression of joy in self and life, which hardly reached in its impulsive (*nothwendig*) utterance to Art's self-consciousness.   In the prime of the Doric State, the Spartan Lyric bent so irresistibly towards the original basis of all Art, the living *Dance,* that— characteristically enough!—it has scarcely handed down to us one single literary memento of itself ; precisely because it was a pure, physical expression of lovely life, and warded off all separation of the art of Poetry from those of Dance and Tone.   Even the transitional stage from the Lyric to the Drama, such as we may recognise in the Epic songs, remained a stranger to the Spartans ; and it is sufficiently significant, that the Homeric songs were collected

woman was satisfied in accordance with nature, arose the spiritual demand for man.—R. WAGNER.

in the Ionic, not the Doric dialect. Whereas the Ionic peoples, and notably in the event, the Athenians, developed themselves into political States under influence of the liveliest mutual intercourse, and preserved in Tragedy the artistic representation of the religion which was melting out of Life : the Spartans, as a shut-off inland people, kept faithful to their old-hellenic character, and held their unmixed Nature-state, as a living monument of art, against the changeful fashionings of the newer life of politics. Whatever in the hurry and confusion of the destructive restlessness of these new times sought rescue or support, now turned its gaze toward Sparta. The Statesman sought to scrutinise the forms of this primeval State, to convey them artificially to the political State of his day ; while the *Artist*, who saw the common artwork of the Tragedy sloughing and crumbling before his very eyes, looked forth to where he might descry the kernel of this artwork, the beauteous old-hellenic * man, and preserve it for his art. As Sparta towered up, a living monument of older times : so did the art of Sculpture crystallise in stone the old-hellenic human being which she had recognised within this living monument, and garner up the lifeless monument of bygone beauty for coming times of quickening barbarism.

But when Athens turned its eyes to Sparta, the worm of general egoism was already gnawing its destructive path into this fair State too. The Peloponnesian War had dragged it, all unwilling, into the whirlpool of the newer times ; and Sparta had only been able to vanquish Athens by the very weapons which the Athenians had erewhile made so terrible and unassailable to *it*. Instead of their simple iron-bars—those tokens of contempt for money, as compared with human worth—the minted gold of Asia was heaped within the Spartan's coffers ; leaving behind the

---

* One feels almost tempted to concoct a hybrid equivalent for this expressive "*ur-hellenisch*," and boldly write it down as "*ur*-hellenic ;" but the fear of a literary Mrs Grundy is too powerful for the rash desire. We cannot, however, help envying the Germans their pregnant prefix "*ur*," a shadow of which we fancy we may still detect in our English "early," "*ere*-while" or "erst" ; again perhaps in our "hoary" ; and almost certainly in "yore."—Tr.

ancient, frugal "public mess," he retired to his sumptuous
banquet between his own four walls; and the noble love of
man to man—whose motive had been an even higher one
than that of love to woman—degenerated, as it had already
done in the other Hellenic states, into its unnatural
counterpart.

This is the Man, lovely in his person but unlovely in his
selfish isolation, that the Sculptor's art has handed down
to us in marble and in bronze,—motionless and cold, like a
petrified remembrance, like the *mummy of the Grecian
world.*

This art, the hireling of the rich for the adornment of
their palaces, the easier won a troop of practisers as its
creative process lent itself to speedy degradation to a mere
mechanical labour. Certainly, the subject of the Sculptor's art is Man, that protean host of countless hues of
character and myriad passions: but this art depicts alone
his outer physical stature, in which there only lies the husk
and not the kernel of the human being. True, that the
inner man shows out most palpably through all his outward
semblance; but this he only does *completely* in, and by
means of, *motion.* The Sculptor can only seize and reproduce *one single* moment from all this manifold play of
movements, and must leave the real motion itself to be
unriddled from the physical relief of the work of art, by a
process of mathematical computation. When once the
most direct and surest mode of reaching from this poverty
of means to a speaking likeness of actual life had been
found,—when once the perfect measure of outward human
show had been thought into the bronze and marble, and
the power to persuade us of the truth of its reflection had
been wrested from them,—this method, once *discovered,*
could easily be *learned;* and Sculpture could live on from
imitation to copy *ad infinitum,* bringing forth her store of
products, graceful, beautiful, and true, without receiving
any sustenance from real creative force. Thus we find
that in the era of the Roman world-empire, when all
artistic instinct had long since died away, the art of

Sculpture brought a multitude of works to mart in which there seemed to dwell an artist soul, despite their really owing all their being to a mere mechanical gift of imitation. She could become a lovely handicraft when she had ceased to be an art—and the latter she was for only just so long as she had aught to discover, aught to invent. But the repetition of a discovery is nothing more nor less than imitation.

Through the chinks of the iron-mailed, or monk-cowled, Middle Ages there shone at last the glimmer of the marble flesh of Grecian bodily beauty, and greeted hungry human-kind with its first new taste of life. It was in this lovely *stone*, and not in the actual Life of the ancient world, that the modern was to learn fair Man again. Our modern art of Sculpture sprang from no lively impulse to portray the actual extant man, whom it could scarcely see beneath his modish covering, but from a longing to copy the counterfeit presentment of a physically extinct race of men. It is the expression of an honourable wish to reach back from an unlovely present to the past, and therefrom to reconstruct lost beauty. As the gradual vanishing of human beauty from actual existence was the first cause of the artistic development of Sculpture, which, as though in a last effort to fix the fading image of a common good, would fain preserve it in a monumental token,—so the *modern* impulse to reproduce those monuments could only find its motive in the total absence of this beauteous man from modern life. Wherefore, since this impulse could never spring *from* life and find *in* life its satisfaction, but for ever swayed from monument to monument, from image to image, stone to stone : our Modern Sculpture, a mere plagiarism of the genuine art, was forced to take the character of a craftsman's trade, in which the wealth of rules and canons by which her hand was guided but bared her poverty as *art*, her utter inability to *invent*. But while she busily set forth her self and products, in place of vanished beauteous Man,—while, in a sense, her art was only fostered by this lack,—she fell at last into her present

selfish isolation, in which she, so to say, but plays the
barometer to the ugliness that still prevails in life; and,
indeed, with a certain complacent feeling of her—*relative*
—necessity amid such atmospheric conditions.

Modern Sculpture can only answer to any vestige of a
need, for precisely so long as the loveliness of man is not
at hand in actual life: the resurrection of this beauty,
its immediate influence on the fashioning of life, must
inevitably throw down our present "plastics." For the
need to which alone this art can answer—nay, the need
which she herself concocts—is that which yearns to flee
the unloveliness of life; not that which, springing from an
actual lovely life, strives toward the exhibition of this life in
living artwork. The true, creative, artistic craving proceeds
from fulness, not from void: while the fulness of the
modern art of Sculpture is merely the wealth of the monuments bequeathed to us by Grecian plastic artists. Now,
from this fulness she cannot *create*, but is merely driven
back to it from lack of beauty in surrounding life; she
plunges herself within this fulness, in order to escape from
lack.

Thus bare of all inventive power, she coquets at last
with the forms to hand in present life, in her despairing
attempt to invent—cost what it may. She casts around
her the garment of Fashion, and so as to be recognised
and rewarded by this life, she models the unbeautiful; in
order to be *true*—that is to say, true according to *our*
notions—she gives up all her hopes of *beauty*. So, during
the continuance of those same conditions which maintain
her in her artificial life, Sculpture falls into that wretched,
sterile, or ugliness-begetting state in which she must
inevitably yearn for nothing but redemption. The life-
conditions, however, into which she desires to be released
are, rightly measured, the conditions of that very life in
presence of which the art of Sculpture must straightway
cease to be an independent art. To gain the power of
creating, she yearns for the reign of loveliness in actual
life; from which she merely hopes to win the living matter

for her invention. But the fulfilment of this desire could only lay bare the egoism of its indwelling self-delusion; inasmuch as the conditions for the *necessary* operation of the art of Sculpture must, in any case, be utterly annulled when *actual life shall itself be fair of body.*

In present life the independent art of Sculpture but answers to a relative need: although to this she stands indebted for her existence of to-day, nay, for her very prime. But that other state of things, the antithesis of the modern state, is that in which an imperative *need* for the works of sculptural art cannot be so much as reasonably imagined. If man's whole life pay homage to the principle of beauty, if he make his living body fair to see, rejoicing in the beauty that he himself displays: then is the subject and the matter of the artistic exhibition of this beauty, and of the delight therein, without a doubt the whole warm, living man himself. His art-work is the *Drama*; and the redemption of Sculpture is just this: *the disenchantment of the stone into the flesh and blood of man; out of immobility into motion, out of the monumental into the temporal.* Only when the artistic impulse of the Sculptor shall have passed into the soul of the *Dancer*—the *mimetic expositor* who sings alike and speaks—can this impulse be conceived as truly satisfied. Only when the statuary's art no longer exists, or rather, has passed along another direction than that of the human body, namely as "sculpture" into "*architecture*";* when the frozen loneliness of this *solitary* stone-hewn man shall have been resolved into the endless-streaming multitude of actual living men; when we recall the memory of the beloved dead in ever newborn, soul-

---

* The words "*Skulptur*" and "*Architektur*" here appear for the first time, in the original. Hitherto these arts have been spoken of under the terms "*Baukunst*" (the building art) and "*Bildhauerkunst*" (the image- or likeness-hewer's art); but I have found it more convenient to employ, in general, the equivalents "Sculpture" and "Architecture." Here, however, I have deemed it necessary to use the more exact, though more cumbersome expression "the statuary's art," in the opening of the sentence, in order to reserve the term "Sculpture" to render the more general idea of "carving," in which sense it is evident that Wagner has here employed the Latin noun.—W.A.E.

filled flesh and blood, and no more in lifeless brass or marble; when we take the stones to build the living Art-work's shrine, and require them no longer for our imaging of living Man,—then first will the *true Plastique* be at our hand.

3

The Painter's Art.

Just as, when we are denied the pleasure of hearing the symphonic playing of an orchestra, we seek to recall our enjoyment by a pianoforte rendering; just as, when we are no longer permitted to gaze upon the colours of an oil-painting in a picture-gallery, we strive by aid of an engraving to refresh the impression which they have left,*— so had *Painting*, if not in her origination, yet in her *artistic* evolution, to answer to the yearning need of calling back to memory the lost features of the living Human Artwork.

We must pass by her raw beginnings, when, like Sculpture, she sprang from the as yet unartistic impulse toward the symbolising of religious ideas; for she first attained artistic significance at the epoch when the living artwork of Tragedy was paling, and the brilliant tints of Painting sought to fix the vision of those wondrous, pregnant scenes which no longer offered their immediate warmth of life to the beholder.

Thus the Grecian artwork solemnised its after-math in Painting. This harvest was not that which sprang by natural necessity from the wealth of Life; its necessity was the rather that of *Culture;* it issued from a conscious, arbitrary motive, to wit the *knowledge* of the loveliness of Art, united with the *wilful purpose* to force, as it were, this loveliness to linger in a life to which it no longer belonged

---

* The personality of the Zurich exile here peeps out from beneath the robes of the art-philosopher. No one could feel more keenly than Wagner himself, at the time of writing this essay, the insufficiency of the suggested substitute, cut off as he then was from enjoyment of all the higher walks of art.—TR.

instinctively as the unconscious, necessary expression of that life's inmost soul. That Art which, unbidden and of her own accord, had blossomed from the communion of the People's life, had likewise by her active presence, and through the regardal of her demeanour, called up the *mental concept* (*Begriff*) of her essence ; for it was not the *idea* of Art that had summoned her to life, but herself, the actual breathing Art, had evolved the "Idea" from out herself.

The artistic power of the Folk, thrusting forward with all the necessity of a nature-force, was dead and buried ; what it had done, lived only now in memory, or in the artificial reproduction. Whereas the Folk, in all its actions and especially in its self-wrought destruction of national, pent-up insularity, has through all time proceeded by the law of inner necessity, and thus in thorough harmony with the majestic evolution of the human race : the lonely spirit of the Artist—to whose yearning for the beautiful the un-beauteous manifestments of the People's life-stress must ever stay a dark enigma—could only console itself by looking backward to the artwork of a bygone era, and, recognising the impossibility of arbitrarily relivening that artwork, could only make this solace as lasting as might be, by freshening up with lifelike details the harvest of its recollections,—just as through a portrait we preserve to our memory the features of a loved lost friend. Hereby Art herself became an object of art ; the "idea" derived from her became her law ; and *cultured art*—the art that can be learnt, and always points back to itself—began its life-career. The latter, as we may see to-day, can be pursued without a halt in the least artistic times and amid the most sordid circumstances,—yet only for the selfish pleasure of isolated, life-divorced, and art-repining Culture.—

The senseless attempt to reconstruct the Tragic Artwork by purely imitative reproduction—such as was engaged in, for instance, by the poets of the Alexandrian court—was most advantageously avoided by Painting ; for she gave up the lost as lost, and answered the impulse to restore it by the cultivation of a special, and peculiar, artistic faculty of man.   Though this faculty required a greater variety of media for its operation, yet Painting soon won a marked advantage over Sculpture.   The sculptor's work displayed the material likeness of the *whole* man in lifelike form, and, thus far, stood nearer to the living artwork of self-portraying man than did the painter's work, which was only able to render, so to speak, his tinted shadow.   As in both counterfeits, however, the breath of Life was unattainable, and motion could only be indicated to the thought of the spectator, to whose phantasy its conceivable extension must be left to be worked out by certain natural laws of inductive reasoning,—so Painting, in that she looked still farther aside from the reality, and depended still more on artistic illusion than did Sculpture, was able to take a more ideal poetic flight than she.   Finally, Painting was not obliged to content herself with the representation of *this one* man, or of *that particular* group or combination to which the art of Statuary was restricted ; rather, the artistic illusion became so preponderant a necessity to her, that she had not only to draw into the sphere of her portrayal a wealth of correlated human groups extended both in length and breadth, but also the circle of their extrahuman surroundings, the *scenes of Nature* herself.   Hereon is based an entirely novel step in the evolution of man's artistic faculties, both perceptive and executive : namely, that of the inner comprehension and reproduction of *Nature*, by means of *Landscape-painting*.

This moment is of the highest importance for the whole range of plastic art : it brings this art—which began, in Architecture, with the observation and artistic exploitation of Nature for the benefit of Man,—which in Sculpture, as though for the deification of Man, exalted *him* as its only subject—to its complete conclusion, by turning it at last, with ever growing understanding, entirely back from Man to *Nature ;* and this inasmuch as it enabled plastic art to take her by the hand of intimate friendship, and thus, as it were, to broaden Architecture out to a full and lifelike portraiture of Nature. Human Egoism, which in naked Architecture was forever referring Nature to its own exclusive self, to some extent broke up in Landscape-painting, which vindicated Nature's individual rights and prompted artistic Man to loving absorption into her, in order there to find himself again, immeasurably amplified.

When Grecian painters sought to fix the memory of the scenes which had erstwhile been presented to their actual sight and hearing in the Lyric, in the lyrical Epos, and in the Tragedy, and to picture them again in outline and in colour—without a doubt they considered men alone as worthy objects of their exhibition ; and it is to the so-called *historical* tendency that we owe the raising of Painting to her first artistic height. As she thus preserved the *united* art-work green in memory, so when the conditions that summoned forth the passionate preservation of these memories vanished quite away, there yet remained two byways open, along which the art of Painting could carry on her further independent self-development: the Portrait and—the Land-scape. True, that Landscape had already been appropriated for the necessary background of the scenes from Homer and the Tragic poets: but at the time of their painting's prime the Greeks looked on landscape with no other eye than that with which the peculiar bent of the Grecian character had caused them to regard the whole of Nature. With the Greeks, *Nature* was merely the distant background of the human being: well in the foreground stood *Man* himself; and the Gods to whom he assigned the force controlling Nature were anthropomorphic gods. He sought to endue everything he saw in Nature with human shape and human being ; as humanised, she had for him that endless charm in whose enjoyment it was impossible for his sense of beauty to look on her from such a standpoint as that of our modern Judaistic utilism, and make of her a mere inanimate object of his sensuous pleasure. However, he but cherished this beautiful relationship between himself and Nature from an involuntary error : in his anthropomorphosis of Nature he credited her with

M

human motives which, necessarily contrasted with the true character of Nature, could be only arbitrarily assumed as operating within her.

As Man, in all his life and all his relations to Nature, acts from a necessity peculiar to his own being, he unwittingly distorts her character when he conceives Nature as behaving not according to her own necessity but to that of Man. Although this error took a beauteous form among the Greeks, while among other races, especially those of Asia, its utterances were for the most part hideous, it was none the less destructive in its influence on Hellenic life. When the Hellenian broke adrift from his ancestral bond of national communion, when he lost the standard of life's beauty that he had drawn from it instinctively, he was unable to replace this needful standard by one derived from a correct survey of surrounding Nature. He had unconsciously perceived in Nature a coherent, encompassing Necessity for just so long as this same Necessity came before his consciousness as a ground condition of his communal life. But when the latter crumbled into its egoistic atoms, when the Greek was ruled by naught but the caprice of his own selfwill, no longer harmonised by brotherhood, or eventually submitted to an arbitrary outer force that gained its leverage from this general selfwill,—then with his faulty knowledge of Nature, whom he deemed as capricious as himself and the worldly might that governed him, he lacked the certain standard by which he could have learnt to measure out himself again ; that standard which Nature offers as their highest boon to *those* men who recognise her innermost necessity and learn to know the eternal harmony of her creative forces, working in widest compass through every separate unit.

It is from this error alone, that arose those vast excesses of the Grecian mind which we see attaining under the Byzantine empire a pitch that quite obscures the old Hellenic character, yet which were but, at bottom, the normal blemishes of its good qualities. Philosophy might put forth its honestest endeavour to grasp the harmony of

Nature: it only showed how impotent is the might of abstract Intellect. In defiance of all the saws of Aristotle, the Folk, in its desire to win itself an absolute bliss from the midst of this million-headed Egoism, formed itself a religion in which Nature was made the pitiful plaything of the quibbling search for human blessedness. It only needed the Grecian view of Nature's government by selfwilled, human-borrowed motives to be wedded to the Judao-oriental theory of her subservience to human Use,—for the disputations and decrees of Councils anent the essence of the Trinity, and the interminable strifes, nay national wars therefrom arising, to face astounded history with the irrefutable fruits of this intermarriage.

Towards the close of the Middle Ages, the Roman Church raised its assumption of the immobility of the earth to the rank of an article of belief: but it could not prevent America from being discovered, the conformation of the globe mapped out, and Nature's self at last laid so far bare to knowledge that the inner harmony of all her manifold phenomena has now been proved to demonstration. The impulse that led toward these discoveries sought, at like time, to find an utterance in that branch of art which was of all best fitted for its artistic satisfaction. With the Renaissance of Art, *Painting* also, in eager struggle for ennoblement, linked on her own new birth to the revival of the antique ; beneath the shelter of the prosperous Church she waxed to the portrayal of its chronicles, and passed from these to scenes of veritable history and actual life, still profiting by the advantage that she yet could take her form and colour from this actual life. But the more the physical Present was crushed by the marring influence of Fashion, and the more the newer school of Historical painting, in order to be beautiful, saw itself compelled by the unloveliness of Life to construct from its own fancy and to combine from styles and manners twice borrowed from art-history— not from life,—the farther did Painting, departing from the portraiture of modish man, strike out that path to which we owe the loving understanding of Nature in the *Landscape*.

Man, around whom the landscape had erstwhile grouped itself as round its egoistic centre, shrank ever smaller mid the fulness of his surroundings, in direct proportion as he bowed beneath the unworthy yoke of disfiguring Fashion in his daily life ; so that at last he played the role in Landscape which before had been assigned to landscape as a foil to him. *Under the given circumstances,* we can only celebrate this advance of landscape as a victory of *Nature* over base and man-degrading *Culture.*   For therein undisfigured Nature asserted herself, in the only possible mode, against her foe ; inasmuch as, seeking for a sanctuary the while, she laid bare herself, as though from very Want, to the inner understanding of artistic Man.

Modern *Natural Science* and *Landscape-Painting* are the only outcomes of the Present which, either from an artistic or a scientific point of view, offer us the smallest consolation in our impotence, or refuge from our madness.   Amid the hopeless splintering of all our art-endeavours, the solitary genius who for a moment binds them into almost violent union, may accomplish feats the more astounding as neither the need nor the conditions for his art-work are now to hand : the general concensus of the Painter's art, however, takes almost solely the direction of the Landscape.   For here it finds exhaustless subjects, and thereby an inexhaustible capacity ; whereas in every other attempt to shadow Nature forth, it can only proceed by arbitrary sifting, sorting, and selecting, to garner from our absolutely inartistic life an object worthy of artistic treatment.

The more the so-called Historical school of painting is busied with its efforts to build up and explain to us the genuine beauteous Man and genuine beauteous Life, by reminiscences from the farthest past ; the more, with all its prodigious outlay of expedients, it confesses the heaviness of the burden imposed upon it, to seek to be *more* and *other* than behoves the nature of one single branch of art, —so much the more must it long for a redemption which, like that destined for Sculpture, can only consist in its ascension into *that* from which it drew the original force that gave to it artistic life; and this is even the living human Art-work, whose very birth from Life must heave away the conditions that made possible the being and the prospering of Painting as an independent branch of art. The *man-portraying* art of Painting will never find it possible to lead a healthy, necessary life—when, without a pencil or a canvas, in liveliest artistic setting, the beauteous Man portrays *himself* in full perfection. What she now toils to reach by *honest* effort, she then will reach in perfect measure, when she bequeaths her colour and her skill of composition to the living "plastic" of the real dramatic representant; when she steps down from her canvas and her plaster, and stands upon the *Tragic stage;* when she bids the artist carry out in his own person what she toiled in vain to consummate by heaping up of richest means without the breath of actual Life.

But *Landscape-painting,* as last and perfected conclusion of all the plastic arts, will become the very soul of Architecture; she will teach us so to rear the *stage* for the dramatic Artwork of the Future that on it, herself imbued with life, she may picture forth the warm *background of Nature* for *living,* no longer counterfeited, *Man.*—

If we may thus regard the *scene* of the united Artwork of the Future as won by the highest power of Plastic-Art, and therewith as attained the inmost *knowledge of familiar Nature:* we may now proceed to take a closer view of the nature of this Artwork itself.

IV.

OUTLINES OF THE ARTWORK OF THE FUTURE.

F we consider the relation of modern art—so far as it is truly *Art*—to public life, we shall recognise at once its complete inability to affect this public life in the sense of its own noblest endeavour. The reason hereof is, that our modern art is a mere product of Culture and has not sprung from Life itself; therefore, being nothing but a hot-house plant, it cannot strike root in the natural soil, or flourish in the natural climate of the present. Art has become the private property of an artist-caste; its taste it offers to those alone who *understand* it; and for its under-standing it demands a special study, aloof from actual life, the study of *art-learning*. This study, and the under-standing to be attained thereby, each individual who has acquired the gold wherewith to pay the proffered delicacies of art conceives to-day that he has made his own: if, how-ever, we were to ask the Artist whether the great majority of art's amateurs are able to understand him in his best endeavours, he could only answer with a deep-drawn sigh. But if he ponder on the infinitely greater mass of those who are perforce shut out on every side by the evils of our present social system from both the understanding and the tasting of the sweets of modern art, then must the artist of to-day grow conscious that his whole art-doings are, at bottom, but an egoistic, self-concerning business; that his art, in the light of public life, is nothing else than luxury and superfluity, a self-amusing pastime. The daily em-phasised, and bitterly deplored abyss between so-called culture and un-culture is so enormous; a bridge between the two so inconceivable; a reconcilement so impossible; that, had it any candour, our modern art, which grounds itself on this unnatural culture, would be forced to admit, to its deepest shame, that it owes its existence to a life-element which in turn can only base *its own* existence on the utter dearth of culture among the real masses of mankind.

The only thing which, in the position thus assigned to her, our Modern Art should be able to effect—and among honest folk, indeed, endeavours—namely, the *spreading abroad of culture*, she cannot do; and simply for the reason that, for Art to operate on Life, she must be herself the blossom of a *natural* culture, *i.e.*, such an one as has grown up from below, for she can never hope to rain down culture from *above*. Therefore, taken at its best, our "cultured" art resembles an orator who should seek to address himself in a foreign tongue to a people which does not understand it: his highest flights of rhetoric can only lead to the most absurd misunderstandings and confusion.—

Let us first attempt to trace the *theoretic* path upon which Modern Art must march forward to redemption from her present lonely, misprised station, and toward the widest understanding of general public Life. That this redemption can only become possible by the *practical* intermediation of public Life, will then appear self-evident.

We have seen that *Plastic Art* can only attain creative strength by going to her work in unison with *artistic* Man, and not with men who purpose mere *utility*.

Artistic Man can only fully content himself by uniting every branch of Art into the *common* Artwork: in every *segregation* of his artistic faculties he is *unfree*, not fully that which he has power to be; whereas in the *common* Artwork he is *free*, and fully that which he has power to be.

The *true* endeavour of Art is therefore all-embracing: each unit who is inspired with a true *art-instinct* develops to the highest his own particular faculties, not for the glory of these special faculties, but for the glory of *general Manhood in Art.*

The highest conjoint work of art is the *Drama:* it can only be at hand in all its *possible* fulness, when in it each *separate branch of art* is at hand in *its own utmost fulness.*

The true Drama is only conceivable as proceeding from a *common urgence of every art* towards the most direct appeal to a *common public.* In this Drama, each separate art can only bare its utmost secret to their common public through a mutual parleying with the other arts; for the purpose of each separate branch of art can only be fully attained by the reciprocal agreement and co-operation of all the branches in their common message.

Architecture can set before herself no higher task than to frame for a fellowship of artists, who in their own persons portray the life of Man, the special surroundings necessary for the display of the Human Artwork. Only that edifice is built according to Necessity, which answers most befittingly an aim of man : the highest aim of man is the artistic aim ; the highest artistic aim—the Drama. In buildings reared for daily use, the builder has only to answer to the lowest aim of men : beauty is therein a luxury. In buildings reared for luxury, he has to satisfy an unnecessary and unnatural need : his fashioning therefore is capricious, unproductive, and unlovely. On the other hand, in the construction of that edifice whose every part shall answer to a common and artistic aim alone,— thus in the building of the *Theatre*, the master-builder needs only to comport himself as *artist*, to keep a single eye upon the *art-work*. In a perfect theatrical edifice, Art's need alone gives law and measure, down even to the smallest detail. This need is twofold, that of *giving* and that of *receiving*, which reciprocally pervade and condition one another. The *Scene* has firstly to comply with all the conditions of "space" imposed by the joint (*gemein-sam*) dramatic action to be displayed thereon : but secondly, it has to fulfil those conditions in the sense of bringing this dramatic action to the eye and ear of the spectator in intelligible fashion. In the arrangement of the *space for the spectators*, the need for optic and acoustic understanding of the artwork will give the necessary law, which can only be observed by a union of beauty and fitness in the proportions ; for the demand of the collective (*gemeinsam*) audience is the demand for the *artwork*, to whose comprehension it must be distinctly led by everything that meets the eye.* Thus the spectator transplants himself upon the stage, by means of all his visual and aural faculties ; while the performer becomes an artist only by complete absorption into the public. Everything, that breathes and moves upon the stage, thus breathes and moves alone from eloquent desire to impart, to be seen and heard within those walls which, however circumscribed their space, seem to the actor from his scenic standpoint to embrace the whole of humankind ; whereas the public, that representative of daily life, forgets the confines of the auditorium, and lives and breathes now only in the artwork which seems to it as Life itself, and on the stage which seems the wide expanse of the whole World.

Such marvels blossom from the fabric of the Architect, to such enchantments can he give a solid base, when he takes the purpose of the highest human artwork for his own, when he summons forth the terms of its enlivening from the individual resources of his art. On the other hand, how rigid, cold, and dead does his handiwork appear when, without a higher helpmeet than the aim of luxury,

---

* The problem of the Theatrical edifice of the Future can in no wise be considered as solved by our modern stage buildings : for they are laid out in accord with traditional laws and canons which have nothing in common with the requirements of pure Art. Where speculation for gain, on the one side, joins forces with luxurious ostentation on the other, the absolute interests of Art must be cryingly affected ; and thus no architect in the world will be able to raise our stratified and fenced-off auditoria—dictated by the parcelling of our public into the most diverse categories of class and civil station—to conformity with any law of beauty. If one imagine oneself, for a moment, within the walls of the common Theatre of the Future, one will recognise with little trouble, that an undreamt width of field lies therein open for invention.—R. WAGNER.

without the artistic necessity which leads him, in the
Theatre, to invent and range each detail with the greatest
sense of fitness, he is forced to follow every speculative
whim of his self-glorifying caprice ; to heap his masses and
trick out his ornament, in order to stereotype to-day the
vanity of some boastful plutocrat, to-morrow the honours
of a modernised Jehovah!

But not the fairest form, the richest masonry, can
alone suffice the Dramatic Artwork for the perfectly
befitting spacial terms of its appearance.   The Scene
which is to mount the picture of Human Life must, for a
thorough understanding of this life, have power to also
show the lively counterfeit of Nature, in which alone
artistic Man can render up a speaking likeness of himself.
The casings of this Scene, which look down chill and
vacantly upon the artist and the public, must deck themselves with the fresh tints of Nature, with the warm light
of heaven's æther, to be worthy to take their share in
the human artwork.   Plastic *Architecture* here feels her
bounds, her own unfreedom, and casts herself, athirst for
love, into the arms of Painting, who shall work out her
redemption into fairest Nature.

Here *Landscape-painting* enters, summoned by a common
need which she alone can satisfy.   What the painter's expert eye has seen in Nature, what he now, as artist, would
fain display for the artistic pleasure of the full community,
he dovetails into the united work of all the arts, as his own
abundant share.   Through him the scene takes on complete
artistic truth : his drawing, his colour, his glowing breadths
of light, compel Dame Nature to serve the highest claims
of Art.   That which the landscape-painter, in his struggle
to impart what he had seen and fathomed, had erstwhile
forced into the narrow frames of panel-pictures,—what he
had hung up on the egoist's secluded chamber-walls, or had
made away to the inconsequent, distracting medley of a
picture-barn,—*therewith* will he henceforth fill the ample
framework of the Tragic stage, calling the whole expanse
of scene as witness to his power of recreating Nature.   The

illusion which his brush and finest blend of colours could only hint at, could only distantly approach, he will here bring to its consummation by artistic practice of every known device of optics, by use of all the art of ' lighting. The apparent roughness of his tools, the seeming grotesqueness of the method of so-called ' scene-painting,' will not offend him ; for he will reflect that even the finest camel's-hair brush is but a humiliating instrument, when compared with the perfect Artwork ; and the artist has no right to *pride* until he is *free, i.e.,* until his artwork is completed and alive, and *he*, with all his helping tools, has been absorbed into it.   But the finished artwork that greets him from the *stage* will, set within this frame and held before the common gaze of full publicity, immeasurably more content him than did his earlier work, accomplished with more delicate tools.   He will not, forsooth, repent the right to use this scenic space to the benefit of such an artwork, for sake of his earlier disposition of a flat-laid scrap of canvas!   For as, at the very worst, his work remains the same no matter what the frame from which it looks, provided only it bring its subject to intelligible show : so will his artwork, in *this* framing, at any rate effect a livelier impression, a greater and more universal understanding, than the whilom landscape picture.

The organ for all understanding of Nature, is Man : the landscape-painter had not only to impart to men this understanding, but to make it for the first time plain to them by depicting Man in the midst of Nature.   Now by setting his artwork in the frame of the Tragic stage, he will expand the individual man, to whom he would address himself, to the associate manhood of full publicity, and reap the satisfaction of having spread his understanding out to that, and made it partner in his joy.   But he cannot fully bring about this public understanding until he allies his work to a joint and all-intelligible aim of loftiest Art ; while this aim itself will be disclosed to the common understanding, past all mistaking, by the actual bodily man with all his warmth of life.   Of all artistic things, the most directly understandable is the Dramatic-Action (*Handlung*), for reason that its art is not complete until every helping artifice be cast behind it, as it were, and genuine life attain the faithfullest and most intelligible show.   And thus each branch of art can only address itself to the *understanding* in proportion as its core—whose relation to Man, or derivation from him, alone can animate and justify the artwork —is ripening toward the *Drama*.   In proportion as it passes over into Drama, as it pulses with the Drama's light, will each domain of Art grow all-intelligible, completely understood and justified.*

On to the stage, prepared by architect and painter, now steps *Artistic Man*, as Natural Man steps on the stage of Nature.   What the statuary and the historical painter endeavoured to limn on *stone* or *canvas*, they now limn upon *themselves*, their form, their body's limbs, the features of their visage, and raise it to the consciousness of full artistic life.   The same sense that led the sculptor in his grasp and rendering of the human figure, now leads the *Mime* in the handling and demeanour of his actual body. The same eye which taught the historical painter, in drawing and in colour, in arrangement of his drapery and composition of his groups, to find the beautiful, the graceful and the characteristic, now orders the whole breadth of *actual human show.*   Sculptor and painter once freed the

---

* It can scarcely be indifferent to the modern landscape-painter to observe by how few his work is really understood to-day, and with what blear-eyed stupidity his nature-paintings are devoured by the Philistine world that pays for them ; how the so-called "charming prospect" is purchased to assuage the idle, unintelligent, visual gluttony of those same *need*-less men whose sense of hearing is tickled by our modern, empty music-manufacture to that idiotic joy which is as repugnant a reward of his performance to the *artist* as it fully answers the intention of the *artisan*.   Between the "charming prospect" and the "pretty tune" of our modern times there subsists a doleful affinity, whose bond of union is certainly not the musing calm of Thought, but that vulgar slipshod *sentimentality* which draws back in selfish horror from the sight of human suffering in its surroundings, to hire for itself a private heavenlet in the blue mists of Nature's generality.   These sentimentals are willing enough to see and hear everything : only *not* the *actual, undistorted Man*, who lifts his warning finger on the threshold of their dreams. *But this is the very man whom we must set up in the forefront of cur show !*—R. WAGNER.

Greek Tragedian from his cothurnus and his mask, upon
and under which the real man could only move according
to a certain religious convention. With justice, did this
pair of plastic artists annihilate the last disfigurement of
pure artistic man, and thus prefigure in their stone and
canvas the tragic Actor of the Future. As they once
descried him in his undistorted truth, they now shall let
him pass into reality and bring his form, in a measure
sketched by them, to bodily portrayal with all its wealth
of movement.

Thus the illusion of plastic art will turn to truth in
Drama : the plastic artist will reach out hands to the
dancer, to the *mime*, will lose himself in them, and
thus become himself both mime and dancer.—So far as
lies within his power, he will have to impart the inner man
his feeling and his will-ing, to the eye. The breadth and
depth of scenic space belong to him for the plastic message
of his stature and his motion, as a single unit or in union
with his fellows. But where his power ends, where the
fulness of his will and feeling impels him to the *utter*ing of
the inner man by means of *Speech*, there will the Word
proclaim his plain and conscious purpose : he becomes a
Poet and, to be poet, a *tone-artist* (*Tonkünstler*). But as
dancer, tone-artist, and poet, he still is one and the same
thing : nothing other than *executant, artistic Man, who, in
the fullest measure of his faculties, imparts himself to the
highest expression of receptive power.*

It is in him, the immediate executant, that the three
sister-arts unite their forces in one collective operation, in
which the highest faculty of each comes to its highest unfolding. By working in common, each one of them attains
the power to be and do the very thing which, of her own and
inmost essence, she longs to do and be. Hereby : that
each, where her own power ends, can be absorbed within
the other, whose power commences where her's ends,—she
maintains her own purity and freedom, her independence
as *that* which she is. The *mimetic dancer* is stripped of his
impotence, so soon as he can sing and speak ; the creations

of *Tone* win all-explaining meaning through the mime, as well as through the poet's word, and that exactly in degree as Tone itself is able to transcend into the motion of the mime and the word of the poet ; while the *Poet* first becomes a Man through his translation to the flesh and blood of the *Performer :* for though he metes to each artistic factor the guiding purpose which binds them all into a common whole, yet this purpose is first changed from " will " to " can " *by the poet's Will descending to the actor's Can.*

Not one rich faculty of the separate arts will remain unused in the United Artwork of the Future ; in *it* will each attain its first complete appraisement.   Thus, especially, will the manifold developments of Tone, so peculiar to our instrumental music, unfold their utmost wealth within this Artwork ; nay, Tone will incite the mimetic art of Dance to entirely new discoveries, and no less swell the breath of Poetry to unimagined fill.   For Music, in her solitude, has fashioned for herself an organ which is capable of the highest reaches of expression.   This organ is the *Orchestra.* The tone-speech of Beethoven, introduced into Drama by the orchestra, marks an entirely fresh departure for the dramatic artwork. While Architecture and, more especially, scenic Landscape-painting have power to set the executant dramatic Artist in the surroundings of physical Nature, and to dower him from the exhaustless stores of natural phenomena with an ample and significant background,—so in the Orchestra, that pulsing body of many-coloured harmony, the personating individual Man is given, for his support, a stanchless elemental spring, at once artistic, natural, and human.

The Orchestra is, so to speak, the loam of endless, universal Feeling, from which the individual feeling of the separate actor draws power to shoot aloft to fullest height of growth : it, in a sense, dissolves * the hard immobile

---

* It is a little difficult to quite unravel this part of the metaphor, for the same word " *Boden* " is used twice over.   I have thought it best to translate it in the first place as " loam," and in the second as " ground " ; for it appears

ground of the actual scene into a fluent, elastic, impression-able æther, whose unmeasured bottom is the great sea of Feeling itself. Thus the Orchestra is like the *Earth* from which Antæus, so soon as ever his foot had grazed it, drew new immortal life-force. By its essence diametrically opposed to the scenic landscape which surrounds the actor, and therefore, as to locality, most rightly placed in the deepened foreground outside the scenic frame, it at like time forms the perfect complement of these surroundings ; inasmuch as it broadens out the exhaustless *physical* element of Nature to the equally exhaustless *emotional* element of artistic Man. These elements, thus knit together, enclose the performer as with an atmospheric ring of Art and Nature, in which, like to the heavenly bodies, he moves secure in fullest orbit, and whence, withal, he is free to radiate on every side his feelings and his views of life,— broadened to infinity, and showered, as it were, on distances as measureless as those on which the stars of heaven cast their rays of light.

Thus supplementing one another in their changeful dance, the united sister-arts will show themselves and make good their claim ; now all together, now in pairs, and again in solitary splendour, according to the momentary need of the only rule- and purpose-giver, the Dramatic Action. Now plastic Mimicry will listen to the passionate plaint of Thought; now resolute Thought will pour itself into the expressive mould of Gesture ; now Tone must vent alone the stream of Feeling, the shudder of alarm ; and now, in mutual embrace, all three will raise the Will of Drama to imme-diate and potent Deed. (For One thing there is that all the three united arts must will, in order to be free: and that one thing is the Drama : the reaching of the Drama's aim must be their common goal. Are they conscious of this aim, do they put forth all their will to work out that alone :

as though the idea were, in the former case, that of what agriculturists call a "top-dressing," and thus a substance which could break up the lower soil and make it fruitful. The "it" which occurs after the colon may refer either to the "feeling" or to the "orchestra," for both are neuter nouns.—Tr.

so will they also gain the power to lop off from their several stems the egoistic offshoots of their own peculiar being; that therewith the tree may not spread out in formless mass to every wind of heaven, but proudly lift its wreath of branches, boughs and leaves, into its lofty crown.

The nature of Man, like that of every branch of Art, is manifold and over-fruitful : but *one thing* alone is the *Soul* of every unit, its most imperious bent (*Nothwendigster Trieb*), its strongest need-urged impulse.   When this One Thing is recognised by man as his fundamental essence, then, to reach this One and indispensable, he has power to ward off every weaker, subordinated appetite, each feeble wish, whose satisfaction might stand between him and Its attainment.   Only the weak and impotent knows no imperious, no mightiest longing of the soul : for him each instant is ruled by accidental, externally incited appetites which, for reason that they are but appetites, he never can allay; and therefore, hurled capriciously from one upon another, to and fro, he never can attain a real enjoyment. But should this need-reft one have strength to obstinately follow the appeasement of his accidental appetite, there then crop up in Life and Art those hideous, unnatural apparitions, the parasites of headlong egoistic frenzy, which fill us with such untold loathing in the murderous lust of despots, or in the wantonness of—modern operatic music. If the individual, however, feel in himself a mighty longing, an impulse that forces back all other desires, and forms the necessary inner urgence which constitutes his soul and being; and if he put forth all his force to satisfy it : he thus will also lift aloft his own peculiar force, and all his special faculties, to the fullest strength and height that e'er can lie within his reach.

But the individual man, in full possession of health of body, heart, and mind, can experience no higher need than that which is common to all his kind ; for, to be a *true* Need, it can only be such an one as he can satisfy in Community alone.   The most imperious and strongest need of full-fledged artist-man, however, is to impart himself in highest compass of his being to the fullest expression of Community ; and this he only reaches with the necessary breadth of general understanding in the *Drama.* In Drama he broadens out his own particular being, by the portrayal of an individual personality not his own, to a universally human being. He must completely step outside himself, to grasp the inner nature of an alien personality with that completeness which is needful before he can portray it. This he will only attain when he so exhaustively analyses this individual in his contact with and penetration and completion by other individualities,—and therefore also the nature of these other individualities themselves,—when he forms thereof so lively a conception, that he gains a sympathetic feeling of this complementary influence on his own interior being. The perfectly artistic Performer is, therefore, the unit Man expanded to the *essence of the Human Species* by the utmost evolution of his own particular nature.

The place in which this wondrous process comes to pass, is the *Theatric stage ;* the collective art-work which it brings to light of day, the *Drama.* But to force his own specific nature to the highest blossoming of its contents in this *one* and highest art-work, the separate artist, like each several art, must quell each selfish, arbitrary bent toward untimely bushing into outgrowths unfurthersome to the whole ; the better then to put forth all his strength for reaching of the highest common purpose, which cannot indeed be realised without the unit, nor, on the other hand, without the unit's recurrent limitation.

This purpose of the Drama, is withal the only true artistic purpose that ever can be fully *realised ;* whatsoever lies aloof from that, must necessarily lose itself in the sea of things indefinite, obscure, unfree. This purpose, however, the separate art-branch will never reach *alone,** but only *all*

* The modern *Playwright* will feel little tempted to concede that Drama ought not to belong exclusively to *his* branch of art, the art of *Poesy ;* above all will he not be able to constrain himself to share it with the Tone-poet,—to wit, as he understands us, allow the Play to be swallowed up by the Opera.

N

together ; and therefore the most *universal* is at like time the only real, free, the only universally *intelligible* Art-work.

(Continuation of Footnote, page 193).

Perfectly correct !—so long as Opera subsists, the Play must also stand, and, for the matter of that, the Pantomime too ; so long as any dispute hereon is thinkable, the Drama of the Future must itself remain un-thinkable.   If, however, the Poet's doubt lie deeper, and consist in this, that he cannot conceive how *Song* should be entitled to usurp entirely the place of spoken dialogue : then he must take for rejoinder, that in two several regards he has not as yet a clear idea of the character of the Art-work of the Future.   Firstly, he does not reflect that Music has to occupy a very different position in this Art-work to what she takes in modern Opera : that only where her power is the *fittest*, has she to open out her full expanse ; while, on the contrary, wherever another power, for instance that of dramatic Speech, is the most *necessary*, she has to subordinate herself to that ; still, that Music possesses the peculiar faculty of, without entirely keeping silence, so imperceptibly linking herself to the thought-full element of Speech that she lets the latter seem to walk abroad alone, the while she still supports it.   Should the poet acknowledge this, then he has to recognise in the second place, that thoughts and situations to which the lightest and most restrained accompaniment of Music should seem importunate and burdensome, can only be such as are borrowed from the spirit of our modern Play ; which, from beginning to end, will find no inch of breathing-space within the Art-work of the Future.   The Man who will portray himself in the Drama of the Future has done for ever with all the prosaic hurly-burly of fashionable manners or polite intrigue, which our modern " poets " have to tangle and to disentangle in their plays, with greatest circumstantiality.   His nature-bidden action and his speech are : Yea, yea ! and Nay, nay !—and all beyond is evil, *i.e.* modern and superfluous.—R. WAGNER.

V.

THE ARTIST OF THE FUTURE.

AVING sketched in general outline the nature of the Art-work into which the whole art-family must be absorbed, to be there redeemed by universal understanding, it remains to ask: What are the life-conditions which shall summon forth the Necessity of this Art-work and this redemption? Will this be brought about by Modern Art, in impatient need of understanding, from out her own pre-meditated plan, by arbitrary choice of means, and with fixed prescription of the 'modus' of the union that she has recognised as necessary? Will she be able to draw up a constitutional chart, a tariff of agreement with the so-called un-culture of the Folk? And if she brought herself to stoop to this, would such an agreement be actually effected by that 'constitution'? Can Cultured Art press forward from her abstract standpoint *into Life*; or rather, must not *Life press forward into Art,*—Life *bear* from out itself its only fitting Art, and mount up into that,—instead of art (well understood: the *Cultured Art*, which sprang from regions outside Life) *engendering Life* from out herself and mounting thereinto?

Let us therefore first agree as to *whom* we must consider the creator of the Art-work of the Future; so that we may argue back from him to the life-conditions which alone can permit his art-work and himself to take their rise.

Who, then, will be the *Artist of the Future?*

Without a doubt, the Poet.*

---

* We must beg to be allowed to regard the *Tone*-poet as included in the *Word*-poet,—whether personally or by fellowship, is here a matter of indifference.—R. WAGNER.

But *who* will be the Poet?

Indisputably the *Performer* * (*Darsteller*).

Yet *who*, again, will be the Performer?

Necessarily the *Fellowship of all the Artists.*—

In order to see the Performer and the Poet take natural rise, we must first imagine to ourselves the artistic Fellowship of the future; and that according to no arbitrary canon, but following the logical course which we are bound to take in drawing from the Art-work itself our conclusions as to those artistic organs which alone can call it into natural life.—

The Art-work of the Future is an associate work, and only an associate demand can call it forth.   This demand, which we have hitherto merely treated theoretically, as a necessary essential of the being of each separate branch of art, is practically conceivable only in the *fellowship of every artist*; and the union of every artist, according to the exigencies of time and place, and for *one definite aim*, is that which forms this fellowship.   This definite aim is the *Drama*, for which they all unite in order by their participation therein to unfold their own peculiar art to the acme of its being; in this unfoldment to permeate each other's essence, and as fruit thereof to generate the living, breathing, moving drama.   But the thing that makes this sharing possible to all—nay that renders it necessary, and which without their coöperation can never come to manifestment —is the very kernel of the Drama, the *dramatic Action* (*dramatische Handlung*).

The dramatic Action, as the first postulate of Drama, is withal that moment in the entire art-work which ensures its widest *understanding*.   Directly borrowed from *Life*, past or present, it forms the intelligible bond that links

---

* The terms derived from the root "*dar-stellen*"—to set, or show, forth— have been used throughout this essay so frequently and so variously, that I deem it necessary to call attention to the fact that in English we have no thoroughly satisfactory equivalent.   I have, therefore, been obliged to render this concept by distinct expressions : sometimes as "performer," again as "executant," "actor," "representant," &c. ; while in the *verb*al sense I have taken refuge in "portray," "display," "perform," "impersonate," &c.—Tr.

this work therewith ; exactly in degree as it mirrors back the face of Life, and fitly satisfies its claim for understanding. The dramatic Action is thus *the bough from the Tree of Life* which, sprung therefrom by an unconscious instinct, has blossomed and shed its fruit obediently to vital laws, and now, dissevered from the stem, is *planted in the soil of Art ;* there, in new, more beautiful, eternal life, to grow into the spreading tree which resembles fully in its inner, necessary force and truth the parent tree of actual Life. But now, become its ' objectivation,' it upholds to Life the picture of its own existence, and lifts unconscious Life to conscious knowledge of itself.

In the dramatic Action, therefore, the Necessity of the art-work displays itself ; without *it*, or some degree of reference thereto, all art-fashioning is arbitrary, unneedful, accidental, unintelligible. The first and truest fount of Art reveals itself in the impulse that urges from *Life* into the work of art ; for it is the impulse to bring the unconscious, instinctive principle of Life to understanding (*verständniss*) and acknowledgment as Necessity. * But the impulse toward agreement (*verständigung*) presupposes *commonality :* the Egoist has need of no one with whom to agree. Therefore, only from a life in common, can proceed the impulse toward intelligible objectification of this life by Art-work ; the Community of artists alone can give it vent ; and only in communion, can they content it. This impulse, however, can only find its full contentment in the faithful representation of an episode (*Handlung*) taken from Life : whilst only such an episode can be a fitting subject for artistic Treatment as has already come in Life to definite conclusion ; as to which, as a series of causes and effects,†

* If we substitute " Will " for " Necessity " in this sentence (see footnote on page 69) we shall here obtain a complete summary of Schopenhauer's system of æsthetics ; while, even as it stands, it significantly foreshadows E. von Hartmann's " *Philosophy of the Unconscious.*"—TR.

† " Über die als reine Thatsache kein zweifel mehr vorhanden ist "—to translate this sentence literally, " as a matter of fact," could only be misleading. Taken apart from the context, it might then be read as a confession of faith in the realistic school ; whereas the whole passage shows that Wagner

there can no longer be any doubt ; and as to whose possible
issue there is no longer room for arbitrary assumption.
Only when a thing has been consummated in Life, can we
grasp the necessity of its occurrence, the harmony of its
separate movements.   But an episode is not completed,
until the *Man* who brought it about—who stood in the
focus of a series of events which, as a feeling, thinking,
will-ing person, he guided by the force of his own innate
character,—until this man is likewise no longer subject to
our arbitrary assumptions as to his possible doings.   Now,
every man is subject to these so long as he lives : by Death
is he first freed from this subjection, for then we know All
that he did, and that he was.   That action, therefore, must
be the best fitted for dramatic art—and the worthiest object
of its rendering—which is rounded off together with the
life of the chief person that evolved it, and whose denouement is none other than the conclusion of the life of this
one man himself.

Only that action is completely truthful — and can
thoroughly convince us of its plain necessity—on whose
fulfilment a man had set the whole strength of his being,
and which was to him so imperative a necessity that he
needs must pass over into it with the whole force of his
character.   But hereof he conclusively persuades us by this
alone : that, in the effectuation of his personal force, he
literally *went under*, he veritably threw overboard his
personal existence, for sake of bringing to the outer world
the inner Necessity which ruled his being.*   He proves to
us the verity of his nature, not only in his actions—which
might still appear capricious so long as he yet were doing

went strongly for a search below the incidental surface for the broad principles of life that govern human action.   Witness, that, of the two schemes
with which he was at this time busied, *Barbarossa* and *Siegfried*, he abandoned
the historical in favour of the mythical.—Tr.

   * In the original, the passage runs : " um der entäusserten Nothwendigkeit
seines Wesens willen " ; it is impossible, however, to convey the idea of
' renunciation ' connoted by the term " entäusserung " (as employed in the next
sentence) at like time with that of the—so to speak—' turning inside out ' of
a man's character.—Tr.

—but by the consummated sacrifice of his personality to this necessary course of action. The last, completest renunciation (*Entäusserung*) of his personal egoism, the demonstration of his full ascension into universalism, a man can only show us by his *Death ;* and that not by his accidental, but by his *necessary* death, the logical sequel to his actions, the last fulfilment of his being.

The celebration of such a Death is the noblest thing that men can enter on. It reveals to us in the nature of this one man, laid bare by death, the whole content of universal human nature.   But we fix this revelation in surest hold of memory by the conscious *representation* of that Death itself and, in order to make its purport clear to us, by the representation of those actions which found their necessary conclusion in that death.*   Not in the repulsive funeral rites which, in our neo-christian mode of life, we solemnise by meaningless hymns and churchyard platitudes; but by the artistic re-animation of the lost one, by life-glad reproduction and portrayal of his actions and his death, in the dramatic Art-work, shall we celebrate that festival which lifts us living to the highest bliss of love for the departed, and turns his nature to our own.

Though the longing for this dramatic rite is present in the whole brotherhood of artists, and though *that* object alone can be a worthy one, and one that justifies the impulse toward its representation, which awakes in us this impulse *in common :* yet that *Love* which alone can be conceived as the active and effectual power hereto, has its unfathomable seat within the heart of each separate unit ; in whom it exercises its specific motive force in accordance with his individual characteristics.   This specific energy of Love will therefore show itself most strenuously in that unit who, by reason of his general character, or in this particular period of his life, feels drawn by the closest bond of affinity toward this particular Hero ; who by his

---

* We must not forget that, only a few months before writing this essay, Wagner had prepared a sketch for a tragedy on the subject of *Jesus of Nazareth.* —Tr.

sympathy makes the nature of this hero the most especially his own, and trains his artistic faculties the fittest to re-quicken by his impersonation this hero, of all others, for the living memory of himself, his fellows, and the whole community. The *might of individuality* will never assert itself more positively than in the free artistic fellowship ; since the incitation to resolves in common can only issue from precisely that unit in whom the individuality speaks out so strongly that it determines the *free* voices of the rest. The might of Individuality, however, will only be able to operate thus upon the fellowship in those specific cases where it has the wit to bring itself to real, and not to merely artificial, currency. Should an art-comrade pro-claim his purpose to represent this one particular Hero, and thereto crave that mutual co-operation of the fellow-ship which alone can bring this to effect : he will not see his wish fulfilled until he has succeeded in arousing for his project the same love and enthusiasm which inspire him-self, and which he can only impart to others when his individuality stands possessed of a force in complete accord with the specific object.

When once the artist has raised his project to a *common* one, by the energy of his own enthusiasm, the artistic undertaking becomes thenceforth *itself an enterprise in common*. But as the dramatic action to be represented has 'its focus in the Hero of that action, so does the com-mon art-work group itself around the *Representant* of this hero. His fellow-actors, and all his other colleagues, bear to him the same relation in the *art*-work as that which the co-enacting persons—those, that is to say, who formed the foils of the hero's character and the ' objects' of his action, —and, withal, the general human and natural entourage,— bore in *Life* to the Hero ; only with this difference, that the hero's impersonator shapes and arranges *consciously* that which came *instinctively* to the actual hero. In his stress for artistic reproduction of the Action, the performer thus becomes a poet ; he arranges his own action, and all its living outward issues, in accordance with an artistic standard. But he only attains his special purpose in measure as he has raised it to a general aim, as every unit is clamorous to lend himself to the furtherance of this general aim,—therefore in exact measure as he himself, above all others, is able to surrender his own specific personal purpose to the general aim ; and thus, in a sense, not merely *represents* in the art-work the action of the fêted hero, but *repeats* its moral lesson ; insomuch as he proves by this surrender of his personality that he also, in his artistic action, is obeying a dictate of Necessity which consumes the whole individuality of his being.*

The *free Artistic Fellowship* is therefore the foundation, and the first condition, of the Art-work itself. From it proceeds the *Performer*, who, in his enthusiasm for this one particular hero whose nature harmonises with his own, now raises himself to the rank of *Poet*, of artistic *Lawgiver* to the fellowship ; from this height, again, to descend to complete absorption in the fellowship. The function of this lawgiver is therefore never more than *periodic*, and is confined to the one particular occasion which has been prompted by his individuality and thereby raised to a common 'objective' for the art of all ; wherefore his rule can by no means be extended to *all* occasions. The dic-

* Whilst we here have only touched upon the *Tragic* element of the Artwork of the Future, in its evolution out of Life, and by artistic fellowship, we may infer its *Comic* element by reversing the conditions which bring the Tragic to a natural birth. The hero of the Comedy will be the obverse of the hero of the Tragedy. Just as the one instinctively directed all his actions to his surroundings and his foils—as a Communist, *i.e.* as a unit who of his inner, free Necessity, and by his force of character, ascends into the Generality—so the other in his rôle of Egoist, of foe to the principle of Generality, will strive to withdraw himself therefrom, or else to arbitrarily direct it to his sole self-interest ; but he will be withstood by this principle of generality in its most multifarious forms, hard pressed by it, and finally subdued. The Egoist will be *compelled* to ascend into *Community* ; and *this* will therefore be the virtual enacting, many-headed personality which will ever appear to the action-wishing, but never can-ning, egoist as a capriciously changing Chance ; until it fences him around within its closest circle and, without further breathing-space for his self-seeking, he sees at last his only rescue in the unconditional acknowledgment of its necessity. The artistic Fellowship, as the representative of Generality, will therefore have in Comedy an even directer share in the framing of the poem itself, than in Tragedy.—R. WAGNER.

tatorship of the poet-actor comes to its natural close together with the attainment of his specific purpose: that
purpose which he had raised into a common one, and in
which his personality was dissolved so soon as ever his
message had been shared with the community.   Each
separate member may lift himself to the exercise of this
dictatorship, when he bears a definite message which so
far answers to his individuality that in its proclamation he
has power to raise it to a common purpose.   For in that
artistic fellowship which combines for no other aim than
the satisfaction of a joint artistic impulse, it is impossible
that any other thing should come to definite prescription
and resolve, than that which compasses the mutual satisfaction of this impulse: namely, Art herself, and the laws
which summon forth her perfect manifestment by the union
of the individual with the universal.—

In all the mutual federations of the Manhood of the
Future, these selfsame laws of *inner* necessity will assert
their sole determinative might.   A natural and unforced
association of men in larger or in smaller numbers, can
only be called forth by a need they feel in common.   The
satisfaction of this need is the exclusive aim of the mutual
undertaking: toward this aim are directed the actions of
each unit, so long as the common need is alike his strongest
personal need ; this aim will then, and of itself, prescribe
the laws for the associate action.   For these laws are
nothing but the fittest means for reaching the common
goal.   The knowledge of the fittest means is denied to him
who is urged towards this goal by no sincere, imperative
need : but where the latter is at hand, the certain knowledge of these means springs self-taught from the cogence
of the need, and above all, from its communal character.
Natural unions have, therefore, only so long a natural
continuance as the need on which they are grounded is a
common one, and as its satisfaction is still to be accomplished : has the goal been reached, then this specific
union is dissolved *together* with the need that called it

forth ; and first from fresh-arising needs will there likewise rise fresh unions of those who share these novel needs in common.   Our modern *States* are thus far the most un-natural unions of fellow men, that—called into existence by mere external caprice, *e.g.* dynastic interests—they yoke together a certain number of men *for once and all*, in furtherance of an aim which either never answered to a need they shared in common, or, from the change of time and circumstance, is certainly no longer common to them now.—*All* men have but *one* lasting need in common ; a need, however, which only in its most general purport abides in them in equal measure : this is the need *to live and to be happy*.   Herein lies the natural bond of all mankind ; a need to which our mother Earth may give us perfect answer.

In the reasonable state of Future Manhood, the special needs which take their rise, and mount aloft, in time and place and individuality, can alone lay down the bases of those special unions whose sum-total will make out the great association of *all* Mankind.   These Unions will alternate, shape themselves afresh, unloose and knit themselves again, precisely as the Needs shall change and come back on their course.   They will be lasting where they are of material sort, where they are rooted in the common ground and soil, and in general affect the intercourse of men in so far as this is necessarily founded on certain like-remaining, local limitations.   But they will ever shape themselves anew, proclaim more complex and vivacious change, the more do they proceed from higher, universal, spiritual needs.   Against the stiff political union of our time, upheld alone by outward force, the *free* communions of the Future in their pliant change—now spread out to bounds unheard-of, now linked in finest meshes—will display the future Human Life itself, whose inexhaustible charm will be preserved by ceaseless alternation of the richest individualities ; whereas our present life,* with its fashion and red-tape uniformity, affords alas ! the but too

* And especially our modern Theatrical institutions.—R. WAGNER.

faithful likeness of the modern *State*, with its *stations*, its *posts*, its *vested* interests,* its *standing* armies—and whatever else it has of *standing.*

Yet no alliances of men will enjoy a richer, more eventful change than those inspired by *Art.* For in these each individuality, so soon as ever it has wit to utter itself in consonance with the spirit of community, will, by the exposition of its passing purpose, call forth a fresh alliance to realise that *one specific* purpose ; inasmuch as it will widen out its own particular need to the Need of a brotherhood which this very need will have summoned into being. Each dramatic art-work, as it enters upon life, will therefore be the work of a new and never-hitherto-existing, and thus a never-to-be-repeated fellowship of artists : its communion will take its rise from the moment when the poet-actor of the hero's rôle exalts his purpose to the common aim of the comrades whom he needed for its exposition, and will be dissolved the very instant that this purpose is attained.

In this wise naught can pass into a standstill, in this artistic union : it is formed for the one sole aim, attained today, of celebrating this one particular hero ; to be tomorrow, under entirely fresh conditions, and through the inspiring purpose of an entirely different individual, resolved into a fresh association. While this fresh association will be as distinct from that preceding it, as it will bring its work to light of day according to *specific laws* which, constituting the fittest means for the realisation of the new-adopted scheme, will evince themselves as likewise new and never matched quite *thus* before.†

Thus, and thus only, must the future Artist-guild be constituted, so soon as ever it is banded by no other aim than that of the *Art-work.* Who, then, will be the *Artist of*

---

* " *Stand*-rechten," generally employed to signify a ' court-martial.' The whole group of derivatives from the root-idea of 'standing' reads thus :— "das getreue Abbild des modernen *Staates*, mit seinen *Ständen, Anstellungen, Stand*rechten, *stehenden* Heeren—und was sonst noch Alles in ihm *stehen* möge" ; the italics being reproduced from the original.—TR.

† See *Meistersinger*, Act 3.—*Walther :* " Wie fang ich nach der Regel an ? "—*Hans Sachs :* " Ihr stellt sie selbst, und folgt ihr dann."—TR.

the Future? The poet? The performer? The musician?
The plastician?—Let us say it in one word: the *Folk*.
*That selfsame Folk to whom we owe the only genuine Art-
work, still living even in our modern memory, however much
distorted by our restorations; to whom alone we owe all
Art itself.*

When we repiece the past and consummated, in order to
conjure up the picture of a particular object in the light of
its general bearings on the history of mankind, we can depict
its singlest traits with surest touch,—nay, from the minute
regardal of such single traits there often springs for us the
surest understanding of the whole, which we are forced to
rescue from its hazy generalism by holding to this one
particular feature. Thus in our present inquiry into the
phenomena of Art, the wealth of details that confront us is
so excessive that, in order to present our object in its
general bearings, we can only venture to select a limited
portion, and that which seems the best to illustrate our line
of thought; lest otherwise we lose ourselves in branching
by-ways, and our eyes be turned aside from the higher
general goal. Now the case is exactly opposite, when we
desire to portray a future state of things; we have only one
scale for such a picture, and that lies, decidedly not in the
spaces of the Future, on which the combination is to shape
itself, but in the Past and in the Present; even there where
all those conditions are still in lusty life which make the
longed-for future state impossible to-day, and allow its sheer
antithesis to seem an unavoidable necessity. The force of
Need impels us to a general preconception; yet we can
only grasp it, not simply by an ardent aspiration of the
heart, but rather by a logical induction which tells us that
this state will be the very opposite of the evil which we
recognise in our system of to-day. All individual features *

* Whosoever is unable to lift himself above his thraldom to the trivial,
unnatural system of our Modern Art, will be sure to pose the vapidest of
questions anent these details; to throw out doubts; to decline to understand.

must stay, perforce, outside this preconception ; since such could only figure as arbitrary assumptions of our phantasy, and must constantly bewray their nature as borrowed from the bad conditions of the present day. Only the consummated and fulfilled, can be matter of our knowledge ; the lifelike shaping of the Future must be the work of Life itself alone ! When this is brought to pass, we shall conceive at the first glance what to-day we could only palm off upon ourselves by the exercise of whim and fancy, submitted as we are to the insuperable influence of our present plight.

Nothing has been more destructive of human happiness, than this frenzied haste to regulate the Life of the Future by given present laws. This loathly care about the Future, which indeed is the sole heritage of moody, absolute Egoism, at bottom seeks but to *preserve*, to *ensure* what we possess to-day, for all our lifetime. It holds fast to Property—the to-all-eternity to be clinched and riveted, *property*—as the only worthy object of busy human forethought, and therefore seeks to do its best to swathe the Future's self-moved limbs, to pluck out by the roots its self-shaping quick of Life, as a poisonous and maddening sting ; in order to protect from every careless jog this undying fund of Property, that it may ever re-engender and swell out the fodder for its comfortable chewing and devouring, by the natural law of five per cent. Just as in this chief anxiety of the modern State, Man is looked-on, to all future time, as an utterly feeble or eternally to-be-mistrusted being, which can only be maintained by Property, or restrained within the proper path by Law : so, in respect of Art and Artists, we view the *Art-institute* as the only safeguard of their common welfare. Without Academies, Statutes, and Institutions, Art seems to us to run the constant danger of—so to phrase it—giving up the ghost ; for we cannot reconcile a free,

That he should answer in advance the myriad possible doubts and questions of this sort, no one, surely, will demand of an author who addresses himself above all to the *thinking artist*, and not to the thick-headed modern art-industrial— no matter whether the latter's literary calling be critical or creative.—R. WAGNER. (Continuation of Footnote, page 205).

a self-determining activity with our modern notions of an
Artist. The reason of this, however, is that in sooth we
are no genuine Artists, no more than we are genuine Men.
And thus the feeling of our pitiful incapacity, entirely
brought upon ourselves by cowardice and weakness, casts
us back upon the everlasting care to frame fixed canons for
the Future ; by whose forcible upholding we, at bottom,
but ensure that we shall *never* be true Artists, and *never*
truthful Men.

So is it ! We always look towards the Future with the
eye of the Present, with the eye that can only measure all
future generations by the standard it has borrowed from
the Men of the Present, and sets up as the universal
standard of mankind. If we have finally proved that *the
Folk* must of necessity be the Artist of the future, we must
be prepared to see the intellectual egoism of the artists of
the Present break forth in contemptuous amazement at the
discovery. They forget completely that in the days of
national blood-brotherhood, which preceded the epoch when
the absolute Egoism of the individual was elevated to a
religion,—the days which our historians betoken as those of
prehistoric myth and fable,—the Folk, in truth, was already
the only poet, the only artist ; that all their matter, and all
their form—if it is to have any sound vitality—they can
derive alone from the fancy of these art-inventive Peoples.
On the contrary, they regard the Folk exclusively under
the aspect lent it nowadays by their culture-spectacled
eyes. From their lofty pedestal, they deem that only their
direct antithesis, the raw uncultured masses, can mean for
them " the Folk." As they look down upon the people,
there rise but fumes of beer and spirits to their nostrils ;
they fumble for their perfumed handkerchiefs, and ask with
civilised exasperation : " What ! The *rabble* is in future to
replace us in Art-making ? The rabble, which does not so
much as understand us, when *we* provide its art ? Out of
the reeking gin-shop, out of the smoking dung-heap, are we
to see arise the mould of Beauty and of Art ? "—

Quite so ! Not from the filthy dregs of your Culture of

to-day, not from the loathsome subsoil of your modern 'polite education,' not from the conditions which give your modern civilisation the sole conceivable base of its existence, shall arise the Art-work of the Future. Yet reflect! that this rabble is in no wise a normal product of real human nature, but rather the artificial outcome of your denaturalised culture; that all the crimes and abominations with which ye now upbraid this rabble, are only the despairing gestures of the battle which the true nature of Man wages against its hideous oppressor, modern Civilisation ; and that these revolting features are nowise the real face of Nature, but rather the reflection of the hypocritical mask of your State-, and Criminal-Culture. Further reflect : that, where one portion of the social system busies itself alone with *superfluous* art and literature, another portion must necessarily redress the balance by scavenging the dirt of your useless lives; that, where fashion and dilettantism fill up one whole unneedful life, there coarseness and grossness must make out the substance of another life,—a life ye cannot do without ; that, where need-less luxury seeks violently to still its all-devouring appetite, the natural Need can only balance its side of the account with Luxury by drudgery and want, amidst the most deforming cares.

So long as ye intellectual egoists and egoistic purists shall blossom in your artificial atmosphere, there must needs be somewhere a " stuff " from whose vital juices ye may distil your own sweet perfumes ; and this stuff, from which ye have sucked out all its inbred scent, is but that foul-breathed rabble whose approach inspires you with disgust, and from whom ye only ward yourselves by that very perfume ye have squeezed from out its native comeliness. So long as a great portion of any nation, installed in State, Judiciary, and University-posts, squanders its precious vital forces on the most useless of employments : so long must an equally great, or even greater portion replace those squandered forces by its own employment in the harshest tasks of bare Utility. And—saddest tale of all !—when in this disproportionately burdened section of the Folk the sheerest utilitarianism has thus become the moving spirit of all its energy, then must the revolting spectacle be exhibited of absolute Egoism enforcing its laws of life on every hand and, from the visage of the town and country rabble, reflecting back its hatefullest grimaces upon yourselves.*

However, neither you nor this rabble do we understand by the term, *the Folk :* only when neither Ye nor It shall exist any longer, can we conceive the presence of the Folk. Yet even now the Folk is living, wherever ye and the rabble are not; or rather, it is living in your twin midst, but ye wist not of it. Did ye *know* it, then were ye yourselves the Folk ; for no man can know the fulness of the Folk, without possessing a share therein. The highest educated alike with the most uneducated, the learned with the most unlearned, the high-placed with the lowly, the nestling of the amplest lap of luxury with the starveling of the filthiest den of Hunger, the ward of heartless Science with the wastrel of the rawest vice,—so soon as e'er he feels and nurtures in himself a stress which thrusts him out from cowardly indifference to the criminal assemblage of our social and political affairs, or heavy-witted submission thereunder,—which inspires him with loathing for the shallow joys of our inhuman Culture, or hatred for a Utilitarianism that brings its uses only to the need-less and never to the needy,—which fills him with contempt for those self-sufficient thralls, the despicable Egoists! or wrath against the arrogant outragers of human nature, —he, therefore, who *not* from this conglomerate of pride and baseness, of shamelessness and cringing, thus not from the *statutory rights* which hold this composite together, but from the fulness and the depth of naked *human nature* and the irrefutable right of its absolute Need, draws force for resistance, for revolt, for assault upon the oppressor of this nature,—he then who *must* withstand, revolt, and deal

* It would almost seem that the author had caught a slight foreboding of the character of the latest Parisian " Commune."—The Editor. (Tr.—*i.e.* of the edition of 1872 ; in other words—Richard Wagner.)

assault, and openly avows this plain necessity in that he
gladly suffers every other sorrow for its sake, and, if need
should be, will even offer up his life,—*he, and he alone
belongs to the Folk ;* for he and all his fellows feel a common *Want.*

This *Want* will give the Folk the mastery of Life, will
raise it to the only living might. *This Want* once drove
the *Israelites,* already turned to dull and sordid beasts of
burden, through the waters of the salt Red Sea ; and
through the Red Sea also must Want drive *us,* if we are
ever, cleansed from shame, to reach the promised land.
We shall not drown beneath its waves ; it is fatal only to
the Pharaohs of this world, who once with host and cap-
tains, with horse and rider, were swallowed up therein,—
those haughty, overweening Pharaohs who had forgotten
that once a poor herdsman's son had through his prudent
counsels saved their land and them from death by hunger !
But the *Folk,* the *chosen people,* passed scathless through
that sea towards the Land of Promise : and reached it
when the desert sand had washed its body of the last
remaining stain of slavery.—

Since the poor Israelites have led me thus into the region
of the fairest of all poetry, the ever fresh and ever truthful
poems of the Folk, I will take my leave—by way of moral
—with the outline of a glorious Saga which long ago the
raw, uncultured Folk of oldtime Germany indited for no
other reason than that of inner, free Necessity.

Wieland the Smith, out of very joy in his handiwork,
forged cunning trinkets for himself, and weapons keen and
fair to see.   One day as he was bathing on the shore, he
saw a Swan-maiden (*Schwanenjungfrau*) come flying with
her sisters through the air and, putting off her swan-
apparel, plunge down into the sea.   Aflame with sudden
love, he rushed into the deeper waters ; he wrestled with,
and won the wondrous woman.   Love, too, broke down

her pride; in tender care for one another, they lived in blissful union.

A ring the Swan-maid gave to Wieland: this must he never let her win back from him; for greatly as she loved him, she had not lost her yearning for her ancient Freedom, for wind-borne passage to her happy island home; and this ring it was, that gave her strength to wing her flight. So Wieland wrought a goodly store of rings alike to that his Swan-wife gave him, and strung them on a hempen cord against his wall: amongst them all she should not recognise her own.

He came home once from journeying. Alack! There lay his house in ruins; his wife had flown away to farthest distance!

There was a King, *Neiding* (Envy) by name, who had heard much talk of Wieland's skill; he burned to trap the Smith, that thenceforth he might work for him alone. He found at last a valid pretext for such a deed of violence: the vein of gold which Wieland wrought into his smitheries belonged to Neiding's ground and soil; thus Wieland's art was a robbery of the royal possessions.—It was he who burst into the smithy; and now he fell upon the Smith himself; bound him with chains, and bore him off.

Set down in Neiding's court, Wieland must hammer for the King all kinds of objects, useful, strong, and durable: harness, tools, and armour, by aid of which the King might broaden-out his realm. But since, for such a labour, Neiding must loose the captive's bonds, his care was how to leave his body free to move, yet hinder him from flight: and so he craftily bethought him of severing the sinews of poor Wieland's feet. For he rightly guessed that the Smith had only need of hands, and not of feet, to do his work.

Thus sate he then, in all his misery, the art-rich Wieland, the one-time blithesome wonder-smith: crippled, behind his anvil, at which he now must slave to swell his master's wealth; limping, lamed, and loathly, whene'er he strove to stand erect! Who might measure all his suffering, when he thought back to his Freedom, to his Art,—to his beloved wife! Who fathom all his grudge against this King, who had wrought him such an untold shame!

From his forge he gazed above to Heaven's blue, through which the Swan-maid once had flown to him; this air was her thrice-happy realm, through which she soared in blissful freedom, the while he breathed the smithy's stench and fume—all for the service of King Neiding's use! The shamed and self-bound man, should he never find his wife again!

Ha! since he was doomed to wretchedness for ever, since nevermore should joy or solace bloom for him,—if he yet might gain at least one only thing: Revenge, revenge upon this Neiding, who had brought him to this endless sorrow for his own base use! If it were only possible to sweep this wretch and all his brood from off the earth!—

Fearsome schemes of vengeance planned he; day by day increased his misery; and day by day grew ranker the desperate longing for revenge.—But how should he, the halting cripple, make ready for the battle that should lay his torturer low? One venturous forward step; and he must fall dishonoured to the ground, the plaything for his foeman's scorn!

"Thou dearest, distant wife! Had I thy wings! Had I thy wings, to wreak my vengeance, and swing myself aloft from out this shame!"—

Then *Want itself* bent down its mighty pinions above the tortured Wieland's breast, and fanned its inspiration about his thoughtful brow. From *Want*, from terrible, all-powerful Want, the fettered artist learnt to mould what no man's mind had yet conceived. *Wieland found it: found how to forge him WINGS. Wings* whereon to mount aloft to wreak revenge on his tormentor,—*Wings*, to soar through Heaven's distance to the blessed island of his Wife!—

He did it: he fulfilled *the task that utmost Want had set*

within him. Borne on *the work of his own Art,* he flew aloft; he rained his deadly shafts into King Neiding's heart;—he swung himself in blissful, daring flight athwart the winds, to where he found the loved one of his youth.—

O sole and glorious Folk! This is it, that thou thyself hast sung. Thou art thyself this Wieland! Weld thou thy wings, and soar on high!

WIELAND THE SMITH,

A DRAMATIC SKETCH.

"WIELAND DER SCHMIEDT,

ALS DRAMA ENTWORFEN."

In a letter to Uhlig, of Dec. 27th, 1849, Wagner writes: "*So on January 16th I go to Paris, and I shall take my completed opera-scheme: it is* Wiland der Schmied."—*And again, March 13th, 1850:* "*I have now only to write the verses to my* Wiland; *otherwise the whole poem is finished— German, German! How my pen flew along! This Wiland will carry you all away on his wings, even your friendly Parisian hopes." In a letter to the Princess Wittgenstein (Wagner-Liszt Correspondence), Oct. 8th, 1850, he says:* "*You ask me about my* Wiland. *I have more designs than I have the power to execute. I beg you to persuade Liszt to undertake the musical execution of* Wiland *in my stead. . . . It takes me back to a time to which I do not want to be taken back. I cannot finish the poem* now, *either in words or music. . . . The design is quite complete; all that remains to be done is simple versification; . . . in the more important places I have already written the verses myself. To do more is at present impossible to me; even the copying out cost me many a pang." On Jan. 3rd, 1851, Liszt writes:* "*Great as is the temptation to weld at your* Wiland, *I must abide by my resolution* never *to write a German opera.*"

The above extracts will explain the circumstance that some portions of this play are set out in dialogue, partly alliterative, while others are merely sketched in.

TRANSLATOR'S NOTE.

DRAMATIS PERSONÆ:

WIELAND,	.	.	.	.	a Smith.
EIGEL,	.	.	.	.	an Archer.
HELFERICH,	.	.	.	a Leech.
SCHWANHILDE.				
NEIDING,	.	.	.	.	King of the Niaren.
BATHILDE,	.	.	.	.	his Daughter.
GRAM,	.	.	.	.	his Marshal.

WIELAND, a Smith.
EIGEL, an Archer. } Brothers.
HELFERICH, a Leech.

FIRST ACT.

(The Mark of Norway. Forest-fringed sea-shore; in the fore-ground, at one side, Wieland's hut with its Smithy, open towards the front.)

First Scene.

IELAND, seated, hammers at a toy of gold; his brothers, *Eigel* and *Helferich* recline beside him, and watch his movements.—The Smith sings at his work, which is nearing its completion; he wishes it all power to lend the woman who shall wear it an ever newborn charm in the eyes of her beloved, for :—" Ye must avow that wives have need of charm and beauty, would they bind their husbands to them. Therefore a prudent man will have a care that the fair he 'd love for ever, shall never want for any charm. See, my brothers, how I care for you : these trinkets have I forged for your dear wives. Two bracelets are they; I share them 'twixt you twain."

Eigel and *Helferich* express their joy and praise; they thank their brother, and ask how they may recompense him ?

Wieland. "Have I not wrought from love to you ? Your wives can I rightly homage from naught but loyal

love! No King has power to bid me what I gladly do.—
But Eigel, fathom what I 've forged for thee?"

Eigel. "A fresh-won boon? For sure, thou 'st sat too
long a-lonely, there by th' forge; famish'd wert thou, had
I not brought my chase-spoils to thee! Tell then, what so
toilfully thou madest?"

Wieland. "See here, this bow of steel for thee, when to
the hunt thou go'st!"

Eigel, enraptured, proves the bow, and lauds it as the
strongest, the farthest-straining and the fairest, that man
could ever gain.

Wieland. "So, for to-day, bring home a quiv'ring
quarry! To braver deeds thou once shalst bend it.—
Thou, Helferich, who wrest'st from fragrant herbs their
gifts of healing, for thee I 've shaped this graven flask of
gold, that thou mayest store the drink therein!"

Helferich, in marvel at the beauty of the phial, breaks
out in thanks that he now may bear the potion with him.

Wieland. "Soon shalt thou prove the potence of thine
art; for soon shall bloody strife arise in Viking's land, and
many a gaping wound shalst heal for Viking's noble scions!
One hero still there is, and him I love; see here this sword
that I have shaped for him. Dear brothers, bear this to
King Rothar! Against the Neidings shall he swing it,
who turn free Norseland's men to thralls!"

The Brothers. "What knowest thou of Rothar?"

Wieland. "Wachilde, sweetest of all sea-wives, who
bore our father once to royal Viking, arose from out those
waves to greet me, and gave me tidings. Full much has
she revealed to me,—of Wate, our lov'd father; how Viking
willed this coast to us for our free birthright; and how the
sons of Viking, born him by the daughter of a King, were
trodden down by evil chance; but Rothar blooms in hero's
manhood, and all are gathering around him who fain would
make a stand 'gainst Neiding's growing might. All this
and more I 'll tell ye, when evening falls, around our loving
board!"—

Helferich. "So come with us; the sun is sinking fast,

and thou hast surely brought to close the labours of thy
day. Who e'er has wrought such countless wonder-works
as thou?"

Eigel. "Yet let me hansel first my new-won bow, by
laying low some lordly prey! This even's meal 't shall,
Wieland, grace for thee!"

Helferich. "And thou shalt give us promise, to take
thee soon a wife ; that so our loving care may wax around
thee."

Wieland (whose gaze has bent regardful toward the sea, now cries
in haste). "See ye what flies there through the heavens?"

Eigel (following his glance). "Three wondrous fowl; their
like I ne'er yet saw!"

Helferich. "They draw nearer!"—

Eigel. "Hei! In troth they're maidens, soaring on the
breeze with wings of swan!"

Helferich. "Westwards goes their swift-wing'd flight!"

Wieland. "Meseems, that swiftness makes one sister
swoon ; her force is flagging!"—

Eigel. "Now they're vanished ; forestwards was bent
their flight."

Helferich (returning to the front with Eigel). "Whence-e'er
they came, *there* welters many a warrior."—

Eigel. "Shield-maidens were they, surely ; in Northland
stirred they strife." (To Wieland, who gazes still into the distance). "Up, Wieland, come! What star'st thou in the
sky? Where mine eye can spy out nothing, there truly
seest thou naught!"

Wieland (rapt and mournful, sighing deeply). "O that I too
could fly! I'd woo a wife upon the winds!"

Helferich. "Come with us to our meal!"

Wieland (without changing his posture). "Nay, then, prepare it ; anon I'll follow!" (The Brothers go.—Wieland ever
peers towards the sea.) "Ha! I see her hover down :—what
the archer saw not, that I sensed.—She's weary—wounded :
cannot hold her flight against the breeze!—She lags behind—sinks ever deeper—the wind is wafting her into the
waters!—Her strength is leaving her ; she plunges down

already to the flood !—Quick, Wieland ! In the sea-foam
thou, too, shalt net thy game ! "

(He dives into the sea, and swiftly swims ahead. After a span, one
sees him swimming back again. With one arm he bears the Swan-
maid, and gains with her the shore.)

Second Scene.

Schwanhilde (is brought fainting to the land by Wieland ; her
arms are swathed in mighty swan-wings, which hang down limp and
leaden). *Wieland* (lays her gently down upon a bank of moss,
beside the stithy). He discovers that she is wounded beneath
the left wing ; and, looking closer, recognises that the
Wings may be detached, and also how to effect this. He
tenderly removes the wings from arms and neck ; and sees,
enraptured, a lovely, perfect-shapen woman. Now he can
reach the wound securely, and finds that it has been dealt
by a spear-thrust. He recalls to mind the remedy that
Helferich had given him for such wounds ; and returns
with a healing herb. He lays it on the wound, and binds
it there. Then he listens to Schwanhilde's breathing. She
gradually regains her senses ; her eyelids open, and she
sees Wieland keeping ward. She shudders at her present
situation, for she deems that she is caught in Neiding's
toils. Wieland pacifies her :—tells her that she is rescued
from the sea and her wound is healed ; that she would
sorrily requite his saving deeds, by anger.—She weeps to
find her wings are stolen from her, and herself within a
stranger's power. "O Sisters, dearest, cruel Sisters !
Alack, ye 've left me helpless here behind ! How shall I
e'er our Mother find again ! " She sobs convulsively.

Wieland comforts her : "Though cast aside by loving
sisters, take thou my strength for shield. Thee, fairest,
sweetest maid, let me shelter with my life ! "—He succeeds
at last in calming her : he softly bids her spare herself,
that so the cure may be completed.—

Schwanhilde. "Then art thou not of Neiding's stem ? "
Wieland. "Nay, nay ! A foe to every Neiding am
I ; I 've newly forged the sword to mow them down. Free

dwell I with my brothers here ; no King can call us ' serf.'
—Yet tell thou me : who art thou, wondrous maid ? "

Schwanhilde is deeply moved by Wieland's love; she
would fain forget who she is and whence she came, since
now she feels that oblivion can but yield her higher comfort
than any memory !—She narrates to Wieland, who has
sate him down beside her, the story of her life :—King
Isang, in the North-land, was her mother's sire ; for this
mother the Prince of the Light-elves burnt with love : in
the form of a Swan he drew anigh her, and bore her off
across the sea to his distant " island home."   Close knit by
love, they dwelt there three full years ; until the mother,
seized with foolish doubting, hotly pressed her spouse to
tell her of his birthplace—a question he had from the first
forfended.   Then swam the Elf-prince down the flood, in
form of Swan once more ;—in reachless distance, saw the
sorrowing mother her husband rising on his wings into the
sea of clouds.   Three daughters had she borne him,
Schwanhilde and her sisters twain : and every year their
swan-wings sprouted ; and every year their mother stripped
their pinions and buried them from sight, for fear lest her
dear nestlings, too, might fly away.   But now they got
them tidings over sea : that good King Isang was fallen
prey to Neiding, was done to death, and his lands despoiled
from his heirs.   Then flamed the mother's breast with rage
and vengeance ; she longed to punish Neiding, and loud
bewailed that she had borne but daughters and no son ;
she therefore gave the maidens back their stored-up wing-
apparel, and bade them northwards fly as fleet Valkyrie,
to stir up vengeful strife against the Neiding.   So had
they stirred men's wrath, and with them striven against the
thievish King ; nor had they turned them homewards until
Schwanhilde met her wound.   Alack ! her force had failed,
as Wieland knew already, to follow farther in their flight.—
" Now am I at thy mercy ! "

Wieland is profoundly touched ; he swears to love her,
and never to forsake her.

Schwanhilde.   " Lov'st thou me truly ? "   She draws a

Ring from off her finger, and reaches it to Wieland.   "Lo!
this Ring will rouse thee Love's enchantment: wears it a
woman, the man who nighs her must straightway glow with
love to her-wards.   This, surely, 'twas alone that won for
me thy love."

Wieland, who has taken the Ring into his hand, feels
that his love is only heightened by her disarming; he begs
of her to never wear it more; he loves her even greater still
without it.

Schwanhilde, moved and quieted, yet counsels him to
never give the Ring away,—for it holds, for the *man* who
wears it, the victor-stone ensuring him the victory in every
combat.

Wieland will neither profit by this its virtue for himself;
he hangs it up behind his dwelling's door, upon a thread of
bast: "there hang thou; neither I, nor yet my Wife, have
need of thee!"—

Schwanhilde.   "My Wieland, must I now rejoice me in
thy love, and can I never wish to rouse thee pain or sorrow;
must I now will to dwell for ever with thee,—so take this
wingèd raiment; bury it deep, and close it fast!   For
should I gaze upon its plumes, and know them in my keeping,—how great soe'er my love for thee, I ne'er could lay
my heartfelt longing to swing myself aloft upon them.   So
blissful is the sense of flight, so sweet the soaring in the
clear blue sea of sky, that whoso once has tasted of it, can
never tear the yearning out; he needs must one day still
it, finds he the means to hand!"

Wieland, in terror at Schwanhilde's fervour, crushes the
feathered mail together.   "And Love, then, would not hold
thee?"—

Schwanhilde (sinks shuddering on Wieland's breast. She weeps
and cries): "Now fare ye well, beloved Sisters! Farewell,
thou dear forsaken Mother!   Schwanhilde see ye never
more!"

Wieland is unnerved by her love and grief.   Yet his care
for her arouses him once more: she is not wholly healed as
yet,—her brow is hot with fever.   He prays her that she

will pass into his hut, and rest her on his couch, the while he goes to seek his brother Helferich : the best-skilled leech is he, and soon will heal her ill completely.—He bears the tired maiden, who lays her loving arms around him, into the hut.—

Third Scene.

(Evening has completely fallen. A ship puts-to, at one side of the background ; from it *Bathilde* and her *Waiting-women* step cautiously to land. They peer around, to discover whether Wieland be present. When they shortly see him passing out of the hut again, they conceal themselves behind the bushes).

Wieland (in act to close the door, pauses and battles with the feeling that prompts him to turn back). " The Wings I have not hidden :—yet, sleeps she not, the tired sick one ? And come I not again before she wakens ?—Or should I nurse suspicion 'gainst her ? Should I fast-bind her as a captur'd prey ?—Nay, nay, in freedom shall she love me !" In a transport of joy, he quits the door. Then he turns round once more. "Still, should I close the door ?—Forsooth to hold her ?—Thou fool ! would she take wing, her flight should lightly find its way through chink or chimney to the open !—Yet sleeps she ; therefore close I fast the friendly door, that none disturb her." He turns the key, and passes swiftly from the scene, shouting aloud : "Now, Brothers, shall ye hear a wonder, how quickly I 've found me a Wife ! "

Bathilde (clad in armour, steps forward with her Women). "My runes I 've read aright ; hither flew the wounded Shield-maid, for well this shore is known for healing. For Wieland—Gram may entrap him ; the weightiest work I alone. Win I the Ring of the Swan-maid, then mistress am I of the mightiest gem ; my father shall thank me alone for his might."—(She approaches the door, and examines its lock.) " In troth, the cunningest lock that locksmith ever wrought ! Yet what is art of Man against the power of Magic ? "—She brushes the lock with a sprig of spurge ; the door opens

outwards of itself. On its rear flange Bathilde sees at once
Schwanhilde's Ring, hanging on the bast that Wiland had
fastened ; she recognises it and, loosing it from off the
thread, she closes fast the door once more.—

Fourth Scene.

(Fresh ships have reached the shore. *Gram* and his weaponed
Warriors set foot upon the land.—*Bathilde*, hiding the ring, goes
joyously towards them.)—" Now rightly have I led thee, Gram;
and speeds thy deed, my Father owes thee utmost thanks :
trapp'st thou the cunning Smith, that so he serve him must,
thou 'st won him more than doubled kingdom. Haste
forward to the forest; I thither saw him wend. That he
may willing follow, lay low whate'er he here holds dear or
worth. Burn down his house and home, that elsewhere he
must seek his weal."—The Warriors have withdrawn, to
search for Wieland ; burning brands are hurled into the
house.—

Gram declares in passionate heat, that for Bathilde and
at her bidding he is ready to fulfil the most daring, alike
with the most fearsome of deeds, might he ever hope to
win her hand.

Bathilde redes aright the magic power of the Ring o'er
him who erst was cold and sullen, and rejoices in the proof
of such a might. She bids him staunchly stand by her,
and she will give him guerdon ; with her he once shall rule
her Father's land. She takes her leave of him ; and with
her Women mounts her ship, on which she quits the shore.

From the hut is heard Schwanhilde's anguished cry :
" Wieland, Wieland !"—Shouts of tumult from the wood-
lands. Wieland is dragged-on by Gram's retainers ; to
overpower him, they have been compelled to throw a hood
across his eyes, which robs him yet of vision. He is bound
hand and foot, and in this condition is laid before Gram.

Gram. " Art Wieland, then, the wonder-smith ? "—
Wieland. " Who be ye, that ye should bind the Free ? "
Gram. " Art Wieland, who has wrought so many mar-
vels, then say whence thou hast won thy gold, if not by

theft from out these mountains' bosom, the booty of a King ?"—

Wieland. "The Gold ?—That will I truly tell thee. Thou know'st that once the Gods were robbed of fair Iduna, her who gave them youth eternal so long as e'er she tarried with them. Then agèd grew the Gods, their beauty faded, and Odur quitted Freia's side, since now no more her charm could bind him. The Gods re-won Iduna ; with her their youth and beauty came again,—but Odur turned not back to Freia. Upon those crags now sits the sad yet glorious Goddess, and weeps full many a hot and golden tear for her lost spouse ; these tears I reap from out the rivers whereinto they fall, and forge from them a store of winsome works, to gladden happy mortals !"

Gram. "Thou featly wagg'st thy tongue, yet liest not thyself into freedom ; for won'st thou e'en from Freia's tears the gold, yet these too are my master's booty, and for him alone shalst thou henceforth forge !"—He commands his men to bear the Smith to ship.

Wieland resists with all his might, and demands to know what has befallen his Wife.

Gram. "Where stayed thy Wife ?"

Wieland. "Within my home she sleeping lay."

Gram laughs in scorn, and tears the bandage from his eyes. "Look up ; there lies thy home !"

Wieland beholds his hut aglow with flame. He cries in horror : "Schwanhilde ! Schwanhilde ! Give me answer !" —No answer comes.—"Dead ! Burnt to ashes !—Vengeance !"—With terrible force he tears his fetters. "A bungler beat-out the iron !"—He snatches a sword from a stander-by, and sets upon Gram, who avoids the blow. Wieland sounds his horn. All draw back before his fury. His brothers, Eigel and Helferich, bring friends to his aid. Many of Gram's followers are slain ; Gram and the survivors flee towards the strand, leap on board ship, and row swiftly away. Wieland thunders curses at the routed, reviling them as cowards and murderers. He then turns hastily back to the front : his hut is a heap of burn-

P

ing ruins; no trace of Schwanhilde is left to sight. He
deems that she is burnt to death, and, seized with despair,
he fain would cast himself into the embers. His brothers
hold him back. He bursts away from them and, bent on
vengeance, determines to pursue the fugitives. He rushes
to the shore; no boat is there. A fallen tree-stem
lies on the brink: he thrusts it into the waves, to embark
thereon to smite the foe. His brothers warn him of the
impossibility of such a voyage: that in such wise he can
never overtake the dastards' flight; that he knows not
in what land to seek them, since none has recognised the
foemen or wots from whence they came. They pray him
go at once to Rothar, and bear him Wieland's Sword.
Wieland will not hearken to them. He calls upon his
grandam, the ocean-wife Wachilde; to her he commits his
care: may she stir the waves from the sea's deepest
bottom, that so they urge him to the distant shore where
he may wreak revenge.—He springs upon the log, and
with a stake he thrusts it off so sturdily that it gains the
open waters in a trice. While the Brothers wish him speed
on such a madcap venture, Wieland from the distance
shouts them back a last farewell.— —

Second Act.

(In Niarenland; King *Neiding's* court. The foreground shows the
Palace-hall; steps lead up from it, on the right to *Neiding's*, on the
left to *Bathilde's* dwelling-rooms. At the back, a broad stairway leads
to the courtyard below; this is surrounded with high walls of stone,
surmounted by a watch-tower.—It is shortly before daybreak.)

First Scene.

(*Bathilde* ushers *Gram* from out her chamber, down the steps,
into the Hall.)—Gram has been banished from court and
office by Neiding, in wrath at the failure of his attack on
Wieland. He has now ventured to approach Bathilde, to
pray her intercession with her father.—

Bathilde engages to fulfil his wish, and doubts not of
her mission's speed. She tells him that she holds a

potent jewel, which shall bend her Father to her will. Only one misgiving has she : Wieland is already here.

Gram is amazed and horror-stricken.

Bathilde. "Naught heardst thou of the wondrous advent of a man, who landwards came afloat upon a log ? The King has ta'en him friendly to him, for that he promised goodly service. Through precious works he wrought for him, the stranger hath made sure King Neiding's favour ; already hath my Sire forgot his trouble, that Wieland he could not trap. 'Goldbrand' dubs himself the Smith ; but Wieland is 't ; mine eyes be witness ! "

Gram. "What seeks he here, beneath a masking name ? "

Bathilde. "On vengeance set he forth, although at hazard ; for little weens he who his foeman is."

Gram. "Yet what withholds that he should farther journey ? "

Bathilde. "Revenge is reft him, now that Love enchains.—His wife he deemeth dead ; and thus forgets her, since another woman lights his love."

Gram. "Who worked such wonders on the wrathful ? "

Bathilde. "My presence only."

Gram. "So is he then my rival ? "

Bathilde. "That is he ; therefore shouldst thou help me to destroy him. Have trust in me ! This day shalt thou be callèd back, and taste again of highest honours. This win I from King Neiding, by power of the Ring."

Gram. "Sad is my mood, since I from Wieland fled."

Bathilde. "That let me venge upon him ! "

Gram. "E'er since I burnt so swift with love to thee, mischance hath dogged my ev'ry step."

Bathilde. "Yet for sake of that same love, shalt thou be lifted up by me ! Be thou but faithful ; spy on Wieland—how thou mayst venge thyself, and him destroy : with me shalt thou anon be ruler here ! "

Gram. "Shall then a stout and fearless man, as once I was, but thank at last a woman for his fame and honour ? "—

Bathilde. "Yet know, how stout and brave may be a woman!—Day breaks! So flee for now! This key take with thee for the postern; hide thee anigh: seest thou a kerchief waving white from out my window, then fearless come, and openly, into this hall; be that the token of thy weal!" He seeks to embrace her; she wards him off: "Once Wieland fallen, I am thine!"—(They part. *Bathilde* retires to her chamber; *Gram* descends into the courtyard, and passes out of sight.—Daybreak.)—

Second Scene.

(A loud knocking is heard at the great Gate of the courtyard. Two of Neiding's *Courtiers* leap up from the steps that lead to the King's apartments—on which they had hitherto lain stretched in sleep—and shout:) "Who's there?"

Answer. "Envoys from the land of Viking."

A Courtier. "To whom your envoie?"

Answer. "To the Bailie of the Niars, King Rothar sends us."

(The two Courtiers sound their horns; one of them goes toward Neiding's chamber, to rouse the King; the other descends into the court, to unbolt the great gate.)

(*Eigel* and *Helferich* rush in, on horseback; they dismount, and are conducted into the Hall by the Courtiers. In answer to the horn-call, Neiding's men have trooped on from different sides. The morning-drink is offered to the Envoys.)—

Neiding (descends the steps from his chamber). He greets the Envoys, and expresses his joy at receiving tidings from King Rothar. He orders the morning meal to be prepared, and takes his seat at the table head. The repast is served, and the Envoys and Courtiers take their places around the board, below the daïs.

Neiding asks:—the message must in truth have pressing moment, since the messengers take horse at night-time, when every man would rather rest?

Eigel. "Rest have we long renouncèd; 'twas robbed us, when an evil deed aroused our vengeance."

Helferich. "By day, by night, we seek the herb to heal a deadly hurt, which direful loss has wrought upon us."

Neiding. "What message woo ye for King Rothar?"

(During this dialogue the speakers have repeatedly struck each other's drinking-horns, and pledged.)

Eigel. "A goodly Sword we brought him, forged by our smith-skill'd brother."—

Helferich. "That Sword will Rothar wield in battle, and right full many a wrong."—

Neiding. "A noble guerdon is a goodly sword, but nobler still a Smith who welds such weapons!—Hath Rothar housed your brother?"

Eigel. "Nay, for he hath 'scaped us."

Helferich. "'Tis him we seek."

Neiding (aside). "Had I not sent a dolt on errand, now Wieland, sure, had forged me weapons!" (aloud:) "Where then hath Wieland hidden?"—

Eigel. "By villains was he set upon; his wife they slaughtered."—

Helferich. "Now hath he sped to farthest lands for vengeance."—

Neiding. "So let him speed; his time's foreby! For know ye this: another Smith there lives, who Wieland's art hath overtopt, and gladly gives me willing service."—

Helferich. "How's hight the hero?"

Neiding. "Goldbrand.—This message take to Rothar: Goldbrand is of Smiths the featest, and *he* it is that welds me weapons."

Eigel. "Yet was't a bailie of the Niars, who struck at Wieland?"—

Neiding. "Are ye his brothers, then throughly must ye know it."—

Helferich. "We lonely coastmen knew the caitiffs not; King Rothar taught us first to track them. If Wieland but had reapt that aid!"

Neiding. "And guides the clue you lonely ones Niarenwards?"

Eigel and Helferich (spring swiftly to their feet, and stand defiantly in face of Neiding). "To Neiding, Bailie of the Niars, sent us king Rothar. Now, Neiding, hear his message!"

Neiding. "Two sorry churls he's sent me; no grateful tidings may they bear. Speak on, ye champions bold!"

Eigel. "First asketh Rothar, Viking's scion: Who gave thee, Bailie of the Niars, the right to reign as King in Northland?"

Neiding. "The fretful question thus I answer: my princeship chose—the free."

Helferich. "Full well we know, how their choice thou guidedst; Wieland, too, wouldst thou chain to choose thee lord."

Eigel. "By lies and fraud thou hurl'dst the freemen 'gainst each other, that so they forced themselves to serve thee. Too late they now repent them of their folly. Envoys have they sent to Rothar, to crave him come to succour them and cut their thraldom short."—

Neiding (with ill-concealed wrath). "Three wanton women flew into my land, and madden'd by their sorcery many a man, that troth he broke to me; they stirred up strife and winged their way. Full many a traitor, left by them in sorry fix, may well have fled to Rothar, to hide him from my hand."

Eigel. "For second, Rothar bids us say: Since thou hast slain King Isang and filched the entail of his heirs, so will he now fill full the vengeance that spurred the daughters of Isang's daughter to flight as Shield-maids to the Northlands."

Helferich. "Blood-payment claims he for the slain. King Rothar's yoke shalt thou bear freely, and freely wive thy daughter to him: else, so swears he, or e'er the moon retrace her course will he set foot in land of Niars, thy heart make over to the ravens, and to the owls thy court."

Neiding (mastering his rage and terror). "Yourselves are owls and ravens, who bring such graceless greeting to my land! Is Rothar wonted thus to woo, the world is rich in brides for him to win. But rest ye now, ye cherish'd envoys; I still have room for rest for you, where owls will not as yet affright you. Rest and repose ye! the while I think upon mine answer." (Eigel and Helferich are led to the royal apartments. Neiding rises restlessly from his seat, and paces swiftly to and fro.) He vents his hatred against Rothar and his rash, heroic youth. Such madcap mood may well destroy with one bold stroke *all* that a careful man, by cunning, craft and violence, has toilfully built up through many a year!—"Who helps me now to beard the beardless, who fain would hunt the father from his home and take to wife the child?—Come hither, ye my heroes! I gave ye store of goods and rich dominion! Sons have I none: so ye shall be mine heirs—and, mated with Bathilde, shall that man reign in Norseland after me, who now obtains me victory over Rothar; that so we weigh him back his haughty wooing!"—

Wieland (steps forward from among the men). "For victory man needs a goodly weapon: now prove, my king, the mettle of my making!" (He reaches to Neiding a naked sword; the king handles it, tests the keenness of its edge, and waves it joyously above him.)

Neiding loads the Smith with praises. A sword like this had never yet been smithied! How it whets the thirst for battle, and bodes of victory to him who swings it! He feels himself a youth again, and hero's lifeblood coursing through his veins! "O Goldbrand, dearest of all friends! The God who sent thee to my land, sent with thee might and blessing!—Come, Rothar, come! I fear thee not."

Wieland. "Like as I forged for thee this sword, that fills thee with the bliss of triumph—so will I forge a myriad like it, for thine whole host within a month. This I engage thee!"

Neiding. "Thus were success made doubly certain! But how could I reward thee? I'd give thee gold above what thou couldst ever weld for pleasure."

Wieland. "O King, if thou shouldst conquer, then be thy daughter wed to me for wife!"—

Neiding. "Such payment have I set, and will observe it; to scorn the Swedish upstart!"—

Third Scene.

Bathilde (comes down hastily from her chamber; as she approaches, Wieland is spell-bound. The Courtiers make way for her, in respectful silence). *The other characters as before.*

Bathilde draws her father to one side, and begs him give her private audience, as she has weighty tidings for him.

Neiding. "My best-loved lords, I pray you wait me: that I may counsel take with this my child, for Rothar's answer!"—

(All the rest withdraw from the Hall into the hinder, lower enclosure.)

(*Wieland*, his yearning gaze directed toward *Bathilde*, who on her part furtively watches him, is the slowest in departing:—at last she sees him leave the court completely, heavy at heart. *Neiding* and *Bathilde* alone in the foreground.)

Bathilde. "Recallest thou the day when thou upbraid'dst my Mother that she bore me Maid?—'Why gave me might the gracious Gods, since they denied to me a Son?!'—So criedst thou bluntly out.—For grief, my Mother died."

Neiding. "What boots that now? No Son will ever bloom for me!"

Bathilde. "This boots it—that I further mind thee, how anon thou chidedst *me*, when runes I carved and learnt the hidden arts of magic: 'What profits all thy wisdom? A Son thou ne'er wilst rede me!' So criedst thou; whilst thy cruel scoffs weighed down my heart with sorrow!"

Neiding. "Why com'st thou here, to heap my care with railing?"

Bathilde. "Nay, rather laud thy Daughter, laud her wisdom! For I alone to-day can save thee; and count upon thy thanks.—To seal thee conquest over Rothar, I 've urged my wisdom to its utmost:—lo here, this Ring upon my finger! It stores a stone which, shouldst thou wear it, will win thee victory in every strife. My runes, it was, that gain'd it for thee."

Neiding. "I 've heard tell, ofttimes, of a victor-stone; how gain'dst thou it, that thou canst count upon its virtue?"

Bathilde. "A Swan-maid bore it on her, when three they came to stir up latest strife in Norseland."

Neiding. "A plague upon the miscreants, who wellnigh overmanned me!"

Bathilde. "Wieland then she wedded, she whom thy spear had wounded; she gave to him the Ring. Though 'scaped the Smith thy Marshal, yet won I still the Ring."

Neiding. "Thou wisest of all daughters; what fortune hast thou dealt me!"

Bathilde. "The Ring I vow to thee; but cannot give it till—thou'st made this Wieland harmless."

Neiding. "Why vex thy soul for Wieland? And how should I attaint him?"

Bathilde. "Where wert thou, read thy daughter not her runes for thee? 'Tis Wieland, whom a moment past thou'st pledged to me as mate!"

Neiding. "Ha! The man who, wonder-like, came swimming on a tree-stem to my land? How might that be?"

Bathilde. "None else is it but Wieland; in his own home I saw him!"

Neiding (overjoyed). "So! Hold I Wieland's self?— Rest calm, my child; he weens not who I am, nor that 'twas I that sent to trap him; he yields me glad and willing service: so let the trouble sleep!"

Bathilde. "Thee serves he not; for *me*, it is, he slaves. On vengeance sailed he, he so fearsome in his wrath! Yet magic'lly did Love compel him to this strand; for he is forced to love me, so long as e'er I bear this ring upon my finger, this Ring which lends to maids a love-spell, to men the mastery in fight. Now go'st thou into battle and give I thee the Ring, I lose my magic power o'er Wieland; he wakes from out his blindness, and wreaks a fell revenge:— the swords the which he forgeth, he turns their edge 'gainst us!"

Neiding. "Alack! then would he never serve me more, the wonder-working Smith!—Now see I clearly: Wieland must I bind—nay, guard myself against him—that so I

have him in my grasp, when he awakes !—O, priceless child !
What gifts I thank to thee !   Thou giv'st me victory,
giv'st the man without a peer in all the world !   Now name
the guerdon of thy gifts ! "

Bathilde.   " What thou 'st decreed in wrath, that word
recall ; from Gram remove thy ban ! "

Neiding.   " He fee'd me sorry service, when erst the
Smith he fled ! "

Bathilde.   " Behold in that the reach of Wieland's rage,
when e'en the bravest of thy warriors blenched before it !
Let Gram now lead thy host ; and as my forethought won
for thee the Ring, so grant me Gram for husband ! "

Neiding.   " Fain must I hearken to thee, yet do it with
sore grudge ; some mighty King I 'd wished to mate with
thee as bridegroom ! "

Bathilde.   " Let *me* become that mighty man : I need
alone a woman for my mate."

Neiding.   " Thou braggart, dauntless child ! Wilt thou
re-bear thyself as Man ? "

Bathilde.   " What use to thee were all thy Men, were *I*
not by ?   Think well upon it, King, whom 'twas thy wife
once bore ! "—(She returns to her chamber.)

Neiding is sorely troubled at his daughter's choice.   He
mistrusts Gram and his fidelity, and resolves to remove him
from his path by some crafty device, without arousing
Bathilde's suspicion.   He decides to inflame Wieland
against Gram, before the former's own downfall.—In
lightened mood he calls up his men from the courtyard,
and acquaints them with the certainty which he has won
of triumph : He has resolved to send the Envoys back to
Rothar with a defiant challenge, by way of answer.—His
Warriors promise him fame and increased might ; for he
must surely reign o'er all the realm of Norseland, when he
shall once have felled the haughty Vikings root and branch.
Neiding promises them fresh riches and new lands.

Fourth Scene.

Gram (steps forward). "The King has sent to call his servant?"

Neiding. "Full swiftly was the message borne thee! (aside:) A secret path he knows; of him be on my guard!" (aloud:) "Yea, Gram, my ban I loose from thee. Yet hearken: Rothar sends me challenge, on tidings trusting which have told him, the Niars themselves are ill-disposed towards me. Now surely know I none I should mistrust, since thou wilt truly serve me. Had ever I misprised thee, so will I now teach Rothar how he tricks himself; since to thee above all others give I, in firmest faith, the conduct of my host. My Leader shalt thou be! Winn'st thou the fight, then give I thee the promised prize; Bathilde by thy side, shalst share the throne with me."

Gram. "And ne'er shalt thou repent thee: I give thee truest service, and win for thee the fight!"

Neiding. "Now call me Goldbrand here!—Thou, Gram, must stand aside, and well keep watch if thou canst tell the fellow's features!" (Wieland comes forward.) "My wonder-working Smith, 'tis time! With ugly answer send I Rothar's envoys home. Within a month must I await the mighty legions of the Viking: they'll swarm my land and make my court a wasteheap, do we not smite them hip and thigh! When weld'st thou, then, the promised swords!"

Wieland (swift and blithely). "Give me but back the sword to-day I gave thee, that made thy heart beat high for joy; upon its model smite I swords a myriad, or e'er the month is out!"

Neiding (hands him the Sword). "Great is thy art, and glad the King whom such a Smith yields lifelong service!"

Wieland. "Thrice-glad the Smith, who for thy Daughter's sake makes bold to tender lifelong service!"

Neiding. "Bathilde have I pledged to *him* who gains me vict'ry; not merely him who welds me swords.

Another is there, vows me victory like thee ; with him must thou wage combat, if't be thou lose not else the prize. Ward thee well, Wieland, wily Smith ! "

Wieland (starts up amazed). " Who names me Wieland ? "

Neiding. " Here's one who knows thee nighly. 'Tis him I will to thank that now thou weld'st me swords ; for all that once unmannerly he fled thee, whom yet I sent him forth to lime. Such recreance must he blot by vict'ry over Rothar, if he would win Bathilde.—Look round thee, Wieland ! "

Wieland espies Gram, who casts black looks of hate upon him. Rage and loathing overmaster him ;—his memory reawakens, though as yet unclear. Savagely he stares around, as though to satisfy himself what place he is in. Suddenly he perceives Eigel and Helferich, who are just descending the steps from the chamber on the left. " My Brothers !—There my foeman ! " He has wellnigh called to mind his Swan-wife, when he turns toward the right hand and sees Bathilde coming terror-stricken from her chamber. He fears that he is going mad.—His senses swirl in wild confusion ; and all his passions gather up at last into one outburst of jealous, frenzied hate against Gram. " Learn ye, how Wieland's swords can cleave ! "—(With a stroke that pierces through the iron armour, he stretches Gram upon the ground a lifeless corpse.)

Bathilde had placed herself between them, stretching out her hand to shelter Gram ; in the blindness of his rage, Wieland has grazed her finger with the Sword. She shrieks aloud.

Wieland hurls away the Sword ; he clutches at Bathilde's hand ; she draws it hastily back—to conceal the Ring, which is injured by the blow. Wieland sinks upon his knees before her, dazed and helpless.

Neiding, in hypocritical wrath at Wieland's deed of violence, commands to bind him.

Eigel and *Helferich* rush forward, horrified ; they defend Wieland against his assailants.

Neiding shouts to them, as Royal Envoys, not to break

the peace: " for peace I give ye, that so ye tell to Rothar :
He may come whene'er he lists. Wieland himself welds
swords for me; swords which shall cleave the steel of
Vikings, as lightly as your eyes have seen this sampler cut
in twain my Marshal's harness ! "

Bathilde, beside herself with rage, demands Wieland's
instant death.

Neiding. " Not so ! What would a lifeless Wieland
boot me ? The living Smith is worth a kingdom ! Weapons
fair and armour shall he weld me; sad is it with a ruler
whom such an artist fails : he gives to sway its only touch
of sweetness ! No artist limb shall come to harm :—yet, so
of him I make me sure, and so he flee not, hew me the
sinews of his feet ! Limps he a little, what hurts it ? The
stithy needs but hands and arms ! These graciously I
leave him ! "

Wieland, already overmanned and bound, is about to be
carried off by the Courtiers.

Eigel and *Helferich* throw themselves once more upon
them : they conjure Neiding not to commit so dastardly a
crime, and threaten him with Rothar's vengeance.

Neiding arrogantly orders them to be scourged.

(All the men set upon them.) The Brothers shout to Wieland their vows of vengeance for him, and hack their way
through the men to the courtyard, where they swing themselves on horse and gallop off.

Wieland cries despairingly to them : Not Men have
bound him, but a Woman's bonds !—Wieland, with agonis-
ing gaze fixed upon Bathilde, is dragged off.

THIRD ACT.

(Wieland's Smithy, with a broad forge-chimney in its middle, taking
up almost the whole of the roof-vault.)

First Scene.

Wieland, propped by crutches, sits and hammers, beside
his hearth. The hammer falls from his hands. His heart

stands wellnigh still, for rage and grief.—He, the free
artist-smith who, of very joy in his art, had forged the
most wondrous of smithery, to arm and gladden withal
those dear ones whom he dowered thus with fame and
victory,—here must he, spurned and spat upon, smite out
the chains for his own body, and swords and trappings to
adorn the man who cast him into shame.—And yet, though
deepest grudge and thirst for vengeance consumed his
bosom, still one unconquerable feeling held him back: a
love, past rooting out, for this King's Daughter who hated
him the while,—unrestful yearning for a woman whom yet
he—loved not! This feeling barbed his sharpest pang.
For ever must he think upon her,—and thought he on her,
then he lost all memory besides: his youth, his whilom
freedom, his blithe and gladsome art, and all that e'er had
stirred his pulses,—all, all was blurred before his senses,
and fled far from his thought. Yea, this stanchless, mad
love-yearning spurred him on at last to labour, and let him
hug his very drudgery; by which it ofttimes seemed as
though, despite his serfdom, he yet might one day win this
princely Daughter! Yea, fain would he frame the richest
work that Art had ever fashioned, to see it trodden under
foot by this fair dame: if only she might smile on him
above its ruins!—Then with all his oldtime glee, he
snatches up his tools; he sings a brisk and lusty lay to
the soughing of the bellows, to the sputtering of the fire-
sparks, to the clanking of his hammer.—Once more there
throng shrill, savage cries into his song: a hideous loathing of his slave-toil gives him sudden pause. In frenzied
wrath he casts the tools away;—lamenting sighs now
overman him!—He longs for—death!—

Second Scene.

A knocking is heard at the door. He refuses to open:
"A fresh tormenter!"—A woman's voice demands admission. (*Wieland* recognises it as that of *Bathilde;* amazed and
enraptured, he hobbles quickly to the door upon his crutches, and
unbolts it.)

Bathilde enters, deeply perturbed :—she has ventured on this unattended journey to help herself in direst need. She counts on Wieland's love to her, not only that he will not harm her, but will also lend the needful aid. She knows, however, that, for her to gain her end without the utmost peril, his love towards her must be proved both true and staunch. She therefore proceeds with the greatest caution, in order to assure herself of this.

Wieland excuses his disfigured form ; with bitter sorrow, he reproaches her for her share in his sufferings. She must, forsooth, have well loved Gram, since she venges thus his death on *him !*

Bathilde, with feigned good wishes, counsels him to woo afresh her favour by a task whereof she wots that his art alone can compass it. But first she must know that loyally he loves her, and in naught will work against her will.—

Wieland. She knows full well with what bitter love he hangs upon her every look. But he, he cannot fathom why she should fret herself about his love?—

Bathilde. " Bethink thee how, when Gram was slain, thou graz'dst my hand, too, with the gruesome sword : a ring, which then I bore upon my finger, bent off the brunt. Yet that ring was splintered by the stroke ; its stone now almost 'scapes the setting."

Wieland. " A scant mishap ! To make atonement, I 'll gladly weld a ring a hundredfold its better."

Bathilde. " 'Tis *that* ring, of all others, that I fancy ; and this so much that favour high and love I 'll show thee, dost thou set firm the stone afresh."—

Wieland. " Why flout me thus ? For sake of such a paltry service ? In sooth, thou cam'st but to contemn me."—

Bathilde. " Nay, Wieland ! Doubt me not ! What I have promised, hold I steadfast. Believe me : know I well thy worth ! "

To quiet Wieland's amazement and mistrustful doubts, Bathilde now sees herself compelled to lay bare to him the value which she sets upon the stone. " A victor-stone this

jewel is: wears it my Father in such sorry setting, to
combat Rothar, so fear I he must lose at once both stone
and conquest."

Wieland now recognises the virtue of the Ring; he thus
conceives the greatness of the service claimed from him,
and—hopes.—He asks to see the Ring.

Bathilde still holds it anxiously back: "Wieland, my
promise is myself,—say thou then if thou truly lov'st me?"

Wieland avows his love with passionate ardour.

Bathilde. "Thou nursest evil schemes: swear me thy
fealty, and that thou vengeance quit'st for ever!"

Wieland. "Naught have I to venge, apart my laming:
does that not lower me in thine eyes, then fair I am again
to look on, and all my vengeance so forswear I!"—

Bathilde, in utmost tremor, throws her arms around him
with fawning softness, and asks: "Wieland, was thine oath
sworn freely?"

Wieland (aflame with passion, snatches the Ring from her hand).
"Upon this Ring I swear it!"

Bathilde fastens her glance, in dread suspense, on
Wieland. He gazes closer at the Ring. A terrible emotion
masters him. In a transport of horror, he thunders forth:
"Schwanhilde; my Wife!" (Bathilde utters one piercing
shriek; then stands as though struck dumb.)

Wieland. "Scoundrels burnt my house—my Wife!
Thieves robbed me of the Ring—and it betrayed me!—
Through it, revenge forgot I!—Ha! Well did Wachilde,
my grandam, guide me! Hither led her waves my way!—
And I, who came on vengeance bent, fell featly in my
foemen's springes!—All, all, through power of this cursèd
Ring!—Bathilde, shameless woman, how wonnest thou
the Ring?"

Bathilde (scarcely mistress of herself). "From the bast on
the door I stole it!"—

Wieland (swings himself in frenzy to the door; closes it fast;
and seizes *Bathilde*). "My curse upon thee, thievish hell-
wife!—Ha! how sly thou thought'st to snare me in thy net
of love; thou who'st never felt its flame! How great,

forsooth, thy love for Gram, whom *thus* thou wreak'st on me! So much as I, was he to thee!—For stones and rings thou lam'st free men, and murderest their wives! My Wife, and not myself, I now venge on thee!—Die!" (He raises the hammer above her.)

Bathilde (with a cry of utmost terror). "Thy wife lives!" (*Wieland* stands confounded.) "Thy senses cheated thee, when dead thou deem'dst her!"—

Wieland. "What liest thou?"

Bathilde. "Slay me! But believe me still: she lives!"

Wieland. "She lives?—And where?"

Bathilde. "That night, upon my homeward journey, I gazed across the wooded shore and saw the swanlike sisters, as they dived into the forest depths: twain were they then; but three they mounted, over wood and sea to wing them westwards."

Wieland. "In flight to home! The pinions found she! Herself she saved—and me, her lame and fettered husband, she left for ever!—Alas, why have I learnt it! Now haps my lot more cruel than before! Had I but blind remainèd, as slave I'd played the Smith; mayhap, at last, had kiss'd the fetters of my chains. Now ween I who I was, and what a free, blest Man! Now wot I that the sweetest Wife is living, but wretched I may never reach her, never see her more!—Perish then, thou lame and limping cripple! Thou sport of scoffers! By men derided, by women pointed at and children! Away with thee! But gibes shall greet thee, never vengeance,—never Love!" (He falls prostrate, in a paroxysm of grief.)

Bathilde stands as though turned to stone; she feels the fearful reality of human misery, now laid before her. Profound sorrow pierces into her soul. Wieland lies speechless upon the ground.—She looks around her—there is naught to stay her flight—but flee she cannot. Horrified, she takes Wieland for dead: she bends down over him, and listens to his breathing. With breaking heart, she cries to him in deep compassion:—he hears her not.—She weeps bitterly.—Slowly Wieland lifts his head a little, and stares vacantly before him ; with scarcely audible voice he then begins :

Wieland. "Schwanhilde, brightest, fairest! Soar'st thou in bliss athwart the breeze? Dost hover happy o'er the sea? Seest thou me crawling here upon the soil, the worm whom crafty foes have trodden? Shame warns him off from crying to thee, that he loves thee! The sturdy swimmer on the sea-waves,—he in very sooth might win thee: but how should now the cripple cleave the flood? How steer'd he straight his seaward way, if thou shouldst leave the clouds for wave-crests? Chained to myself, my feet hang lifeless, to my shame: my rudder-strings are hewn asunder!"—(With growing emphasis.) "Schwanhilde! Schwanhilde! Could I but lift myself from Earth, that only greets my foot with anguish, laid low in shameful impotence!—As erst I swam across the billows, ah! could I fly now through the clouds! Strong are mine arms, to ply thy pinions, and fearsome is my need! Thy Wings! Thy Wings! Had I thy wings, a warrior then would stoutly cleave the clouds, and venging soar above his foemen!"—

In wild excitement he gazes upwards, speechless.— Bathilde calls him softly; he commands her, by a hasty gesture, to keep silence. She peers anxiously into his face :—she sees his lips tremble violently, his eyes light up with ever brighter glow. In waxing inspiration, he raises himself upon his crutches, to the full height of his stature.

Bathilde (awestruck). "A God it is, that stands before me!"

Wieland (with heaving breast). "A Man! A Man in highest Need!" (Then with a terrible outburst:) "'Tis Need! Need swayed her pinions, and fanned her inspiration round my brain! I 've found 't, what never man devis'd!— Schwanhilde! Sweetest Wife, to thee I 'm nigh! I swing me up to thee!"—

Bathilde. "Nay, can I help thee? Say, how I may save thee!"

Wieland. "What wouldst thou, woman? Why feed thine eyes on me? Avaunt thee!"

Bathilde (beside herself). "O Wieland! Wieland! See my sorrow! See the grief that cuts my heartstrings! Pity, pardon the unhappy maid, thou godlike man! In pangs that nigh consume her, she casts her love before thy feet!"—

Wieland. "Is't the Ring in my hand, that so enflames thee?" (He flings it on the hearth.) "Lo! *that* shall yield me other service, than to light false love in thee!"

Bathilde. "Nay, not the magic of the Ring, the magic of thine anguish bids me love thee!—yet not as mate,— as Man must I love thee!—Wieland, Wieland! Glorious, woe-filled Man! How expiate my guilt?"—

Wieland. "Love thou! So shalt from guilt be freed!"

Bathilde (humbly). "Whom should I love then?"

Wieland. "'Tis out, with all thy Father's might; as victor and deliverer, King Rothar comes into the land: despise him not, who sues thy hand! Of mine own stem is he! Stand proudly by his side as happy bride, and bear him blithesome heroes!"

Bathilde (in sorrowful submission). "Say I to him that Wieland grants me pardon?"

Wieland. "So say, and tell him of my deeds!"

Bathilde falls on her knees before him; he raises her, and bids her hurry forth, for now must he lay hand to work.—He ushers her through the door: she casts a last mournful look toward Wieland, and leaves the stithy with sunken head.

Third Scene.

Wieland places himself beside the hearth, plies the bellows, rakes the embers, and sets to his work with eager ardour. He is bent on creating his highest masterpiece. The swordblades that he had forged so keen and sharp for Neiding, he now will beat them out to pliant, soaring pinions; they shall be joined together, for the arms, by bands of steel; in the neck, where the bands are to fit into each other, the Wonder-stone from Schwanhilde's Ring

shall form the clasp, the magic axis round which the pair
of Wings shall stir.—Suddenly he pauses : through the
chimney of the forge he hears his name borne down the
breeze ; he looks up—the smoke prevents his seeing.—He
listens :

Schwanhilde's Voice is heard from on high : " Wieland !
Wieland ! Remember'st me ? "

Wieland (entranced). " Schwanhilde ! Dearest Wife !
Art nigh to me ? Seek'st thou for me, whom thou hadst
fled so far ? "

Schwanhilde's Voice : " Tempests wafted me afar :—from
happy homeland yearned I forth to thee ! "—

Wieland. " Wing'dst thy way hither from blissful home ?
Sought'st thou me out in want and woe ? "

Schwanhilde. " I hover nigh thee in the air above, to
comfort thee in woe and want ! "

Wieland. " In want am I ; yet taught me Want to
swing myself above my woe."

Schwanhilde. " Weldest thou weapons, sturdy Smith,
to take thy stand in strife and war ? "

Wieland. " Weapons shaped I for mine own foe ! I
wot not how to stand in strife ! Hewn are the sinews of
my feet,—on horse ne'er more can I hie to battle ; nor
stoutly steer me through the waves, to woo a sweetest
woman ! "

Schwanhilde. " O Wieland ! Saddest ! What work'st
thou now, to win thee freedom ? "

Wieland. " A work I work at, which shall help me : woo
I revenge below on robbers, woo I a sweetest wife who
soars on high above my head ! " (With growing confidence and
gladness) " Ne'er more shall she flee the cripple ; he 'll follow
her where'er she flies."

Schwanhilde. " Wieland ! Thou bravest ! Forgest thou
wonders, featest of men ? "

Wieland (exultingly). " I forge me Wings, thou dearest
Wife ! On wings I 'll mount into the sky ! Death and
destruction dealt to the Neidings, I swing myself aveng'd
to thee ! "

Schwanhilde. "Wieland! Wieland! Mightiest man! Wooest thou me in the free wide heavens, ne'er will I flee thee away!"

Wieland. "In the heavens await me, thou fairest! There will I win thee afresh.—Sink thee down above yon forest; soon see'st thou me floating through the breezes, with mighty wing-strokes beating their bountiful waves!"

Schwanhilde. "Farewell, belovèd! I tarry for thee in the forest, thou godlike wonder-smith!"

During this dialogue Wieland, with ever-waxing agitation, has completed his work. A loud rapping is heard at the door.

Neiding demands admission. Wieland springs up, in terrible glee; lets Neiding and his retainers into the forge; then, unnoticed, shuts the door behind them, and throws the key into the fire upon the hearth.—

Fourth Scene.

Neiding is delighted at Wieland's arduous toil; far and wide had his hammering been heard. The Courtiers laugh at Wieland, jesting over his marvellous agility in the use of crutches: how well he knows to help himself; he could scarce have been so nimble, even when his feet were sound. Neiding quells their scoffing: the wondrous force of the man astounds him. Any other would have died, mayhap, through what he suffered; but the force of will, with which Wieland fits himself to his evil plight, shows a high and noble race.—He flatters him, and wishes that he may ever remain in so good a mood, work stout and briskly; for then he may be sure of finding all go well with him.

Wieland (gradually deepening the grimness of his scorn). "How *well* should I have things go with thee? Perchance like a bird whom thou'st snared in the woods? Thou clippest his wings, that he may not fly thee;—yet, so that his song may fill thine ears with sweetest sounds, thou blind'st forsooth his eyes; that out of endless night he cry in anquish'd yearning for his mate? Then sugar'd berries thou

reachest him, to pay for maim and blinding? How well
'tis, Neiding, that I had but feet, not also wings. Thou 'd
find it fit that I should sing too, like the glad songster of
the forest!"

Neiding. "What means this, Wieland? Fret'st thou
then, and los'st thy cheer already?"

Wieland. "I sing thee songs, so good as I may!"

Neiding. "So leave thy lays; they 'll gain no liking.
For reason of thy goodly swords thou find'st me friendly.
What thou hast promised, claim I now. The truce is o'er;
with mighty hosts has Rothar march'd already into North-
land. Mad'st thou the swords we need?—E'en still with
Bathilde mayst thou mate thee!"

Wieland. "Hold'st to thy bird the sugar'd berries?
In sooth, in the wood he 'll soon pluck them himself!"—

Neiding. "Out on thy song! Come show us the
sword-blades!"

Wieland. "What boot thee swords then? Since thou
canst boast the Victor-Stone! But bear it soothly on thy
finger, King of heroes, and joy to see how Rothar's men
shall fall before thy merest wish!"

Neiding. "'Tis true, I prize the Ring Bathilde guards
me. Yet what is that to thee? Thou, knave, hast naught
to know but thy smithy!"

Wieland. "Small use are swords, to him who van-
quishes by Stones-of-Vict'ry! More need was mine of
newer crutches; that nimbler still about thy business I 'd
hither flit and fro, than e'er I could upon these stumps of
willow.—Lo! from thy blades I 've forged me crutches;—
they 'll let me gladly lack my feet."

Neiding. "Art thou raving? Thou 'st beat the sword-
blades into toys?"

Wieland (standing behind the hearth, and thrusting his arms into
the wing-bands). "Such toys a lonely cripple makes to play
with!—Hé! How the crutches' swing delights me!"
(He sways the wings with ever wider stroke, and fans therewith the
embers on the hearth to higher flames, which he directs towards
Neiding and his Courtiers.)

Neiding. "Why heat'st thou flames so furious on the hearth?"

Wieland. "With my crutches fan I the fire; no more I need the bellows; that cost, my King, I'll spare thee!"

Neiding. "Why hunt'st thou the blaze to us hither?"

Wieland (with terrible intent in his voice). "I do but prove the strength of their sway, if they'll mightily bear me from hence through the chimney, when once ye have fall'n to the fire!" (A rush of smoke conceals the hearth, with Wieland, behind it. Tongues of fire lick the walls and ground.)

Neiding (dashes in horror to the door). "Betrayed! we're trapped past helping! Seize ye the traitor, or e'er we stifle!"—

Wieland has become completely invisible amid the smoke. As the men press toward the hearth to seize on Wieland, the chimney falls in with a fearful crash, leaving only the side-walls standing. A dense body of flame leaps up on every hand. Above the smoke, Wieland is seen soaring into the air with outspread Wings.—

Neiding (in the death-agony). "Wieland, rescue me!"—

Wieland (whose form shines bloodred in the glow). "Perish, O Neiding! Done is thy living,—done is thy rule! The Victor-stone now clasps the Wings around my neck!—Lo there my Brothers! Rothar nighs! Thy Daughter his bride,—she curseth thee!—Naught rests of thee and all thy might, but the tale of the vengeance a free Smith forg'd him for end of his thraldom! Pass over, O Neiding, for aye!"

Fifth Scene.

(The entire Stithy now crashes together, and buries Neiding and his men beneath its ruins.)

Eigel and *Helferich* rush on, at the head of Rothar's host. Eigel leaps to the edge of the ruins; he sees Neiding struggling with death, and shoots down an arrow into his heart. The tumult of victory fills the stage.

Rothar, advancing, is greeted by the Niars as their

deliverer.—Sun-drenched, brilliant morn.   In the background a Forest.   All gaze, in transport and amazement, up to Wieland.   He has swung himself still higher ; the dazzling steel of his Wings shines like the sun in the morning splendour.

Schwanhilde hovers, on her broad-spread swan-wings, towards him from the Wood.   They meet, and fly into the distance.

ART AND CLIMATE.

"*KUNST UND KLIMA.*"

(1850)

In a letter to Uhlig, dated February 8th, 1850, Wagner writes: " To the March number of the Deutsche Monatsschrift *(Stuttgart) I have promised to contribute an article, 'Art and Climate.' The good friend in the* Allgemeine Zeitung *has determined me to expose the lazy, cowardly, preposterous objection of 'climate,' in all its emptiness." A nervous illness intervened between this letter and the following, undated but apparently written towards the end of the month, where he says: " Since yesterday I have been writing away at the article for the March number of the* Monatsschrift." *In the succeeding letter (March 13th, 1850), in which he also refers to " Wieland" as previously cited, Wagner says: "Kunst und Klima appears in the Stuttgart* Deutsche Monatsschrift, *in the March, or, at latest, in the April number. The article is important."—In the April number of that review (edited by Adolph Kolatschek) the article accordingly appeared.—*

Upon referring to the Deutsche Allgemeine Zeitung, *we find in the issue for Jan. 15, 1850 a criticism of* Art and Revolution *containing the remarks here referred to by our author. They run as follows: " Whence, beneath our Northern skies, shall we derive that rapt intoxication of the sense of beauty, which even upon the Ionic horizon did not loom so pure as we are wont to conceive when we sum up the æsthetic life of olden times in the principle of Hellenism ? ... These wailings are fantastic, unfruitful, and can be answered by no kind of Revolution, excepting by that of the whole* Earth-rind, *and a new cycle of the world."—*

TRANSLATOR'S NOTE.

THE author's publicly expressed views on the future of Art, in step with the advance of the human race to perfect Freedom, have been met with this objection, among others: that he has failed to take account of the *influence of Climate upon man's capacity for Art*, and has, for instance, presupposed of the modern Northern-European nations a future imaginative and constructive art-faculty to which the natural characteristics of their native skies are entirely opposed.

It may therefore be deemed of some importance to lay bare the lack of understanding which lies at the bottom of this objection, by a general survey of the actual relations between Art and Climate; leaving, for the present, the kindly reader to complete the individual details by their further consequences.

Just as we know that there are heavenly bodies which have not as yet, or never will have, attained the birth of those conditions fundamentally necessary to the existence of human beings: so do we know that at one time our own Earth, also, had not as yet evolved such attributes. The present physiognomy of our planet shows us that, even now, the life of Man is by no means permitted on every portion of its surface: where its climatic mood proclaims itself in unbroken exclusiveness, as on the fiery plains of the Sahara, or mid the Northern ice-steppes, there Man is an impossibility. Only where this 'Climate' resolves the fixed and all-dominating uniformity of its influence into a

pliant chain of broken contrasts, do we see arise that
infinitely manifold series of organic creations whose highest
grade is conscience-gifted Man.

Yet where Climatic Nature draws Man beneath the all-
sheltering influence of her rankest prodigality, and rocks
him in her bosom as a mother rocks her child,—where we
must therefore place the cradle of newborn mankind :—
there has Man remained a child forever—as in the Tropics,
—with all an infant's good and evil qualities.   First where
she drew this all-conditioning, over-tender influence back,
when she handed Man, like a prudent mother her adult
son, to himself and his own free self-devisings,—where
Man, then, mid the waning warmth of the directly fostering
care of Climate, was forced to cater for himself,—do we see
him ripening to the full unfoldment of his being.   Only
through the force of such a Need as surrounding Nature
did not, like an over-careful mother, both listen for and
still at once ere it had scarcely risen, but for whose appeasement he must himself provide, did he gain consciousness not only of that need but also of his *power*.   This
consciousness he reached through learning *the distinction
between himself and Nature ;* and thus it was that she, who
no more *offered* him the stilling of his need, but from whom
he now must *wrest* it, became the object of his observation, inquiry, and dominion.

The progress of the human race in the development of
its innate capabilities of winning from Nature the contentment of those needs that waxed with its ever-waxing
powers, is the *history of Culture*.   In it Man evolves his
own qualities in *counterpoise* to Nature, and thus acquires
independence of her.   Only man become independent of
Nature by his personal energy, is the *historical* Man ; and
only the historical Man has summoned *Art* to life, but not
the primitive Man in Nature's leading-strings.

Art is the highest common life-expression of the man
who, after self-fought-out contentment of his natural needs,
displays himself to Nature in all the flush of triumph.
His art-works as though fill up the gaps which she had

left for Man's free personal activity; they form the closing harmony of her majestic whole, in which self-conscious, independent Man is thus included as her highest factor. Wherefore, where *Nature* in her overfill was All, we neither light upon free Man nor genuine *Art;* but where —as we have phrased it—she left those empty gaps, where she thus made room for the free self-evolution of Man and of his need-grown energy, was Art first born.

Granted, that Nature has also had her share in the birth of Art, just as the highest expression of the latter is the brilliant 'close,' the conscious reunion of Nature with Man, effected by his understanding of her.   Her share, however, was this: that she abandoned Man, the creator of Art, to the conditions which must necessarily spur him on to self-gained consciousness,—inasmuch as she retreated before him and merely exerted a conditional influence over him, in place of holding him a prisoner in the bosom of her full and unconditional sway.   From the over-tender mother, she became to him a bashful bride, whom he now must win by vigour and love-worthiness for his—endlessly enhanced —fruition; a bride who, vanquished thus by mind and valour, made offering of herself to Love's embraces.   Not, therefore, in the teeming Tropics, not in the sensuous flower-land of India, was born *true Art;* but on the naked, sea-plashed rocks of Hellas, upon the stony soil and beneath the scanty shadows of the olive-trees of Attica, was set her cradle:—*for here, amid privations, strove Hercules and suffered*—here was the first *true Man* begotten.— —

When we survey the history of Hellenic culture, we are above all struck by *those* circumstances which favoured the development of Man to his highest energy, and thereby to independence of Nature and finally of those cramping human relationships which sprang directly from his natural surroundings.   We certainly shall find these circumstances markedly involved in the characteristics of the 'scene of action' of Hellenic history; but the decisive feature of these characteristics lies herein, that Nature did not *pamper* (*v e r wöhnte*) the Hellenes by her 'influence, but *weaned* (*e n t wöhnte*) them from her care ; that she *be-schooled* (*e r zog*), and not *be-lapped* (*v e r zog*) them like the softer Asiatics. Every other determining factor in the Hellenic evolution may be referred to the individual manysidedness of the numerous racial stems which crowded close together in rich variety. The natural characteristics of their respective dwelling-places had, sure enough, an essential effect upon their individuality, and therefore upon that of the whole nation, but only in the sense of spurring them to free activity ; so that the work of forming and developing these diverse individualities must be ascribed far more to History than to Nature.

The motive force of Hellenic history is thus the *vigorous* (*thätige*) *Man* ; and its fairest fruit, the crown of Hellenic self-consciousness, is the *purely human Art, i.e.* that art which found its stuff and object in actual Man, man self-acknowledged as Nature's highest product. The later *Plastic art* was the luxury and superfluity of Hellenic Art : in it the flower of Greece shed down on its surroundings the overfill of its rich sap, secreted by the fibres of the humanistic art-work, and erstwhile kept close-locked within its maiden chalice : it is the squandered seed of bursting, over-ripe Hellenic Art. This seed glanced off from Man, fell back upon surrounding Nature, and on her soil twixt trees and bushes, from mountain, brook and meadow, brought forth those teeming pictures of man's art which signal for us, to this very day, the tidings of the overfill of human faculty.

In the plastic arts, Man undoubtedly brought himself once more into direct relationship with surrounding climatic Nature ; but only herein, that he weighed his needs and forces against hers, and set his purely human will and pleasure in unison with the Necessity of her demeanour. *Only the free and full-fledged man*, however, such as he had evolved himself by combat with the parsimony of Nature, could throughly understand her, and wist at last to spend the overfill of his own being on that harmonic complement

of Nature which should answer to his power of enjoyment.
The creative faculty lay therefore ever grounded on Man's
independence of Nature—yea, on the overfill of that quality
—and not in any directly productive *operation of natural
Climate.*

But the voiding of that overfill was also the death-knell
of this art-creative man : the more he strewed his seed
beyond the confines of his Hellenic motherland, the farther
he shed this overfill toward Asia, and led back thence its
lavish stream into the pragmatic-prosaic and grossly sensual
world of Rome : so much the more visibly did his creative
force die out ; to make place, at his eventual death, for the
worship of an *abstract God* who, in melancholy joy of immortality, wandered aimlessly between the splendid works
of statuary and architecture which decked the burying-
place of this departed Man.   Thenceforth God *ruled* the
world,—God, who had *made* all Nature for the glory of his
name.   From that time forward, man's affairs are governed
by the '*incomprehensible will*' of God ; no longer by the
instinct and necessity of Nature,—and it is therefore a highly
unchristian action, on the part of our modern Christian art-
producers, to appeal to "Climate" and "Natural soil" as
hindering or favouring conditions for the birth of Art.—
Let us consider what has become of art-fit Man, under the
dispensation of Jehova !

The first thing that strikes us, in glancing at the evolution of our modern nations, is this : that it has only most
conditionally been governed by the influence of *Nature*,
but quite unconditionally by the confounding and distort-
ing operation of an alien Civilisation ; that, as a matter of
fact, our Culture and Civilisation have not sprung upwards
from the nether soil of Nature, but have been poured down
upon us from above, from the Heaven of the priests and
the *Corpus Juris* of Justinian.

With its entrance upon history, the natural stock of each
new European nation was grafted with a cutting from the
tree of Roman-dom and Christendom, and the fruit of the
thus-engendered artificial shoot, which bushed out on

every hand in cripple-like monstrosity, we are now tasting in our barbaric civilisation. Hindered from the first in their self-unfolding, we can form no estimate of the shape which the original characteristics and climatic idiosyncracies of those nations might perchance have evolved. Even though we should set down the degree of artistic culture, which they might be trusted to have attained on the path of self-unfolding, at ever so little (an assumption, however, which would be thoroughly onesided and unjust !), yet we have here no need to vex ourselves with that question ; but simply to confess that such an undisturbed self-development has actually had no chance of taking place. Whosoever may choose to reply, that at all events our native idiosyncracy has had a well-marked influence on the shaping of imported elements of culture, is completely in the right when, for example, he asserts that the Christianity of Nicæa was a different matter from that of Berlin ; but he would only make himself ridiculous, if he should attempt—as has already occurred to certain pious persons—to prove an innate predisposition of the Germanic races toward Christianity from the contents of the Eddas.

True, that into the evolutionary channel of the modern nations their 'climatic' origin poured its waters too,* and that from the perennial torrent of the Folk, with its own peculiar strain of poetry and intuition ; only—it was but in an incomplete and spasmodic, a fragmentary and unsubstantial manner, that the true Folk-spirit could ever manifest itself, beneath the 'influences' that pressed upon it from outside and above. Our spiritual development has

---

* The original text runs : "Wohl ist im Entwickelungsgange der modernen Nationen ihre klimatische Originalität ebenfalls mit eingeflossen, und zwar aus dem unversiegbaren Strome des Volkes, . . ." The author has here indulged in a rhetorical play of words, quite impossible to reproduce in another tongue ; taking the word "influence" from the mouths of his opponents, he has, in this sentence, restored it to its primitive meaning, viz., "to flow into " (cf. *influx*), a sense still preserved in the German verb "einfliessen." To complete his metaphor, he has further employed the "gang" of "Entwickelungsgang" (course of evolution) in its sense of "conduit," a meaning retained in the English "water-*course*."—TR.

therefore been a mass of tangled contradictions: *not* the product of Nature and Climate, nor of a cycle of culture that had shaped itself in strict conformity therewith; but the result of a violent counter-thrust against this Nature, of a wilful disregard of both Nature and Climate, of the frenzied strife twixt soul and body, "will" and "can." The desolate battlefield, across which this crazy fight swept howling, is the plain of the Middle Ages. Undecided, as of its very nature it could not but remain, the battle wavered to and fro; until the Turks came to our help, and hunted over to us, in the Occident, the last professors of Hellenic art.

Art's *renaissance*—mark well! not any *birth*—now set in with full force: the last remains of Greek art-beauty were *taught* to us. The tombstones from the burial-place of long-deceased Greek art, those weather-beaten forms of bronze and marble, denuded of their living garb of colour, —were unriddled for us by these learned men, so well as their own scant stock of understanding still permitted. And just as those monuments were, as we said, the merest gravestones of the once living Hellenic artist-man,—the last ghostlike, pallid death-abstraction from his onetime warmly-feeling, nobly-doing life,—so have we learnt from them to regard *Art* itself as an *abstract notion*, which we fancy we must pour down from above—as we had erstwhile done with the immaterial god of Heaven—into the mould of actual Life. From this abstract notion has our Modern Art been *constructed* : meaning thereby our *plastic* art, i.e. that art which, of our need of Luxury, we have *imitated* from the plastic art of Greece, itself the mere luxurious appanage of Grecian Art; and, in troth, have not imitated in the fulness wherewith it once took rise from Life and stood erect in living bloom,—but according to the sorrowful disfigurement in which alone it offered itself to us, beaten by the storms of time, torn from its natural bearings, and scattered in capricious fragments here a little and there a little. And thus we take these monuments— robbed of their warming and protecting deckery of tint—

drag them naked and frostbitten through the Christian-German sand of " Mark " Brandenburg, set them up amidst the windy firs of " Sans-Souci," and chatter from between our teeth a learned sigh anent the *unfavourableness of our climate*.   But that, midst this " unfavourableness," our Berlin art-pedants have not yet gone completely crazy, we ascribe with justice to the undeserved grace of God !

By all means these learned men are right, when, beholding the work of their own luxurious caprice, they find that in that work we are merely bunglers, prompted by neither necessity nor self-dependence ; that in our " climate " the imitated plastic art of Greece can only be a hothouse growth, and not a natural plant.   This verdict, however, can but open the eyes of any man of common sense, to the fact that our whole art is good for nothing *because* it has had no origin in our actual being, nor in any harmonic supplementing of the " climatic " Nature which surrounds us.   But this in nowise proves that, in our climate, an art could not unfold itself in answer to our veritable human needs ; for we have never yet reached the point of developing our artistic powers, without let or hindrance, according to *our own* associate need.

A survey of our modern art thus teaches us that we absolutely do *not* stand under the influence of climatic *Nature*, but of a *History* at entire variance with that Nature· We must, therefore, first realise that our history of to-day is made by the selfsame *men* who once brought forth the Grecian art-work, and, that done, ask ourselves : *what* is it, that has changed these men so utterly, that Those created works of Art whilst We but turn-out costly wares of Industry ?   Then shall we also recognise that, as our essence is at bottom one and the same, so, however wide apart our starting-points, our termini must one day light upon each other, though approached on different paths. The Greek, proceeding from the bosom of Nature, attained to Art when he had made himself independent of the immediate influence of Nature : *we*, violently debarred from Nature, and proceeding from the drillground of a heaven-rid and juristic Civilisation, shall first reach Art when we completely turn our backs on such a civilisation and once more cast ourselves, with conscious bent, into the arms of Nature.

We have not, therefore, to turn to the consideration of Climatic Nature, but of *Man*, the only creator of Art, in order to discover what has made this modern European man art-impotent. Then shall we perceive with full distinctness, that this evil influence is none other than our present *Civilisation*, with its complete indifference to Climate. It is not our atmosphere, that has reduced the proud warriors of the North, who shattered once the Roman world, to servile, crass, weak-nerved, dim-eyed, deformed and slovenly cripples;—not it, that has turned the blithesome, action-lusting, dauntless sons of heroes, whom we cannot now conceive aright, into our hypochondriacal, cowardly and cringing citizens;—not it, that has brought forth from the hale and hearty Teutons our scrofulous linen-weavers, weaved themselves from skin and bones; from the Siegfried of olden days a " Gottlieb"; from spear-throwers our logic-choppers, our counsellors and sermon-spinners. No, the glory of this splendid work belongs to our clergy-ridden *Pandect-civilisation*, with all its fine results; among which, beside our Industry, our worthless, heart-and-soul-confounding *art* fills out its seat of honour. For the whole posse must be set down to this Civilisation, in its entire variance with our nature, and not to any Nature-born *necessity*.

Wherefore, not from that Civilisation, but from the future true and genuine *Culture, which shall bear a right relation to our climatic Nature,* will one day also bloom that Artwork which is now denied both breath and air to breathe in, and as to whose peculiar properties we shall never be able to form a notion until *we Men*, the creators of that artwork, can conceive ourselves as developed to a rational concord *with this Nature.*

From the kernel of our history therefore, have we, for now, to draw conclusions on our Future; from the character of Man, such as our history shows us working-out himself to free self-destination, under the merest conditional influence of Nature, have we to enquire how the free and veritable Men of the Future will take their stand twixt Art and Nature.

What then is the kernel of this history?

We shall surely not go far astray, if we describe it briefly thus :—

In Greekdom, we find Man evolving to full and conscious self-discrimination from Nature : the artistic monument in which this conscious man objectified himself, is the tintless marble statue,—the idea, expressed in stone, of the pure human form ; which idea Philosophy, again, dissolved from out the stone and resolved into a pure 'abstraction' of the human essence. Into this solitary man, existing at last in naught but the idea,—this man in whom, amid the physical lack of all community of the species, the essence of the sheer personality was represented as the essence of the species,—the People's Christianity instilled the lifebreath of passionate heart's-desire. The error of the philosopher became the madness of the masses. This frenzy's scene of action is the Middle Ages : on it we see the Nature-sundered man—taking his personal, egoistic, and therefore impotent being for the essence of the human species—with greed and haste, by physical and moral mutilation,* hunt after his redemption into *God;* under whose image, by an instinctive error, he expressed the idea of the in truth consummate essence of the human race and Nature.†

---

* Compare *Parsifal*, Act i. "an sich legt er die Frevelhand," where Gurnemanz refers to Klingsor's egoistic endeavours to force his way to the *Gral.*—Tr.

† " Unter welchem er das in Wahrheit vollkommene Wesen der menschlichen Gattung und der Natur nach unwillkürlichem Irrthume begriff."—The meaning of this passage, and of that which follows, will become clearer by reference to Ludwig Feuerbach's *Essence of Christianity* (for Wagner's partial thought-indebtedness whereto, see the Preface to the present volume and also p. 25), in the first chapter of which we find : " Religion is nothing else than the consciousness which man has of his own, not finite and limited, but infinite nature " ; again : " The antithesis of divine and human is nothing else than the antithesis between human nature in general and the individual " ; and

As the only possible, true, therefore unconsciously and at last consciously striven-for, redemption from this state of misery, we then see loom before us the ascension of the *egoistic* essence of the individual into the *communistic* essence of the human race; the concretion of the abstract idea of Man into the actual, true and blissful common-being of *Mankind*. If, therefore the kernel of the world's history, from the Asiatic down to the close of the Grecian period, was the emanation of the *unit Man* from Nature: so is the kernel of the newer European history the resolution of this idea into the actuality of *Men*.

But to men who know themselves united in one all-capable species, the natural character of this or that particular Climate can no longer set up cramping bounds: to them, as a species at one with itself, the total like-united Nature of this Earth alone can form a confine. To this whole Earth-Nature, in measure as she is known to them in all her wide connexion with the World-All, will the Men and Brothers of the Future turn; yet no longer turn as to a barrier—such as the Egoist deemed the circle of his natural surroundings—but as the prime condition of their existence, their life and handiwork.

In this vast and blest conjunction, shall we first attain the artist's true creative-force ; when first *the Artists* are to hand, then will *Art* herself be present. But these Artists are *human beings ;* not trees, nor waves, nor skies. This brotherhood of artist-men will mould its works of art in unison with, in complement and rounding-off of Mother Nature ; accenting every quality and individual trait evoked by special need, in answer to the special call of Nature's individual features, but marching forward from the base of

later : " God is the concept of the species as an individual : the idea, or rather the essence of the species, that, while a universal being, the epitome of all perfections, of all attributes set free from the limits existing in the mind and feeling of the individual, is withal an individual *personal* being . . . . . Man supplies the absence of the idea of the species by the idea of God,—as of a Being who is free from the limits and wants which oppress the individual, and, in his judgment (since he identifies the species with the individual), the species itself."—Tʀ.

this particularity towards a common pact with common Nature—as toward the utmost fulness of man's being.

Before, however, men shall once more shape their art-works by their Need, and not as now by Luxury and Caprice, they will neither have the wit to bring their works to needful unison with Nature. But if they shape from Need —and the true need of Art can only be one felt in common —then no Climate upon earth, that allows at all of man's existence, can hinder them from Art-work ; the rather will the niggardness of outward Nature but whet the more their purely human artist-zeal.

As for the objection that, even for the generation of the *art-need*, peculiar favouring conditions of Climate—such as Ionic skies—are indispensable : it is, in the sense in which it is nowadays brought forward, either bigoted or hypo-critical, and in its very gist unmanly. Wherever Climate does not forbid men living *free* and *healthy* lives, neither will it hinder them from bodily beauty and the feeling of the need of art. Climate can only pronounce its fatal veto where, through the invincibility of its influence, it stays true Men from being bred, and merely lets the human *animal* vegetate. Yet even these men-beasts will one day vanish before the march of truer culture ; just as so many of their like have already vanished, or through exchange of climate and intermingling of varieties, have thriven into normal men. But, as we have said above, where men attain to mastery of their dependence on climatic Nature, they will necessarily—in their ever broader *historical* con-tact with all those men who have reached like independ-ence—stride onward also to the mastery of each dependence on those oppressive tenets which have clung to them as the result of erroneous conceptions harboured in the time of that war-of-emancipation with Nature, and have ruled both the religious and political conscience of mankind with equal cramping dictates of authority. The common creed of those Men of the Future must therefore necessarily take this form :—

There exists no higher *Power* than *Man's Community ;* there is naught so *worthy Love* as the *Brotherhood of Man.*

But only through the *highest power of Love* can we attain to *perfect Freedom ;* for there exists no genuine Freedom but that in which *each Man hath share.*

The mediator between Power and Freedom, the redeemer without whom Power remains but violence, and Freedom but caprice, is therefore—*Love ;* yet not that revelation from above, imposed on us by precept and command,—and therefore never realised, — like the Christian's : but *that* Love which issues from the Power of true and undistorted human nature ; which in its origin is nothing other than the liveliest utterance of this nature, that proclaims itself in pure delight at physical existence and, starting from marital love, strides forward through the love for children, friends and brothers, right on to *love for Universal Man.*

This Love is thus the wellspring of all true Art, for through it alone can the natural flower of *Beauty* bloom from Life. Yet Beauty, too, is now only one of our abstract notions, and verily no notion deduced from actual Life, but from the *lesson-ed* Grecian art. That which can only be perceived and felt in the full warm joy of all the senses, has become the object of æsthetic speculation ; and, confronted with the axioms of the Metaphysician, our modern art-professor sighs again for Ionic skies, beneath which alone (in his opinion) can Beauty ever thrive. But here, again, he keeps his eyes involuntarily fixed on the only remaining, dull and faded link that connects the art of Greece with our own time, the *plastic* art and notably the natural Material from which it fashioned forms. He thus forgets entirely that the fashioner of those statues was first and foremost an artist Man, and that he only *copied* in those works the actual artwork he had *carried out* upon and with his own warm, living body. The Beauty to which the artist at last erected marble statues, he had *felt* before, and *tasted,* with the highest joy of sense ; to him this tasting had been a true instinctive *need,* and this need was none other than—*Love.* How high this love-need could mount

within the exclusive circle of the Grecian nation, we learn
from the course of their historical evolution. Because it was
no more than the need of a peculiar people, it remained
hedged about with Egoism ; and could therefore only squander, so to speak, its force on wantonness at last, and, after
all this prodigality, die out in philosophical abstractions,
renewed by not one spark of counter-love.   If, on the other
hand, we weigh the instinctive impulse of the men of present history,—if we recognise that they can only reach
redemption by the realisation of God in the physical verity
of the Human Race,—that their most burning need can
only still itself in Universal Human Love, and that, by an
infallible necessity, it must one day attain this stilling,—
then we can but look with full assurance to a future element
of life in which this Love, extending its own need into the
widest circles of broad humanity, must needs give birth to
works undreamt as yet ; works which, moulded by unheard-
of manysidedness of *felt and living* sense of Beauty, shall
turn those mouldering remains of Grecian art to unregarded
playthings for peevish children.

Let us therefore conclude thus :—

That which a man loves, that *deems* he beautiful ; that
which strong, free *Men*—who in community are all that of
their essence they can be—that which *they* love in common,
that *is* in very surety beautiful.   No other natural standard
exists for true, not inculcated, Beauty.   In their joy at this
beauty, will the Freemen of the Future fashion works of Art
such as they needs *must* fashion to content their measure-
lessly heightened need.   Everywhere, in every Climate,
will these works be suchwise fashioned as to answer to the
purely human need inspired by native skies : they will be
beautiful alike and perfect, for reason that in them the
highest need of Man is *satisfied*.   But in the boundless
intercourse of Future Men, the thousand individual qualities
that shall have sprung from human Need, in answer to the
divers idiosyncracies of Climate,—*so soon as ever they have
raised themselves to the height of the universal Human, and
therefore universally Intelligible,*—will mutually react on one

another in fertilising interchange, and blossom forth to joint 'all-human' artworks, of whose amplitude and splendour our art-sense of to-day, with its eternal clinging to the fetters of the old and dead, can conceive no jot or tittle.

To clear the ground for such a Work of the Future, must the Earth, then, take the human race once more into her womb, and bear herself and it anew ?

In troth, she 'd play us thus a sorry trick !—for then would Mother Earth destroy at one fell swoop all those conditions whose actual presence, just as they are, now shows us — rightly understood — the Necessity of such a framing of the human Future as we have here but barely hinted. For we can gain no hope, no courage, no confident assurance of the Future, till we convince ourselves that the fulfilment of our soul's best wish hangs not upon the old erroneous supposition that men must needs be what our wilful notions, abstracted from the Past, dictate that they *should* be ; but on the certain knowledge, that they require alone to be what by their very nature they *can* be, and *therefore shall and will be.* Not *Angels ;* but precisely *Men !*

The *Climate* about which alone we can talk, in any reasonable fashion, as fundamentally conditioning Art, is therefore :

The actual—and not the fancied—essence of the Human Race.

A
COMMUNICATION TO MY FRIENDS.

"EINE MITTHEILUNG AN MEINE FREUNDE."

(1851)

From among the many references to the Mittheilung, *in the* Correspondence of Wagner and Liszt *and the* Letters to Uhlig, Fischer and Heine, *I select the following :*—

To Liszt, Nov. 25, 1850, " *When I have finished* Opera and Drama, *I intend, provided I can find a publisher, to bring out my three romantic opera-poems with a Preface introducing them and explaining their genesis.*"—*To Uhlig, (undated, but apparently written in August '51),* " *My* Mittheilung *was ready soon after you left. The part you do not know is actually the most important. This is a decisive work !—The copying took me over a week.*"—*To Uhlig, Nov.* 1, *'*51, " *Well !* — *Härtels have only just read the* Vorwort, *and will not venture to publish it.*"—*To Liszt, Nov.* 20, *'*51, " *The timidity of Messrs Härtel, the proposed publishers of the book, has taken exception to certain passages in that Preface to which I did not wish to have any demonstrative intention attributed, and which I might have expressed just as well in a different way ; and the appearance of the book has in consequence been much retarded, to my great annoyance. . . . . But, although the Preface, written at the beginning of last August, appears in the present circumstances too late, the aforesaid declaration* " *(as to the intended destiny of* Siegfried) " *will be given to the public without any change.*"—*To Liszt, Dec.* 14, *'*51, " *The three operatic poems, with a Communication to my Friends, will appear at the end of this month. . . . The conclusion I have recently altered a little, but in such a manner that everything referring to Weimar remains unchanged.*"— *To Uhlig, Jan.* 1, *'*52, " *Yesterday I received the book :* ' *Three opera poems.*' *. . . This Preface was really the most important message I had to deliver, for it was absolutely necessary in completion of* Opera and Drama *. . . What can I still say, if now my friends do not clearly understand ?*"—

TRANSLATOR'S NOTE.

A COMMUNICATION TO MY FRIENDS.

Y motive for this detailed "Communication" took rise in the necessity I felt of explaining the apparent, or real, contradiction offered by the character and form of my hitherto published opera-poems, and of the musical compositions which had sprung therefrom, to the views and principles which I have recently set down at considerable length and laid before the public under the title : "*Opera and Drama.*"

This explanation I propose to address to my *Friends*, because I can only hope to be understood * by those who feel a need and inclination to understand me ; and these, again, can only be my Friends.

As such, however, I cannot consider those who pretend to love me as *artist*, yet deem themselves bound to deny

---

* I must explain, once and for all, that whenever in the course of this Communication I speak of "understanding me" or "not understanding me," it is not as though I fancied myself a shade too lofty, too deep-meaning, or too high-soaring ; but I simply demand of whosoever may desire to understand me, that he will look upon me no otherwise than as I am, and in my communications upon Art will only regard as essential precisely what, in accordance with my general aim and as far as lay within my powers of exposition, has been put forth in them by myself. R. WAGNER.—The latter portion of this sentence is somewhat ambiguous in the German, running thus : "und in meiner künstlerischen Mittheilungen genau eben nur Das als wesentlich erkenne, was meiner Absicht und meinem Darstellungsvermögen gemäss in ihnen von mir kundgegeben wurde." It will be seen that the expression "künstlerischen Mittheilungen" admits of two interpretations, viz. : either "artistic communications,"—in other words, his operas,—or "communications upon the subject of Art." After some hesitation, I have chosen the latter, as it seems to me that Wagner is here referring to the distortions of his views promulgated by hostile critics—and nearly all his critics were both crafty and malicious—*e.g.* Professor Bischoff and his perversion of the title : "Artwork of the Future" into "Music of the Future," together with the consequences he deduced from this wilful misunderstanding of the author's aim.—TR.

me their sympathy as *man*.*　If the severance of the Artist
from the Man is as brainless an attempt as the divorce of
soul from body, and if it be a stable truth that never was
an Artist loved nor his art comprehended, unless he was
also loved—at least unwittingly—as Man, and with his art
his life was also understood: then at the present moment
less than ever, and amid the hopeless desolation of our
public art-affairs, can an artist of my endeavour be loved,
and thus his art be understood, if this understanding and
that love which makes it possible be not above all grounded
upon sympathy, *i.e.* upon a fellow-pain and fellow-feeling
with the veriest human aspect of his life.

Least of all, however, can I deem those to be my friends
who, led by impressions gathered from an incomplete
acquaintance with my artistic doings, transfer the nebulous
uncertainty of this their understanding to the artistic
object itself, and ascribe to a peculiarity of the latter
that which finds its only origin in their own confusion
of mind.　The position which these gentry take up against
the artist, and seek to fortify by all the aids of toilsome
cunning, they dub "impartial criticism," seizing on every
opportunity of posing as the only "true Friends" of the
artist,—whose actual Foes are therefore those who take
their stand beside him in full sympathy.—Our language
is so rich in synonymes that, having lost our intuitive
understanding of their meaning, we fancy we may use
them at our pleasure and draw private lines of demarcation between them.　Thus do we employ and separate

* For the matter of that, they understand by the expression "Man," strictly
speaking, nothing but a "Subject" ("*Unterthan*"); and perhaps also, in
my particular case, one who has his own opinions and follows them without
regard of consequences.—R. WAGNER.—Considerable light is thrown upon
both these notes, when we reflect that Wagner, at the period of writing, was in
exile for attempting to introduce ethical considerations into politics, whilst
actually—think on it!—a court-salaried Musical Conductor.　As regards the
present note, its second half (*i.e.* the words following "Unterthan") does not
appear in the original edition, of the "Three Opera-Poems with a Preface;"
and it should be added that the opening line of the essay referred, in that
edition, to the necessity of publishing in self-defence the opera-poems themselves—not merely, as now, the "Communication."—TR.

"Love" and "Friendship." For my own part, with the attainment of years of discretion I have lost the power of imagining a Friendship without Love, to say nothing of experiencing such a feeling; and still harder should I find it, to conceive how modern Art-Criticism and Friendship for the artist criticised could possibly be terms of like significance.

The Artist addresses himself to the Feeling, and not to the Understanding. If he be answered in terms of the Understanding, then it is as good as said that he has not been *understood;* and our Criticism is nothing else than the avowal of the misunderstanding (*Geständniss des Unverständniss*) of the artwork, which can only be really understood by the Feeling—admitted, by the formed, and withal not mis-formed feeling. Whosoever feels impelled, then, to bear witness to his lack of understanding of an artwork, should take the precaution to ask himself one simple question, namely: what were the reasons for this lack? True, that he would come back at last to the qualities of the artwork itself; but only after he had cleared up the immediate problem of the physical garb in which it had addressed itself to his feelings. Was this outward garb unable to arouse or pacify his feelings, then he would have, before all else, to endeavour to procure himself an insight into a manifest imperfection of the artwork; namely, into the grounds of a failure of harmony between the purpose of the artist and the nature of those means by which he sought to impart it to the hearer's Feeling. Only two issues could then lie open for his inquiry, namely: whether the means of presentation to the senses were in keeping with the artistic aim, or whether this aim itself was indeed an artistic one?

We are not here speaking of the works of plastic art, in which the technical execution is part and parcel of the creation of the artist himself; but of the Drama, whose physical garb is merely planned-out by the technique of the poet, but not—as in the case of the plastic artist— realised also by him; since it first gains this realisation

at the hands of a specific art, the art of dramatic portrayal.
Now if the Feeling of our critical friend has not received
a sure and definite impression from the physical show
(*sinnliche Erscheinung*), in the present case the province
of the art of dramatic portrayal, he ought before all things
to perceive that the execution was at any rate inadequate ;
for the very essence of physical portrayal consists in this,
that it should exert a sure and definite impression upon
the Feeling. The shortcoming of the means once recognised, it then would only remain for him to inquire, on
what the disproportion between aim and means was
grounded : whether the aim was of such a character that
it was either unworthy of realisation, or generally unfit
for realisation by the means of Art,—or whether the disproportion simply rested on the *mis*character of the means
which, at a given time and place, and under given circumstances, had proved themselves insufficient to realise a
given artistic aim. In the latter case, it would be a
question of distinctly understanding an artistic aim which
had been only so far realised as the limited technical
means of the dramatic poet allowed of. But, from the
nature of every *artistic* aim, this understanding cannot
be compassed by the sheer unaided Intellect (*mit dem
reinen Verstande*), but only by the Feeling ; and indeed
by that more or less *artistically* cultured feeling which
can only be the property of those who find themselves
in a predicament more or less akin to that of the artist,
who have developed amid conditions of life like his, and
who in their inmost being so heartily sympathise with
him that they are prepared, under certain circumstances,
to adopt that aim as their very own, and are able to take
an intimate and weighty share in the struggle for its
realisation.

Manifestly these can only be the artist's actual loving
Friends, and not the Critics who place themselves at an
intentional distance from him. When the 'absolute'
Critic looks out upon the Artist from his private peep-
hole, he as good as sees *nothing ;* for the only thing he

can espy, namely his own likeness on the mirror of his vanity, is—take it reasonably—naught.   The imperfection of the artwork's semblance (*Erscheinung*) he by no means traces to its actual source ; he discerns it, at the utmost, in the felt imperfection of his impression, and endeavours to vindicate the latter by defects in the artist's aim, which he is the very last person to be in a position to understand.   In fact he has already so thoroughly practised himself in this procedure, that he finally gives up the attempt to let himself be influenced by the physical appearance of the artwork; but fancies that, with his acquired professional aptness, he may make shift with the written or printed pages on which the poet or musician —so far as his technical powers permitted—had set down his aim as such   transferring to this aim itself so much of his discontent—unconsciously developed in advance—as he desires to base especially thereon.   Though this position is that least fitted for the understanding of any work of art, particularly in the Present, yet it is the only one which enables our modern art-critics to maintain their eternal paper life.   But even with this my Communication—alas ! likewise on paper—I do not address myself to them, so proud in their exalted station : I decline to accept one iota of their critical Friendship.   What I might have to tell them, even *about* myself and my artistic doings, they would not deign to understand ; for the very good reason that they make it a point of honour to know everything in the world already.

By thus explaining—to whom I do *not* address myself, I have *ipso facto* defined those to whom I do.   They are those who so far sympathise with me both as man and artist, that they are able to understand my *aims*, even though I cannot bring these before them in the perfect realisation of a fitting physical embodiment because the conditions prior thereto are lacking in the public art-life of the Present, and I can therefore only appeal to those who think and feel with me,—in short: *to my Friends, who love me*.

Only those Friends, however, who above all feel an

S

interest in the Man within the Artist, are capable of understanding him ; and that not only in the Present, which
forbids the realisation of any high poetic aim, but at all
times and in all places.—The *absolute artwork*, i.e. the art-
work which shall neither be bound by time and place, nor
portrayed by given men in given circumstances, for the
understanding of equally definite human beings,—is an
utter *no*thing, a chimera of æsthetic phantasy.   Its sponsors
have distilled the idea of Art from the actuality of the art-
works of diverse epochs : to give this idea an imagined
reality again, since one otherwise could not have kept it
handy even in the imagination, they have clothed it around
with a conceptual body which, under the firma of the
'absolute artwork,' avowedly or unavowedly makes out
the brain-spook of our æsthetic critics.   Moreover, as this
hypothetical body has taken all the features of its imaginary
physical form from the actual attributes of the artworks of
the Past, so also is the æsthetic belief therein essentially
conservative ; and therefore the reduction of this creed to
practice, the completest artistic unfertility.

Only in a truly inartistic era, could the belief in such an
artwork arise within the heads—naturally, not within the
hearts—of men.   We descry its first historical traces in the
era of the Alexandrians, after the demise of Grecian art.
To the dogmatic character, however, which this conception
has taken-on in our own time,—to the rigour, obstinacy,
and persecuting savagery with which it mounts the tribune
of our journalistic criticism, it could only grow in an era
when Life itself began to face it with fresh-budding germs
of the genuine artwork, whose qualities every man of
healthy feeling could recognise—though not, for obvious
reasons, our art-criticism that lives upon the refuse of
the old and outlived.   That the new germs, especially in
the teeth of such a criticism, cannot as yet reach full unfoldment into flowers, it is, that brings to its speculative energy
a constant store of fresh apparent vindication ; for, amongst
its other abstractions from the artworks of the Past, it has
also bottled-off the notion of the actuality of physical show

being indispensable to the artwork. Now it observes that this condition, with whose fulfilment itself must certainly cease to exist, is as yet unfulfilled by the germs of a new and living art, and for that very reason it denies them the right to life, or in other words, the right to that impulse which spurs them onward to the blossom of physical manifestment. Herewith the Science of Æsthetics assumes a truly art-murderous activity, and carries it to the pitch of fanatical barbarity; inasmuch as it hugs to its breast the conservative phantasm of an 'absolute art-work' which it can never see realised, for the simple reason that its realisation lies already far behind us in the realm of History, and with reactionary zeal would sacrifice to that the reality of natural beginnings of fresh works of art. That which alone can bring those beginnings to completion, alone those germs to blossom,—That which must consequently throw the æsthetic phantasm of the absolute artwork for ever on the dustheap of the ages, is this: the winning of the *conditions* for the complete and full appearance of the physical artwork amid and from our actual Life.

The absolute, i.e. the *un*conditioned artwork, existing but in Thought, is naturally bound to neither time nor place, nor yet to definite circumstance. It can, for instance, be indited two thousand years ago for the democracy of Athens, and performed to-day before the Prussian Court at Potsdam. In the conception of our æsthetists it must bear exactly the same value, possess exactly the same essential features, no matter whether here or there, to-day or in the days of old; nay, they go farther, and imagine that, like certain sorts of wine, it gains by being cellared, and can to-day and here be first entirely understood aright, because they now forsooth can think into it the democratic public of Athens, and gain an endlessly augmented store of knowledge from the criticism of both this phantom public and the to-be-assumed impression once exercised upon it by the artwork.*

---

* Thus, even now, our literary dilettantists know no more refreshing entertainment for themselves and their æstheto-political public of idling readers, than for ever and a day to jog round *Shakespeare* with their writings. It

Now however elevating all this may be to the modern intellect, yet for one thing it forms a sorry outlook, namely the factor of artistic enjoyment; that factor naturally not coming into play, since such an enjoyment can only be won through the Feeling, and not through antiquarian Research. Wherefore if, in contradistinction to this arid, critical enjoyment of the ghost of art, we are ever to come to a genuine enjoyment; and if the latter, in keeping with the nature of Art, can only be approached through Feeling : then nothing remains for us but to turn to that Art-work whose attributes present as great a contrast to the fancied monumental artwork as the living Man to the marble Statue. But these attributes consist herein, that it proclaims itself in sharpest definition by Time, by Place, by Circumstance ; therefore that it can never come to living and effective show, if it come not to show at a given time, in a given place, and amid given circumstances ; in a word, that it strips off every vestige of the *monumental*.

We shall never gain a clear perception of the necessity of these attributes, nor shall we ever advance that claim for the genuine Art-work which such perception must engender, if we do not first arrive at a proper understanding of what we are to connote by the term " Universal-human." Until we come to recognise, and on every hand to demonstrate in practice, that the very essence of the human species consists in the diversity of human Individuality, —instead of placing the essence of the individuality in its conformity to the general characteristics of the species, and consequently sacrificing it to the latter, as Religion and State have hitherto done,*—neither shall we comprehend that the fully and wholly Present must once and for

never occurs to them for a moment, that *that* Shakespeare whom they suck dry with their critical sponges, is not worth a rushlight, and serves at utmost as the sheet of foolscap for the exhibition of those proofs of their intellectual poverty which they take such desperate pains to air. The Shakespeare, who alone can be worth somewhat to us, is the ever new-creating poet who, now and in all ages, is That which Shakespeare once was to his age.—R. WAGNER.

* " Wie es bisher in Religion und Staat der Fall war, das Wesen der Individualität in die Gattung setzen, folgerichtig es dieser aufopfern."—In connection with the footnote to *Art and Climate*, page 260, I would draw attention

all supplant the half or wholly Absent, *the monumental*. In truth, our entire ideas on Art are now so bound up in the "monumental," that we fancy we may only assign a value to works of art in measure as we are justified in imputing to them a monumental character. Though this view may be right as applied to the offspring of frivolous *Mode*, which never can content a human need, still we cannot but see that it is at bottom but a mere reaction of man's nobler feeling of natural shame against the motley utterances of Mode, and with the ceasing of the reign of Mode itself, must stand confessed of no more right, because of no more reason. An absolute respect for the Monumental is entirely unthinkable : at best, it can only bolster itself upon æsthetic revulsion against an uncontenting Present. But this feeling of revulsion has not the needful strength to take victorious arms gainst such a Present, so long as it merely shows itself as a passion for the monumental. The utmost which that passion can eventually effect, is the perversion of the Monumental itself into another Mode,—such as, to tell the truth, is the case to-day. And thus we never leave the vicious circle from which the noblest impulse of the 'monumental' craze itself is striving to withdraw, regardless that no rational exit is so much as thinkable except by violent withdrawal of their life-conditions both from Mode and Monument ; for even the Mode has its full justification in face of the Monumental, to wit as the reaction of the im-

to page 152 of George Eliot's translation of *The Essence of Christianity* (Ludwig Feuerbach) : "All divine attributes are attributes of the species, attributes which in the individual are limited, but the limits of which are abolished in the essence of the species. My knowledge, my will is limited ; but my limit is not that of another man, to say nothing of mankind." In the first chapter of Feuerbach's book we also read, "Certainly the human individual—and herein consists his distinction from the animal—can and must feel himself confined by limits ; but he can only become conscious of his limits in that he takes the perfection, the infinitude of the species as his 'object,' be it the object of his feeling, his conscious experience, or his reflection. That he nevertheless confounds *his* limits with the *limits of the species*, rests upon the illusion whereby be *directly* identifies himself with the species—an illusion which is intimately bound up with the indolence, the vanity, and the self-seeking of the individual."—Tr.

mediate vital impulse of the Present from the coldness of that unfelt sense of beauty which proclaims itself in the passion for the monumental. But the annihilation of the Monumental together with the Mode is, in other terms : the entry upon life of the ever freshly present, ever new-related and warm-appealing Art-work ; which, again, is as much as to say : the winning of the conditions for this art-work *from Life itself.*

To map out the character of this Art-work: that it could not be the work of our plastic art of nowadays—in so far as that art is compelled to proclaim itself as monumental, and owes its bare existence to our monumental craze,—but could only be *the Drama;* further, that this Drama could only find its proper attitude toward Life, when in its every moment it should be completely present with that Life, in its remotest relations so bound therewith and issuing therefrom, in its individuality of time and place and circumstance so characteristic thereof, that for its understanding (*Verständniss*), *i.e.,* for its enjoyment, there should be no longer need of the reflecting Intellect (*Verstand*) but only of the directly seizing Feeling; in fine, that this understanding could only be brought about when the contents, in themselves strictly emotional, should be presented to the senses in their own most fitting form, to wit, by man's universal-artistic faculty of expression to man's universal-artistic faculty of reception, and not by one severed attribute of that one faculty to another fenced-off attribute of this :—to show all this in general terms, was the object of my essay " The Art-work of the Future." The nature of the difference between this art-work and that *monumental* artwork which hovers in the mist before our critical Æsthetes, lies there exposed for any one who will trouble himself to understand me; and to assert that the thing I there demanded is already extant, could only occur to those for whom true art itself is absolutely non-extant.

Only *one* situation, in which I necessarily found myself herewith, could give to even less prejudiced persons a colour for the cry of " contradictions." It is this : I place *Life* as the first and foremost condition for the appearance of the Artwork, and not indeed its wilful reflection in the thought of the philosopher, but the most real and sentient Life of all, the freest fount of natural Will (*den freiesten Quell der Unwillkürlichkeit*) ; yet from my standpoint of artist of the Present, I sketch the outlines of the "art-work of the future," and this with reference to a form which only the artistic instinct of that future Life itself can ever shape aright. Against this reproach I not merely advance the plea that I have only suggested the barest *general* features of the Art-work, but I go farther and observe—not alone for my justification, but as essential to the understanding of my aim—that the Artist of the Present must certainly have an influence, determinative in every respect, upon the Art-work of the Future, and that he may well count up this influence in advance, for the very reason that he must grow conscious of it even now. Amid his noblest striving, this consciousness waxes in him from his inward feeling of deepest discontent with the life of the Present: he sees himself pointed to the life of the Future alone, for the realisation of possibilities whose existence has come to his consciousness from the promptings of his own artistic powers.

Now he who cherishes the fatalistic view anent this Life of the Future, that we can conceive absolutely nothing of it, thereby confesses that he has not got so far with his human development as to possess a *reasonable Will* (vernünftigen Willen): for the reasonable Will is the willing of the recognised Spontaneous and Natural, and only he who has reached the point of grasping its substance for himself can presuppose this Will as fashioning the Life of the Future. Whosoever does not conceive this fashioning of the Future as a necessary consequence of the reasonable will of the Present, neither has he the shadow of a reasonable conception of the Present or the Past : whosoever possesses no initiative in his own character, neither can he perceive in the Present any initiative for the Future. But the initiative for the Art-work of the Future must come from the Artist of the Present who is in the position to grasp this Present, who takes up its powers and its necessary Will into himself, and withal remains no slave to the Present but shows himself as its moving, willing, and fashioning organ, as a consciously-operating portion of that vital impulse which urges it to reach forth from out itself.

To recognise the Life-stress (*Lebenstrieb*) of the Present, is to be impelled to put it into action.   But, with *our* Present, such a setting-in-action cannot possibly proclaim itself in any other way than as a foreshadowing of the Future ; and, indeed, of such a Future as shall not depend upon the mechanism of the Past, but, in all its movements free and self-dependent, shall shape from out itself, i.e., from out of Life.   This setting-in-action is the annihilation of the Monumental, and, in the case of Art, must take that path which brings it into most immediate contact with ever-present Life ; this path is that of *Drama*.   The recognition of the necessity of Art's taking this direction, to set it in an ever fruitful interaction with Life, and lift it from the Monumental rut, must naturally also lead the artist to recognise the inability of present public life either to further such an artistic tendency or itself to fall in therewith ; for our public life, so far as it comes into any contact with the phenomena of Art, has shaped itself under the exclusive influence of the Monumental and its counterpoise, the Mode.   Wherefore only such artists can work in harmony with present public life as either imitate the monuments of the past, or stamp themselves as servants of the mode : but both are, in very truth, no artists at all.   The genuine artist, on the other hand, who moves along the said true path of Drama, cannot but show himself at variance with the spirit of present public life.   But just as he recognises the true Artwork to be *that* which can unveil to Life its meaning in fullest physical show, so must he necessarily throw forward to the Future the realisation of his highest artistic wish, as to a life enfranchised from the tyranny of both Monument and Mode ; he thus must turn his artist Will straight toward the Art-work of the Future, no matter whether it shall be himself or others to whom it first is granted to set foot upon the soil of that Life of the Future which shall bring both means and consummation.

It is certainly not the professional thinker or critic, who can ever reach this Will; but only the actual artist, to whom, from his artistic standpoint in the life of the Present, thought and criticism have become an indispensable attribute of his general artistic activity. This attribute is necessarily developed in him through the survey of his position towards our public life, which he cannot look on with the cold indifference of a sheer critical experimentalist, but with the warm desire to address himself intelligibly thereto. What this artist most perceives, when he looks upon the public life of the Present, is the utter impossibility of thus addressing himself by means of the mechanical implements of prevailing monumental, or modish art. As I am here dealing with the genuine dramatic poet alone, I allude to the absence of *that* theatric art, and *that* dramatic platform, which would be equal to the task of realising his aim. Our modern theatres are either the tools of monumental criticism—as witness, the Berlin Sophocles, Shakespeare &c.—or of absolute fashion. The possibility of entirely dispensing with these theatres he can only embrace by an abandonment of every, even the remotest, attempt to realise his specific purpose: in other words, he must write dramas for the reading-desk. But since the Drama is just that thing which only in its fullest physical manifestment can ever become a work of Art, he is forced at last to content himself with an *incomplete* realisation of his purpose, so as not to bid entire farewell to his main endeavour.

But the poet's purpose would first be fully realised, when he not only saw it adequately expressed upon the stage, but when this should happen withal at a definite time, under definite conditions, and before a gathering of spectators connected by a definite measure of affinity with himself. A poetic aim which I have conceived with a view to certain relations and surroundings, can only expend its full effect when I impart it amid the same relations and to the same surroundings : then alone can this aim be understood apart from the critic's art, and its human purport be perceived ; but not when all these vital conditions shall have vanished, and the relations changed. When, for instance, before the first French Revolution, there existed amongst an entire class of frivolous pleasure-seekers that mood (*Stimmung*) in which a *Don Juan* could be deemed an entirely comprehensible phenomenon, the true expression of that mood ; when this type was seized by artists and, in its last process of realisation, embodied by an actor whose whole temperament was as fitted to this personality as was the Italian tongue to give this personality an adequate expression,—the emotional effect of such an exhibition, at such a time, was certainly most definite and unmistakable. But what is the complexion of affairs when, to-day, before the entirely altered Public of the Present composed of members of the Bourse or State-officialdom the same Don Juan is played again, by a performer who treats his leisure to beer and skittles and thus escapes all temptation to be unfaithful to his wife ; a Don Juan transposed, to boot, to the German tongue, and disguised in a translation from which every trace of the Italian linguistic character has been washed completely out ? Will not this Don Juan be understood at least *quite otherwise* than as the poet meant ; and is not this quite other understanding —at best depending on the critic's aid—in truth *no* understanding of the real Don Juan ? Or can ye, perchance, enjoy a lovely landscape, when ye look on it in darkest midnight ?—

In the haphazard and piecemeal fashion in which the artist now attains the public's ear, he must become the less intelligible, the more the artistic aim from which his work took rise has an actual connexion with Life ; for such an aim can never be an accidental, abstract one, conceived amid the generalisms of æsthetic caprice, but only ripens to the force requisite for artistic manifestment when it has borrowed from time and circumstance an individual shape.   If the realisation of such an aim can only have its full effect when it comes to manifestment while the relations which awoke it in the poet are still warm with life, and when it is brought before those who were included, consciously or unconsciously, amongst those relations : then the artist who sees his work treated as a monumental one, which may indifferently be given at any convenient time or before any audience one pleases, must be exposed to every conceivable peril of misunderstanding. Then can he cleave alone to those who, by reason of their general sympathy with him, *can understand this situation also, and through their sharing in his endeavour*—which they find made infinitely more difficult by this his situation—*make good to him* in self-creative generosity *the fulness of those furthering conditions* which are denied his artwork by the actual times.—It is therefore to these fellow-feeling and fellow-creating Friends alone, that I feel impelled to here address myself.

To them, whom I have never been able to address in that fashion which alone could satisfy my wish, I have thus, in order to make myself completely understood, to explain the contradictions presented by my hitherto enacted opera-poems to my recently expressed views upon the operatic *genre* in general. I speak chiefly of the *poems*, not only because the bond between my art and my life lies plainest shown in them, but also because I have to call on them to witness that my musical working-out, my method of operatic composition, was conditioned by the very nature of those poems.

The contradictions to which I here allude, do not at all events exist for any one who has accustomed himself to regard a phenomenon with due allowance for its development *in time*. Whosoever in his verdict on a phenomenon takes this development also into consideration, can only light on contradictions when the phenomenon is one divorced from time and place, unnatural, or illogical. But to leave the evolutionary factor completely out of count, to jumble phases separated by time and well-marked

difference into one conglomerate mass, is certainly itself
an unnatural or illogical mode of viewing things, and
such as can only belong to our monumental-historic
criticism, not to the healthy criticism of the sympathetic,
feeling heart. This uncritical demeanour of our modern
Criticism is due, among other things, to the standpoint from which she applies to each and every object
the monumental foot-rule. For her, the artists and masterpieces of all ages and nations stand piled beside and
on each other, and their differences she treats as merely
art-historical, to be computed by the abstract date, not felt
as warm and living ; for with any truth of feeling, their
simultaneous exhibition must needs be utterly insupportable,—about as painful as when we hear Sebastian Bach
performed at a concert by side of Beethoven.   In my own
case, also, certain critics, who pretend to judge my art-
doings as a connected whole, have set about their task
with this same uncritical heedlessness and lack of Feeling :
views on the nature of Art, that I have proclaimed from a
standpoint which it took me years of evolution step-by-
step to gain, they seize-on for the standard of their verdict,
and point them back upon those very compositions from
which I started on the natural path of evolution that led me
to this standpoint. When, for instance—not from the standpoint of abstract æsthetics, but from that of practical artistic
experience—I denote the Christian principle as hostile to or
incapable of Art (*kunstunfähig*), these critics point me out
the contradiction in which I stand towards my *earlier* dramatic works, which undoubtedly are filled with a certain
tincture of this principle, so inextricably blended with our
modern evolution.   But it never occurs to them that, if they
would only compare the new-won standpoint with that abandoned, the two are certainly distinct enough yet the one is
organically connected with the other, and that far rather were
the new standpoint to be *explained* from the old, than were
this relinquished to be judged by that adopted.   No,—
thinking fit to take my older works as planned and carried
out in the light of the newer standpoint, they find in them

an inconsequence with, a contradiction to my present views, and derive the clearest proof of the erroneous nature of those views from my own contradiction of them in the practice of my art; and thus, in the most easy-going fashion in the world, they kill two birds with one stone, inasmuch as they brand both my artistic and my theoretic labours as the acts of a critically untrained, confused, and extravagant person. But the product of their own acumen they call true " Criticism," forsooth, and criticism of the " historical " school !—

I have here touched on one essential point of the above-mentioned contradictions. Since I now wish to address my friends alone, I might perhaps have left it wholly unregarded; for in truth no one can be my friend who is not able to detect for himself the phantom nature of this 'contradiction.' This insight, however, is immeasurably hindered by the incomplete and fragmentary fashion in which alone I am able to impart my purpose even to my Friends. One has witnessed a performance of this, another of that, of my dramatic works, as chance might hap; his inclination towards me has sprung from his acquaintance with just this one work; even this one work has come before him in a halting fashion, at the best; he has had to fill up many a gap, by drawing on the store of his own feelings and endeavours, and to gain himself at last a full enjoyment by importing a perchance preponderating share of himself and his hobbies into the object of enjoyment. But here comes the point where we must clearly understand each other : my friends must see the *whole* of me, in order to decide whether they can be *wholly* my friends. I can no longer content myself with half arrangements; I cannot consent that things which were necessities in my development should appear to good natured people as accidentals, which they may twist to my advantage according to their degree of inclination toward me. Thus I face towards *my Friends*, to render them a clear account of my path of evolution, in course of which those apparent contradictions, also, must be thoroughly unriddled.

I will not, however, attempt to reach this end by the paths of abstract criticism ; but will point out my evolutionary career, as faithfully as I can now survey it, by reviewing my works, and the moods of life which called them forth, in series—not tossing everything upon one heap of generalities.

Of my earliest efforts I shall have but a brief report to make : they were the usual attempts of an as yet undeveloped individuality, to find, with advancing adolescence, its bearings toward those general impressions of art which affect us from our youth up. The first artistic Will is nothing else than the contentment of the instinctive impulse to imitate what most attracts us.—

If I seek to gain myself a fairly satisfactory explanation of the artistic faculty, I can only do so by attributing it chiefly to the *force of the receptive faculty* (die Kraft des Empfängnissvermögens). The un-artistic, political temperament may be characterised thus : that from youth up it sets a check upon impressions from outside, which, in the course of the man's development, mounts even to a calculation of the personal profit that his withstanding of the outer world will bring him, to a talent for referring this outer world to himself and never himself to it. On the other hand, the un-political, artistic temperament is marked by this one feature : that its owner gives himself up without reserve to the impressions which move his emotional being (*Empfindungswesen*) to sympathy. The motive power of these impressions, again, is in direct ratio to the force of the receptive faculty, which latter only gains the strength of an *impulse to impart* (*Mittheilungsdrang*) when they fill it to an ecstatic excess (*entzückenden Übermaase*).* The

* We have here another instance of the unconscious identity of Wagner's thought with that of Schopenhauer, who has said in " *Die Welt als Wille und Vorstellung* " :—" It is as if, when genius appears in an individual, a far greater measure of the power of knowledge falls to his lot than is necessary for the service of an individual will ; and this superfluity of knowledge, being free, now becomes *subject* purified from will, a clear mirror of the inner nature of

artistic force is conditioned by the measure of this excess, for it is nothing else than the need to make away to others the over-swelling store (*Empfängniss*). This force may operate in either of two directions, according as it has been set in motion by *exclusively* artistic impressions, or finally by impressions *also* harvested from Life itself. That which first decides the *Artist*, as such, is certainly the purely artistic impression ; if his receptive force be completely absorbed thereby, so that the impressions to be later received from Life find his faculty already exhausted, then he will develop as an *absolute* artist along the path which we must designate the feminine, i.e. that which embraces alone the feminine element of art. On this we meet all those artists of the day whose deeds make out the catalogue of modern art ; it is the world of art close fenced from Life, in which Art plays with herself, drawing sensitively back from every brush with actuality—not merely the actuality of the modern Present, but of Life in general—and treats it as her *absolute* foe ; believing that Life in every age and every land is waging war against herself, and therefore that any toil to fashion Life is labour lost, and consequently unbeseeming to the artist. In this class we find above all Painting and, pre-eminently, Music. The case is otherwise, where the previously developed artistic receptive-force has merely formed and focussed the faculty for receiving Life's impressions ; where in place of weakening, it has the rather strengthened it—in the highest sense of the term. On the path along which this force evolves, Life itself is at last surveyed in the light of artistic impressions, and the impulse towards imparting which gathers from the overfill of these impressions is the only true *poetic force*. This divorces not itself from Life, but from the standpoint of Art it strives to tender Life a fashioning hand. Let us denote this as the masculine, the generative path of Art.—

the world. This explains the activity, amounting even to disquietude, of men of genius ; for the present can seldom satisfy them, because it does not fill their consciousness. This gives them that longing for men of similar nature and of like stature to whom they might communicate themselves."—Tr.

Whosoever may choose to think that with my present Communication I propose to make out for myself a title to the halo of a "Genius," I flatly and distinctly contradict him in advance. On the contrary, I feel prepared to prove that it is a piece of uncommonly vapid and superficial criticism, to ascribe, as we customarily do, the definitive operation of a particular artistic force to a gift (*Befähigung*) which we fancy we have fathomed when we briefly call it "Genius." In other words, we treat this Genius as a pure and absolute windfall, which God or Nature casts hither and thither at pleasure, often without the favoured bounty falling even to the right man: for how frequently we hear, that "So-and-so does not know what to be about with his genius."—I attribute the force which we commonly call Genius solely to the faculty which I have just described at length. That which operates so mightily upon this force that it must finally come forth to full productiveness, we have in truth to regard as the real fashioner and former, as the only furthering condition for that force's efficacy, and this is the Art already evolved outside that separate force, the Art which from the artworks of the ancient and the modern world has shaped itself into a universal Substance, and hand in hand with actual Life, reacts upon the individual with the character of the force that I have elsewhere named the *communistic*. Amid these all-filling and all-fashioning influences of Art and Life, there thus remains to the Individual but one chief thing as his own: namely Force, vital force, force to assimilate the kindred and the needful; and this is precisely that receptive-force which I have denoted above, and which—so soon as it opens its arms in love without reserve—must necessarily, with the attainment of its perfect strength, become at last productive-force.

In epochs when this force, like the force of Individuality in general, has been entirely crushed out by state-discipline, or by the complete fossilisation of the outward forms of Life and Art—as in China, or in Europe towards the end of the Roman world-dominion—neither have those phenomena

which we christen by the name of "Genius" ever come to
light: a plain proof that they are not cast upon life by the
caprice of God or Nature. On the other hand, these phenomena were just as little known in those ages when both
creative forces, the individualistic and the communistic,
reacted on each other with all the freedom of unfettered
Nature, forever fresh-begetting and ever giving birth anew.
These are the so-called prehistoric times, the times when
Speech, and Myth, and Art were really born. Then, too, the
thing we call Genius was unknown: no one man was a
Genius, since all men were it. Only in times like ours, does
one know or name these "Geniuses"; the sole name that we
can find for those artistic forces which withdraw themselves
from the drillground of the State and ruling Dogma, or from
the sluggard bolstering-up of tottering forms of Art, to open
out new pathways and fill them with their innate life. Yet
if we look a little closer, we shall find that these new
openings are in no wise arbitrary and private paths, but
continuations of a long-since-hewn main causeway; down
which, before and with these solitary units, a joint and
many-membered force of diverse individualities has poured
itself, whose conscious or unconscious instinct has urged
it to the abrogation of those forms by fashioning newer
moulds of Life and Art. Here, then, we see again a
common force, which includes within its coefficients that
individual force we have erstwhile foolishly dismissed with
the appellation "Genius," and, according to our modern
notions thereof, utterly annuls it. By all means, that
associate, communistic force is only brought into play
through the medium of the individual force; for it is, in
truth, naught other than the force of sheer human Individuality in general. The form, however, that comes
eventually to manifestment is nowise, as we superficially
opine, the work of the solitary individual; but the latter
takes his share in the common work—namely that of most
palpably revealing, by its realisation, an existing potentiality—only by virtue of that one quality which I have
already denoted above, and whose prime energy I wish

T

now to express still more distinctly. An ancient myth which I will now relate—despite the comminations of the historico-political school—shall serve me in the stead of definition.

The fair sea-wife Wachilde had born a son to good King Viking : the three Norns came to greet the child, and dower it with gifts. The first Norn gave it strength of body, the second wisdom ; and the grateful father bade them take their seat beside his throne. But the third bestowed upon the child "the ne'er-contented mind that ever broods the New." Viking, aghast at such a gift, refused the youngest Norn his thanks; indignant, she recalled her gift, to punish his ingratitude. The son grew up to strength and mighty stature ; and whate'er there was to know, he mastered it betimes. But never did he feel the spur to change or venture ; with every turning of his life he was content, and found his home in all. He never loved, and neither did he hate : but, since he lit by chance upon a wife, he, too, begat a son, and sent him to take schooling from the Dwarves, that he might learn what's fit ;—this son was that Wieland whom Want was once to teach to forge himself his wings. But the Ancient soon became the sport of fools and children, since every one might plague him, without it moving him to ire ; for he was so wise that he knew that fools and children love to scoff and tease. Only when they said light words about his mother, did he kindle into wrath ; about *her*, he would bear no jesting. When he came upon the Sound, it never dawned on him to build a boat and ship across it, but he waded plump into the waters, shoulder-high ; so the people called him "Wate." One day he wished to get him news about his son, if the child was well-behaved and making progress with his lessons ; he found the gateway closed, that led into the cavern of the Dwarves, for they were planning mischief against the child and wished to balk the father's visit. But he felt no care, for he was always satisfied : he laid him down beside the entrance, and fell asleep. His mighty snoring shook a boulder that hung above his head; it hurtled down on him and killed him. Such was the life of the sage and sturdy giant Wate: thereto had Viking's father-care brought up the son of the sweet sea-wife Wachilde; and thus art thou brought up, to this very day, my German Folk!

That one rejected gift: "the ne'er contented mind, that ever broods the New," the youngest Norn holds out to all of us when we are born, and through it alone might we each, one day, become a "Genius;"* but now, in our craze for education, 'tis Chance alone that brings this gift within our grasp,—the accident of *not becoming educated* (erzogen). Secure against the refusal of a father who died beside my cradle, perchance the Norn, so often chased away, stole gently to it, and there bestowed on me her gift; which never left poor untrained me, and made Life and Art and mine own self my only, quite anarchic, educators.—

I may pass over the endless variety of impressions which exercised a lively effect upon me in my earliest youth; they were as diverse in their operation as in their source. Whether, under their influence, I ever appeared to any one an "Infant prodigy" ("*Wunderkind*"), I very much doubt: mechanical dexterities were never drubbed into me, nor did I ever show the slightest bent towards them. To play-acting I felt an inclination, and indulged it in the quiet of my chamber; this was naturally aroused in me by the close connection of my family with the stage. The only remarkable thing about it all, was my repugnance against going to the theatre itself; childish impressions which I had imbibed from the earnestness of classical antiquity, so far as I had made its acquaintance in the 'Gymnasium,' may have inspired me with a certain contempt, nay, an abhorrence of the rouge-and-powdered ways of the Comedian.

*At this assertion, in his time, Professor Bischoff of Cologne waxed mighty wroth; he considered it a most unbecoming suggestion to make to himself and his friends.—R. WAGNER.—This sly little sarcasm does not appear in the original edition. As to our author's want of "education" (perhaps "bringing-up" would better express the idea), the statement in the next sentence must not be taken too literally; see the "*Autobiographic Sketch*."—TR.

But my passion for imitation (*Nachahmungseifer*) threw itself with greatest zest into the making of poetry and music,—perhaps because my stepfather, a portrait-painter, died betimes, and thus the pictorial element vanished early from among my nearer models; otherwise I should probably have begun to paint too, although I cannot but remember that the learning of the technique of the pencil soon went against my grain.   First I wrote plays ; but the acquaintance with Beethoven's Symphonies, which I only made in my fifteenth year, eventually inflamed me with a passion for music also, albeit it had long before this exercised a powerful effect upon me, chiefly through Weber's "*Freischütz.*"   Amidst my study of music, the poetic 'imitative-impulse' never quite forsook me ; it subordinated itself, however, to the musical, for whose contentment I only called it in as aid. Thus I recollect that, incited by the Pastoral Symphony, I set to work on a shepherd-play, its dramatic material being prompted by Goethe's " Lovers' Fancies " (" *Laune der Verliebten* ").   I here made no attempt at a preliminary poetic sketch, but wrote verses and music together, thus leaving the situations to take their rise from the music and the verses as I made them.

After many a digression to this side and to that, toward the commencement of my eighteenth year I was confronted by the Revolution of July 1830.   The effect upon me was both violent and stimulating ; especially keen was my enthusiasm for the struggling, my sorrow for the vanquished, Poles.   But these impressions were not as yet of any perceptible formative influence upon my artistic evolution ; in that respect they were stimulators only in a general sense.   Indeed, so much were my receptive and imitative faculties still under the sole dominion of artistic impressions, that it was precisely at this time that I occupied myself the most exclusively with music, wrote Sonatas, Overtures, and a Symphony, and in fact declined a proffered opera-text on the subject of " Kosziusko."*

---

* The author of this libretto (or sketch for a libretto ?) was Heinrich Laube mentioned by Wagner on page 9 of the present volume.—TR.

My passion for reproduction, however, soon turned towards the drama—at least, towards the opera. On the model of one of Gozzi's fairy-tales,* I wrote for myself an opera - text in verse, "*Die Feen*" ("The Fairies "); the then predominant "Romantic"- Opera of Weber, and also of Marschner — who about this time made his first appearance on the scene, and that at my place of sojourn, Leipzig — determined me to follow in their footsteps. What I turned out for myself was nothing more than barely what I wanted, namely an opera-text ; this I set to music according to the impressions made upon me by Weber, Beethoven, and Marschner.† However, what took my fancy in the tale of Gozzi, was not merely its adaptability for an opera-text, but the fascination of the 'stuff' itself.—A Fairy, who renounces immortality for the sake of a human lover, can only become a mortal through the fulfilment of certain hard conditions, the non-compliance wherewith on the part of her earthly swain threatens her with the direst penalties ; her lover fails in the test, which consists in this, that however evil and repulsive she may appear to him (in an obligatory metamorphosis) he shall not reject her in his unbelief. In Gozzi's tale the Fairy is now changed into a snake ; the remorseful lover frees her from the spell, by kissing the snake : thus he wins her for his wife. I altered this denouement by changing the Fairy into a stone, and then releasing her from the spell by her lover's passionate song ; while the lover — instead of being allowed to carry off his bride into his own country—is himself admitted by the Fairy-King to the immortal bliss of Fairyland, together with his fairy wife.—At the present time, this feature seems to me of some importance : though it was only the music and the ordinary traditions of opera,

* By an oversight, the title of this story was given by me, on page 8 (*Autobiographic Sketch*) in the German form, instead of in the Italian ; it should there read : "*La Donna Serpente*," in place of "*Die Frau als Schlange.*"—W. A. E.

† Note to the orginal edition :—" Whom people most unjustifiably take for a *mere* imitator of Weber."

that gave me then the notion, yet there lay already here the germ of a weighty factor in my whole development.—

I had now attained that age when the mind of man, if ever it is to do so, throws itself with greater directness upon the immediate surroundings of life. The fantastic looseness of German student-life, after a turbulent bout or two, had quickly filled me with disgust: *Woman* had begun to dawn on my horizon. The longing which could nowhere still itself in life found an ideal food in the reading of Heinse's "*Ardinghello*," as also the works of Heine, and other members of the then "Young-German" school of literature. The effect of the impressions thus received, expressed itself in my actual life in the only way wherein Nature can utter herself under the pressure of the moral bigotry of our social system. On the other hand, my artistic 'impulse-to-impart' unburdened itself of these life-impressions along the line of the artistic impressions which I received at the like time; among these, the most vivid were those derived from the newer French, and even Italian, operas. As this genre had, in effect, gained the upper hand on the German operatic stage, and figured in its repertoire almost exclusively, so was its influence inevitable upon one who found himself in a life-mood such as that I have referred to as mine at that period; there spoke out in this music, at least for me, all that which I then felt: the joyous throb of life, emprisoned in the makeshift garment of frivolity.—But it was a living personality, that kindled this inclination of mine into an enthusiasm of nobler intent: this was the *Schröder-Devrient*, in a 'star' engagement (*Gastspiel*) on the Leipzig stage. The remotest contact with this extraordinary woman electrified me; for many a long year, down even to the present day, I saw, I heard, I felt her near me, whenever the impulse to artistic production seized me.

The fruit of all these impressions, and all these moods, was an opera: the "*Liebesverbot, or the Novice of Palermo*." I took its subject from Shakespeare's "Measure for

Measure." It was Isabella that inspired me: she who leaves her novitiate in the cloister, to plead with a hardhearted Stateholder for mercy to her brother, who, in pursuance of a draconic edict, has been condemned to death for entering on a forbidden, yet Nature-hallowed love-bond with a maiden. Isabella's chaste soul urges on the stony judge such cogent reasons for pardoning the offence, her agitation helps her to paint these reasons in such entrancing warmth of colour, that the stern protector of morals is himself seized with passionate love for the superb woman. This sudden-flaming passion proclaims itself by his promising the pardon of the brother as the price of the lovely sister's favours. Aghast at this proposal, Isabella takes refuge in artifice, to unmask the hypocrite and save her brother. The Stateholder, whom she has vouchsafed a fictitious indulgence, still thinks good to withhold the stipulated pardon, so not to sacrifice his stern judicial conscience to a passing lapse from virtue.— Shakespeare disentangles the resulting situation by means of the public return of the Duke, who had hitherto observed events from under a disguise: his decision is an earnest one, and grounded on the judge's maxim, "measure for measure." I, on the other hand, unloosed the knot without the Prince's aid, by means of a revolution. The scene of action I transferred to the capital of Sicily, in order to bring in the southern heat of blood to help me with my scheme; I also made the Stateholder, a puritanical German, forbid a projected carnival; while a madcap youngster, in love with Isabella, incites the populace to mask, and keep their weapons ready: "Who will not dance at our behest, Your steel shall pierce him through the breast!" The Stateholder, himself induced by Isabella to come disguised to their rendezvous, is discovered, unmasked, and hooted;—the brother, in the nick of time, is freed by force from the executioner's hands; Isabella renounces her novitiate, and gives her hand to that young leader of the carnival. In full procession, the maskers go forth to meet their home-returning

Prince, assured that he will at least not govern them so crookedly as had his deputy.*

If one compares this subject with that of the *Feen,* one will see that there was a possibility of my developing along two diametrically opposite lines : to the reverent earnestness (*heiligen Ernste*) of my original promptings there here opposed itself, implanted by impressions gained from Life, a pert fancy for the wild turmoil of the senses, a defiant exuberance of glee which seemed to offer to the former mood a crying contrast.   This becomes obvious to myself, when I compare the musical working-out of the two operas.   Music always exercised a decisive influence upon my emotional fund (*Empfindungsvermögen*) ;   and indeed this could not well be otherwise, at a period of my evolution when the impressions of Life had not as yet made so sharp and definite an effect upon me, that they could lend me the imperious force of individuality to hold that receptive power to a definite field of outward action. The effect of the impressions produced on me by Life was still of general, and not of individual sort ;   therefore 'general' music as yet must dominate my individual powers of artistic fashioning.   Even in the case of the *Liebesverbot,* the music had exercised a prior sway upon the fashioning and arranging of the subject-matter ; and this music was nothing else than the reflex of the influence of modern French and (as concerns the melody) Italian Opera upon my physically-excited receptive faculties. Whosoever should take the pains to compare this composition with that of the *Feen,* would scarcely be able to understand how in so short a time so surprising a reverse of front could have been brought about : the balancing of the two tendencies was to be the work of my further course of evolution as an artist.—

* Note to original edition.—"Delicious was the spirit of the negotiations upon which I was compelled to enter with the then-time Director of the Leipzig theatre, with a view to the production of this opera.   He declared that the Town Council would never grant permission for the representation of such things, and that he, as a father, would demolish all the principles in which he had brought his daughter up, should he allow her to appear in such an opera,—a condition upon which, for the rest, I by no means insisted."

My path led first to utter frivolity in my views of art; this coincides with my earliest practical contact with the theatre, as Musical-director.* The rehearsing and conducting of those loose-limbed French operas which were then the mode, the piquant prurience of their orchestral effects, gave me many a childish thrill of joy when I could set the stew a-frothing right and left from my conductor's-desk. In Life, which henceforth meant for me the motley life of the stage, I sought by distraction to content an impulse which, as regards the things of everyday, took the form of a chase after pleasure, and as regards music, of a prickling, sputtering unrest. My *Feen*-composition became utterly indifferent to me, until at last I gave up all idea of getting that work produced. A performance of the *Liebesverbot*, carried out with headstrong obstinacy under the most unfavourable conditions, and completely unintelligibly rendered, caused me much vexation; yet this experience was quite insufficient to cure me of the lightmindedness with which I then set about everything.—The modern requital of modern levity, however, soon knocked at my unready door. I fell in love; married in feverish haste; distressed myself and others with the trials of a poverty-stricken home; and thus fell into that misery whose nature it is to bring thousands upon thousands to the ground.

One strong desire then arose in me, and developed into an all-consuming passion: to force my way out from the paltry squalor of my situation. This desire, however, was busied only in the second line with actual Life; its front rank made towards a brilliant course as Artist. To extricate myself from the petty commerce of the German stage, and straightway try my luck in Paris: this, in a word, was the goal I set before me.—A romance by H. König, "*die Hohe Braut*," had fallen into my hands; everything which I read

---

* Our author is here somewhat too hard upon himself, having apparently forgotten the exact bearing of an article, "*Pasticcio*," which he wrote at this period (1834) for the *Neue Zeitschrift für Musik* (see No. XVI. of *The Meister*). That article, though certainly advocating the Italian *method* of singing (with reservations), by no means looks upon Opera with a "frivolous" eye.—Tr.

had only an interest for me when viewed in the light of its adaptability for an operatic subject : in my mood of then, the reading of this novel attracted me the more, as it soon conjured up in my eyes the vision of a grand-opera in five acts, for Paris. I drafted a complete sketch, and sent it direct to Scribe in Paris, with the prayer that he would work it up for the Grand Opera there, and get me appointed for its composition. Naturally this project ended in smoke.

My home troubles increased ; the desire to wrest myself from a humiliating plight now grew into an eager longing to begin something on a grand and inspiring scale, even though it should involve the temporary abandonment of any practical aim. This mood was fed and fostered by my reading Bulwer's " Rienzi." From the misery of modern private-life, whence I could nowhere glean the scantiest stuff for artistic treatment, I was borne away by the picture of a great historico-political event, in lingering on which I needs must find a salutary distraction from cares and conditions that appeared to me as nothing else than absolutely fatal to art. In accordance with my particular artistic bent, however, I still kept more or less to the purely musical, or rather : operatic standpoint. This Rienzi with great thoughts in his head, great feelings in his heart, amid an entourage of coarseness and vulgarity, set all my nerves a-quivering with sympathy and love ; yet my plan for an artwork based thereon sprang first from the perception of a purely lyric element in the hero's atmosphere. The " Messengers of Peace," the Church's summons to awake, the Battle-hymns, — these were what impelled me to an *opera :* " Rienzi."

Before I set about the prosecution of my plan, however, much thrust itself into my outward life that distracted me from my inner resolve. I went to Riga, to take up the post of Musical director to a stage-company just formed there. The somewhat more orderly state of affairs, and the manifest desire of the directorate to give at least good performances, prompted me once more to write something for the forces at my disposal. So I began the composition

of a comic opera, the libretto for which I had founded on
a droll story in the "Thousand and one Nights," although
with a complete modernisation of the subject.—Even here,
however, my relations with the theatre soon proved a thorn
in my side. The thing we understand by the term, "the
traffic of the stage" (*Komödiantenwirthschaft*), took no
length of time in showing me the depth and breadth of its
economy ; and my composition, begun with a view to this
"traffic," suddenly so revolted me that I threw the whole
thing on one side and, as regards the theatre, confined
myself more and more to the bare fulfilment of my conducting duties. I thus stood more and more completely
aloof from intercourse with the stage *personnel*, and withdrew into that inner fortress of my being where the yearning to tear myself loose from everyday relations found both
its nurture and its goad.—At this period I made my first
acquaintance with the legend of the "Flying Dutchman";
Heine takes occasion to relate it, in speaking of the representation of a play, founded thereon, which he had
witnessed—as I believe—at Amsterdam.* This subject
fascinated me, and made an indelible impression upon my
fancy : still, it did not as yet acquire the force needful for
its rebirth within me.

To do something grand, to write an opera for whose
production only the most exceptional means should suffice
—a work, therefore, which I should never feel tempted to
bring before the public amid such cramping relations as
those which then oppressed me, and the hope of whose
eventual production should thus incite me to make every
sacrifice in order to extricate myself from those relations,
—this is what resolved me to resume and carry out with
all my might my former plan for "*Rienzi*." In the pre-
paration of this text, also, I took no thought for anything
but the writing of an effective operatic libretto. The
"Grand Opera" with all its scenic and musical display, its
sensationalism and massive vehemence, loomed large before

* For an attempt at elucidation of the hypothesis of a Fitzball origin of
Heine's version, see *The Meister*, No. XVII., Feb. 1892.—TR.

me; and not merely to copy it, but with reckless extravagance to outbid it in its every detail, became the object of my artistic ambition.—However, I should be unjust to myself, did I represent this ambition as my only motive for the conception and execution of my *Rienzi*. The stuff really aroused my enthusiasm, and I put nothing into my sketch which had not a direct bearing on the grounds of this enthusiasm. My chief concern was my Rienzi himself; and only when I felt quite contented with him, did I give rein to the notion of a "grand opera." Nevertheless, from a purely artistic point of view, this "grand opera" was the pair of spectacles through which I unconsciously regarded my Rienzi-stuff; nothing in that stuff did I find enthral me, but what could be looked at through these spectacles. True, that I always fixed my gaze upon the stuff itself, and did not keep one eye open for certain ready-made musical effects which I might wish to father on it by hook or crook; only, I saw it in no other light than that of a "five-act-opera," with five brilliant "finales," and filled with hymns, processions, and musical clash of arms. Thus I bestowed no greater care upon the verse and diction than seemed needful for turning out a good, and not a trivial, *opera-text*. I did not set out with the object of writing Duets, Trios, &c.; but they found their own way in, here and there, because I looked upon my subject exclusively through the medium of "Opera." For instance, I by no means hunted about in my stuff for a pretext for a Ballet; but with the eyes of the opera-composer, I perceived in it a self-evident festival that Rienzi must give to the People, and at which he would have to exhibit to them, in dumbshow, a drastic scene from their ancient history : this scene being the story of Lucretia and the consequent expulsion of the Tarquins from Rome.*
Thus in every department of my plan I was certainly ruled

* That this Pantomime has had to be omitted from all the stage-performances of *Rienzi*, has been a serious drawback to me ; for the Ballet that replaced it has obscured my nobler intentions, and turned this scene into nothing more nor less than an ordinary operatic spectacle.—R. WAGNER.

by the stuff alone ; but on the other hand, I ruled this stuff according to my only chosen pattern, the form of the Grand Opera. My artistic individuality, in its dealings with the impressions of Life, was still entirely under the influence of purely artistic, or rather art-formalistic, mechanically-operating impressions.

I had scarcely finished the composition of the first two Acts of this opera, when my outward affairs at last compelled me to break entirely with my former surroundings. Without being provided with anything like sufficient means, without the smallest prospect, nay, without even the expectation of meeting so much as an acquaintance there, I set out from Riga for Paris. I passed through four weeks of the severest hardship upon the sea, in the course of which we were driven upon the coast of Norway. Here the " flying Dutchman " once more arose before me. From my own plight he won a psychic force ; from the storms, the billows, the sailors' shouts and the rock-bound Northern shore, a physiognomy and colour.

Paris, however, washed out this figure for a time.—It is unnecessary to give a detailed account of the impressions which Paris, with its art-life and art-doings, was bound to make upon a man in my condition ; their influence will be best recognised in the character of my immediate plans and undertakings.—The half-finished *Rienzi* I laid at first upon one side, and busied myself in every way to make myself known in the world's metropolis. But, for this I lacked the necessary personal qualifications; I had scarcely even learnt the French tongue, instinctively distasteful to me, sufficiently for the most ordinary needs of everyday. Not in the remotest degree did I feel tempted to assimilate the Frenchman's nature, though I flattered myself with the hope that I could appeal to it *in my own* way ; I confided in Music, as a cosmopolitan language, to fill up that gulf between my own and the Parisian character which my inner feeling could not be blind to.—When I attended the dazzling performances of the Grand Opera—a thing which did not happen very often—a pleasurable warmth would steal into my brain and kindle the desire, the hope, aye, even the certainty, that I, also, could one day triumph there. This splendour of means, once animated by the fire of an artistic aim, appeared to me the highest summit of Art; and I felt myself nowise incapable of reaching that summit. Beyond this, I call to mind a readiness to warm myself at any of that artworld's *ignes fatui* which showed the least resemblance to my goal: their sickly unsubstantiality was mantled with a glittering show, such as never had I seen before. It was only later, that I became conscious how greatly I deceived myself in this respect, through an almost artificial state of nervous excitation. This gratuitous excitement, mounting glibly to the verge of transport, was nourished, all unawares to myself, by the feeling of my outward lot; which I must have recognised as *completely hopeless*, if I had suddenly acknowledged to myself that all this artistic tinsel, that made up the world in which I was striving to press forward, was inwardly an object of my deepest loathing. But my outward Want compelled me to hold this admission aloof; and I was able to do it with the ready placability of a man and artist whom an instinctive need of love allows to see in every smiling semblance the object of his search.

In this mood and situation, I was prompted to revert to standpoints I had already travelled past. Prospects were held out to me of getting an opera of lighter genre produced at a theatre of minor rank; I therefore harked back to my *Liebesverbot*, and its translation was commenced. I felt all the more humiliated inwardly by this transaction, as I was forced to put on the outward mask of hope for its success.—In order to gain the graces of the Parisian salon-world through its favourite singers, I composed several French 'romances,' which, after all my efforts to the contrary, were considered too out-of-the-way and difficult to be actually sung.—Out of the depth of my inner uncontent, I armed myself against the crushing reaction of this outward art-activity by the hasty sketch, and as hasty composition, of an orchestral piece, which I called an

"Overture to Goethe's Faust," but which was in reality intended for the first section of a grand Faust-Symphony.

Owing to the complete failure of all my outer efforts, financial straits at last compelled me to a still deeper degradation of the character of my artistic activity: I declared my willingness to concoct the music for a slangy *vaudeville* at a Boulevard-theatre. But even this step was frustrated by the jealousy of a musical money-grubber. So I had to look on it almost as my salvation, that I obtained the chance of doing violence to myself with the arrangement of melodies from "favourite" operas for the cornet-à-pistons. The time which these arrangements left upon my hands I expended on the completion of the second half of my *Rienzi*, for which I gave up all thoughts of a French translation, looking only toward its adoption by some German Court-Theatre. The last three Acts of this opera were finished, amid the circumstances I have mentioned, in a proportionately brief space of time.

After completing *Rienzi*, and while each day was still occupied by hack-work for the music-publishers, I hit upon a new vent for my pent-up energy. With the Faust-Overture, I had sought this before in 'absolute' music; with the musical completion of an older dramatic plan, the *Rienzi*, I had endeavoured to give due artistic effect, and at the same time bid farewell, to the tendency which first led my steps to Paris, and ahead of which I now saw every opening blocked. That opera once finished, I stood entirely outside the territory of my recent past. I was entering upon a new path, *that of Revolution against our modern Public Art*, with whose traffic I had erstwhile sought to familiarise myself when I rushed to Paris, there to seek its glittering crest.—It was the feeling of the *necessity* of my revolt, that turned me first into a writer. The publisher of the *Gazette Musicale* commissioned me, besides arranging melodies for my daily bread, to write him articles for his paper. To him, it was a matter of indifference *which* I sent: to me, not. Just as I found my deepest humiliation in the one task, I greedily snatched at the other to revenge myself for that humiliation. After a few general articles upon music, I wrote a kind of art-novelette, "*A Pilgrimage to Beethoven*," and followed it up by a sequel, "*The End of a Musician in Paris.*" In these I described, in a fictitious garb and with a dash of humour, my personal fate, especially in Paris; excepting in so far as touched the actual death by hunger, which, at any rate, I had been lucky enough to escape. Every line that I wrote was a cry of revolt against the conditions of our modern art: I have been told that this caused much amusement. To the handful of true friends, however, who gathered cheerily around me of an evening in the triste retirement of my home, I had herewith passed the word that I had completely broken with every wish and every expectation of success in Paris, and that the young man who had come there with such wishes and expectations in his head was virtually dead and buried.*

It was a sorrowful mirth—the mood to which I then was tuned; it bore me the long-since brooding *Flying Dutchman.*—All the irony, all the bitter or humoristic sarcasm which, in a kindred plight, is all that remains to our literary poets to spur them on to work, I first unburdened in the above-named, and in certain directly subsequent literary effusions;† and thus put it so far behind me, for a while, that I was again in a position to follow my inner bent toward real artistic fashioning (*Gestalten*). Seemingly—after what I had gone through, and from the standpoint on which my experiences of life

---

* In a letter to Ferd. Heine (*Wagner's Letters to Uhlig &c.*—H. Grevel & Co.) dated Paris, Jan. 4th, 1842, Wagner writes "If you or any other person exactly realised how my whole situation, all my plans, and all my resolutions were destroyed by such procrastination, some pity would be surely shown me. . . . I am truly quite exhausted! Alas, I meet with so little that is encouraging, that it would really be of untold import to me if at least in Dresden things should go according to my wish."—Tr.

† Note to the original edition (1852):—"Among these I may mention the articles which I wrote for Lewald's magazine, *Europa*, under the name of 'Freudenfeuer.'"—A translation of these articles is now (1892) appearing in "*The Meister*," and will be included, together with Wagner's other early writings, in the last volume of this present series.—Tr.

had set me—I should not have been able to do this, if I had devoted myself from youth up to the acquirement of a knack for literary poetry; mayhap I should have trodden in the footsteps of our modern scribes and playwrights, who, under the petty influences of our stereotyped social system, take the field, with every stroke of their prose- or rhyme-trimmed quills, against the mere formal surface of that system, and thus conduct a war like that which General Willisen and his volunteers have lately waged against the Danes; * to express myself in the vernacular, I should probably have followed the example of the donkey-driver who beats the bundle in place of the beast:—had I not been blessed with Something higher. This Something was my preoccupation with *music*.

I have recently said quite enough about the nature of music; I will here refer to it simply as the good angel which preserved me as an artist, nay, which really first made me an artist when my inner feeling commenced to revolt, with ever greater resolution, against the whole condition of our modern art. That this revolt did not find its sphere of action outside the realm of Art, did not take the coign of vantage either of the criticising man of letters or the art-denying, socialistically calculating, political mathematician of our day; but that my revolutionary ardour itself awoke in me the stress and power for artistic deeds,—this, as I have said, I owe to Music alone. I have just called it my good angel: this angel was not sent down to me from Heaven; it came to me from out the sweat of centuries of human " Genius." It did not, forsooth, lay the feather-light touch of a sun-

---

* In the revolt of Schleswig-Holstein against Denmark, General Willisen (a Prussian officer who had been unsuccessful in his dealings with Poland) was appointed Commander-in-Chief of the Schleswig-Holstein army of volunteers, in April 1850. General Willisen's tactics were so ill-conceived and disastrous, that he was removed from the command in December of that year. Wagner, writing the *Mittheilung*—at all events, its first portion—only two or three months after these events, has fixed upon this particular Commander as a current representative of red-tape incapacity.—TR.

steeped hand upon my brow; in the blood-warm night of my stifling heart, it girt itself for action in the world outside.

I cannot conceive the spirit of Music as aught but *Love.* Filled with its hallowed might, and with waxing power of insight into human life, I saw set before me no mere formalism to criticise; but, clean through the formal semblance, the force of sympathy displayed to me its background, the Need-of-Love downtrodden by that love-less formalism. Only he who feels the need of Love, can recognise that need in others : my art-receptive faculty, possessed with Music, gave me the power to recognise this need on every hand, even in that art-world from the shock of contact with whose outer formalism my own capacity for love drew smarting back, and in which I felt my love-need roused to action by that very smart. Thus I revolted out of sheer love, not out of spite or envy ; and thus did I become an *artist*, and not a carping man of letters.

The influence which my sense of music (*musikalisches Empfindungswesen*) exerted on the trend of my artistic labours, especially upon the choice and moulding of the poetic material, I will specify after I have first cleared the way for its understanding by an account of the origin and character of those works to which I gave birth under that influence. I shall therefore pass at once to the said account.—

To the path which I struck with the conception of the *Flying Dutchman* belong the two succeeding dramatic poems, *Tannhäuser* and *Lohengrin.* I have been reproached as falling *back*, in all three works, upon a path already trodden bald—as the opinion goes—by Meyerbeer in his *Robert the Devil*, and already forsaken by myself in my *Rienzi :* the path, to wit, of "romantic opera." Those who level this charge against me are naturally more con-cerned with the classification, Romantic *Opera*, than with the *operas* thus conventionally classified as "romantic." Whether I set about my task with the formal intention of constructing "romantic" operas, or did nothing of the kind, will become apparent if I relate in detail the history of the origin of these three works.

The mood in which I adopted the legend of the "Flying Dutchman," I have already stated in general terms : the adoption (*Empfängniss*) was exactly as old as the mood itself, which, at first merely brooding within me and battling against more seductive impressions, at last attained the power of outwardly expressing itself in a cognate work of art.—The figure of the "Flying Dutchman" is a mythical creation of the Folk : a primal trait of human nature speaks out from it with heart-enthralling force. This trait, in its most universal meaning, is the longing after rest from amid the storms of life. In the blithe world of Greece we meet with it in the wanderings of Ulysses and his longing after home, house, hearth and —wife : the attainable, and at last attained reward of the city-loving son of ancient Hellas. The Christian, without a home on earth, embodied this trait in the figure of the "Wandering Jew" : for that wanderer, forever doomed to a long-since outlived life, without an aim, without a joy, there bloomed no earthly ransom ; death was the sole remaining goal of all his strivings ; his only hope, the laying-down of being. At the close of the Middle Ages a new, more active impulse led the nations to fresh *life :* in the world-historical direction its most important result was the bent to voyages of discovery. The sea, in its turn, became the soil of Life ; yet no longer the narrow land-locked sea of the Grecian world, but the great ocean that engirdles all the earth. The fetters of the older world were broken ; the longing of Ulysses, back to home and hearth and wedded wife, after feeding on the sufferings of the "never-dying Jew" until it became a yearning for Death, had mounted to the craving for a new, an unknown home, invisible as yet, but dimly boded. This vast-spread feature fronts us in the mythos of the "Flying Dutchman" ; that seaman's poem from the world-historical age of journeys of discovery. Here we light upon a remarkable mixture, a

blend, effected by the spirit of the Folk, of the character
of Ulysses with that of the Wandering Jew. The Hollandic
mariner, in punishment for his temerity, is condemned by
the Devil (here, obviously, the element of Flood and
Storm *) to do battle with the unresting waves, to all
eternity. Like Ahasuerus, he yearns for his sufferings to
be ended by Death ; the Dutchman, however, may gain
this redemption, denied to the undying Jew, at the hands
of—*a Woman* who, of very love, shall sacrifice herself for
him. The yearning for death thus spurs him on to seek
this Woman ; but she is no longer the home-tending
Penelope of Ulysses, as courted in the days of old, but the
quintessence of womankind ; and yet the still unmanifest,
the longed-for, the dreamt-of, the infinitely womanly
Woman,—let me out with it in one word : *the Woman of
the Future.*

This was that " Flying Dutchman " who arose so often
from the swamps and billows of my life, and drew me to
him with such resistless might; this was the first *Folk-
poem* that forced its way into my heart, and called on me
as man and artist to point its meaning, and mould it in
a work of art.

From here begins my career as *poet,* and my farewell to the
mere concoctor of opera-texts. And yet I took no sudden
leap. In no wise was I influenced by reflection ; for reflection comes only from the mental combination of existing
models : whereas I nowhere found the specimens which
might have served as beacons on my road. My course
was new ; it was bidden me by my inner mood (*Stimmung*),
and forced upon me by the pressing need to impart this
mood to others. In order to enfranchise myself from
within outwards, i.e. to address myself to the understanding of like-feeling men, I was driven to strike out for
myself, as artist, a path as yet not pointed me by any out-

---

* Note to the original edition :—" A critic recently considered this Devil
and this Flying Dutchman as an orthodox (*dogmatischer*) Devil and an orthodox
ghost."

ward experience; and that which drives a man hereto is
Necessity deeply felt, incognisable by the practical reason,
but overmastering Necessity.

In thus introducing myself to my Friends, as a poet, I
almost ought to hesitate before making my bow with a
work like the *Flying Dutchman*. In it there is so much as
yet inchoate, the joinery of the situations is for the most
part so imperfect, the verse and diction so often bare of
individual stamp, that our modern playwrights—who construct everything according to a prescribed formula, and,
boastful of their formal aptitude, start out to glean that
matter which shall best lend itself to handling in the
lesson-ed form—will be the first to count my denomination
of this "poem" as a piece of impudence that calls for
strenuous castigation. My dread of such prospective
punishment would weigh less with me than my own
scruples as to the poetical form of the *Dutchman*, were it
my intention to pose therewith as a fixed and finished
entity; on the contrary, I find a private relish in here
showing my friends myself in process of 'becoming' (*in
meinem Werden*). The form of the poem of the *Flying
Dutchman*, however, as that of all my later poems, down
even to the minutiæ of their musical setting, was dictated
to me by the subject-matter alone, insomuch as that had
become absorbed into a definite colouring of my life, and
in so far as I had gained by practice and experience on
my own adopted path any general aptitude for artistic
construction.—To the characteristics of such construction
I purpose, as said above, to return later on. For the
present, having satisfied my wish to indicate the decisive
turning-point of my evolutionary career, alike in its formal
as in its material bearings, I will return to the history of
the origin of my dramatic poems.—

Amid outward circumstances which I have already
described elsewhere,* I rapidly composed the verse and
music for my *Flying Dutchman*. I had withdrawn from

* See the "Autobiographic Sketch."—R. WAGNER

Paris into the country, and it was there that I was once more brought into contact with my German home. My *Rienzi* had been at last accepted for production in Dresden. This acceptance, broadly speaking, meant for me an almost amazingly encouraging omen, and withal a friendly greeting from Germany that made my feelings all the warmer for my native home as the worldly blast of Paris was daily freezing me the more. Already, with all my hopes and all my thoughts, I lived in Germany alone. An ardent, yearning patriotism awoke within me, such as I had never dreamt before. This patriotism was free from any political tinge; for I was alive, at any rate, to the fact that political Germany had not the slightest attraction to offer me, as compared with, say, political France. It was the feeling of utter homelessness in Paris, that aroused my yearning for the German home-land; yet this longing was not directed to any old familiar haunt that I must win my way *back* to, but onward to a country pictured in my dreams, an unknown and still-to-be-discovered haven, of which I knew this thing alone: that I should certainly *never* find it here in Paris. It was the longing of my Flying Dutchman for "*das Weib*,"—not, as I have said before, for the wife who waited for Ulysses, but for the redeeming Woman, whose features had never presented themselves to me in any clear-marked outline, but who hovered before my vision as the element of Womanhood in its widest sense. This element here found expression in the idea: one's *Native Home*, i.e. the encirclement by a wide community of kindred and familiar souls; by a community, however, which as yet I knew not in the flesh, which I only learnt to yearn for after I had realised what is generally meant by "home;"* whereas in my

---

* As this passage is somewhat obscure, I append the original, in case that any German scholar might prefer to substitute another rendering for that which—after considerable pondering—I have here adopted :—"und diess Element gewann hier den Ausdruck *der Heimath*, d. h. des Umschlossenseins von einem innig vertrauten Allgemeinen, aber einem Allgemeinen, das ich noch nicht kannte, sondern eben erst mir ersehnte, nach der Verwirklichung des Begriffes 'Heimath.'"—TR.

former straitened lot it was the remote and alien that had hovered before me as the redeeming element, and the stress to find it had driven me to Paris. Just as I had been undeceived in Paris, so was I doomed to disappointment in Germany. My Flying Dutchman, sure enough, had not as yet unveiled the *newer* world : *his* Wife could only redeem him by plunging together with him beneath the waves of life.—But to proceed !

After completing the *Flying Dutchman*, although entirely pre-occupied with my return to Germany and with getting together the necessary wherewithal, I was obliged, for very sake of the latter, to betake myself once more to hackwork for the music-sellers. I made arrangements from Halévy's operas. Yet a new-won pride already saved me from the bitterness with which this humiliation had erstwhile filled me. I kept of good cheer, and corresponded with the home-land about the advancing preparations for the production of *Rienzi ;* while I was further encouraged by the news that my *Flying Dutchman* itself had been accepted for Berlin. Already I lived entirely in the longed-for, now soon to be entered world of Home.—

In this mood, the German Folk's-book * of "Tannhäuser" fell into my hands. This wonderful creation of the Folk at once usurped my liveliest emotions : indeed it was now that it first *could* do so. Tannhäuser, however, was by no means a figure completely new to me : I had early made his acquaintance through Tieck's narration. He had then aroused my interest in the same fantastically mystic manner in which Hoffmann's stories had worked upon my young imagination ; but this domain of romance had never exercised any influence upon my art-productive powers. I now read through again the utterly modern poem of Tieck, and understood at once why his coquettish

---

* This "Volksbuch," alluded to again a few lines lower down, can nowhere be traced. For the arguments for and against its existence, I must refer my readers to Dr Wolfgang Golther's article in the " *Bayreuther Taschen-Kalender* " for 1891, and to my article on " The Tannhäuser Drama " in No. XIV. of " *The Meister.*"—W. A. E.

mysticism and catholic frivolity had not appealed in any
definite way to my sympathy ; the Folk's-book and the
homely *Tannhäuserlied* explained this point to me, as
they showed me the simple genuine inspiration of the
Tannhäuser-legend in such swiftly-seizable and undisfigured traits.—But what most irresistibly attracted me
was the connection, however loose, between Tannhäuser
and the "Singers'-Tourney in the Wartburg," which I
found established in that Folk's-book. With this second
poetic subject also I had already made an earlier acquaintance, in a tale of Hoffmann's ; but, as with Tieck's
Tannhäuser, it had left me without the slightest incitation
to dramatic treatment. I now decided to trace this
Singers'-Tourney, whose whole entourage breathed on me
the air of home, to its simplest and most genuine source ;
this led me to the study of the *mittelhochdeutsch* * (middle-
high-German) poem of the "*Sängerkrieg*," into which one
of my friends, a German philologist who happened to
possess a copy, was fortunately able to induct me.—This
poem, as is well known, is set in direct connection with a
larger epos, that of "*Lohengrin.*" That also I studied, and
thus with one blow a whole new world of poetic stuff was
opened out to me ; a world of which in my previous
search, mostly for ready-made material adapted to the
genre of Opera, I had not had the slightest conception.—
I must describe a little more minutely the impressions I
derived therefrom.

* One of the three divisions into which the German literature and mode of
speech are classified, in order of time, by literary historians ; that preceding it
being called the *Althochdeutsch*, and that following it the *Neuhochdeutsch*.
According to *Brockhaus*, the integral distinction between the *M. h. d.* and its
predecessor consisted in the weakening of the inflectional vowels, after the
root-syllable, into a colourless ' e.' The period lasted from the commencement of the 12th century to about the middle of the 15th. As regards
literature, however, the epoch best known as the *M. h. d.* is that covered
chiefly by the 13th century and coincident with the glories of the Hohenstaufian
reign. Its treasures are represented by the ballads of the strolling singers
from among the Folk (*Der Nibelunger Not, Wolfdietrich* &c.), and by the
lyrics and epics of the courtly minstrels, among whom Wolfram von
Eschenbach, Gottfried von Strassburg, Walther von der Vogelweide, and
Albrecht von Scharffenberg are of special interest to the Wagnerian
student.—TR.

To many a hanger-on of the historico-poetical school it will appear of some weight that, between the completion of the *Flying Dutchman* and the conception of *Tannhäuser*, I had busied myself with the sketch for a *historical* opera-text; but it will be a disappointment for him, and another proof of my incapacity, when I inform him that I discarded this sketch in favour of that for *Tannhäuser*. For the present I will merely narrate the incident, since I shall have occasion to treat more fully the æsthetical question therein involved when I come to discuss a later mental conflict of like kind.

I have said that my yearning for home had nothing of the character of political patriotism in it; yet I should be untruthful, did I not admit that a political interpretation of the German Home was among the objects of my indefinite longing. This I naturally could not find in the Present, and any justification of the wish for such a rendering I—like our whole historical school—could only seek-out in the Past. In order to assure myself of what it was, in particular, that I held dear in the German Home for which I was yearning, I recalled the image of the impressions of my youth, and, to conjure up a clearer vision, I turned the pages of the book of History. I also took advantage of this opportunity to *seek* again for an operatic subject: but nowhere in the ample outlines of the old German Kaiser-world could I find one; and, although without distinctly realising it, I felt that the features of this epoch were unfitted for a faithful and intelligible dramatisation in exact measure as they presented a dearth of seizable motive to my musical conception.—At last I fastened on *one* episode, since it seemed to offer me the chance of giving a freer rein to my poetic fancy. This was a moment from the last days of the Hohenstaufian era. Manfred, the son of Friedrich II., tears himself from his lethargy and abandonment to lyric luxury, and, pressed by hot need, throws himself upon Luceria; which city, in the heart of the realms of Holy Church, had been assigned by his father to the Saracens, after their dis-

lodgement from Sicily. Chiefly by aid of these warlike
and lightly kindled Sons of Araby, he wins back from the
Pope and ruling Guelphs the whole of the disputed realm
of Sicily and Apuleia; the dramatic sketch concluding
with his coronation. Into this purely historical plot I
wove an imaginary female figure: I now recall the fact
that her form had taken shape in my mind from the
memory of an engraving which I had seen long
previously; this picture represented Friedrich II. surrounded by his almost exclusively Arabian court, amongst
which my fancy was principally attracted by the oriental
forms of singing and dancing women. The spirit of this
Friedrich, my favourite hero, I now embodied in the
person of a Saracen maiden, the fruit of the embraces of
Friedrich and a daughter of Araby, during the Kaiser's
peaceful sojourn in Palestine. Tidings of the downfall of
the Ghibelline house had come to the girl in her native
home; fired with that same Arabian enthusiasm which
not long since gave the East its songs of ardent love for
Bonaparte, she made her way to Apuleia. There, in the
court of the dispirited Manfred, she appears as a prophetess, inspires him with fresh courage, and spurs him on
to action; she kindles the hearts of the Arabs in Luceria,
and, instilling enthusiasm whithersoever she goes, she
leads the Emperor's son through victory on victory to
throne. Her descent she has kept enwrapt in mystery,
the better to work on Manfred's mind, by the riddle of
her apparition; he loves her passionately, and fain would
break the secret's seal: she waves him back with an
oracular saying. His life being attempted, she receives
the death-thrust in her own breast: dying, she confesses herself as Manfred's sister, and unveils the fulness
of her love to him. Manfred, crowned, takes leave of
happiness for ever.

This picture which my homesick phantasy had painted,
not without some warmth of colour, in the departing light
of a historical sunset, completely faded from my sight
so soon as ever the figure of Tannhäuser revealed itself

to my inner eye. That picture was conjured from outside : this figure sprang from my inmost heart. In its infinitely simple traits, it was to me more wide-embracing, and alike more definite and plain, than the richly-coloured, shimmering tissue—half historical and half poetic—which like a showy cloak of many folds concealed the true, the supple human form my inner wish desired to look on, and which stepped at once before me in the new-found Tannhäuser. Here was the very essence of the *Folk's*-poem, that ever seizes on the *kernel* of the matter (*Erscheinung*), and brings it again to show (*Erscheinung*) in simple plastic outlines ; whilst there, in the history—i.e. the event not such as it was, but such alone as it comes within *our* ken—this matter shows itself in endless trickery of outer facings, and never attains that fine plasticity of form until the eye of the Folk has plunged into its inner *soul*, and given it the artistic mould of Myth.

This Tannhäuser was infinitely more than Manfred ; for he was the spirit of the whole Ghibelline race for every age, embraced within one only, clearly cut and infinitely moving form; but in this form a *human being*, right down to our own day, right into the heart of a poor artist all athirst for life. But more of that anon !

For the moment I merely note that, in the choice of the Tannhäuser-stuff also, I acted entirely without re-flection; and thus simply emphasise the fact that I had hitherto proceeded without any critical consciousness, following absolutely the dictates of instinctive feeling. My recital alone will have shown how completely with-out an axiom I had commenced, in the *Flying Dutchman*, to strike out my new pathway. With the "*Sarazenin*" I was on the point of harking back, more or less, to the road of my *Rienzi*, and again writing a "historical Grand Opera in five acts"; only the overpowering subject of Tannhäuser, grappling my individual nature with far more energetic hold, kept my footsteps firm upon the path which Necessity had bid me strike. This happened, as I will now relate, amid an active combat—not yet over—with accidental outer influences, which were destined to gradually enlighten my consciousness, also, as to the inner nature of that path itself.— —

At last, after a stay of well-nigh three years, I left Paris, nine-and-twenty years of age. The direct route to Dresden took me through the Thuringian valley from which one sees the Wartburg towering above. How unspeakably homelike and inspiring was the effect upon me of this castle, already hallowed to me, but which—strangely enough!—I was not to actually visit until seven years later when, already proscribed, I cast therefrom my last look upon that Germany which I had once entered with such warm affection : only to leave it in contumely, an exile fleeing from his native land !— —

I arrived in Dresden, to hasten forward the promised production of my *Rienzi*. Before the actual commencement of the rehearsals, I made an excursion into the Bohemian mountains ; there I jotted down the complete dramatic sketch of *Tannhäuser*. Before I could proceed to its working out, however, I was doomed to be interrupted in a hundred ways. Preceded by many a trimming and paring of that excessively protracted composition, the practical study of my *Rienzi* began. Concernment with the long-awaited production of one of my operas, under conditions so sufficient as those the Dresden Court-theatre afforded me, was an entirely new element for me, and proved a source of active distraction from my inner thoughts. At this time, I felt myself so buoyantly lifted from out my fundamental nature, and attracted toward the practical, that I even took up again an earlier, long-since forgotten sketch for an opera founded on König's romance "*die hohe Braut*," and cast it into racy opera-verse for my future colleague * in the office of Dresden *Hof-kapellmeister*, who just then thought himself in need of an

---

* Gottlieb Reissiger, successor to Carl Maria von Weber in that post.—Tr.

opera-text, and whom I thus endeavoured to win over.*— The growing goodwill of the singers towards my *Rienzi*, and especially the amiable expressions of enthusiasm elicited from the pre-eminently gifted singer of the title-rôle,† affected me to an uncommonly pleasant degree. After long battling amid the paltriest surroundings, after severest struggles, sufferings and privations in the loveless commerce of Paris art and Paris life, I suddenly found myself surrounded by an appreciative, inspiriting, and often quite affectionate group. How pardonable, if I began to yield to illusions from which, however, I was doomed to wake with poignant pain! But if one thing was more calculated than another to deceive me as to my true position towards the existing state of affairs, it was the remarkable success of the production of my *Rienzi* in Dresden:—I, a lonely, homeless waif, found myself suddenly beloved, admired, nay, by many looked on with amazement; and, according to our general notion of things, this success was to win me for my whole span of life a solid basis of social and artistic well-being,—for, to cap it all, I was nominated to the post of Kapellmeister of the Royal Saxon Court-band.

It was here that a great self-delusion, forced upon me by circumstances, though not completely unawares to myself, became the cause of a fresh development, painful but decisive, of my character both as artist and as man. My earliest experiences, then those of Paris, and lastly those already made in Dresden, had not left me in the dark as to the real nature of our entire public art, especially as regards its practice in our official institutions. My repugnance to any concernment with it, farther than what was absolutely called-for by the production of my operas, had already

---

* This is the same text that—after my colleague had apparently found it beneath his dignity to carry out a cast-off project of mine—was set to music by *Kittl*, who could nowhere obtain a libretto more to his mind than just this one. It was brought to a hearing in Prag, after divers Royal-Imperial-Austrian alterations, under the title of "*die Franzosen vor Nizza*" (The French before Nice).—R. WAGNER.

† Joseph Tichatschek.—TR.

developed to a considerable pitch. It had been brought plainly enough before my own eyes that it was not Art such as I had learnt to know it, but a completely different set of interests, which only cloaked themselves with an artistic semblance, that was ministered-to in the daily traffic of our public art-affairs. But I had not as yet thrust down to the fundamental cause of this phenomenon, and therefore rather held it as a mere accident, remediable by a little pains. It was now that I was first to gradually and sorrowfully discover the cause itself.

To a few more intimate friends I openly declared my inner aversion, and consequent hesitation, to take up the proffered post of *Hofkapellmeister* (Conductor of the Royal orchestra). They could not understand me ; and this was natural, for I myself could only express my inner distaste, without being able to assign any reasons in terms of the practical understanding. A glance back to my quondam troublous and disjointed outer circumstances, which henceforth promised to take on a surer ordering ; and further, the assumption that, in the favourable mood of my surroundings, and especially considering the brilliant nature of the artistic forces at my disposal, I should at any rate be able to do many a good stroke of work for art, soon conquered my avowed disinclination : a result explicable enough, in view of my still scanty stock of experience in the last regard. My recognition of the high opinion that is customarily held of such a post ;* and finally the signal honour which my selection appeared to represent in the eyes of all the rest of you, ended by dazzling me also, and making me behold an unwonted piece of good fortune in what was but too soon to be for me the source of gnawing pain. I became—in highest spirits!—a Royal Kapellmeister.—

---

* The subordinate post of *Musikdirector*, i.e. conductor of the playhouse-music and the weekday church-music, was that which was first offered to Wagner, for a probationary year ; this he declined, in a manly letter addressed to v. Lüttichau, Jan. 5, 1843, three days after the production of the *Flying Dutchman* (see R. Prölss' " *Beitrage zur Geschichte des Hoftheaters zu Dresden* "). Lüttichau thereupon offered him the higher post, in which he shared with Reissiger the supreme control of the Court orchestra.—TR.

The sense of physical comfort, which stole over me in consequence of the rebound in my outward lot, and grew into a pleasurable feeling of self-content through my first taste of a settled position in life—and especially of public favour and admiration—soon betrayed me into a more and more complete repudiation and abuse of my inner nature, such as it had hitherto evolved in necessary consecution. I was chiefly deceived by the not altogether unreasonable assumption of a speedy—or, if more tardy, yet bound to come at last—pecuniary success of my operas through their gaining themselves a footing on the wider German stage. While this obstinate belief betrayed me, in the long run, into ever-increasing sacrifices and undertakings, which were destined, in the absence of success, to dislocate afresh my outward circumstances : its mainspring, a more or less impatient quest for pleasure, for a long time led my steps astray from the artistic path I had already struck out. This episode seems worth narrating, as it affords a not un-weighty contribution to the developmental history of an artist's individuality.

Immediately after the success of *Rienzi* at the Dresden Court-theatre, the management determined to bring out at once my *Flying Dutchman*. The acceptance of this opera by the Berlin Court-theatre directorate had been nothing more nor less than a cheap compliment, devoid of any serious meaning. The Dresden directorate being in earnest, I willingly accepted their proposal and rehearsed the opera as quickly as possible, without any special care about the material for its production ; the work seemed to me so immeasurably simpler for performance than its predecessor *Rienzi*, its scenic arrangements so much easier to grasp. The chief male rôle I almost forced upon a singer who had sufficient experience and self-knowledge to declare him-self unfitted for the part.—The main point of the repre-sentation was completely missed. This performance the public felt all the less inclined to applaud as it was disap-pointed in the *genre* of the work itself, having expected and desired something akin to *Rienzi*, not something directly opposite in style. My friends were crestfallen at the result; almost all they could think about, was to wipe out its impression upon themselves and the public, and that by an eager resumption of *Rienzi*. I myself was so disconcerted, that I held my peace and left the *Dutchman* undefended. In the mood described above, it was natural that I should prefer the sweets of immediate success, and benumb my conscience with the hopes held out by that earlier successful path. Under the influence of these outward impressions I again began to vacillate, and my unrest was largely increased by my intercourse with the *Schröder-Devrient.—*

I have already alluded to the extraordinary and lasting impression which the artistic genius of this in every respect exceptional woman had made upon me in my youth. Now, after an interval of eight years, I came into personal contact with her, a contact prompted and governed by the deep significance of her art to me. I found this gifted nature involved in the most manifold contradictions, which were as disquieting to myself as in her they took the form of passionate unrest. The motley hollowness of our modern theatrical life had the less remained without influence on this artist as, neither as artist nor woman, did she possess that cold and egoistic composure with which, for example, a Jenny Lind can place herself entirely outside the frame of the modern stage and keep free from any compromising intercourse therewith. The Schröder-Devrient was neither in life nor art an embodiment of that virtuosodom which flourishes alone in isolation, in it alone can shine : here as there, she was dramatic through and through, in the fullest meaning of the word. She was born for intercourse, for blending with the Whole ; and yet this Whole was, both in life and art, *our* social life, and *our* theatric art. I have never seen a greater-hearted human being, nor one in battle with more trivial conceptions, than this woman with those ideas which she had imbibed from her contact, necessary as her nature made it, with her surroundings. Upon myself the effect of my deep sympathy with this artistic woman was less stimulating than tormenting; and tormenting because it roused, without contenting me. She studied the "Senta" of my *Flying Dutchman*, and gave this rôle with such creative perfection of finish, that her performance alone saved the opera from being completely misunderstood by the public, and even evoked the liveliest enthusiasm. This inspired me with the wish to write a piece expressly for her, and with this object I reached back to my abandoned sketch for the "*Sarazenin*," the scenic draft of which I now hastily completed. But this poem, when submitted, had but little attraction for her; chiefly on account of certain references which, in her situation at that time, she would not allow to pass current. One typical feature of my heroine was expressed in the sentence: "the *Prophetess* can never more become a *woman*." This artist, however—without putting it in so many words—would not completely throw aside the woman; and it is only at the present that I have learnt to rightly value her instinctive judgment, now that those circumstances which brought that instinct into play have faded from my sight; whereas at that time their utter triviality jarred on me to such a degree that, looking from them to the artist herself, I could not help regarding her as caught in the toils of a desire unworthy of her.*

Under such impressions, I fell into a conflict with myself; a conflict peculiar to our modern evolution, and only not experienced, or regarded as already out of date, by those who have not a vestige of evolutionary force within them and, for their philosophy of life, content themselves with borrowed plumes—however new—of theory. I will attempt to describe, in brief, this conflict, and the mode in which it expressed itself in my relations to the outer world.

---

* Lest any misconception should arise, it may be as well to state that the unworthy object of Schröder-Devrient's affections was a certain Saxon officer, von Döring by name, who first inspired her with a passion for him in 1842, and for the next seven years dragged her from one 'starring' engagement to another, only to squander her money on the gaming-tables (vide—Glasenapp's "*Life of Wagner*").—TR.

Through the happy change in the aspect of my outward lot ; through the hopes I cherished, of its even still more favourable development in the future ; and finally through my personal and, in a sense, intoxicating contact with a new and well-inclined surrounding, a passion for enjoyment had sprung up within me, that led my inner nature, formed amid the struggles and impressions of a painful past, astray from its own peculiar path. A general instinct that urges every man to take life as he finds it, now pointed me, in my particular relations as Artist, to a path which, on the other hand, must soon and bitterly disgust me. This instinct could only have been appeased in Life on condition of my seeking, as artist, to wrest myself renown and pleasure by a complete subordination of my true nature to the demands of the public taste in Art. I should have had to submit myself to the Mode, and to speculation on its weaknesses ; and here, on this point at least, my feeling showed me clearly that, with an actual entry on that path, I must inevitably be engulfed in my own loathing. Thus the pleasures of life presented themselves to my feeling in the shape alone of what *our modern world* can offer to the senses; and this again appeared attainable by me, as artist, solely along the direction which I had already learnt to recognise as the exploitation of our public art-morass. In actual life I was at like time confronted—in the person of a woman for whom I had a sincere admiration—with the phenomenon that a longing akin to my own could only imagine itself contented with the paltriest return of trivial love ; a delusion so completely threadbare, that it could never really mask its nature from the inner need.

If at last I turned impatiently away, and owed the strength of my repugnance to the independence already developed in my nature, both as artist and as man : so did that double revolt, of man and artist, inevitably take-on the form of a yearning for appeasement in a higher, nobler element ; an element which, in its contrast to the only pleasures that the material Present spreads in modern Life and modern Art, could but appear to me in the guise of a pure, chaste, virginal, unseizable and unapproachable ideal of Love. What, in fine, could this love-yearning, the noblest thing my heart could feel—what other could it be than a longing for release from the Present, for absorption into an element of endless Love, a love denied to earth and reachable through the gates of Death alone? * And what, again, at bottom, could such a longing be, but the yearning of Love ; aye, of a real love seeded in the soil of fullest sentience (*Sinnlichkeit*),—yet a love that could *never* come to fruitage on the loathsome soil of *modern* sentience? —How absurd, then, must those critics seem to me, who, drawing all their wit from modern wantonness, insist on reading into my " Tannhäuser " a specifically Christian and impotently pietistic drift! They recognise nothing but the fable of their own incompetence, in the story of a man whom they are utterly unable to comprehend.—

The above is an exact account of the mood in which I was, when the unlaid ghost of Tannhäuser returned again, and urged me to complete his poem. When I reached the sketch and working-out of the *Tannhäuser* music, it was in a state of burning exaltation (*verzehrend üppige Erregtheit*) that held my blood and every nerve in fevered throbbing. My true nature—which, in my loathing of the modern world and ardour to discover something nobler and beyond-all noblest, had quite returned to me—now seized, as in a passionate embrace, the opposing channels of my being, and disembouched them both into *one* stream : a longing for the highest form of Love.—With this work I penned my death-warrant : before the world of Modern Art, I now could hope no more for life. This I *felt ;* but as yet I *knew* it not with full distinctness :—that knowledge I was not to gain till later.

I have meanwhile to relate how I was confirmed in my tendency by further experiences from outside.—My hopes of a rapid success, through the circulation of my operas on the German stage, remained entirely unfulfilled ; my scores

---

* One scarcely need emphasise this forecast of the poem of *Tristan und Isolde,* except to compare it with page 116, *Art-work of the Future.*—TR.

were returned to me by the principal Theatrical Directors, unaccepted—often with even their wrappers unopened. It was only the patient toil of personal friendship, that brought *Rienzi* to a production in Hamburg: an utterly unsuitable singer played havoc with the title-rôle, and the Director found his hopes and all his persevering efforts demolished by the inadequate result. I then saw, to my astonishment, that even this "Rienzi" was above folk's heads. Yet, however coldly I may now look back upon this earlier work of mine, I cannot shut my eyes to the youthful, heroic strain of enthusiasm that breathes throughout it. Our public, however, nourished on the masterpieces of modern operatic manufacture, has accustomed itself to seek the object of its stage-enthusiasm in something very different to the dominant mood of a dramatic work. In Dresden I was succoured by something quite aloof from this; to wit, the purely physical *verve* of the whole thing, which there, under circumstances favourable in this respect, and especially by reason of the brilliance of the stage-material and the personal characteristics of the chief singer, worked in an intoxicating fashion on the public.

On the other hand, I had quite a different experience with my *Flying Dutchman*. The old master *Spohr* had already produced this opera at Cassel, almost immediately after its original appearance. This happened without any overtures on my side; nevertheless I feared that I must remain a stranger to Spohr, since I could not see how my novel bent could fall in with his taste. What, then, was my astonishment and glad surprise, when this grey-haired master, although wrapt in a cold but honourable seclusion from the world of modern music, expressed to me by letter his unqualified approval, and explained it simply by his heart-felt joy at meeting with a young artist who plainly showed that he was taking art in earnest! Spohr, the aged Spohr, remained the only German Kapellmeister who received me with any warmth of affection, who nursed my works as far as he was able, and who, amid all changes, preserved for me a true and faithful friendship.

At Berlin, also, the *Flying Dutchman* was placed upon the boards ; I had no grounds for absolute discontent with this affair. My experience of the effect upon the public, however, was here most significant : the mistrustful Berlin chill, only too prone to fault-finding, lasted throughout the whole First Act, but gave way in the course of the Second to the fullest warmth of emotion ; in fact, I could not but regard the result as completely favourable. Yet the opera very soon disappeared from the repertory. A keen instinct for matters theatrical must have prompted the management, when, even though this opera pleased, they looked upon it as unfitted for the regular routine. I recognise today how correct a verdict upon the general nature of our theatric art was herewith expressed. A piece intended for the operatic repertoire, to be played before the public throughout a long season, perhaps for ever, in alternation with other pieces of its like, must have no *Stimmung*,* and require for its understanding no *Stimmung*, that is of any markedly individual character. To this end, one must provide pieces which are either of a generally-current *Stimmung* or, in fact, of none at all, and therefore which do not pretend to arouse the feeling of the public to any particular mood, but afford a pleasurable distraction by the brilliance of their ' mounting ' and the more or less personal interest taken in the performing virtuosi. The revival of earlier so-called " classical " works, which certainly cannot attain a real understanding without awaking such an individual *Stimmung*, is never due to the convictions of the Theatre-directors themselves, but both laborious revival and success are the artificial outcome of compliance with the demands of our æsthetical

---

* We have no single word that will adequately replace the German "*Stimmung*" ; the meaning being partly "drift" or "tendency," and partly "mood," "impression," or "frame of mind." The term is gradually finding its way into our conversation, wherefore I may perhaps be forgiven for occasionally adopting it in print.—TR.

critics. The 'stimmung,' however, which my *Flying Dutchman* was at times so fortunate as to arouse, was so pregnant, so unaccustomed, and so searching, that it was highly improbable that those who had experienced it most fully would place themselves in the way of its recurrence at frequent and brief intervals. An audience, in its every member, demands that such impressions shall take it *unawares :* the sudden *shock* of this surprise, and its lasting after-effects—which form the object of the artwork—constitute the elevating factor in any dramatic performance. But the same feeling of surprise either does not recur at all, or only after a considerable period has been allowed to intervene, and the events of daily life have gradually effaced the vividness of the first impression ; whereas the deliberate attempt to galvanise oneself into this feeling, is one of the pathological symptoms of our modern artdebauchery. With men who follow in their lives the natural course of evolution, the same effect is—strictly speaking—never to be obtained from the performance of one and the same dramatic work ; their renewed demand can be met alone by a fresh work of art, a work proceeding in its turn from a new developmental phase in the mind of the artist.—Here I touch on what I have said in the Introduction, with regard to the Monumental and its manifestments in our art-doings : for I adduce the logical result of investigation into the above phenomena as witness to the need of an ever fresh-born Artwork of the Future, springing directly from, and belonging only to the Present ; an Artwork which shall not be fettered by the Monumental, but, mirroring the face of Life itself in all its countless traits, shall proclaim itself in infinitely changeful multiformity, and thus be understood.

Though I did not clearly formulate the notion at this time, yet it began to thrust itself upon my inner observation, the more especially through my perception of the uncommonly strong impression which my *Flying Dutchman* had made on *individuals.* In Berlin, where for the rest I was entirely unknown, I received from two persons

—a gentleman and a lady, previously total strangers to me, whom the impressions produced by the *Flying Dutchman* had made my instant friends—the first definite expression of satisfaction at the new path which I had struck out, and the first exhortation to continue thereon. From that time forward I lost more and more the so-called " Public " from my view : the judgment of definite, individual human beings usurped, for me, the place of the never to be accurately gauged opinion of the Mass, which hitherto—without my own full consciousness—had floated before me, in vague outlines, as the object to which I should address myself as poet. The *understanding* of my aim became each day more clearly the chief thing to be striven for, and, to ensure myself this understanding, involuntarily I turned no longer to the stranger *Mass*, but to the individual persons whose moods and ways of thought were familiar to me.

Again, this better defined position toward those whom I wished to address, exercised a most weighty influence upon the future bent of my constructive faculties (*künstlerisches Gestaltungswesen*). If the impulse to *intelligibly* impart his aim be the true constructive standard of the artist, its exercise will necessarily be governed by the character of those *by whom* he wishes that aim to be understood. If he picture them as an indefinite, never plainly cognisable mass, whose tastes are never to be accurately gauged and whose character it is therefore impossible *for himself* to understand, in fact as the medley that constitutes our modern theatrical public : then, in his efforts to expound his aim, the artist must inevitably be driven to a hazy mode of treatment which often strays aside into purposeless generalities, nay—for the matter of that—to a choice of subject-matter dictated by naught else than its peculiar fitness for this washy treatment. The artistic defects resulting from such a position were now apparent to me, upon re-examining my earlier operas. As compared with the products of modern theatric art, I recognised, it is true, the greater significance of the subjects of my own

creations, but at like time the undecided, often unclear
nature of the treatment of those subjects, which therefore
still were lacking in the necessary features of a sharply-
chiselled individuality.   Thenceforward, by addressing
myself instinctively to [definite individuals allied to me by
community of feeling, I at the same time won the power of
casting my subjects in a more distinct and stable mould.
Without going to work with any deliberate purpose, 1
divested myself more and more of the customary method of
treating my characters in the gross ; I drew a sharper line
of demarcation between the surroundings and the main
figure, which erewhile had frequently been swamped by
them ; I raised it into bolder relief, and thus attained the
power of rescuing these surroundings themselves from their
operatic diffuseness, and condensing them into plastic
forms.

It was under influences such as these, and proceeding as
just stated, that I worked away at my *Tannhäuser*, and,
after many and varied interruptions, completed it.—

With this work, I had passed another stage in the new
evolutionary path that I had opened with the *Flying
Dutchman.* My whole being had been so consumed with
ardour for my task that, as I cannot but call to mind, the
nearer I approached its completion the more was I haunted
by the fancy that a sudden death would stay my hand
from finishing it ; so that, when at last I wrote its closing
chord, I felt as joyful as though I had escaped some mortal
danger.—

Immediately after the conclusion of this task, I obtained
leave to visit a Bohemian wateringplace, for the benefit of
my health.   Here, as whenever I could snatch myself away
from the footlights and my "duties" in their dense atmosphere, I soon felt light of heart and gay ; and, for the first
time in my life, the strain of cheerfulness (*Heiterkeit*) in-
herent in my disposition took visible shape in an artistic
plan.   Almost with wilful premeditation, I had already of
late resolved to write a *comic* opera, so soon as I could set
about it ; I remember that this determination had been

assisted by the well-meant advice of certain good friends of mine, who wished me to compose an opera of "lighter genre," since they believed that such a work would open the doors of most German theatres to me and thus effect a beneficial change in my outward circumstances, which had certainly begun to take on a threatening aspect owing to the obstinate default of that success. Just as a jovial Satyr-play was wont at Athens to follow on the Tragedy, so on that pleasure-trip there suddenly occurred to me the picture of a comic piece which well might form a Satyr-play as pendant to my "*Sängerkrieg auf Wartburg*" (i.e. Tann-häuser). This was "The Meistersingers of Nuremberg," with Hans Sachs at their head. I took Hans Sachs as the last manifestation of the art-productive spirit of the Folk (*Volksgeist*), and set him, in this sense, in contrast to the pettyfogging bombast of the other Meistersingers ; to whose absurd pedanticism, of *tabulatur* and prosody, I gave a concrete personal expression in the figure of the "Marker." This "Marker," as is well-known (or as per- haps is *not* known to our critics), was the examiner appointed by the Singers' Guild to "mark" each breach of rule in the effusions of the members, and particularly of fresh candidates, noting them down with crosses : whoso- ever was adjudged a certain number of these crosses, had "out-sung" himself.—In my story, the oldest member of the guild offered the hand of his young daughter to that "Meister" who should win the prize at a forthcoming public singing-contest. The Marker himself had already paid his court to the damsel, but is now confronted by a rival in the person of a young nobleman who, inspired by the *Heldenbuch* and the songs of the ancient Minne- singers, forsakes the ruined castle of his ancestors to learn the Meistersingers' art at Nuremberg. He applies for admission into the guild, determined chiefly by a swiftly- kindled passion for the prize-maiden, "whom none but a Master of the Guild may win." Put to the test, he sings an enthusiastic song in praise of Woman ; but from the first his verse offends the Marker's ear, so that when

the aspirant has got but halfway through his song, he
is "plucked." Hans Sachs, who has taken a fancy
to the young man, now frustrates — in the latter's
best interest — his despairing attempt to elope with the
damsel; Hans finds occasion, at like time, to mightily
annoy the Marker. For the latter, who had before this
made a savage attack upon Sachs on account of a never-
finished pair of shoes, with the sole object of humiliating
him, stations himself below the maiden's window at night,
in order to serenade her with a foretaste of the song by
which he hopes next day to win her; since he is most
anxious to make sure of her casting-vote in the decision
of the prize. At the first note of the Marker's lay, Sachs,
whose cobbler's-stall lies opposite the house be-sung, begins
in his turn to sing aloud, explaining to the indignant wooer
that this is necessary to keep himself awake when he works
so late at night; while no one can know better that the
job is pressing than the Marker, who had rated him so
roundly for the non-delivery of his shoes. At last Sachs
promises the unhappy wretch to hold his peace, provided
only that he be allowed to mark according to *his* mode—as
cobbler—the faults which, according to *his* feeling, he may
detect in the Marker's song: namely, to signal each by a
hammer-stroke upon the lasted shoes. The Marker now
sings on; Sachs strikes repeatedly upon the last. Out of
all patience, the Marker makes a rush at him; the Cobbler
calmly asks, Whether the song is done then? "Not by a
long way yet," shouts the other. Sachs lays down the
shoes upon the board, with a roar of laughter, and tells him
that they have just been finished by the "Marker's-crosses."
Of the rest of his song, which he bawls out without a pause,
the Marker makes an utter bungle, in his despair at the
violent head-shakings of the female figure at the window.
In deepest dudgeon, he next day begs of Sachs a new song
wherewith to woo the bridal prize; the Cobbler gives him
a poem of the young noble's, pretending not to know how
he has come thereby: only he warns him to be very
careful in the selection of a fitting "tune" to which to sing

it. As to that, the conceited Marker is perfectly confident in himself, and proceeds to sing the poem before the full assembly of Meisters and Folk ; but he chooses such an ill-suited and sense-confounding tune, that again he comes to grief, and this time decisively. Boiling over with rage, he accuses Sachs of fraud, in having foisted upon him an infamous poem ; the latter declares that the verse is good enough, but it must be sung to a becoming tune. It is then decided that whoever can fit it with the right tune, shall be the victor. The young noble performs this feat, and wins the bride ; but he scorns admission to the Guild, now that it is proffered him. Sachs champions the Meister-singerhood in a humorous address, concluding with the couplet :

" Tho' Holy Roman Empire's pride depart,
  We 'll hold on high our holy German Art."—

Such was my swiftly planned, and swiftly traced design. But scarcely had I written it down, when peace forsook me until I had sketched-out the more detailed plan for *Lohengrin*. This was during the same brief visit to the baths, and despite the doctor's warnings against my engaging in any work of the kind. There is something strange in the fact that, at the very time when I made that refreshing little excursion into the realms of mirth, I was driven back so quickly to the earnest, yearning mood which impelled me to the absorbing task of *Lohengrin*. The reason now is clear to me, why the cheerful mood which sought to vent itself in the conception of the *Meistersinger* could make no lasting stay with me. At that time it took alone the shape of *Irony*, and, as such, was busied more with the purely formal side of my artistic views and aims, than with that core of Art whereof the roots lie hid in Life itself.

The only form of Mirth (*Heiterkeit*) which our public of today can understand, and thus the only form in which an underlying truth can appeal thereto, is that of Irony. It seizes the formal aspect of our public offences against Nature, and is in so far effective, as Form, being directly

cognisable by the senses, is the thing most patent to the
ordinary understanding; whereas the Content of this form
is that hidden mystery at which we fumble all perplexed,
and wherefrom we are involuntarily thrust back again to
utterance in that very form at which we jeer. Thus Irony
is *that* form of Mirth through which the latter can never
break to open revelation of its inner essence, to vivid,
individual exposition as a vital force. But the core that
lies beneath the unnatural semblance of our public intercourse, that kernel which all Irony must needs leave unex-
plored, is at like time unseizable by the power of Mirth, in
the latter's purest, most specific manifestment ; it is only to
be seized by *that* power which expresses itself as resistance
to an element of life whose very pressure suffocates the
pure breath of Mirth. Thus when we feel this pressure, we
are driven by the primal force of Mirth itself, and in our
endeavour to regain its pristine purity, to a withstanding
whose utterance, in face of modern life, can only proclaim
itself in tones of yearning and finally of revolt, and therefore in a tragic mood.

My whole nature instantly reacted against the incomplete
attempt to unburden myself of the contents of a mirthful
mood by means of irony; and I must now consider the
attempt itself as the last expression of that desire for enjoyment which fain would reconcile itself with the triviality of
its surroundings, and from which I had already escaped, by
a painful exercise of energy, in my *Tannhäuser.*—

If it is now clear to me, after reflection upon my then-
prevailing frame of mind, why I so suddenly relinquished
this attempt, and threw myself with such consuming passion
upon the shaping of the Lohengrin-'stuff': on the other
hand, the peculiarity of that subject itself makes plain to
me why it was that *it*, of all others, so irresistibly attracted
and enthralled me. It was not the mere memory, how this
stuff was first brought before me in intimate connection
with Tannhäuser ; least of all was it a frugal husbandry,
which might forsooth have bidden me to make the
most of gathered stores : for it is obvious, from the
account of my artistic labours, that, if anything, I was

in this regard inclined to prodigality. On the contrary, I must here attest that at the time when I first learnt the story of Lohengrin, in connection with that of Tann-häuser, the tale indeed affected me, but in no wise prompted me to store the 'stuff' for future working-up. Not only because I was then completely saturated with Tannhäuser, but also because the form in which Lohengrin first stepped before me made an almost disagreeable im-pression upon my feeling, did I not at that time keep a sharper eye upon him. The medieval poem presented Lohengrin in a mystic twilight, that filled me with sus-picion and that haunting feeling of repugnance with which we look upon the carved and painted saints and martyrs on the highways, or in the churches, of Catholic lands. Only when the immediate impression of this reading had faded, did the shape of Lohengrin rise repeatedly, and with grow-ing power of attraction, before my soul ; and this power gathered fresh force to itself from outside, chiefly by reason that I learnt to know the myth of Lohengrin in its simpler traits, and alike its deeper meaning, as the genuine poem of the Folk, such as it has been laid bare to us by the dis-coveries of the newer searchers into Saga lore. After I had thus seen it as a noble poem of man's yearning and his longing—by no means merely seeded from the Christian's bent toward supernaturalism, but from the truest depths of universal human nature,—this figure became ever more endeared to me, and ever stronger grew the urgence to adopt it and thus give utterance to my own internal long-ing ; so that, at the time of completing my *Tannhäuser*, it positively became a dominating need, which thrust back each alien effort to withdraw myself from its despotic mastery.

This "Lohengrin" is no mere outcome of Christian meditation (*Anschauung*), but one of man's earliest poetic ideals ; just as, for the matter of that, it is a fundamental error of our modern superficialism, to consider the specific Christian legends as by any means original creations. Not one of the most affecting, not one of the most distinctive

Christian myths belongs by right of generation to the Christian spirit, such as we commonly understand it: it has inherited them all from the purely human intuitions (*Anschauungen*) of earlier times, and merely moulded them to fit its own peculiar tenets.   To purge them of this heterogeneous influence, and thus enable us to look straight into the pure humanity of the eternal poem : such was the task of the more recent inquirer,* a task which it must necessarily remain for the poet to complete.

Just as the main feature of the mythos of the " Flying Dutchman " may be clearly traced to an earlier setting in the Hellenic Odyssey ; just as this same Ulysses in his wrench from the arms of Calypso, in his flight from the charms of Circe, and in his yearning for the earthly wife of cherished home, embodied the Hellenic prototype of a longing such as we find in " Tannhäuser " immeasurably enhanced and widened in its meaning: so do we already meet in the Grecian mythos—nor is even this by any means its oldest form—the outlines of the myth of " Lohengrin."   Who does not know the story of " Zeus and Semele " ?   The god loves a mortal woman, and for sake of this love, approaches her in human shape ; but the mortal learns that she does not know her lover in his true estate, and, urged by Love's own ardour, demands that her spouse shall show himself to physical sense in the full substance of his being.   Zeus knows that she can never grasp him, that the unveiling of his godhead must destroy her ; himself, he suffers by this knowledge, beneath the stern compulsion to fulfill his loved one's dreaded wish : he signs his own death-warrant, when the fatal splendour of his godlike presence strikes Semele dead.—Was it, forsooth, some priestly fraud that shaped this myth ?   How insensate, to attempt to argue from the selfish state-religious, caste-like exploitation of the noblest human longing, back to the origin and the genuine meaning of ideals which

---

* In view of the author's preface to the two volumes in which this *Communication* was included (see page 25 of the present volume), it would appear that the allusion is to Ludwig Feuerbach's *Essence of Christianity.*—TR.

blossomed from a human fancy that stamped man first as Man! 'Twas no *God*, that sang the meeting of Zeus and Semele; but *Man*, in his humanest of yearnings. Who had taught Man that a God could burn with love toward earthly Woman? For certain, only Man himself; who, however high the object of his yearning may soar above the limits of his earthly wont, can only stamp it with the imprint of his human nature. From the highest sphere to which the might of his desire may bear him up, he finally can only long again for what is purely human, can only crave the taste of his own nature, as the one thing worth desiring. What then is the inmost essence of this Human Nature, whereto the desire which reaches forth to farthest distance turns back at last, for its only possible appeasement? It is the *Necessity of Love;* and the essence of this love, in its truest utterance, is the *longing for utmost physical reality*, for fruition in an object that can be grasped by all the senses, held fast with all the force of actual being. In this finite, physically sure embrace, must not the *God* dissolve and disappear? Is not the mortal, who had *yearned* for God, undone, annulled? Yet is not *Love*, in its truest, highest essence, herein *revealed?*—Marvel, ye erudite Critics, at the omnipotence of human minstrelsy, unfolded in the simple *Mythos of the Folk!* Things that all your Understanding can not so much as comprehend, are there laid bare to human Feeling, with such a physically perfect surety as *no other means could bring to pass.*—

The ethereal sphere, from which the god is yearning to descend to men, had stretched itself, through Christian longing, to inconceivable bounds of space. To the Hellenes, it was still the cloud-locked realm of thunder and the thunderbolt, from which the lusty Zeus moved down, to mix with men in expert likeness: to the Christian, the blue firmament dissolved into an infinite sea of yearning ecstasy, in which the forms of all the gods were melted, until at last it was the lonely image of his own person, the yearning Man, that alone was left to greet him from the ocean of his phantasy. One primal, manifold-repeated trait runs through the Sagas of those peoples who dwelt beside the sea or sea-embouching rivers : upon the blue mirror of the waters there draws nigh an Unknown-being, of utmost grace and purest virtue, who moves and wins all hearts by charm resistless ; he is the embodied wish of the yearner who dreams of happiness in that far-off land he can not sense. This Unknown-being vanishes across the ocean's waves, so soon as ever questioned on his nature. Thus— so goes the story—there once came in a swan-drawn skiff, over the sea to the banks of the Scheldt, an unknown hero : there he rescued downtrod innocence, and wedded a sweet maiden ; but since she asked him who he was and whence he came, he needs must seek the sea once more and leave his All behind.—Why this Saga, when I learnt it in its simplest outlines, so irresistibly attracted me that, at the very time when I had but just completed *Tannhäuser*, I could concern myself with naught but it, was to be made clearer to my feeling by the immediately succeeding incidents of my life.—

With the finished sketch for the poem of *Lohengrin*, I returned to Dresden, in order to produce *Tannhäuser*. This production was prepared with no inconsiderable outlay on the part of the directorate, who cherished great hopes of the work. The public, by their enthusiastic reception of *Rienzi* and cooler welcome of the *Flying Dutchman*, had plainly shewn me what I must set before them if I sought to please. I completely undeceived their expectations : they left the theatre, after the first performance of *Tannhäuser*, in a confused and discontented mood.—The feeling of the utter loneliness in which I now found myself, quite unmanned me. The few friends who gave me hearty sympathy, felt so depressed by the painfulness of my situation, that the involuntary exhibition of their own disappointment was the only sign of friendly life around me. A week passed by, ere a second performance of *Tannhäuser* could take place ; a thing so needed to correct erroneous impressions, and pave the way for better under-

standing. To me this week was fraught with the burden of
a lifetime. Not wounded vanity, but the shock of an utter
disillusionment, chilled my very marrow. It became clear
to me that my *Tannhäuser* had appealed to a handful of
intimate friends alone, and not to the heart of a public to
whom, nevertheless, I had instinctively turned in the production of this my work. Here was a contradiction which
I could not but deem insoluble. There seemed but one
possibility of winning the public also to my side, namely
—to secure its *understanding:* but I here felt, for the
first time with any great distinctness, that the character
to which we have grown accustomed in operatic performances was completely at variance with what *I* demanded of a representation.—In our Opera the *singer*,
by virtue of the purely material attributes of his voice,
usurps the first place ; whilst the *actor* takes the second, or
even a quite subsidiary rank. On the other side of the line,
stands, logically enough, a public that looks chiefly for satisfaction of the purely sensuous demands of its nerve of
hearing, and thus almost entirely abjures the enjoyment
of a dramatic portrayal. My claim, however, was diametrically opposed to this whole state of affairs : I required
the Actor (*Darsteller*) in the forefront, and the Singer only
as the actor's aid ; lastly, therefore, a public who should
join me in this claim. For I was forced to see that not
until such claim were met, could there be the remotest
question of an impression by the story told ; whereas any
impression must be nothing but a chaos of confusion, when
the fulfilment of that claim was disregarded upon every
hand. Thus I could only look upon myself as a madman
who speaks to the wind and expects it to understand him ;
for I was openly speaking of things which were all the
more doomed to stay uncomprehended as not even the
tongue in which I uttered them was understood. The
gradually awakened interest in my work, displayed by a
portion of the public, appeared to me like the good-
natured sympathy shewn to a lunatic by his friends : this
sympathy impels us to enter into the spirit of the sufferer's

Y

wanderings, to try to unriddle some meaning therefrom, and in this unriddled sense at last to answer, in order thus to make his sad condition a little bearable to him ; then throngs around the indifferent crowd, to whom it is a piquant entertainment to catch the utterances of a madman, and from the odds and ends of intelligible matter in his talk to fall into a pleasurable bewilderment as to whether the madman has suddenly become sane, or they themselves have lost their reason.   This was the precise manner in which I thenceforth interpreted my position towards the general " public."   The benevolent intentions of the direc- torate, and, above all, the friendly zeal and exceptional talent of the performers, succeeded in gradually establishing my opera in public favour.   But no more could this success deceive me ; I now *knew* what I and the public were to one another, and even if I had still been left in any doubt, my further experiences would have well enough dispelled it.

The consequences of my earlier blindness as to my true position toward the public now made themselves appall- ingly evident : the impossibility of procuring *Tannhäuser* a popular success, or even a circulation among the German theatres, was clear as day ; and therewith I was con- fronted with the complete downfall of my outer circum- stances.   Almost solely to stave off that downfall, I still made further efforts to spread this opera ; and, with that end in view, I turned towards Berlin.   By the Intendant of the Royal Prussian Stage I was waved aside with the critical verdict that my opera was too " epically " con- structed to be suitable for production in Berlin.   The General-Intendant of the Royal Prussian Court-music,* however, appeared to be of another opinion.   When, in order to gain the royal interest for the production of my work, I begged him induce the King to allow me to dedicate *Tannhäuser* to his Majesty, I received for reply the advice that—seeing, on the one hand, the King only

---

* In view of the accusation so often levelled against Wagner, of *ingratitude* toward Meyerbeer, it is as well to bear in mind that Meyerbeer was at this time ' Generalmusikdirector ' at the Berlin Court.—TR.

accepted works which were already known to him, but on
the other, there were obstacles in the way of producing
this opera upon the Berlin Court-stage—I had better assist
His Majesty to an acquaintance with the work in question
by arranging something from it for a military band, which
something could then be played before the King during
the ' change of guard.'—I could scarcely have been more
deeply humbled, nor brought to a preciser knowledge of my
situation! Henceforth our entire modern art-publicity
began to vanish more and more completely from my
purview.—But what, then, was my position? And what
sort of a mood must that have been which, precisely at this
time, and amid these facts and these impressions, urged
me on with headlong haste to carry out the project of
my *Lohengrin?*—I will endeavour to make it clear to
myself and friends, in order to explain the meaning that
the Lohengrin legend bore for me; and the light in which
alone I could regard it, both as man and artist.

I was now so completely awoken to the utter *loneliness*
of my position as an artist, that the very feeling of this loneliness supplied me with the spur and the ability to address
myself to my surroundings. Since this prompting spoke
so loud within me that, even without any conscious prospect
of compassing an intelligible message, I yet felt passionately impelled to unbosom myself,—this could only proceed from a mood of wellnigh fanatical yearning, which
itself was born of that feeling of isolation.—In *Tannhäuser*
I had yearned to flee a world of frivolous and repellent
sensuousness,—the only form our modern Present has to
offer ; my impulse lay towards the unknown land of pure
and chaste virginity, as toward the element that might
allay a nobler, but still at bottom sensuous longing : only,
a longing such as our frivolous Present can never satisfy.
By the strength of my longing, I had mounted to the
realms where purity and chastity abide : I felt myself outside the modern world, and mid a sacred, limpid æther
which, in the transport of my solitude, filled me with that
delicious awe we drink-in upon the summits of the Alps,

when, circled with a sea of azure air, we look down upon the lower hills and valleys. Such mountain-peaks the Thinker climbs, and on this height imagines he is "cleansed" from all that's "earthly,"* the topmost branch upon the tree of man's omnipotence : here at last may he feed full upon himself, and, midst this self-repast, freeze finally beneath the Alpine chill into a monument of ice ; as which, philosopher or critic, he stonily frowns down upon the warm and living world below. The desire, however, that had driven *me* to those heights, was a desire sprung from art and man's five senses : it was not the warmth of *Life*, I fain would flee, but the vaporous morass of trivial sensuousness whose exhalations form *one definite* shape of Life, the life of modern times. Upon those heights, moreover, I was warmed by the sunny rays of Love, whose living impulse alone had sped me up. And so it was, that, hardly had this blessed solitude enwrapt me, when it woke a new and overpowering desire, the desire *from peak to valley*, from the dazzling brilliance of chaste Sanctity to the sweet shadows of Love's humanest caresses. From these heights my longing glance beheld at last—*das Weib* : the woman for whom the "Flying Dutchman" yearned, from out the ocean of his misery; the woman who, star-like, showed to "Tannhäuser" the way that led from the hot passion of the Venusberg to Heaven;

---

* In a foot-note to page 286, I drew attention to the similarity of Wagner's description of the "artistic temperament" to that given by Schopenhauer in Chapter 30 of Vol. II. "*Die Welt als Wille und Vorstellung*" ; in like manner he has here unconsciously approached, though by an opposite path, the same idea as Schopenhauer expounds in § 34, Vol. I. of that work, where he refers to the man "who has so plunged and lost himself in contemplation of Nature, that he is now nothing more than the sheer perceiving *Subject*, and thus becomes directly conscious that, as such, he is the bearer of the world and all *objective* existence, since it shows itself as dependent on his own. He draws all Nature into his own self, so that he now regards it as an *accidental* of his being [or essence]. In this sense it is, that Byron says : Are not the mountains, waves and skies, a part Of me and of my soul, as I of them ?"—It is significant that to both these thinkers the solitude of the Alps should have suggested the same line of thought ; but perhaps it may be carried farther back, to the idea underlying the Temptation on the Mountain. —TR.

the woman who now drew Lohengrin from sunny heights
to the depths of Earth's warm breast.—

Lohengrin sought the woman who should *trust* in him ;
who should not ask how he was hight or whence he came,
but love him as he was, and because he was whate'er she
deemed him. He sought the woman who would not call
for explanations or defence, but who should *love* him with
an unconditioned love. Therefore must he cloak his higher
nature, for only in the non-revealing of this higher (*höheren*)
—or more correctly, heightened (*erhöhten*)—essence, could
there lie the surety that he was not adored because of it
alone, or humbly worshipped as a Being past all understanding—whereas his longing was *not* for worship nor for
adoration, but for the only thing sufficient to redeem him
from his loneliness, to still his deep desire,—for *Love*,
for *being loved*, for *being understood through Love*. With
the highest powers of his senses, with his fullest fill of
consciousness, he would fain become and be none other
than a warmly-feeling, warmth-inspiring Man ; in a word,
a *Man* and not a God—i.e. no ' absolute ' artist. Thus
yearned he for Woman,—for the human Heart. And thus
did he step down from out his loneliness of sterile bliss,
when he heard this woman's cry for succour, this heart-cry
from humanity below. But there clings to him the tell-tale
halo of his ' heightened ' nature ; he can not appear as
aught but suprahuman ; the gaping of the common herd,
the poisoned trail of envy, throw their shadows even across
the loving maiden's heart ; doubt and jealousy convince
him that he has not been *understood*, but only *worshipped*,
and force from him the avowal of his divinity, wherewith,
undone, he returns into his loneliness.—

It seemed then to me, and still it seems, most hard to
comprehend, how the deep tragedy of this subject and this
character should have stayed unfelt ; and how the story
should have been so misunderstood that Lohengrin was
looked on as a cold, forbidding figure, more prone to
rouse dislike than sympathy. This reproach was first made

to me by an intimate friend, whose knowledge and whose intellectual gifts I highly prize.*   In his case, however, I reaped an experience which has since been verified by repetition : namely, that upon the first direct acquaintance with my poem the impression produced is thoroughly affecting, and that this reproach only enters when the impression of the artwork itself has faded, and given place to cold, reflective criticism.†   Thus this reproach was not an instinctive act of the immediate-feeling heart, but a purposed act of mediate reflection.   In this occurrence I therefore found the tragedy of Lohengrin's character and situation confirmed, as one deep-rooted in our modern life : it was reproduced upon the artwork and its author, just in the same way as it had borne down upon the hero of the poem.   The character and situation of this Lohengrin I now recognise, with clearest sureness, as the *type of the only absolute tragedy*, in fine, of the *tragic element of modern life ;* and that of just as great significance for the *Present*, as was the " Antigone "—though in another relation—for the life of the Hellenic State.‡   From out this sternest tragic moment of the Present one path alone can lead : the full reunion of sense and soul, the only genuinely *gladsome* element of the Future's Life and Art, each in its utmost consummation.—

I must admit that I myself was so far infected with the doubting spirit of Criticism, that I seriously thought of forc-

---

* According to the late Mr F. Praeger's " *Wagner as I knew him* " (page 145) this friend was August Roeckel ; but it seems far more likely to have been Theodor Uhlig or Eduard Devrient.—TR.

† Of this I have recently been assured again by a talented reporter, who *during* the performance of *Lohengrin* at Weimar—according to his own confession—felt nothing calling for an adverse criticism, but gave himself without restraint to the enjoyment of a touching story.   The doubts that *afterwards* arose in him, I am delighted to say, in dearest self-defence, have never attacked the *actual artist*.   The latter could *throughly* understand me : a thing that was impossible to the critic.—R. WAGNER.

‡ Exactly as my critic, may the Athenian citizen have felt, who under the immediate influence of the artwork was seized with unquestioning sympathy for Antigone, yet in the Areopagus, upon the following day, would certainly have voted to death the living heroine.—R. WAGNER.

ing on my poem a complete change of motive. Through
my sharing in this criticism, I had fallen, for a short time,
so far out of touch with the essence of the story, that I
actually strayed into the sketch of a new denouement,
according to which Lohengrin should be allowed to put
aside his higher nature, so soon as revealed, in favour of
a sojourn upon earth with Elsa. The utterly unsatisfac-
tory, and in the highest sense unnatural character of this
denouement, however, not only was felt by myself—who
had conceived it in a moment of variance with my inner
being—but also by my critical friend. We came to the
joint conclusion, that That which jarred upon our modern
critical conscience lay in the unalterable idiosyncrasy of the
Stuff itself; but on the other hand, that this 'stuff' exerted
so precise and stimulating an effect upon our Feeling that, in
truth, it must have for us a meaning sufficient to make its
artistic exposition a desirable enrichment of our emotional
impressions, and therewith of our powers of emotion.—

In effect, this "Lohengrin" is an entirely new phenomenon to the modern mind; for it could only issue from the
Stimmung and the life-views of an artist who, at none
other than the present time, and amid no other relations
to Art and Life than those which had sprung from my own
peculiar situation, had developed to exactly that point
where this legend faced me with an imperative demand
for treatment. Wherefore, only he who is able to free
himself from all our modern abstract generalisms, and look
Life straight into the eyes, can understand this Lohengrin.
Whoso can *only* class under one general category the
manifold phenomena that spring from the individual
fashioning-force of Life's most active interactions, can
comprehend as good as nothing of them : to wit, not the
phenomenon itself, but only the mere category; whereto—
as to an order laid down in advance—it in truth does
not belong. He to whom there seems nothing comprehensible in Lohengrin beyond the category "Christian-
Romantic," comprehends alone an accidental surface, but
not its underlying essence. This essence, the essence of

a strictly new and hitherto unbroached phenomenon, can be comprehended by that faculty alone whereby is brought to man, in every instance, the fodder for his categorical understanding : and this is the purely physical faculty of Feeling. But only an artwork that presents itself in fullest physical show, can convey the new ' stuff,' with due insistence, to this emotional faculty ; and only he who has taken-in this artwork in that complete embodiment— i.e. the emotional-man who has thus experienced an entire satisfaction of his highest powers of receiving—can also compass the new ' stuff' in all its bearings.

Here I touch the tragic feature in the situation of the true Artist towards the life of the Present, that very situation to which I gave artistic effect in the Lohengrin story.—The most natural and urgent longing of such an artist is, to be taken up without reserve into the Feeling, and by it understood ; and the *impossibility*—under the modern conditions of our art-life—of meeting with this Feeling in such a state of freedom and undoubting sureness as he needs for being fully understood,—the *compulsion* to address himself almost solely to the critical Understanding, instead of to the Feeling : this it is, that forms the tragic element in his situation ; this it is, that, as an artist made of flesh and blood, I could not help but feel ; and this, that, on the pathway of my further evolution, was to be forced so on my consciousness that I broke at last into open revolt against the burden of that situation.—

I now approach the account of my latest evolutionary period, which I must treat at somewhat greater length ; since the chief aim of this Communication has been to correct the apparent contradictions which might be discovered betwixt the nature of my artistic works and the character of my recently-uttered views on Art and its true position toward Life,— contradictions which have already, in part, been held up to opprobrium by superficial critics. In strict connection with what I have already said, I shall proceed to this account, by way of the unbroken history of my artistic doings and the moods of mind from which they sprang.—

Criticism had proved itself unequal to alter the denouement of my *Lohengrin*, and by this victorious issue of the
encounter between my instinctive artistic Feeling and the
modern Critical conscience, my zeal for its artistic completion was kindled to yet brighter flame. In this *completion*, I felt, would lie the *demonstration* of the rightness
of my feeling. It was clear to my inner sense, that an
essential ground of misunderstanding of the tragical significance of my hero had lain in the assumption that Lohengrin,
having descended from a glittering realm of painlessly-
unearned and cold magnificence, and in obedience to an
unnatural law that bound him will-lessly thereto, now
turned his back upon the strife of earthly passions, to
taste again the pleasures of divinity. As the chief lesson
that this taught me, was the wilfulness of the modern
critical mode of viewing things, which looks away from
the instinctive aspect and twists them round to suit its
purpose; and as it was easy for me to see that this misunderstanding had simply sprung from a wilful interpretation of that binding law, which in truth was no
outwardly-imposed decree, but the expression of the
necessary inner nature of one who, from the midst of
lonely splendour, is athirst for being understood through
Love : so, to ensure the desired correct impression, I held
all the faster to the original outlines of the legend, whose
naïve innocence had made so irresistible an impression
upon myself. In order to artistically convey these outlines in entire accordance with the effect that they had
made on me, I observed a still greater fidelity than in
the case of " Tannhäuser," in my presentment of those
half-historical, half-legendary features by which alone a
subject so out of the beaten path could be brought with due
conviction to the answering senses. This led me, in the
conduct of the scenes (*scenische Haltung*) and dialogue
(*sprachlichen Ausdruck*), to a path which brought me later
to the discovery of possibilities whose logical sequence was
certainly to point me out an utter revolution in the adjust-
ment of those factors which have hitherto made up our

operatic mode of speech. But toward this path, also, I was led by *one* sole impulse, namely to convey to others as vividly and intelligibly as possible, what my own mind's eye had seen; and here, again, it was always the subject-matter that governed me in my every choice of form. Utmost clearness was the chief endeavour of my working-out; and that not the superficial clearness wherewith a shallow object greets us, but the rich and many-coloured light wherein alone a comprehensive, broad-related subject can intelligibly display itself, and yet which cannot help but seem superficial, and often downright obscure, to those accustomed to mere form without contents.—

It was midst this struggle for clearness of exposition, as I remember, that the essence of the heart of Woman, such as I had to picture in the loving *Elsa*, first dawned upon me with more and more distinctness. The artist can only attain the power of convincing portraiture, when he has been able to sink himself with fullest sympathy into the essence of the character to be portrayed.* In "Elsa" I saw, from the commencement, my desired antithesis to Lohengrin,— yet naturally, not so absolute an antithesis as should lie far removed from his own nature, but rather the *other half* of his being,—the antithesis which is included in his general nature† and forms the necessarily longed-for complement of his specific *man*-hood. *Elsa* is the Unconscious, the Undeliberate (*Unwillkürliche*), into which Lohengrin's conscious, deliberate (*willkürliche*) being yearns to be redeemed; but this *yearning*, again, is itself the unconscious, undeliberate Necessity in Lohengrin, whereby he feels himself akin to Elsa's being. Through the capability of this "unconscious consciousness," such as I myself now felt

* Compare *Art-work of the Future*, page 149.—TR.

† At first sight this looks as though it were written under the influence of the Hegelian doctrine, of every Reality being the "unification of two contradictory elements," and every true Idea containing a "coincidence of opposites"; but there is, so far as I can see, no warrant for believing that Wagner ever studied Hegel's system of philosophy, excepting in so far as it had been transformed by Feuerbach, who seems to have discarded the formula of "Thesis, antithesis, and synthesis."—TR.

alike with Lohengrin, the nature of Woman also—and that precisely as I felt impelled to the faithfullest portrayal of its essence—came to ever clearer understanding in my inner mind. Through this power I succeeded in so completely transferring myself to this female principle, that I came to an entire agreement with its utterance by my loving Elsa. I grew to find her so justified in the final outburst of her jealousy, that from this very outburst I learnt first to throughly understand the purely-human element of love; and I suffered deep and actual grief—often welling into bitter tears—as I saw the tragical necessity of the parting, the unavoidable undoing of this pair of lovers. This woman, who with clear foreknowledge rushes on her doom, for sake of Love's imperative behest,—who, amid the ecstasy of adoration, wills yet to lose her all, if so be she cannot all-embrace her loved one; this woman, who in her contact with this Lohengrin, of all men, must founder, and in doing so, must shipwreck her beloved too; this woman, who can love but thus and not otherwise, who, by the very outburst of her jealousy, wakes first from out the thrill of worship into the full reality of Love, and by her wreck reveals its essence to him who had not fathomed it as yet; this glorious woman, before whom Lohengrin must vanish, for reason that his own specific nature could not understand her,—I had found her *now :* and the random shaft that I had shot towards the treasure dreamt but hitherto un-*known*, was my own Lohengrin, whom now I must give up as lost; to track more certainly the footsteps of that *true Woman-hood*, which should one day bring to me and all the world redemption, after Man-hood's egoism, even in its noblest form, had shivered into self-crushed dust before her.—Elsa, the Woman,—Woman hitherto un-understood by me, and understood at last,—that most positive expression of the purest instinct of the senses,*—made me a Revolutionary at one blow. She was the Spirit of the

---

* "Diese nothwendigste Wesenäusserung der reinsten sinnlichen Unwill-kür."

Folk, for whose redeeming hand I too, as artist-man, was longing.—

But this treasure trove of Knowledge lay hid, at first, within the silence of my lonely heart : only slowly did it ripen into loud avowal.—

I must now recall the outward situation of my life, at that time when—with long and frequent interruptions —I was working out my *Lohengrin.* This situation was at the utmost variance with my inner mood. I drew back into ever greater seclusion, and lived in intimate communion almost solely with one friend, * who went so far in his sympathy with *my* artistic evolution as to quell the natural impulse to develop, and gain credit for, his own artistic talents—as he himself confessed to me. Nothing could I wish so much, as to create in undisturbed retirement ; the possibility of intelligibly conveying the result to others, albeit the one thing needful, then scarcely troubled me at all. I consoled myself by saying that my loneliness was no egoistic, self-sought thing, but absolutely imposed upon me by the wilderness around. But *one* distasteful bond still chained me to our public art-affairs,— the obligation of taking thought for pecuniary profit from my works, in order to eke out my ways and means. Thus had I still to care for outer success, although I had already renounced it for myself and inner needs.

Berlin had declined my *Tannhäuser :* no longer for myself, but for the sake of others,† I bestirred myself to secure the production there of my *Rienzi,* a work I had long since done with. My sole reason for this step was the experience of this opera's success in Dresden, and a calculation of the outward advantage which a like success in Berlin would bring me, in the shape of the *tantièmes* I should there secure from the receipts of the performances.

* By all accounts, this " friend " was August Roeckel ; and according to Ferdinand Praeger, he withdrew his opera " Farinelli " before its production, in humble recognition of the supremacy of Wagner's genius.—TR.

† For his creditors, who had advanced money for the publication of the scores of *Rienzi, The Flying Dutchman,* and *Tannhäuser.* See the *Letters to Uhlig and Fischer.*—TR.

—I remember with horror, into what a sludge of contradictions of the vilest sort I was plunged by this sheer solicitude for outward gain, amid my already fixed ideas regarding human-things artistic. I was forced to yield myself to the entire modern crime of hypocrisy and deceit: people whom I despised from the bottom of my heart, I flattered, or at least sedulously concealed from them my inner sentiments, because, as circumstances were, they had within their hands the success or failure of my enterprise; crafty men, who were ranged upon the side the farthest from my own true nature, and of whom I knew that they as mistrustfully disliked me as they themselves were repugnant to my inner feeling, I sought by an assumed ingenuousness to rob of their suspicion,—though with small chance of actually effecting this, as I pretty soon discovered. Naturally, this whole behaviour stayed without its only intended result, since I was but a 'prentice hand at lying: my candid opinion, which had a knack of always breaking out, just simply turned me from a dangerous into a ridiculous being. For instance, nothing did me more harm than a remark which, conscious of the better work I now could do, I made in an address to the performers at the commencement of the general rehearsal; when I described the excessive demands made by *Rienzi* on their strength, and only to be met by great exertion, as an "art-crime of my youth." The reporters served this saying to the public steaming-hot, and gave it thus the cue for its demeanour towards a work which the composer himself had characterised as "a miserable failure" (*ein "durchaus verfehltes"*), and whose presentation to the art-cultured public of Berlin was therefore a piece of audacity that cried for chastisement.—Thus I had, in truth, to ascribe my ill success in Berlin more to my badly-acted rôle of diplomat, than to my opera itself; which, if I had only gone to work with a complete belief in its merits and in my own eagerness to bring them forward, would possibly have made as good a 'hit' in that city as other works of far less effectiveness (*Wirkungskraft*) have done.

It was a hideous state of mind, in which I returned from Berlin. Only those who have misread my often lasting outbursts of unbridled ironical mirth, could shut their eyes to the fact that I now felt all the more wretched as I had made shipwreck with my enforced attempts at self-dishonouring—commonly called worldly wisdom. Never was the ghastly curb that the unbreakable connection of our modern Art and modern Life imposes on a man's free heart, and makes him bad, more clear to me than at that time. Was there any possible outlet for a single-handed man to find, but—Death? How laughable must seem to me those knowing gabies, who deemed it a point of honour to see nothing in the yearning for this Death but a "residue of Christian exaltation, already overcome by Science," and thus objectionable! If, in my longing to escape from the worthlessness of the modern world, I showed myself a *Christian*,—then I was a more honest Christian than any of those who now, with smug impertinence, upbraid me for my lapse from Christianity.—

One thing, only, kept me on end : *my art*, which for me was no mere mean to fame and gain, but to the proclamation of my thoughts to feeling hearts. When, therefore, I had exorcised that *outer* fiend which had lately tempted me to speculate on outward profit, I for the first time became plainly conscious of how imperative a necessity it was to me, to busy myself about the formation of that artistic organ through which I might impart my aim to others. This organ was *the theatre*, or better still : the Art of Stage-portrayal, which I recognised each day more clearly as the only redeemer of the Poet, who through it alone can see the object of his Will contented in the certainty of physically-accomplished Deed. On this weightiest point of all, I had hitherto been yielding myself more and more to the hazards of Chance : *now* I felt that it was a question of here, at a definite place and under definite conditions, bringing the right and needful thing to pass ; and that it never could be brought to pass, if one's hand were not stretched out at once to work that lay the closest. The

winning of the possibility of seeing my artistic views completely realised in the flesh, by the art of Stage-portrayal,
no matter where—and therefore best at Dresden, where I
was and worked,—seemed henceforth to me my nighest
worthy goal ; and in the struggle for its reach, I for the
moment looked quite away from the constitution of that
Public which I thought to gain myself by the mere fact of
setting scenic performances so intellectually and physically
complete before it, that the sympathy to be wrested from
its purely-human Feeling would let it easily be led towards
a higher plane.

In this sense I turned back to that art-institute in whose
guidance I had already shared, as Kapellmeister, for nigh
upon six years. I say : turned *back* to it; since my experiences, reaped thus far, had already reduced me to a
state of hopeless indifference in its regard.—The ground
of my inner repugnance to taking the post of Kapellmeister
to any theatre, especially a Court theatre, had become ever
clearer to my perception, in the course of my practical
discharge of the duties of that office. Our theatrical institutions have, in general, no other end in view than to cater
for a nightly entertainment, never energetically demanded,
but forced down people's throats by the spirit of Speculation, and lazily swallowed by the social Ennui of the
dwellers in our larger cities. Whatever, from a purely
artistic standpoint, has rebelled against this mission of the
stage, has always shown itself too weak for any good.
The only regulator of distinctions, has been the *section*
for whom this entertainment was to be provided : for the
rabble, brought up in tutored grossness, coarse farces and
crass montrosities were served ; the decorous *Philistines* of
our bourgeoisie were treated to moral family-pieces ; for the
more delicately cultured, and art-spoilt *higher* and *highest
classes*, only the most elegant art-viands were dished up,
often garnished with æsthetic quips. The genuine Poet,
who from time to time sought to make good his claim,
among those of the three above-named classes, was always
driven back with a taunt peculiar to our theatre-public,

the taunt of Ennui—at least until he had become an antiquarian morsel wherewith conveniently to grace that art-
repast.

Now the special feature of our *greater* theatrical institutions consists in this, that they plan their performances to
catch the taste of all three classes of the public ; they are
provided with an auditorium wherein those classes range
themselves entirely apart, according to the figure of their
entrance-money, thus placing the artist in the predicament
of seeking-out his hearers now among the so-called ' Gods,'
now in the Pit, and again in the Boxes.   The Director of
such institutions, who proximately has no other concern
than to make money, has therefore to please each section
of his public in its turn : this he arranges, generally with an
eye to the business character of the day of the week, by
furnishing the most diverse products of the playwright's
art, giving today a vulgar burlesque, tomorrow a piece of
Philistine sensationalism, and the day after, a toothsome
delicacy for the epicures.   This still left one thing to be
aimed at, namely from all three mentioned *genera* to concoct a *genre* of stage-piece which should satisfy the whole
public at one stroke.   That task the modern Opera has with
great energy fulfilled : it has thrown the vulgar, the philis-
tinish, and the exquisite into one common pot, and now sets
the broth before the entire public, crowded head on head.
The Opera has thus succeeded in fining down the mob, in
vulgarising the genteel, and finally in turning the whole conglomerate audience into a superfinely-mobbish Philistine ;
who now, in the shape of the Theatre-public, flings his confused demands into the face of every man who undertakes
the guidance of an Art-institute.

This position of affairs will not give a moment's uneasi-
ness to *that* Stage-director whose only business is to charm
the money out of the pockets of the " Public " : the said
problem is solved, even with great tact and never-failing
certainty, by every Director of the un-subventioned theatres
of our large or smaller cities.   It operates confusingly,
however, upon those who are called by a royal Court to

manage an exactly similar institution, differing only in that
it is lent the Court ægis to cover any contingent deficiency
in the 'takings.' In virtue of this protecting ægis, the
Director of such a Court-theatre ought to feel bound to
look aside from any speculation on the already corrupted
taste of the masses, and rather to endeavour to improve
that taste by seeing to it that the spirit of the stage
performances be governed by the dictates of a higher art-
intelligence. And, as a matter of fact, such was originally
the good intention of enlightened princes, like Joseph II.
of Austria, in founding their Court-theatres ; as a tradition,
it has also been transmitted to the Court-theatre Intendants
even of our later days. Two practical obstacles, however,
have stood in the way of realising this—in itself more
munificently chimerical than actually attainable—object :
firstly, the personal incapacity of the appointed Intendant,
who is chosen from the ranks of court-officials mostly
without any regard to acquired professional skill, or even
so much as natural disposition to artistic sensibility; and
secondly, the impossibility of really dispensing with speculation on the Public's taste. In fact, the ampler
monetary support of the Court-theatres has only led to an
increase in the price of the artistic *matériel*, the systematic
cultivation whereof, so far as concerns theatric art, has
never occurred to the else so education-rabid leaders of
our State ; and thus the expenses of these institutions
have mounted so high, that it has become a sheer necessity to the Director of a Court theatre, beyond all others,
to speculate upon the paying public, without whose active
help the outlay could not possibly be met. But on the
other hand, a successful pursuit of this speculation, in the
same sense as that of any other theatrical manager, is
made impossible to the distinguished Court-theatre-
intendant by the feeling of his higher mission ; a mission,
however, which—in his personal incapacity for rightly
fathoming its import—has been only taken in the sense of
a shadowy Court dignity, and could be so interpreted that,
for any particularly foolish arrangement, the Intendant

z

would excuse himself by saying that in a Court-theatre this was nobody's business.   Thus a modern Court-theatre-intendant's skill can only, and inevitably, result in the perpetual exhibition of a conflict between a *second-rate* spirit of speculation and a courtier's red-tape arrogance. An insight into this dilemma is so easy to be gained, that I here have merely alluded to the situation, without any wish to throw its details into higher relief.

That no one, even the best intentioned, and—to give every man his due—the most accessible to good advice, can wrest himself from the iron grip of this unnatural situation, without he finally decide to give his office up for good : this could not but become perfectly plain to me from my Dresden experiences.   These experiences, themselves, I scarcely think it necessary to describe more closely ; hardly will it need assurance that, after constantly renewed, and as constantly proved fruitless, endeavours to gain from the good-will of my Intendant toward myself a definitely favourable influence on the affairs of the theatre, I at last fell into a quagmire of torturing cross-purposes, from which I could only free myself again by giving up the attempt entirely, and adhering strictly to the letter of my duties.—

When, then, I left this temporary reserve, and turned my thoughts again towards the Stage, this—in view of the proved fruitlessness of all detached attempts—could only be in the sense of a fundamental and *complete* reform thereof.   I could but see that I here had not to do with isolated phenomena, but with a wide connexus of phenomena, whereof I was gradually forced to recognise that *it*, also, was inextricably involved in the endless-branching system of our whole social and political affairs.   While pondering on the possibility of a thorough change in our theatrical relations, I was insensibly driven to a full perception of *the worthlessness of that social and political system which, of its very nature, could beget no other public art-conditions than precisely those I then was grappling with.* —This knowledge was of decisive consequence for the further development of my whole life.

Never had I occupied myself with politics, strictly so called. I now remember that I only turned my attention to the phenomena of the political world in exact measure as in them was manifested the spirit of Revolution—*i.e.*, as pure Human Nature rebelled against politico-juristic Formalism. In this sense a criminal case had the same interest for me as a political action ; I could only take the side of the suffering party, and, indeed, in exact measure of vehemence as it was engaged in resisting any kind of oppression. I have never been able to relinquish this manner of ' taking sides,' in favour of any politically constructive notion. Therefore was my interest in the world of politics always in so far of an artistic nature, as I looked beneath its formal expression into its purely human contents. Only when I could strip off from the phenomena their formal shell, fashioned from the traditions of Juristic Rights, and light upon their inward kernel of purely human essence, could they arouse my sympathy ; for here I then saw the same impelling motive which drove myself, as artist-man, to wrest from the evil physical form of the Present a new physical mould which should correspond to the true essence of humanity—a mould which is only to be gained through destruction of the physical form of the Present, and therefore through Revolution.

Thus, from my artistic standpoint, and specially on the forementioned path of pondering on the reconstruction of the Stage,* I had arrived at a point where I was in a position to thoroughly recognise the necessity of the commencing Revolution of 1848. The formal political channel into which—particularly in Dresden—the stream of agitation first poured itself, did not indeed deceive me as to the true nature of the Revolution ; still I held myself at first aloof from any manner of share therein. I set about drawing up a comprehensive plan for the reorganisation of the theatre, in order to be fully equipped so soon as ever

* I lay stress on this, how tasteless soever it may appear to those who make merry over me as "a revolutionary for the sake of the theatre."—R. WAGNER

the revolutionary question should reach this institution
also. It did not escape me that, in a new arrangement of
the Civil List, such as was to be expected, the object of
the subvention for the Theatre would be submitted to a
searching criticism. As it was to be foreseen that, so soon
as this question arose, the public utility of the employment
of that money would be disputed, my proposed plan was
to start with an admission of this uselessness and aimless-
ness, not only from the standpoint of political economy,
but also from that of purely artistic interests; but it was
at like time to show the true social aim of theatric art, and
to bring the necessity of providing such an aim with all
the needful means for its attainment before those who, with
righteous indignation, could see nothing in our *existing*
Theatre but a useless, or even harmful public institution.

All this was prompted by the assumption of a peaceful
solution of the imminent, more reformatory than revolutionary questions, and of the serious will of those in power,
to themselves set on foot an actual reform. The course of
political events was soon to teach me a different lesson;
Reaction and Revolution set themselves squarely face to
face, and the necessity arose, to either return completely
to the Old, or throughly break therewith. My observation
of the utter haziness of the views of the contending parties,
as to the essential contents of the Revolution, decided me
one day to openly declare myself *against* the purely formal
and political conception of this Revolution, and *for* the
necessity of keeping its purely human kernel plainly in the
eye. From the results of this step I now saw, for the first
time unmistakably, how our politicians were situated with
regard to a knowledge of the true spirit of Revolution, and
that genuine Revolution could never come from Above,
from the standpoint of erudite intellect, but only from
Below, from the urgence of true human need. The lying
and hypocrisy of the political parties filled me with a
disgust that drove me back, at first, into the most utter
solitude.

Here my energy, unsatisfied without, consumed itself

once more in projects for artistic work.—Two such projects, which had occupied my thoughts for some time previously, now claimed my attention wellnigh at the same moment; indeed, the character of their subjects made them almost seem to me as one. Even during the musical composition of *Lohengrin*, midst which I had always felt as though resting by an oasis in the desert, *both* these subjects had usurped my poetic fancy: they were "Siegfried" and "Frederic Barbarossa."—

Once again, and that the last time, did Myth and History stand before me with opposing claims; this while, as good as forcing me to decide whether it was a musical drama, or a spoken play, that I had to write. A closer narration of the conflict that lay behind this question, I have purposely reserved until this stage, because it was *here* first that I arrived at its definite answer, and thus at a full consciousness of its true nature.

Since my return to Germany from Paris, my favourite study had been that of ancient German lore. I have already dwelt on the deep longing for my native home that filled me then. This Home, however, in its actual reality, could nowise satisfy my longing; thus I felt that a deeper instinct lay behind my impulse, and one that needs must have its source in some other yearning than merely for the modern homeland. As though to get down to its root, I sank myself into the primal element of Home, that meets us in the legends of a Past which attracts us the more warmly as the Present repels us with its hostile chill. To all our wishes and warm impulses, which in truth transport us to the *Future*, we seek to give a physical token by means of pictures from the Past, and thus to win for them a form the modern Present never can provide. In the struggle to give the wishes of my heart artistic shape, and in the ardour to discover *what* thing it was that drew me so resistlessly to the primal source of old home Sagas, I drove step by step into the deeper regions of antiquity, where at last to my delight, and truly in the *utmost* reaches of old time, I was to light upon the fair young form of

Man, in all the freshness of his force. My studies thus bore me, through the legends of the Middle Ages, right down to their foundation in the old-Germanic Mythos ; one swathing after another, which the later legendary lore had bound around it, I was able to unloose, and thus at last to gaze upon it in its chastest beauty. What here I saw, was no longer the Figure of conventional history, whose garment claims our interest more than does the actual shape inside ; but the real naked Man, in whom I might spy each throbbing of his pulses, each stir within his mighty muscles, in uncramped, freest motion : the type of the true *human being*.

At like time I had sought this human being *in History too*. Here offered themselves *relations*, and nothing but relations ; the *human being* I could only see in so far as the relations ordered him : and not as he had power to order *them*. To get to the bottom of these 'relations,' whose coercive force compelled the strongest man to squander all his powers on objectless and never-compassed aims, I turned afresh to the soil of Greek antiquity, and here, again, was pointed at the last *to Mythos*, in which alone I could touch the ground of even these *relations :* but in that Mythos, these social relations were drawn in lines as simple, plastic and distinct as I had earlier recognised therein the human shape itself. From this side, also, did Mythos lead me to this Man alone, as to the involuntary *creator* of those relations, which, in their documento-monumental perversion, as the excrescences of History (*Geschichtsmomente*), as traditional fictions and established rights, have at last usurped dominion over Man and ground to dust his freedom.

Although the splendid type of *Siegfried* had long attracted me, it first enthralled my every thought when I had come to see it in its purest human shape, set free from every later wrappage. Now for the first time, also, did I recognise the possibility of making him the hero of a drama ; a possibility that had not occurred to me while I only knew him from the medieval *Nibelungenlied.* But at like time with him, had *Friedrich I.* loomed on me from the study of our History: he appeared to me, just as he had appeared to the Saga-framing German Folk, a historical rebirth of the old-pagan Siegfried. When the wave of political commotion broke lately in upon us, and proclaimed itself at first, in Germany, as a longing for national unity, it could not but seem to me that Friedrich I. would lie nearer to the Folk,* and be more readily understood, than the downright human Siegfried. Already I had sketched the plan for a drama in five acts, which should depict this Friedrich's life, from the Roncalian Diet down to his entry on the Crusade. But ever and again I turned in discontentment from my plan. It was no mere desire to mirror detached historical events, that had prompted my sketch, but the wish to show a wide connexus of relations, in such a fashion that its unity might be embraced in easy survey, and understood at once. In order to make plainly understandable both my hero and the relations that with giant force he strives to master, only to be at last subdued by them, I should have felt compelled to adopt the method of Mythos, in the very teeth of the historic material: the vast mass of incidents and intricate associations, whereof no single link could be omitted if the connection of the whole was to be intelligibly set before the eye, was adapted neither to the form, nor to the spirit of Drama. Had I chosen to comply with the imperative demands of History, then had my drama become an unsurveyable conglomerate of pictured incidents, entirely crowding out from view the real and only thing I wished to show; and thus, as artist, I should have met precisely the same fate in my drama as

---

* The connection of this subject with the events of 1848 is made obvious by the prefatory note to the *Wibelungen* essay: " I, too, in the late arousing times, shared the ardent wishes of so many, for the re-awakening of *Frederick the Red-beard.*" The tradition ran (though now proved to have been originally connected with Friedrich II.) that the first and greatest Hohenstaufian Kaiser was still sleeping in the heart of the Kyffhäuser hills, and would one day come again to free his people and knit them once more into a sovereign nation.—Tr.

did its hero: to wit, I should myself have been crushed by the weight of the very *relations* that I fain would master— i.e. portray—, without ever having brought my *purpose* to an understanding; just as Friedrich could not bring his *will* to carrying-out.   To attain my purpose, I should therefore have had to reduce this mass of relations by *free* construction, and should have fallen into a treatment that would have absolutely violated History.*   Yet I could not but see the contradiction involved herein; for it was the main characteristic of Friedrich, in my eyes, that he should be a *historical* hero.   If, on the other hand, I wished to dabble in mythical construction, then, for its ultimate and highest form, but quite beyond the modern poet's reach, I must go back to the unadulterated Mythos, which up to now the Folk alone has hymned, and which I had already found in full perfection—in the "Siegfried."

I now returned to "Siegfried"—at the selfsame time as, disgusted with the empty formalistic tendency of the doings of our political parties, I withdrew from contact with our public life—and that with a full conviction of History's unsuitedness to Art.   But at like time I had definitely solved for myself a problem of artistic formalism: namely, the question of the applicability of the pure, i.e. the merely spoken, Play (*Schauspiel*) to the Drama of the Future.   This question by no means presented itself to me from the formal æsthetic standpoint, but I happened on it through the very character of the poetic 'stuff' to be portrayed; which character alone, henceforth, laid down my lines of treatment.   When outward instigations prompted me to take up the sketch of "Friedrich Rothbart," I did not for a moment doubt that it could only be dealt with as a spoken play, and by no manner of means as a drama to be set to music.   In that

---

* The studies that I made upon these lines, and whose very necessity decided me to abandon my proposal, I a short while since laid publicly before my friends—at least, not at the feet of historico-juristic criticism—in a little essay entitled "*Die Wibelungen.*"—R. WAGNER.

period of my life when I conceived *Rienzi*, it might perhaps have struck me to regard the " Rothbart," also, as an opera subject: now, when it was no longer my purpose to write operas, but before all to give forth my poetic thoughts (*Anschauungen*) in the most living of artistic forms, to wit in Drama, I had not the remotest idea of handling a historico-political subject otherwise than as a spoken play. Yet when I put aside this 'stuff,' it was nowise from any scruple that might perchance have come to me as opera-poet and composer, and forbidden me to leave the trade that I was versed in : no, it came about— as I have shown—simply because I learnt to see the general unfitness of the Stuff *for drama ;* and this, again, grew clear to me, not merely from any scruple as to the artistic form, but from dissatisfaction of that same sheer human feeling that in actual life was set on edge by the political formalism of our era.   I felt that the highest of what I had seen from the purely human standpoint, and longed to show to others, could *not* be imparted in the treatment of a historico-political subject ; that the mere intellectual exposition of *relations* made impossible to me the presentment of the purely human Individuality ; that I should therefore have had to leave to be *unriddled* the only and essential thing I was concerned with, and not to bring it actually and sensibly before the Feeling.   For these reasons, together with the historico-political *subject* I necessarily also cast aside that dramatic *art-form* with which alone it could have been invested : for I recognised that this form had issued only from that subject, and by it alone was justifiable, but that it was altogether incapable of convincingly imparting to the Feeling the purely-human subject on which alone my gaze was henceforth bent ; and thus that, with the disappearance of the historico-political subject, there must also necessarily vanish, in the future, the spoken form of play (*die Schauspielform*), as inadequate to meet the novel subject, incongruous and halting.

I have said that it was not my profession of Opera-composer that caused me to give up a story merely fitted for the Play : nevertheless I must avow, that a recognition of the essence of the spectacular play and of the historico-political subject that demands this form, such as had now arisen in me, could certainly *not* have come to any absolute playwright or dramatic litterateur, but only to a man and artist who had passed through a development like mine, under the influence of the spirit of *music.*—Already in speaking of my Paris period, I have mentioned how I looked on Music as the good angel, who, amid my revolt against the baseness of modern public art, preserved me as an artist and saved me from the mere literary activity of the critic. In that paragraph, I reserved to myself the opportunity of describing somewhat more closely the influence that my musical predisposition (*Stimmung*) exerted on the fashioning of my artistic works. Although the character of this influence can scarcely have escaped any-one who has attentively followed the account of the origina-tion of my poems, yet I must here return to the matter still more explicitly, since it was precisely now that, in forming an important artistic decision, this influence came to my full consciousness.

As far as my *Rienzi*, I had it only in my mind to write an "opera." To this end I sought out my materials, and, merely concerned for "opera," I chose them from ready-made stories, and indeed from such as had already been fashioned with deliberate attention to artistic form : * a dramatic fairy-tale of Gozzi's, a play of Shakespeare's, and finally a romance of Bulwer's, I arranged for the sole end of Opera. With regard to the *Rienzi*, I have already said that I manipulated the story—as, for the matter of that, was unavoidable, from the very nature of a historical romance—according to my own impressions, and in such a manner as—to recall my expression—I had seen it through the "opera-glasses." With the *Flying Dutchman*, whose origin from specific moods of my own life I have already suffi-

---

* Here I got no further in the formalities of my trade than did the skilful Lortzing, who likewise adapted ready-made stage-pieces for his opera-texts.— R. WAGNER.

ciently described, I struck out a new path ; inasmuch as I became, myself, the artistic modeller of a 'stuff' that lay before me only in the blunt and simple outlines of Folk-Saga. Henceforward, with all my dramatic works, I was in the first instance *Poet*, and only in the complete working-out of the poem, did I become once more. Musician. Only, I was a poet who was conscious in advance of the faculty of *musical* expression, for the working-out of his poems. This faculty I had exercised so far, that I was fully aware of my ability to employ it on the realisation of a poetic aim, and not only to reckon on its help when drafting a poetic sketch, but in that knowledge to draw such sketch itself more *freely*, and more in accordance with poetic necessity, than if I had designed merely with an eye to the musical effect. Before this, I had had to acquire facility of musical expression in the same manner as one learns a language. He who has not made himself thoroughly at home with a foreign, unaccustomed tongue, must pay heed to its idiosyncrasies in everything he says ; to express himself intelligibly, he must keep a constant watch upon this mode of utterance itself, and deliberately reckon for it *What* he desires to say. Wherefore, for every sentence he is entangled in the formal rules of speech, and cannot as yet speak out from his instinctive Feeling, and altogether *how* he means to, *what* he feels and what he sees. The rather, for their utterance, he must model his feelings and seeings, themselves, on a form of expression whereof he is not so completely master as of his mother-tongue; in which latter, entirely careless of expression, he finds the correct expression without an effort.

Now, however, I had completely learnt the speech of Music ; I was at home with it, as with a genuine mother-tongue ; in what I wished to utter, I need no more be careful for the formal mode: it stood ready at my call, exactly as I needed it, to impart a definite impression or emotion (*Anschauung oder Empfindung*) in keeping with my inner impulse. But one can never speak a foreign tongue without fatigue, and at like time thoroughly correctly, until one has taken up its spirit into oneself, until one feels and thinks in this tongue, and thus desires to utter nothing but that which can be uttered in its spirit When, however, we have arrived at speaking entirely from out the spirit of a tongue, at feeling and thinking quite instinctively therein, there also springs up in us the power of broadening this very spirit, of enriching and extending at once the mode of utterance and the utter-able in that tongue. Yet that which is utterable in the speech of Music, is limited to *feelings* and *emotions :* it expresses, in abundance, that which has been cast adrift from our Word-speech (*Wortsprache*) at its conversion into a mere organ of the Intellect, namely, the emotional contents of Purely-human speech.   What thus remains unutterable in the absolute-musical tongue, is the exact definement of the *object* of the feeling and emotion, whereby the latter reach themselves a surer definition. The broadening and extension of the Musical form of speech (*musikalischer Sprachausdruck*), as called for by this Object, therefore consists in the attainment of the power to outline sharply and distinctly the Individual and the Particular ; and this it gains alone by being wed to Word-speech.   But then only can this marriage prove a fruitful one, when the Musical-speech allies itself directly to its kindred elements in Word-speech ; the union must take place precisely *there*, where in Word-speech itself there is evinced a mastering desire for real utterance of Feeling to the senses.   This, again, is governed by the *matter* to be uttered (*Inhalt des Auszudrückenden*), and the degree in which it becomes, from a matter of the intellect, a matter of the feeling.   A Matter that is only seizable by the Understanding, can be conveyed alone by means of Word-speech ; but the more it expands into a phase of Feeling, the more definitely does it also need a mode of expression that Tone-speech alone can, at the last, confer on it with answering fulness.   Herewith is laid down, quite of itself, the Matter of what the Word-Tone poet has to utter : it is, *the Purely-human, freed from every shackle of Convention.*

With the attained facility of speaking in this Tone-speech

freely from my heart, I naturally could only have to give my message also in the spirit of that speech ; and where, as artist-man, I felt the most peremptorily urged to its delivery, the Matter of my message was necessarily dictated by the Spirit of the means of expression that I had made my own. The poetic 'stuffs' which urged me to artistic fashioning, could only be of such a nature that, before all else, they usurped my emotional, and not my intellectual being : only the Purely-human (*Reinmenschliche*), loosed from all historical formality, could—once it came before my vision in its genuine natural shape, unruffled from outside—arouse my interest, and spur me on to impart what I beheld. What I beheld, I now looked at solely with the eyes of Music ; though not of *that* music whose formal maxims might have held me still embarrassed for expression, but of the music which I had within my heart, and wherein I might express myself as in a mother-tongue. With this freedom of faculty, I now might address myself without a hindrance to *that to be expressed ;* henceforth the *object* of expression was the sole matter for regard in all my workmanship. Thus, precisely by the acquirement of facility in musical expression, did I become a *poet ;* inasmuch as I no longer had, as fashioning artist, to refer to the mode of expression itself, but only to its object. Yet, without deliberately setting about an enrichment of the means of musical expression, I was absolutely driven to expand them, by the very nature of the objects I was seeking to express.

Now it lay conditioned in the nature of an advance from musical emotionalism (*Empfindungswesen*) to the shaping of poetic stuffs, that I should condense * the vague, more general emotional contents of these stuffs to an ever clearer and more individual precision, and thus at last arrive at the point where the poet, in his direct concern with Life, takes a firmer hold of the matter to be conveyed through musical expression, and stamps it with his own intent. Who-

---

* Again we have the—logical—play of words between "*dichterisch*" (poetic) and "*verdichten*" (to condense).   Compare page 92.—Tr.

soever, therefore, will carefully consider the construction
(*Bildung*) of the three accompanying poems, will find that
what I drew in haziest outline in the *Flying Dutchman*, I
brought with ever plainer definition into stabler form in
Tannhäuser, and finally in *Lohengrin*. Since by such a
procedure I was enabled to draw nearer and nearer to actual
Life, I must inevitably reach a point of time at last, when,
under certain external impressions, a poetic subject such
as that of "*Friedrich Rothbart*" would present itself to
me, for whose modelling I should have had to downright
renounce all musical expression. But it was precisely here,
that my hitherto *unconscious* procedure came to my *consciousness* as an artistic Necessity. With this 'stuff,' which
would have made me altogether forget my music, I became
aware of the bearings of true poetic stuffs in general; and
*there, where I must have left unused my faculty of musical
expression, I also found that I should have had to subordinate
my poetic attainments to political abstractions, and thus to
radically forswear my artistic nature.*—Here was it, also,
that I had the most urgent occasion to clear my mind as
to the essential difference between the historico-political,
and the purely-human life; and when I knowingly and
willingly gave up the "*Friedrich*," in which I had approached
the closest to that political life, and—by so much the clearer
as to what I wished—gave preference to the "*Siegfried*,"
I had entered a new and most decisive period of my
evolution, both as artist and as man : the period of *conscious artistic will* to continue on an altogether novel path,
which I had struck with unconscious necessity, and whereon
I now, as man and artist, press on to meet a newer world.*

I have here described the influence that my possession
with the spirit of Music exerted on the choice of my poetic
stuffs, and therewith on their poetic fashioning. I have
next to show the reaction that my poetic procedure, thus
influenced, exercised in turn upon my musical expression
and its form.—This reaction manifested itself chiefly in

* To wit, that ideal condition of society which he still considered realisable
in the near future.—Tr.

two departments : in the *dramatic-musical form* in general, and in the *melody* in particular.

Seeing that, onward from the said turning-point of my artistic course, I was once for all determined by *the stuff*, and by that stuff as seen with the eye of Music : so in its fashioning, I must necessarily pass forward to a gradual but complete upheaval of the traditional *operatic form.* This opera-form was never, of its very nature, a form embracing the whole Drama, but the rather an arbitrary conglomerate of separate smaller forms of song, whose fortuitous concatenation of Arias, Duos, Trios, &c., with Choruses and so-called ensemble-pieces, made out the actual edifice of Opera. In the poetic fashioning of my stuffs, it was henceforth impossible for me to contemplate a filling of these ready-moulded forms, but solely a bringing of the drama's broader Object to the cognisance of the Feeling. In the whole course of the drama I saw no possibility of division or demarcation, other than the Acts in which the place or time, or the Scenes in which the dramatis personæ change. Moreover, the plastic unity of the Mythic Stuff brought with it this advantage, that, in the arrangement of my Scenes, all those minor details, which the modern playwright finds so indispensable for the elucidation of involved historical occurrences, were quite unnecessary, and the whole strength of the portrayal could be concentrated upon a few weighty and decisive moments of development. Upon the working-out of these fewer scenes, in each of which a decisive *stimmung* was to be given its full play, I might linger with an exhaustiveness already reckoned-for in the original draft ; I was not compelled to make shift with mere suggestions, and—for sake of the outward economy—to hasten on from one suggestion to another ; but with needful repose, I could display the simple object in the very last connections required to bring it clearly home to the dramatic understanding. Through this natural attribute of the Stuff, I was not in the least coerced to strain the planning of my scenes into any preconceived conformity with given musical forms, since they dictated of themselves their mode of musical completion. In the ever surer feeling hereof, it thus could no more occur to me to rack with wilful outward canons the musical form that sprang self-bidden from the very nature of these scenes, to break its natural mould by violent grafting-in of conventional slips of operatic song. Thus I by no means set out with the fixed purpose of a deliberate iconoclast (*Formumänderer—* lit: changer of forms) * to destroy, forsooth, the prevailing operatic forms, of Aria, Duet, &c. ; but the omission of these forms followed from the very nature of the Stuff, with whose intelligible presentment to the Feeling through an adequate vehicle, I had alone to do. A mechanical reflex (*unwillkürliches Wissen*) of those traditional forms still influenced me so much in my *Flying Dutchman,* that any attentive investigator will recognise how often there it governed even the arrangement of my scenes ; and only gradually, in *Tannhäuser,* and yet more decisively in *Lohengrin*—accordingly, with a more and more practised knowledge of the nature of my Stuff and the means necessary for its presentment—did I extricate myself from that form-al influence, and more and more definitely rule the Form of portrayal by the requirements and peculiarities of the Stuff and Situation.

This procedure, dictated by the nature of the poetic

* Note to the original edition, of 1852 :—" This bugbear of the generality of musical critics, is the rôle they think necessary to ascribe to me, whenever they pay me the honour of their notice. As they never concern themselves about a *whole,* it is only the *part,* the question of Form, that can become the object of *their* reflection ; and the blame, that in matters of music they should be compelled to ' reflect,' they lay on *me,* for stepping before them with a ' reflected ' music. But herein they make a changeling of me, keeping *only the musician* in view, and confound me with certain actual brain-grubbers of Absolute Music, who—as such—can only exercise their inventive ingenuity on a wilful variation and twisting-about of forms. In their agony lest I should upset the forms that keep our musical hotch-potch steady, they go at last so far, as to see in every new work projected by me an imminent disaster ; and fan themselves into such a fury, that they end by fancying my operas, albeit entirely unknown to the directors, are deluging the German stage. So foolish maketh Fear ! "

subject, exercised a quite specific influence on the *tissue* of my music, as regards the characteristic *combination and ramification of the Thematic Motivs*. Just as the joinery of my individual Scenes excluded every alien and unnecessary detail, and led all interest to the dominant Chief-mood (*vorwaltende Hauptstimmung*), so did the whole building of my drama join itself into one organic unity, whose easily-surveyed members were made-out by those fewer scenes and situations which set the passing mood : no mood (Stimmung) could be permitted to be struck in any one of these scenes, that did not stand in a weighty relation to the moods of all the other scenes, so that the development of the moods from out each other, and the constant obviousness of this development, should establish the unity of the drama in its very mode of expression. Each of these chief moods, in keeping with the nature of the Stuff, must also gain a definite musical expression, which should display itself to the sense of hearing as a definite musical Theme.   Just as, in the progress of the drama, the intended climax of a decisory Chief-mood was only to be reached through a development, continuously present to the Feeling, of the individual moods already roused : so must the musical expression, which directly influences the physical feeling, necessarily take a decisive share in this development to a climax ; and this was brought about, quite of itself, in the shape of a characteristic tissue of principal themes, that spread itself not over *one* scene only (as heretofore in separate operatic ' numbers '), but *over the whole drama*, and that in *intimate connection with the poetic aim*.

The characteristic peculiarity of this thematic method, and its weighty consequences for the emotional understanding of a poetic aim, I have minutely described and vindicated, from the theoretic standpoint, in the third part of my book : *Opera and Drama*.   While referring my readers to that work, I have only, in keeping with the object of the present Communication, to underline the fact that in *this* procedure also, which had never before been systematically extended over the whole drama, I was not prompted by reflection, but solely by practical experience and the nature of my artistic aim. I remember, before I set about the actual working-out of the *Flying Dutchman*, to have drafted first the Ballad of Senta in the second act, and completed both its verse and melody. In this piece, I unconsciously laid the thematic germ of the whole music of the opera: it was the picture *in petto* of the whole drama, such as it stood before my soul; and when I was about to betitle the finished work, I felt strongly tempted to call it a " dramatic ballad." In the eventual composition of the music, the thematic picture, thus evoked, spread itself quite instinctively over the whole drama, as one continuous tissue; I had only, without further initiative, to take the various thematic germs included in the Ballad and develop them to their legitimate conclusions, and I had all the Chief-moods of this poem, quite of themselves, in definite thematic shapes before me. I should have had stubbornly to follow the example of the self-willed opera-composer, had I chosen to invent a fresh motiv for each recurrence of one and the same mood in different scenes; a course whereto I naturally did not feel the smallest inclination, since I had only in my mind the most intelligible portrayal of the subject-matter, and not a mere conglomerate of operatic numbers.

Tannhäuser I treated in a similar fashion, and finally *Lohengrin ;* only that I here had not a finished musical piece before me in advance, such as that Ballad, but from the aspect of the scenes and their organic growth out of one another I first created the picture itself on which the thematic rays should all converge, and then let them fall in changeful play *wherever* necessary for the understanding of the main situations. Moreover my treatment gained a more definite artistic form, especially in *Lohengrin*, through a continual re-modelling of the thematic material to fit the character of the passing situation ; and thus the music won a greater variety of appearance than was the case, for instance, in the *Flying Dutchman*, where the reappearance of a Theme had often the mere character of an absolute Reminiscence—a device that had already been employed, before myself, by other composers.—

I have still to indicate the influence of my general poetic method upon the shaping of my Themes themselves, upon *the Melody*.

From the 'absolute-music' period of my youth, I recall that I had often posed myself the question: How must I set about, to invent thoroughly original Melodies, which should bear a stamp peculiar to myself? The more I approached the period when I based my musical construction upon the poetic Stuff, the more completely vanished this anxiety for a special style of melody, until at last I lost it altogether. In my earlier operas I was purely governed by traditional or modern Melody, whose character I imitated and, from the solicitude just mentioned, merely sought to trick with rhythmic and harmonic artifices, and thus to model in a fashion of my own. I had always, however, a greater leaning to broad and long-spun melodies than to the short, broken and contrapuntal *melismus* proper to Instrumental Chamber-music: in my *Liebesverbot*, indeed, I had openly thrown myself into the arms of the modern Italian *cantilena*. In *Rienzi*, wherever the Stuff itself did not already begin to govern my invention, I was governed by the Franco-Italian Melismus, especially in the form in which it appealed to me from *Spontini's* operas. But the Operatic Melody, as stamped upon the modern ear, lost more and more its influence over me, and at last entirely, when I took in hand the *Flying Dutchman*.

While the putting-off of that outer influence followed chiefly from the nature of the general course I opened with this work, on the other hand I derived a reimbursement for my melody from the spirit of the Folk-song, to which I there approached. Already in that Ballad, I was governed by an instinctive feeling (*unwillkürliches Innehaben*) of the peculiarities of national Folk-melismus; yet more decisively in the Spinning-Chorus, and most of all in the Sailors' Song.

That which most palpably distinguishes the Folk-melody from the modern Italian melismus, is principally its sharp and lively *rhythm*, a family feature from the Folk-dance. Our *absolute* melody loses all popular intelligibility, in exact measure as it departs from this rhythmic quality; and, seeing that the history of modern operatic music is nothing else than that of Absolute Melody,* it seems easy to explain why the newer, especially the French composers and their imitators, have been compelled to turn back to the sheer Dance-melody, and now-a-days the *contredanse*, with its derivatives, inspires the whole of modern Opera-melody. For myself, however, I had now no more to do with *operatic melodies*, but with the most fitting vehicle for my subject of portrayal.   In the *Flying Dutchman*, therefore, I touched indeed the rhythmic melody of the Folk, but only where the Stuff itself brought me at all into contact with the Folk-element, here taking more or less a National form. Wherever I had to give utterance to the emotions of my dramatis personæ, as shown by them in feeling discourse, I was forced to entirely abstain from this rhythmic melody of the Folk : or rather, it could not so much as occur to me, to employ that method of expression ; nay, here the dialogue itself, conformably to the emotional contents, was to be rendered in such a fashion that, *not the melodic Expression, per se, but the expressed Emotion* should rouse the interest of the hearer.   The melody must therefore spring, quite of itself, from out the verse ; in itself, as sheer melody, it could not be permitted to attract attention, but only in so far as it was the most expressive vehicle for an emotion already plainly outlined in the words.   With this strict (*nothwendig*) conception of the melodic element, I now completely left the usual operatic mode of composition ; inasmuch as I no longer tried intentionally for customary melody, or, in a sense, for Melody at all, but absolutely *let it take its rise* from feeling utterance of the words.

* See *Opera and Drama*, Part I.—R. WAGNER.

How very gradually this came about, however, as waned the influence of accustomed operatic melody, will be obvious from a consideration of my music to the *Flying Dutchman*. Here I was still so governed by the wonted Melismus, that I even retained the Cadenza, here and there, in all its nakedness ; and to any one who, on the other hand, must admit that with this *Flying Dutchman* I commenced my new departure in the matter of melody, this may serve as proof with how little premeditation I swerved into that path.—In the further evolution of my melody, however un-deliberately I followed it in *Tannhäuser* and *Lohengrin*, at all events I freed myself more and more definitely from that influence, and that in exact measure as the Emotion expressed *in the verbal phrase* (*Sprach-vers*) alone dictated to me its mode of enhancement by musical expression ; nevertheless, here also, and markedly in *Tannhäuser*, a preoccupation with melodic Form, i.e., the felt necessity of aiming at a *strictly melodic* garment for my dialogue, is still distinctly visible. It is clear to me *now*, that this aim was still thrust upon me by an *imperfection in our modern verse*, in which I could find no *sensible* trace of natural melodic source, or standard of musical expression.

Upon the nature of Modern Verse I have spoken at length, in Part III. of *Opera and Drama ;* here, therefore, I shall only touch upon it in so far as concerns its utter lack of *genuine Rhythm*. The rhythm of Modern Verse is a mere *indoctrination ;* and no one could feel this more plainly, than that composer who fain would take from such verse alone the matter wherewithal to build his melody. In face of this Verse, I saw myself compelled either to dispense with melodic rhythm altogether, or, so soon as from the standpoint of sheer Music I felt a need thereof, to borrow wilfully the rhythmic structure of my melody from just that of absolute Opera-melody, and often artificially to bolster it upon the verse. Thus, whenever the expression of the poetry so gained the upper hand, that I could only justify the melody to my Feeling by appeal thereto, this melody must needs lose almost all rhythmic character, if it were not to bear a forced relation to the verse; and in treating it so, I was infinitely more conscientious and true to my purpose, than when contrariwise I sought to enliven my melody by a capricious rhythm.

I was hereby brought into the most intimate, and eventually fruitful concernment with Verse and *Speech*, wherefrom alone a sound Dramatic melody can gain its vindication. My melody's loss in rhythmic definition, or better: *strikingness*, I now made good by a *harmonic* livening of the expression, such as only a man in *my* situation towards melody could feel a need of. Whereas modern opera-composers had merely sought to make the wonted Opera-melody, in its final utter pauperism and stereotyped immutability, just new and piquant by far-fetched artifices,* the harmonic suppleness (*Beweglichkeit*) that I gave my melody had its mainspring in the feeling of a quite other need. I had now completely given up Traditional Melody, with its want of any prop, or vindication of its rhythmic structure, in the spoken text; in place of that *false* rhythmic garb, I gave my melody a harmonic characterisation, which, with its determinant effect upon the sense of hearing, made it the answering expression of each emotion pictured in the verse. Further, I heightened the individuality of this expression by a more and more symbolic treatment of the *instrumental orchestra*, to which latter I assigned the special office of making plain the harmonic 'motivation' of the melody. This method of procedure, at bottom directed to *dramatic* melody alone, I followed with the most decision in my *Lohengrin*, in which I have thus pursued to its necessary consequences the course struck-out in the *Flying Dutchman.*—One thing alone remained to be discovered, in this quest for artistic Form: namely, a new *rhythmical* enlivenment of the melody, to be won from its justification *by the verse*, by the *speech* itself. This also, I was to attain;

---

* Take for instance the hideously contorted harmonic variations, wherewith folk have sought to make the old and threadbare Rossinian Closing-cadence into something '*à part.*'—R. WAGNER.

and that by no turning back upon my road, but by logical
pursuit of a course whose idiosyncrasy consisted herein :
that I derived my artistic bent, not from the *Form*—as
almost all our modern artists have—but from the poetic
Stuff.—

When I sketched my "*Siegfried*"—for the moment
leaving altogether out of count its form of musical completion—I felt the impossibility, or at least the utter un-
suitability, of carrying-out that poem in modern verse.
With the conception of "Siegfried," I had pressed forward
to where I saw before me the Human Being in the most
natural and blithest fulness of his physical life. No historic
garment more, confined his limbs ; no outwardly-imposed
relation hemmed his movements, which, springing from
the inner fount of Joy-in-life, so bore themselves in face of
all encounter, that error and bewilderment, though nurtured
on the wildest play of passions, might heap themselves
around until they threatened to destroy him, without the
hero checking for a moment, even in the face of death, the
welling outflow of that inner fount ; or ever holding anything the rightful master of himself and his own movements,
but alone the natural outstreaming of his restless fount of
Life. It was "Elsa" who had taught me to unearth this
man : to me, he was the male-embodied spirit of perennial
and sole creative Instinct (*Unwillkür*), of the doer of true
Deeds, of *Manhood* in the utmost fulness of its inborn
strength and proved loveworthiness. Here, in the promptings of this Man, Love's brooding Wish had no more place ;
but bodily lived it there, swelled every vein, and stirred
each muscle of the gladsome being, to all-enthralling practice of its essence.

Just so as this Human Being moved, must his spoken
utterance need to be. Here sufficed no more the merely
thought-out verse, with its hazy, limbless body ; the fantastic
cheat of terminal Rhyme could no longer throw its cloak
of seeming flesh above the total lack of living bony framework, above the viscid cartilage, here stretched capriciously

and there compressed, that verse's hulk still holds within as makeshift. I must have straightway let my "Siegfried" go, could I have dressed it only in such verse. Thus I must needs bethink me of a Speech-melody quite other. And yet, in truth, I had not to bethink, but merely to resolve me; for at the primal mythic spring where I had found the fair young Siegfried-man, I also lit, led by his hand, upon the physically-perfect mode of utterance wherein alone that man could speak his feelings. This was the *alliterative* verse, bending itself in natural and lively rhythm to the actual accents of our speech, yielding itself so readily to every shade of manifold expression,—that *Stabreim** which the Folk itself once sang, when *it* was still both Poet and Myth-Maker.†

Upon the nature of this verse, how it wins its shape from the deep begetting force of *Speech* itself, and how it pours that force again into the female element of Music, to bring forth there the perfect melody of Rhythmic Tone, I have likewise dwelt in the said Part III. of *Opera and Drama ;* and, now that I have shown the discovery of this form-al innovation, too, as being a necessary consequence of my artistic labours, I might perhaps consider the general aim of this Communication reached. Since I cannot as yet lay "Siegfried's Death" before the public, all further reference thereto must needs to me seem objectless, or at any rate

---

* In a footnote to page 132 I have endeavoured to give a slight idea of the meaning of this term.—TR.

† Note to the first German edition :—"A newest critic, having by chance obtained a glimpse of its manuscript, has had the questionable taste to publish his opinion of my poem ' *Siegfried's Tod* ' ; whereas I myself am here careful not to enter closer on the subject of that work, for the very reason that I cannot as yet present it to the public in the fashion I should like. Among other things, this unwarranted critic calls that verse ' old-Frankish rubbish.' Truly he could not have found a better term to characterise the blindness that makes him *there* see nothing but the Old, where we are already living and moving in the wholly *New !* "—The reference is to an unsigned critique in the *Grenzboten*, for the "24th week" of 1851 ; this article is also alluded to, by Wagner, in the footnote to page 308 of the present volume. A reply, by "Bw" (? Hans von Bülow ?), was printed in the *Neue Zeitschrift für Musik* of Oct. 10 and 17, 1851.—TR.

exposed to every kind of mis-understanding. Only in so far as an allusion to my remaining poetic drafts, and the life-moods whence they sprang, seems still to me of some importance for the explanation or vindication of my since-published theoretic writings, do I hold it of any use to continue this narration.

This I shall do—in brief—all the more gladly, since in this Communication, besides the aim I mentioned at the beginning, I have another and a special one: namely, to make my friends so far acquainted with the course of my development right down to the present day, that whenever I shall next come openly before them with a new dramatic work, I may hope to then address myself to folk entirely familiar. For some time past, I have been utterly cut off from this direct artistic intercourse; I could only ad-dress my friends from time to time, and now again, as Essayist. Of the pain this kind of address inflicts upon me, I scarcely need assure those who know me as Artist; they will recognise it in the very style of my literary works, where I must torture myself with circumstantial details to express That which I might show so tersely, easily and trimly in the work of art itself, were only its fitting physical presentment so ready to my hand as is its technical description with the pen on paper. But so hateful to me is the scribblers' art, and the Want that has driven me into their ranks, that I fain would make this Communication my last literary appearance before my friends: wherefore I here take stock of all that, under the prevailing difficulties of my lot, I still think necessary to say, in order to apprise them definitely what they have to expect from my newest dramatic work whenever it shall be set before them in performance; for *that* I wish to then induct to life *without* a Preface.*

I therefore proceed.—

My poem of "Siegfried's Death" I had sketched and

---

* Note to the edition of 1872 :—" This wish, however, was not to be fulfilled."—It should be also remarked that, as noted earlier, the *Communication* originally formed a *preface* to the three Opera-poems.—TR.

executed solely to satisfy my inner promptings, and nowise with the thought of a production on our theatric boards, or with the dramatic means to hand ; which I could not but hold in every respect unsuitable thereto.   Only quite recently has the hope been roused in me, that, under certain favouring conditions, and in due course of time, I may be able to bring this drama before the public ; however, only after those preparations needful to guarantee as far as possible an effective production, shall have come to a happy issue.   This is also the reason why I still keep back the poem.—In those days, in the autumn of 1848, I never dreamt of the possibility of a performance of "Siegfried's Death ; " but merely regarded its technical completion in verse, and some fugitive attempts at its musical composition, as an inner gratification, which I bestowed upon myself at that time of disgust at public affairs, and withdrawal from their contact.—This sad and solitary situation as man and artist, however, could not but be hereby forced all the more painfully upon my consciousness ; and the gnawing torments of that pain I could only quiet by giving rein to my restless impulse towards fresh schemes.   I was burning to write Something that should take the message of my tortured brain, and speak it in a fashion to be understood by present life.   Just as with my "Siegfried," the force of my desire had borne me to the fount of the Eternal Human : so now, when I found this desire cut off by Modern Life from all appeasement, and saw afresh that the sole redemption lay in flight from out this life, in casting-off its claims on me by self-destruction, did I come to the fount of every modern rendering of such a situation—to *Jesus of Nazareth* the Man.

While pondering on the wondrous apparition of this Jesus, I arrived at a judgment particularly resultful for the Artist, inasmuch as I distinguished between the symbolical Christ and *Him* who, thought-of as existing at a certain time and amid definite surroundings, presents so easily embraced an image to our hearts and minds.   When I considered the epoch and the general life-conditions in

which so loving and so love-athirst a soul, as that of Jesus,
unfolded itself, nothing seemed to me more natural than
that this *solitary* One—who, fronted with a materialism
(*Sinnlichkeit*) so honourless, so hollow, and so pitiful as
that of the Roman world, and still more of the world
subjected to the Romans, could not demolish it and build
upon its wrack an order answering to his soul's desire—
should straightway long from out that world, from out the
wider world at large, towards a better land Beyond,—
toward Death. Since I saw the modern world of nowadays a prey to worthlessness akin to that which then
surrounded Jesus, so did I now recognise this longing, in
correspondence with the characteristics of our present state
of things, as in truth deep-rooted in man's sentient nature,
which yearns from out an evil and dishonoured world-of-
sense (*Sinnlichkeit*) towards a nobler reality* that shall
answer to his nature purified. Here Death is but the
moment of despair; it is the act of demolition that we
discharge upon ourselves, since—as solitary units—we can
not discharge it on the evil order of the tyrant world. But
the actual destruction of the outer, visible bonds of that
honourless materialism, is the duty which devolves on *us*,
as the healthy proclamation of a stress turned heretofore
toward self-destruction.—So the thought attracted me, to
present the nature of Jesus—such as it has gained a meaning for *our*, for the consciousness directed to the stir of
Life—in such a fashion that his self-offering should be the
but imperfect utterance of that human instinct which
drives the individual into revolt against a loveless whole,
into a revolt which the altogether Isolated can certainly

---

* *Wahrnehmbarkeit*—literally, 'the qualities that make an object perceptible.' It appears that, by opposing the terms *Sinnlichkeit* and
Wahrnehmbarkeit, our author here seeks to draw a distinction between the
faculties of the lower and the higher senses, and thus between the objects on
which these faculties must be exercised. It is perhaps unnecessary to point
out how intrinsically this passage differs from the views of Feuerbach and his
circle, and how it already foreshadows the transcendentalism of Wagner's later
period, as developed in the *Beethoven* essay, *Religion and Art*, and *Parsifal*.
—Tr.

only seal by self-destruction ; but yet which in this very self-destruction proclaims its own true nature, in that it was not directed to the personal death, but to a disowning of the lovelessness around (*der lieblosen Allgemeinheit*).*

In this sense did I seek to vent my rebellious feelings in the sketch of a drama, "*Jesus of Nazareth.*" Two overpowering objections, however, held me back from filling up the preliminary draft: the one arose from the contradictory nature of the subject-matter, in the guise in which it lies before us ; the other, from the recognised impossibility of bringing this work, either, to a public hearing. The story, such as it has stamped itself once and for all on the mind of the Folk, through religious dogma and popular conception, must be done too grievous a violence, if I fain would give therein my modern reading of its nature ; its popular features must be touched, and altered with a deliberation more philosophic than artistic, in order to insensibly withdraw them from the customary point of view and show them in the light that I had seen them in. Now, even if I had been able to overcome *this*, yet I could not shut my eyes to the fact, that the only thing which could give this subject the meaning I intended, was just our modern life-conditions; and that this meaning could only have a due effect, provided it were set *precisely now* before the Folk, and not *hereafter*, when these same conditions should have been demolished by that very Revolution which at like time—on the shore beyond—should open out the only possibility of publicly producing to the Folk this drama.

For I had already so far come to an agreement with myself, concerning the character of the movement around me, that I deemed we must either remain completely rooted in the Old, or completely bring the New to burst its swathings. A clear glance upon the outer world, freed from all illusions, taught me conclusively that I must altogether give up my *Jesus of Nazareth.* This glance, which, from

---

* It will scarcely fail to be noticed, how much the *artist* was alone concerned in this conception.—R. WAGNER ("The Editor"), 1872.

within my brooding solitude, I cast upon the political world outside, showed me now the near approaching catastrophe, that must inevitably engulf each man who was in earnest for a fundamental change of existing bad conditions, if, even amid such bad conditions, he loved his own existence above all else. In face of the open and shamelessly out-spoken insolence of the outlived Old, which would fain maintain itself at any price, my earlier plans, such as that for a Stage reform, could not but now take for me a childish light. I gave them up, like all besides that had filled me with hope, and thus deceived me as to the true state of affairs. With a foreboding of the unavoidable decision, which, do what I might, must soon confront me also, if only I remained true to my nature and my opinions, I now shunned all drafting of artistic projects; every stroke of the pen that I might have driven, seemed laughable to me now, when I could no longer belie or numb myself with any artistic aspiration. Of a morning I left my chamber with its empty writing-table, and wandered alone in the open, to sun myself in the waking Spring ; and midst its waxing warmth to cast aside all self-seeking wishes that might still have enchained me, with their cheating visions, to a world of conditions from which all my longing was tumultuously urging me forth.

Thus did the Dresden rising come upon me ; a rising which I, with many others, regarded as the beginning of a general upheaval in Germany. After what I have said, who can be so intentionally blind as not to see that I had *there* no longer any choice, where I could only now deter-minately turn my back upon a world to which, in my inmost nature, I had long since ceased to belong ?—

With nothing can I compare the feeling of wellbeing that invaded me—after the first painful impressions had been effaced—when I felt myself free: free from the world of torturing and never-granted wishes, free from the relations in which those wishes had been my sole, my heart-consum-ing sustenance ! When I, the outlawed and proscribed, was bound no more to any lie of any kind; when I had cast behind me every wish and every hope from this now triumphant world, and with unrestrained downrightness could cry aloud and open to it, that I, the Artist, despised it, this world of canting care for Art and Culture, from the bottom of my heart; when I could tell it that in all its life-veins there flowed no single drop of true artistic blood, that it could not draw one breath of human sentiment, breathe out one whiff of human beauty:—then did I, for the first time in my life, feel free from crown to sole, feel hale and blithe in every limb, though I did not even know what hidingplace the morrow might afford me, in which to dare respire the air of heaven.

Like a dark shadow from a long done with, hideous past, did *Paris* once more pass before me; that Paris to which my steps were next guided by the well-meant advice of a friend, who, in this instance, took more thought for my outward fortune than my inward contentment; that Paris which now, on my first re-survey of its mocking features, I put behind me like a midnight spectre, as I fled panting to the fresh Swiss highlands, to shun at least the pestilential breath of modern Babylon.   Here, in the shelter of swift-won sterling friends, I first gathered up my strength to publicly protest against the momentary conquerors of the Revolution, from whom I had to strip at least *that* title of their rulership by which they styled themselves as *Art's* defenders.   Thus did I become once more a Writer, as heretofore in Paris when I cast behind my wishes for Parisian fame, and took arms against the formalism of its ruling art: but now I had to direct my blows against this whole art-system, *in its coherence with the whole politico-social status of the modern world;* and the breath that I must draw herefor, had to be deeper in its draught.

In a shorter essay, *Art and the Revolution,* I devoted myself to unmasking *this coherence,* and did my best to snatch the name of Art from That which nowadays, pro-tected by such title, exploits the misery and baseness of our modern "Public." In a somewhat more detailed treatise, which appeared under the name of *The Art-work of the Future*, I showed the fatal influence of that connexion upon the character of Art herself, and how, in her egoistic parcelling into the modern separate arts, she had become incapable of bringing forth the genuine artwork— the only admissible, because the only *intelligible* and alone capable of holding a purely human content. In my latest literary work, *Opera and Drama*, I then showed, in a preciser handling of the sheer artistic aspect of the matter, how *Opera* had been hitherto mistaken by critics and artists for that artwork in which the seeds, nay even the fruitage of the Artwork of the Future, as I conceived it, had already come to light of day ; and I proved that alone by a complete reversal of the procedure hitherto adopted in Opera, could the artistic Right be done, inasmuch as I based upon my own artistic experiences my demonstration of the logical and only fit relation between the Poet and Musician. With that work, and with the present Communication, I now feel that I have done enough for the impulse which lately made me take the Writer's pen ; for I think I may venture to say, that whoso does not even yet understand me, can never in any circumstances understand me,—because he *will* not.

During this literary period, however, I had never bidden entire farewell to my artistic sketches. Though my eyes were so far open to my general outlook, that I believed the less in a possibility of *now* seeing one of my works produced, as I myself, from personal conviction, had given up all hope of, and therefore all attempt at, successful dealings of any kind with our theatres ; and though I thus no longer cherished inwardly the intention, but rather the utmost disinclination, to make possible the Impossible by fresh endeavours : yet at first there was outward motive in plenty, to place myself at least in a remoter contact with our public art. I had gone completely helpless into exile ; and a possible success in Paris as Opera-composer must needs appear to my friends, and even to myself eventually, the only promise of a lasting guarantee of my existence. Never, in my inner heart, could I conceive the possibility of such a success; and that the less, as even the bare thought of a concernment with Parisian operatic ways revolted me to the core: yet, in face of outer want, and since even my most devoted friends could not view my repugnance to this plan as altogether justified, I at last resigned myself to a final and exhausting war against my nature. However, even here I refused to budge one inch from my path, and I sketched for my Parisian opera-poet the draft for a " *Wieland the Smith*," on lines which my friends already know from the close of *The Art-work of the Future.**

So once again I went to Paris. This was, and will be, the last time that I have ever permitted outward considerations to coerce my inner nature. That coercion weighed so terribly and crushingly upon me, that this while, through the mere burden of its strain, I came nigh to my undoing: an illness, racking all my nerves, attacked me so severely on my arrival in Paris, that even for this cause alone, I was obliged to abandon every step required by my undertaking. My bodily and mental pain grew soon so insupportable, that, driven by one of Life's blind instincts, I was about to seek relief in desperate measures, to break with everything that yet was friendly toward me, to rush out into God knows what wild unknown world. But in this extremity, at which I had arrived, I was grasped by truest friends; with a hand of infinitely tender love, they led my footsteps back. Thanks be to those who know alone of whom I speak!

Yes! I now learnt to know the fullest, noblest, fairest love, the only genuine love; which sets up no conditions, but takes its object altogether as it is, and as it cannot else be, of its very nature. *It* has held me, too, to art!

* This, of course, is the summary given on pages 210-13; the longer "Dramatic Sketch," though written about this time, was not printed until 1872, when it made its appearance in Vol. III. of the *Gesammelte Schriften.*— TR.

Returned, I took up afresh with the thought of completely carrying out the music for "*Siegfried's Death*." Yet still there lurked a half despair in this resolve; for I knew that this music, now, could only have a paper life. That unbearable conviction lamed anew my purpose; and feeling that, in all my endeavours hitherto, I had for the most part been so utterly misunderstood,* I reached back to pen and ink, and wrote my "*Opera and Drama*."—Again, then, was I completely disheartened for the embracing of any artistic project: fresh-gotten proofs of the impossibility of my now addressing any artistic message to the understanding of the public, brought in their train an access of distaste for fresh dramatic labours; and I believed that I must openly avow the End of all my art-creation.—Then rose *one Friend*, and lifted me from out my deepest discontent. Through the most searching and overpowering proof that I did not stand alone, nay, that I was profoundly understood—even by those who else had almost stood the farthest from me—, did he make me anew, and now entirely, an Artist. This wondrous Friend of mine is

FRANZ LISZT.—

I here must touch a little closer on the character of this friendship, since to many it may seem a paradox. I have been unfortunate enough to earn the reputation of being not only on many sides forbidding (*abstossend*), but rightdown malignant (*feindselig*); so that the account of an affectionate relationship becomes, in a certain sense, a pressing need to me.—

I met *Liszt*, for the first time in my life, during my

* Nothing could more thoroughly reveal this—among other matters—to me, than a letter I received from a former friend, a noted composer, in which he adjured me to "leave politics aside, as they brought no good to any one" ("*doch von der Politik zu lassen, bei der im Ganzen doch nichts herauskäme*"). This obstinacy—I know not whether intentional or not—in taking me sheerly as a politician, and studiously passing over the artistic tenour of my already promulgated views, had for me something exasperating.—R. WAGNER.—As may be seen by letter 59 *to Uhlig*, the "former friend" was Ferdinand Hiller. —TR.

earliest stay in Paris ; indeed, not until the second period
of that stay, and at a time when—humiliated and disgusted
—I had given up every hope, nay, all mind for a Paris
success, and was involved in that inward rebellion against
this art-world which I have characterised above. In this
encounter, Liszt came before me as the completest antithesis of my nature and my lot. In that world which I
had longed to tread with lustre, when I yearned from petty
things to grand, Liszt had unconsciously grown up from
tenderest youth, to be its wonder and its charm at a time
when I, already so far repulsed by the lovelessness and
coldness of its contact, could recognise its void and nullity
with all the bitterness of a disillusioned man.   Thus Liszt
was more to me than a mere object of my jealousy.   I had
no opportunity to make him know me in myself and
doings : superficial, therefore, as was the only knowledge
he could gain of me, equally so was the manner of our
interview ; and while this was quite explicable on his part
—to wit, from a man who was daily thronged by the most
kaleidoscopic of affairs—, I, on the other hand, was just
then not in the mood to seek quietly and fairly for the
simplest explanation of a behaviour which, friendly and
obliging in itself, was of all others the kind to ruffle *me*.
Beyond that first time, I visited Liszt no more ; and—in
like manner without my knowing *him*, nay with an utter
disinclination on *my* side, to even the attempt—he remained
for me one of those phenomena that one considers foreign
and hostile to one's nature.

What I repeatedly expressed to others, in this continued
mood, came later to the ears of Liszt, and indeed at the
time when I had so suddenly attracted notice by the
Dresden production of my *Rienzi*. He was concerned at
having been so hastily misunderstood, as he clearly saw
from those expressions, by a man whose acquaintance he
had scarcely made, and whom to know seemed now not
quite unworth the while.—When I now think back to it,
there is to me something exceedingly touching in the
strenuous attempts, renewed with a positive patience, with

which Liszt troubled himself in order to bring me to another opinion of him. As yet he had not heard a note of my works, and therefore there could be no question of any artistic sympathy, in his endeavour to come into closer contact with me. No, it was simply the purely-human wish to put an end to any chance-arisen discord in his relations with another man ; coupled, perhaps, with an infinitely tender misgiving that he might, after all, have really wounded me. Whoso in all our social relations, and especially in the bearing of modern artists to one another, knows the appalling self-seeking and the loveless disregard of others' feelings, as manifested in such intercourse, must be filled with more than astonishment, with the highest admiration, when he hears of personal advances such as those thrust on me by that extraordinary man.

But I was not then in a position to feel as yet the uncommon charm and fascination of these tokens of Liszt's pre-eminently lovable and loving nature : I at first regarded his overtures with a lingering tinge of wonder, to which, doubter that I was, I felt often inclined to give an almost trivial food.—Liszt, however, had attended a performance of *Rienzi*, which he wellnigh had to extort ; and from all the ends of the earth, whithersoever his virtuoso-tour had borne him, I received witness, now from this person, and now from that, of Liszt's restless ardour to impart to others the delight he had experienced in my music, and thus—as I almost prefer to believe—quite unintentionally to set on foot a crusade for me. This happened at a time when, on the other side, it waxed more and more undoubtable to me, that I and my dramatic works would remain without a ghost of external success. But in direct proportion as this utter failure grew more certain, and at the last quite obvious, did Liszt succeed in his personal efforts to found a fostering refuge for my art. He, the favoured guest of Europe's stateliest cities, gave up his royal progresses, and, settling down in modest little Weimar, took up the Musical Conductor's bâton. There did I last meet him, when—uncertain, still, as to the actual nature of the prosecution hanging over me—I halted for a few days on Thuringian soil, in my at last necessitated flight from Germany. On the very day on which I received information that made it more and more indubitable, and at last quite positive, that my person was exposed to the most serious peril, I heard Liszt conduct a rehearsal of my *Tannhäuser*. I was astounded to recognise in him my second self : what I had felt when I conceived this music, he felt when he performed it ; what I had wished to say when I wrote down the notes, he said when he made them sound. Miraculous ! Through the Love of this rarest of all Friends, and at the moment when I became a *homeless* man, I won the true, long yearned for, ever sought amiss, ne'er happed-on *habitation for my art*. Whilst I was banned to wandering afar, the great world-wanderer had cast his anchor on a little spot of earth, to turn it into Home for me. Caring for me everywhere and everywhen, helping ever swiftly and decisively where help was needed, with heart wide opened to my every wish, with love the most devoted for my whole being,—did Liszt become what I had never found before, and in a measure whose fulness we can only then conceive, when it actually surrounds us with its own full compass.—

At the end of my latest stay in Paris, as I lay ill and wretched, gazing brooding into space, my eye fell on the score of my already almost quite forgotten *Lohengrin*. It filled me with a sudden grief, to think that these notes should never ring from off the death-wan paper. Two words I wrote to Liszt. His answer was none other than an announcement of preparations the most sumptuous— for the modest means of Weimar—for *Lohengrin's* production. What men and means could do, was done, to bring the work to understanding there. The only thing that —given the unavoidably halting nature of our present Stage representations—can bring about a needful understanding, the active, willing Fancy of the public, could not, distracted by our modern wont, assert itself at once in helpful strength : mistake and misconception blocked the path of hardly-strived success. What was there to do, to make good the lack, to help on every side to comprehension, and therewith to success ? • Liszt swiftly saw and *did* it : he laid before the public his personal views and feeling of the work, in a fashion unapproached before for convincing eloquence and potent charm. Success rewarded him ; and, crowned with this success, he ran to meet me with the cry : *See ! Thus far have we brought it. Do thou create for us anew a work, that we may bring it farther yet !*

In effect, it was this summons and this challenge, that woke in me the liveliest resolve to set myself to fresh artistic labour. I sketched a poem, and finished it in flying haste ; my hand was already laid to its musical composition. For the production, to be promptly set on foot, I had only *Liszt* in view, together with those of my *friends* whom, after my late experiences, I have learnt to group under the local concept: *Weimar.*—If, then, I have quite recently been forced to change this resolution, in some very essential points, so that in truth it can no longer be carried out in the form in which it had already been publicly announced : the ground hereof lies chiefly in the *character of the poetic Stuff* itself, as to whose only fitting mode of exposition I have but now at last become thoroughly settled in my mind. I think it not unweighty to give my friends, in brief and in conclusion, a communication of my views hereon.

When, at every attempt to take it up in earnest, I was forced to look upon the composition of my " *Siegfried's Death* " as aimless and impossible, provided I held to my definite intention of immediately producing it upon the stage: I was weighted not only by my general knowledge of our present opera-singers' inability to fulfil a task such as I was setting before them in this drama, but in particular by the fear that my poetic purpose (*dichterische Absicht*)— as such—could not be conveyed in all its bearings to the only organ at which I aimed, namely, the Feeling's-understanding, either in the case of our modern, or of any Public whatsoever. To begin with, I had set forth this wide-ranging purpose in a sketch of the Nibelungen-mythos, such as it had become my own poetic property. "*Siegfried's Death*" was, as I now recognise, only the first attempt to bring a most important feature of this myth to dramatic portrayal; in that drama I should have had, involuntarily, to tax myself to *suggest* a host of huge connexions (*Beziehungen*), in order to present a notion of the given feature in its strongest meaning. But these *suggestions*, naturally, could only be inlaid in *epic* form into the drama; and here was the point that filled me with misgiving as to the efficacy of my drama, in its proper sense of a scenic exposition. Tortured by this feeling, I fell upon the plan of carrying out as an independent drama a most attractive portion of the mythos, which in "*Siegfried's Death*" could only have been given in narrative fashion. Yet here again, it was the Stuff itself that so urged me to its dramatic moulding, that it only further needed Liszt's appeal, to call into being, with the swiftness of a lightning-flash, the "*Young Siegfried*," the Winner of the Hoard and Waker of Brünnhilde.

Again, however, I had to go through the same experience with this "*Junge Siegfried*" that had earlier been brought me in the train of "*Siegfried's Tod.*" The richer and completer the means of imparting my purpose, that it offered me, all the more forcibly must I feel that, even with these two dramas, my myth had not as yet entirely passed over into the sensible reality of Drama; but that Connexions of the most vital importance had been left unrealised, and relegated to the reflective and co-ordinating powers of the beholder. That these Connexions, however, in keeping with the unique character of genuine Mythos, were of such a nature that they could proclaim themselves alone *in actual physical situations* (Handlungsmomenten), and thus in 'moments' which can only be intelligibly displayed *in Drama*,—this quality it was, that, so soon as

ever I made its glad discovery, led me to find at last the
final fitting form for the conveyance of my comprehensive
purpose.

With the framework of this form I now may make my
Friends acquainted, as being the substance of the project
to which alone I shall address myself henceforward.

I propose to produce my myth *in three complete dramas,**
preceded by a lengthy *Prelude* (Vorspiel). With these
dramas, however, although each is to constitute a self-
included whole, I have in mind no "Repertory-piece," in
the modern theatrical sense; but, for their performance, I
shall abide by the following plan:—

At a specially-appointed Festival, I propose, some future
time, to produce those three Dramas with their Prelude,
in the course of three days and a fore-evening. The object
of this production I shall consider thoroughly attained, if
I and my artistic comrades, the actual performers, shall
within these four evenings succeed in *artistically conveying
my purpose to the true Emotional* (not the Critical) *Understanding* of spectators who shall have gathered together
expressly to learn it. A further issue is as indifferent to
me, as it cannot but seem superfluous.—

From this plan for the *representation,* every one of my
Friends may now also deduce the nature of my plan for
the poetic and musical *working-out ;* while every one who
approves thereof, will, *for the nonce,* be equally unconcerned
with myself as to the How and When of the public realisation of this plan, since he will at least conceive one item,
namely that with *this* undertaking I have nothing more to
do with our Theatre of *to-day.* Then if my Friends take
firmly up this certainty into themselves, they surely will
end by taking also thought with me : *How and under what
circumstances* a plan, such as that just named, can finally

---

* I shall never write an *Opera* more. As I have no wish to invent an
arbitrary title for my works, I will call them *Dramas,* since hereby will at
least be clearest indicated the standpoint whence the thing I offer should be
accepted.—R. WAGNER.

be carried out ; and thus, perhaps—will there also arise that help of theirs which alone can bring this thing to pass.—

So now I give You time and ease to think it out :—for only *with my Work*, will Ye see me again !

ZURICH, *November* 1851.

APPENDIX.

AUTHOR'S VARIANTS, in the original editions of the works included in this volume; omitting such as either are altogether insignificant, and would have called for no difference in translation, or have already been reproduced in the Footnotes to the text.

Autobiographic Sketch :—

Page 8, last line, after "effect", omitted from the 1871 edition : "in the separate Numbers there was an absence of that free and self-dependent melody in which alone the singer can produce an effect, seeing that he is robbed by the composer, through minutely detailed declamation, of all free agency. A failing common to most Germans who write operas."

Page 12, line 16, "Auber" (original) in place of "Adam,"—evidently a misprint.

Page 14, line 15, "set in train" in place of "seemed prepared to set in train"; line 17, "I should have", for "it seemed to me that I should"; line 21, "sought to", for "wished to",—speaking of Meyerbeer.

Page 15, line 21, after "enthusiasm", "for his art" does not appear in the original article,—referring to Halévy; line 31, after "beauty" the words "and with few exceptions, his music is grimace" are omitted from the reprint, —referring to Berlioz.

Page 17, line 7, "helped where he could" (original) for "desired to help", —speaking of Meyerbeer; line 17, of Heine's version of the Flying Dutchman legend, "a genuinely dramatic invention" for "borrowed from a Dutch play under the same title." The last variant seems to throw some light on the preposterous hypothesis of Heine's derivation of his story from Fitzball, for Wagner wrote the original Autobiographic Sketch only a year or two after his interview with Heine, and when their conversation must have been still fresh in his memory; while the subsequent alteration would be easily accounted for on the supposition that he looked up Heine's *Salon* again, and there found this reference to a "Dutch play."

Page 18, line 8, before "&c., &c." there appeared "'virtuosodom' and 'free composition.'"

Art and Revolution :—

Page 38, line 7 from bottom (also p. 144, l. 10,), "heavenly" for "physical", —an obvious misprint, "*himmlische*" for "*sinnliche*." See LETTERS TO UHLIG pp. 15, 20, 36, 41.

Page 56, line 11, "real" for "worthy", i.e. "*wirklichem*" for "*würdigem*", —see above.

Page 57, line 15, after "weal of all." there appeared "O glorious Jesus ! what grief, to think it was the Poor of Galilee that did not understand thee, but only the Rich of this world, who follow out thy teaching to the letter, and hence uphold the Christian church (*Christenthum*) by might and main !"

Page 60, after the last paragraph appeared the following : "The often lauded, oft contemned *Ideal* is in very truth a no-thing. If in That which we picture to ourselves with the wish of reaching it, there be present as its moving and self-willing force the nature of Man with its genuine impulses, its faculty and bents, then the Ideal is naught else than the actual aim, the unfailing object of our Will ; if the so-called Ideal consist in a purpose, the which to fulfil lies beyond the powers and the bents of Human Nature, then this Ideal is but the utterance of the madness of a diseased imagination (*Gemüth*), not of the healthy human understanding. Such a fit of madness, is that which has hitherto possessed our Art : in verity, the Christian art-Ideal could only proclaim itself as a fixed idea, as the vision of a fever paroxysm ; since it must necessarily set its goal and aim beyond our human nature, and therefore find its end and its negation in that nature. The human Art of the Future, fast-rooting in the ever fresh and verdant soil of hearty Nature, will lift itself aloft to heights undreamt as yet ; for its growth is that which spreads up from below, as the tree's growth from the earth into the air, from the nature of Man into the great spirit of Mankind."

Page 61, lines 6 to 4 from bottom, "or mayhap . . . . functions" are not in the edition of 1849-50.

The Art-work of the Future :—

Dedication of the Original Edition (1850, Otto Wigand, Leipzig).

To LUDWIG FEUERBACH, with grateful esteem.

"To no one but yourself, honoured Sir, can I dedicate this book ; for, in offering it you, I restore to you your own property. Only in so far as that property has become not your own, but that of the *artist*, must I be uncertain how I ought to approach you : whether you would be inclined to receive back from the hand of the artistic man that which you, as philosophic man, have bestowed upon him. The strong desire and deep-felt obligation to at least express to you my thanks for the heart-tonic administered by you to me, have overcome that scruple.

No personal conceit, but a need too great for silencing, has made of me—for a brief period—a writer. In my earliest youth I made poetry and plays ; to one of these plays I longed to write some music : to learn that art, I became a musician. Later I wrote operas, setting my own dramatic poems to music. Musicians by profession, to whose ranks I belonged in virtue of my outer station, ascribed to me poetic talent ; poets by profession allowed currency to my musical faculties. The public I often succeeded in actively arousing : critics by profession always tore me into rags. Thus I derived from myself and my antitheses much food for thought : when I thought aloud, I brought the Philistines upon me, who can only imagine the artist as a dolt, and never as a thinker. By friends I was often begged to publish in type my thoughts on Art and what I wished to see fulfilled therein : I preferred the endeavour to convey my wish by artistic deeds alone. From the circumstance that this my attempt could never quite succeed, I was forced to recognise that it is not the *individual*, but only the *community*, that can bring artistic deeds to actual accomplishment, past any doubting of the senses. The *recognition* of this fact, if *hope* herein is *not* to be entirely abandoned, means as much as : to raise the standard of *revolt* against the whole condition of our present Art and Life. Since the time when I summoned up the necessary courage for this revolt, I also resolved to enter on the field of writing ; a course to which I had already once before been driven by outward want. Literarians by profession, who after the calming of the recent storms are now filling their lungs again with balmy breezes, find it shameless of an opera-poetising musician to go so far out of his way as to invade their own preserves. May they permit me, as an artistic man, to make the attempt to address—by no means them, but—merely *thinking artists*, with whom they have naught in common.

May you, however, honoured Sir, not take it ill of me that, by this dedication, I connect your name with a work that in my own eyes most certainly owes its origin to the impression which your writings have made upon me, yet which may perhaps not meet your views as to how that impression should have been developed. Nevertheless I venture to presume that it will not be quite indifferent to you, to gain a certain proof as to how your thoughts have operated upon an *artist*, and how the latter—as an *artist*—endeavours, in all sincerity of ardour for the cause, to interpret them again to artists, and indeed to no one else. May you attribute to this zeal, which you will be the last to treat with blame, not only whatever may please you, but also whatever may displease you in its expression !

RICHARD WAGNER."

Page 77, line 3, "abstract" (1850 edition) for "deistic."

Page 97, in connection with the top paragraph there stood a footnote: "This cultivated man-consumer is only distinguished from the savage cannibal by a greater daintiness ; inasmuch as he consumes alone the life-sap of his fellow-man, whereas the savage gulps down all the gross accessories. The first, therefore, is able to feast off a goodly number of human victims at one sitting ; while the second, with the best appetite in the world, can hardly get through one."

Page 101, line 2 of second paragraph, "wills to" for "*shall*."

Page 103, line 8, after "corporeal motion", appeared "the movement of motion" (*die Bewegung der Bewegung*).

Page 106, line 11 from bottom, "in public private life", for "in private life".

Page 183, line 16, after "from above." there appeared : "Our art, like our whole culture, bears the same relation to the life of modern Europe, as does their civilisation, imported from outside, to the national character of the Russians. Not only is it, that, beneath the thin veneer of this civilisation, the real Russian remains a barbarian, and for the matter of that, a hideously-enslaved barbarian ; but that any member of the Folk who shares in it, thereby becomes at once the most abandoned rascal, since he only sees therein a school of over-reaching and hypocrisy, in which he also learns his part. But, taken at its best . . ."

Page 186, line 7, "abstract God", for "modernised Jehova!"—A similar substitution of "Jehova" for "God" has been made in that page of the *Ges. Schr.* which corresponds to 255 of *Art and Climate.*

A Communication to my Friends :—

The opening sentence in the edition of 1852 ran as follows : " *The reason that decided me to undertake this present publication of three of my opera-poems lay* in the necessity I felt of explaining the apparent, or real, contradiction offered by the character and form of *these* opera-poems, and of the musical compositions which had sprung therefrom, to the views and principles which I have recently set down at considerable length and *shall presently—perhaps simultaneously with them—lay* before the public under the title of OPERA AND DRAMA."—The italicised words are those that differ from the 1872 edition (as translated on page 269), and are to be explained by the fact that the original *Communication*—as stated in the words : " which I set before the poems as a Preface "—formed an introduction to the poems of the *Flying Dutchman*, *Tannhäuser* and *Lohengrin*, and that the *Communication* and *Opera and Drama* were in the hands of two different publishing firms, J. J. Weber and Breitkopf und Härtel, at the same time. As a matter of fact, *Opera and Drama* was published in November '51 and the *Communication* at the end of the following month.

Page 291, line 17, after " educators.—" appeared " Look ye ! herein lies all Genius ! " (*Seht, hierin liegt alles Genie !*)

Page 294, line 8, after "horizon." appeared : " The timid reserve towards the female sex, that is inculcated into all of us—this ground of all the vices of the modern male generation, and no less of the stunting of Woman's nature (*Verkümmerung des Weibes*)—my natural temperament had only been able to break through by fits and starts, and in isolated utterances of a pert impetuosity (*kecke Heftigkeit*) : a hasty, conscience-stinging snatch of pleasure must form the unrequiting substitute for instinctively-desired delight."

Ibidem, line 15, after "social system" appeared "to wit, as—using a current expression : unfortunately to-be-put-up-with—vice."

Page 306, line 10 from bottom ran as follows : "belong the three dramatic poems which, in this publication, I lay before my friends in the order wherein they arose : namely, besides the just-named *Flying Dutchman*, *Tannhäuser* and *Lohengrin*."

Page 309, line 2 from bottom, " in the *Zeitung für die elegante Welt*, 1843," for "elsewhere."

SUMMARY.

AUTOBIOGRAPHIC SKETCH.

Birth. Deaths of father and step-father. Geyer's prophecy. Schooldays at Dresden. Weber often passes the house. Never learnt to play the piano properly. *Don Giovanni* and its Italian text. Greek, Latin &c. Early poem on death of a schoolfellow. Translation of twelve books of Odyssey and Romeo's monologue. "Shakespeare remained my exemplar." An early tragedy : a "medley of *Hamlet* and *King Lear*"; ghosts of dramatis personæ (4). Moves to Leipzig ; school disappointments. First acquaintance with Beethoven's music and Mozart's *Requiem*. A week's private study of thorough-bass, to provide music for his tragedy ; its difficulties. Resolves to become a musician. Family unearth the tragedy. Composes in silence. Announcement of musical studies meets with opposition from relatives (5). E. A. Hoffmann and mysticism ; visions of ' Key-notes,' ' Thirds ' &c. Musical tutor engaged, who shakes his head. Overtures for full orchestra, one written in three tints of ink ; *fortissimo* big drum every four bars ; performance in Leipzig theatre ; public amusement (6). July-Revolution ; political Overture. Musical career decided on. Goes to Leipzig University, to attend lectures on philosophy and æsthetics. Excesses of student-life; "I speedily came to my senses." Methodic musical study under Theodor Weinlig for six months ; counterpoint. Love for Mozart. Composes a Sonata. Weinlig's verdict : "You have learnt self-dependence." An Overture modelled on Beethoven, performed at Gewandhaus. Writes a Symphony ; "lucidity and force" (7). Journey to Vienna ; Straussian pot-pourris on *Zampa*. Prague ; visits Dionys Weber and Tomatschek ; performance there of his Symphony. Writes libretto, *Die Hochzeit*; composes for it a Sextet that pleases Weinlig; destroys textbook at sister's instigation. Symphony performed at Gewandhaus, Jan. '33. Meets Laube. Wurzburg and brother Albert. Composes *Die Feen* ; excerpts given at a Wurzburg concert (8). Returns to Leipzig; *Feen* shelved by Theatre-director. German composers submerged by foreigners. Schröder-Devrient in Bellini's *Romeo*. Italian "glow" v. German "pedantry" (9). Life and its pleasures ; *Ardinghello* and *Das Junge Europa*. Germany a very tiny portion of this earth. Matter v. mysticism. French and Italian music v. Beethoven. Mendelssohn's smaller form. Fermenting period. Bohemia and *Das Liebesverbot*. Frank physicalism v. puritanical hypocrisy. Music-director at Magdeburg ; singers and the footlights. Composition of *Liebesverbot*. Public success of Overture to *Feen ;* the opera itself forgotten (10). Music for New Year's day, '35 ; its success. *Liebesverbot* completed and hastily produced at Magdeburg ; fiasco, but applauded. " Earnestness of Life," follies, and debts. Offers *Liebesverbot* to Berlin ; hollow promises. Music-director at Königsberg. Marries Minna Planer, autumn 1836. A year lost to art by petty cares.

Overture, *Rule Britannia* (11). Visit to Dresden and first thoughts of *Rienzi*. Music-director at Riga; writes passages for his singers, and libretto for *Die Glückliche Bärenfamilie*. "Music à la Adam." Provincial public and minor theatres; *Rienzi* sketched for a "large" theatre. "Necessity." Rehearses Méhuls *Jacob*, with enthusiasm. Composition of first two acts of *Rienzi;* "no model." Triviality abhorrent. Opera-sketch (*Bianca und Giuseppe*) sent to Scribe. Leaves Riga for Paris (13). Storms at sea; Norwegian coast; sailors' tales of 'Flying Dutchman.' London; Houses of Parliament. Meets Meyerbeer at Boulogne; *Rienzi* shown, and support promised. Paris; Meyerbeer mostly away. Théâtre de la Renaissance accepts *Liebesverbot;* Dumersan's French translation; theatre goes bankrupt. *Faust*-Overture; French ballads; Heine's *Two Grenadiers*. *Rienzi* not for Paris. "Wait five or six years"; bereft of prospects. Habeneck, Halévy, Berlioz. "Renown is everything in Paris." Berlioz "makes no music for gold," and "creator of a brand-new musical system" (15). Rubini disgusts him for Italian music. Paris Grand Opéra "middling," except *mise en scène*. Opéra Comique possesses best talents and ensemble. Earlier French composers v. "quadrille rhythms." Conservatoire concerts stand alone; Beethoven's Ninth Symphony. Friendships with other artists, but not musicians. *Rienzi* continued; destined for Dresden. *Liebesverbot* put aside. Meyerbeer returns; introduction to Pillet, Director of Grand Opéra. *Flying Dutchman* sketch, with Heine's consent, handed to Pillet; "the very thing for" *another* composer (17). Writes for Schlesinger's *Gazette Musicale;* "A Pilgrimage to Beethoven." *Rienzi* completed and sent to Dresden. Instrumental arrangements from popular operas. Goes to Meudon; "warm approach of summer" incites to brain-work. Forced sale of French sketch for *Dutchman* to Pillet; the German poem written—"Had I ceased to be a musician?"—the music composed in seven weeks. Munich and Leipzig consider *Dutchman* unfitted for Germany; "Fool that I was!" Meyerbeer gets it accepted for Berlin. *Rienzi* accepted at Dresden. "Paris had been of the greatest service for Germany." The Rhine! (19).

INTRODUCTION TO ART AND REVOLUTION &c.

Thos Carlyle—"Sham-Teachers; Millennium of Anarchies; Heroic Wise." 1849 and *Art and Revolution*. The ruins of a sham-bred art. The flood of Revolution and the peaceful stream of Manhood. State-wisdom and Philosophy. Literary attacks; the *Communication* and *Music of the Future*. Indiscriminate use of abstract terms. Ludwig Feuerbach and his "farewell to Philosophy." Ideal of Artistic Manhood. Precipitance in philosophical systematising (25). Confusion of meaning in " *Willkür*" and " *Unwillkür*"; Schopenhauer's " *Wille*." *Sinnlichkeit* and *Gedanklichkeit*: Art and Learning (27). Communism and Egoism; Paris *Commune*. The Folk, antique brotherhood, and Manhood of the Future. The French: their materialistic interpretation of many an abstract idea; the German mind. *Artistic* ideal; *Wieland der Schmied*. Germany's predestined place in the Council of the Nations. Hopeful equanimity indispensable to the artist. *Opera and Drama*. Carlyle and the French Revolution. The German nation's veracity; spared by its Reformation from necessity of Revolution (29).

ART AND REVOLUTION.

The artists' outcry against the Revolution : Art has no longer the where-withal to live ! Cruel to refuse our sympathy. The hungering mechanic and Nature's gift of tears. Labouring for Art for its own pure sake. Art as a factor in the life of the State (31).

The Art of ancient Greece. The fair, strong manhood of Freedom : Apollo, fulfiller of the will of Zeus. Greek earnestness and Æschylus. Spartan manliness and beauty. Athenian union of the arts in DRAMA. The Tragedy a feast of the god, the Poet his high-priest (33). The *Prometheus*. Grecian individuality and freedom, jealous of even the hoariest tradition. The great story of Necessity, and the Pythian oracle. Better to be for half a day a Greek in presence of this artwork, than to all eternity an un-Greek god !

Dissolution of Athenian State and downfall of Tragedy. The mad laughter of Aristophanes. Philosophy with her gloomy mien. The fetters of convention. True Art is highest Freedom (35). Roman brutal realism and slavery ; Art could not be its expression. Christianity condemns the senses ; the undeserved Grace of God (37). Jesus teaches love, Paul dogma. Christianity could not bring forth the true and living Art. Art comes from very joy in manhood ; how can pure Spirit bring forth something cognisable to the senses ? (38). The Greek amphitheatre and the Christian cloister. Hypocrisy of the Christian era. Chivalric poetry of the Middle Ages, over-idealised. The Renaissance. The Church decks herself with borrowed plumes of Pagan art. Louis XIV., Corneille and Racine. But Art sells herself to a worse mistress—Commerce (41).

Hermes, the embodied thought of Zeus, v. the Roman Mercury : now the god of Five-per-cent. The English banker and his daughter. The essence of Modern-art is Industry ; its pleasaunce in the theatre ; the efflorescence of corruption ; a faithful mirror of the times, but not genuine *Drama*. Opera a chaos of sensuous impressions, serving only for distraction and amusement (44). The art-hero of our times and the honest journeymen of art. Modern Fame, Gold, and Lies. Greek Tragedy the work of Athens. The street-minstrel commonplaces of Opera. The February-Revolution, Cavaignac and the breadless classes (46).

Public art of the Greeks v. modern ; religion and the police. The Greek his own actor : we *pay* ours. The slave of Industry ; the spirit of modern Christianity embodied in a cotton mill (49). The Greek's simple home and culture of body ; beauty, strength and freedom ; the slave the fateful hinge of the world's destiny. Emperor Constantine ; modern manufacturers. Our god is Gold (51). Art conservative and art revolutionary. Drama the perfect work of art ; its splintering into severed arts. The *Revolution of Mankind* and a nobler Universalism (53).

Not slavish *restoration* of sham Greek art. Universal Journeymanhood v. free Manhood with its World-soul. The load of Culture teaching Nature to thrust it off. Is labour to be the religion of society ? (55). Art to guide the social development. The wisdom of mankind its Heavenly Father. Nature, the brotherhood of man, and conquered Knowledge. Each man will become an artist ; Art's focus in Drama, the glorious Tragedy of Man (58).

Utopia of Christendom, and Art of Future. What has revolted the architect, painter &c. ? That he must make his art a handicraft (61). The Theatre the widest-reaching of Art's institutes ; it must be the business of the Community to place it above commercial speculation ; the public must have *unbought* entrance. Art-institutes will thus herald all others.—Jesus and Apollo the two sublimest teachers of mankind (65).

THE ART-WORK OF THE FUTURE.

I. MAN AND ART IN GENERAL.

1. *Nature, Man and Art.*

Nature works without caprice, and of Necessity. Man's oneness with Nature ; his evolution her conscious-growing ; its activation in Art (71).

2. *Life, Science and Art.*

The path of Science lies from Religion back to Nature ; its end the justification of the Unconscious ; its melting away in Life, and Life's expression embodied in Art. The redemption of the artist (73).

3. *The Folk and Art.*

Theology, Philosophy, and Statecraft ; Intellect's divorce from Life. The vital force the Folk ; the Folk all those *who feel a common Want.* Want will cut short the hell of Luxury ; the brother-kiss the Art-work of the Future (77).

4. *The Folk the force conditioning the Art-work.*

The Harmful = the powerlessness of the Necessary ; the want of the poor hurling fresh fodder to the luxury of the rich. The march of human evolution, from need to satisfaction. The Folk the real inventor of Speech, Religion, and State ; has only to turn the Willed-not to a Non-existing. Art the daughter of the noblest Manhood, of men who are all they *can*, and therefore *should* be (82).

5. *Present Life antagonistic to Art.*

Abstract Thought casting aside the link that binds it to the real, physical man. Is Life then a fantastic maskerade ? Fashion the maddest tyranny ; can but *derive*, and not invent ; its ally the Machine. Mind, yearning for redemption into Art, clutches at outlandish Customs ; Mannerism. The solitary artist sets his hope upon the Manhood of the Future (88).

6. *Standard for the Art-work of the Future.*

Two cardinal moments in man's development, the Generic-national and the un-national Universal. Greek art and universal art ; the racial garment of Religion to be stretched into the universal Religion of the Future (90).

II. ARTISTIC MAN AND ART AS DERIVED DIRECTLY FROM HIM.

1. *Man as his own artistic subject and material.*

To the eye appeals the outer man, the inner to the ear. Gesture, Tone, and Speech. Feelings and their expression, general and particular. The pride of Intellect breaks down in presence of man as a Species and an integral factor in

Nature's whole. Wide Love; the egoist becomes a communist, the art-variety Art (94).

2. *The three varieties of Purely-human Art.*

The sister Muses, Dance, Tone and Poetry; the stately menuet of Art. Art free by Love. The Need of Love man's highest life-need; *Men* higher than man; Giving, not Taking. The limits of human faculty and the boundaries of Art's varieties. All-faculty and Universal art. The absolute egoist (99).

3. *The art of Dance.*

The arts of Tone and Poetry first understandable in that of Dance. The highest subject of Art's message is Man himself. ' *Kunst* '=Can. By Rhythm Dance becomes an art; Rhythm the mind of Dance and skeleton of Tone; Tone's flesh the Word (103). The Lyric artwork and its perfected form in Drama. Dance exalts itself to Mimetic-art. The Tower of Babel. Tone takes away, in Voice, the *key* of Dance's soul; Dance keeps the musical *tool*. Tricked-out figure of Modern Dance, depending on its feet alone. The sole remaining *individual* dance the Folk-dance (107). Christian Civilisation nipping Folk-art in the bud. Modern Pantomime; men who cannot talk since stubborn choice forbids; the unflecked sense of Dance's self-dependence. Yet Dance is yearning for redemption into Drama (110).

4. *The art of Tone.*

Tone is the Heart of man, the medium between Dance's motion and Poetry's thought. Tone is the Ocean, its waters Harmony, its shores are Melody and Rhythm. The steam-tamed crests of Music. Man dives into this sea, there finds the infinity of Nature. Desire must have an 'object'; the Greek hugged the coast, the Christian left the shores of Life (113). The compass cast overboard; Bliss in selfish solitude. Yet each immensity strives for Measure; Columbus-Beethoven. The Word drenched by Christian Harmony. Harmony grows from below upwards, as a range of columns; play of colour, but not of Time; no beginning and no end; answers to no other artistic faculty of man (117). Counterpoint the Mathematics of feeling, the cashbook of a market speculation. Operatic Aria and the Folk-ballad: not the beating heart of the nightingale, but only its warbling throat. The harmonised dance and the folk-tune, in the Symphony (120). Mirth and rhythmic dance-melody in Haydn's symphonies; passionate song in Mozart's; elemental storm and stress in Beethoven's. Harmonic-melody and tone-speech. Instrumental, i.e. Absolute Music can only express either Mirth or *endless* Yearning; emotion but not Deed; it lacks the Moral Will (123). Beethoven: *almost* a moral resolve in C-Minor Sym; shuns that infinite yearning in Pastoral Sym; apotheosis of Dance in A-Major Sym; but seeks for *men*, ships across the ocean and throws out the anchor of the Word, in Ninth Sym; "Rejoice!" This word the redemption of Music into Drama, the human evangel of the Art of the Future (126). This was not the work of a Community, but simply of a richly-gifted Individual; therefore remained shamefully misunderstood; Modern Music seized on its form, but not its spirit (128). The ground lies in Modern Music's divorce from human nature, and in its arbitrary canons. Hypocrisy of modern concert-public. 'Schools' and mannerisms ; Symphony, Opera, Oratorio, and the cataclysmic significance of Ninth Sym. Yet in the artwork of the future Music will surely play no minor rôle (131).

5. *The Poetic Art.*

Stabreim of *Tanz-, Ton-, und Ticht-Kunst:* man, wife and child. The Poet cannot create from Nothing ; needs the whole man. Lyrics of Orpheus and the Folk ; Homer, the *Nibelungenlieder* and the Folk-epos. Art-creating and literary Making ; the car of Thespis (135). The Folk and Deed ; brain-racking speculations of modern dramaturgists. Art thrown upon one side for two millennia. Poetry no longer showed, but only described ; a written dialect ; the female Faust ; aphasia-smitten Thought. The poet's thought a human-outlined cloud (138). Poetry turned to Science and Philosophy ; their redemption in the living Drama ; a common longing to impart and a common receptivity. Shakespeare, the Fellowship of Players, and the Phantasy of the audience ; the mightiest poet of all time, but the Thespis of the Tragedy of the Future. The twin Prometheus', Shakespeare and Beethoven, joining hands with Phidias (141). Arrogance of the Poet ; the rebellious pianoforte. Goethe and the performing poodle. Dramas written for dumb reading, half-dead and half-alive. Folk-lyrics and Literary-drama ; Thought the restless mill-wheel of the Wish ; the bookseller's counter and the theatre (145). The art of the Comedian become an egoistic virtuosity ; the battlefield of the two lions. Yet virtuosity more natural than the self-glorification of the 'abstract' poet ; Italian singers and French actors ; the French dramatic school shows uncommon skill in handling Form. The German dramatist's olla-podrida ; the poet who writes down his palpable poetic incompetence. Poetry longing for dissolution *into* the living Artwork (149).

6. *Whilom attempts at re-uniting the three humanistic arts.*

Man, wife and child : one art-variety must give itself *entirely* to the second, ere it can pass into the third. Catholic music and the *Passion*-music. Oratorio an unnatural abortion ; Tone letting Poetry pile the heap of stones for her selection (151). Opera a mutual compact of the egoism of three sister-arts ; so many quarters-of-an-hour apiece to Dance and Music, and Poetry relegated to the printed textbook (153). Gluck and Mozart ; their noble musical deeds remaining without influence, because the sister-arts had not contributed of their best. When the conditions of Life that allow of modern Comedy, Opera and Pantomime, are upheaved, the Drama of the Future will arise of itself (155).

III. MAN SHAPING ART FROM NATURE'S STUFFS.

1. *Architectural art.*

Man extends his longing for artistic portrayal to surrounding Nature. The Asiatic thralls of Nature adored their bondage ; heaped pomp around their human despot. The Greek conquered Nature, and set Man on its pinnacle ; the God's-grove and -temple, the tragic Theatre ; simple dwelling of the individual.

When bonds of common polity dissolved, the egoist built to Plutus, not Athene ; Asia crushed the heart of Europe (159). Roman luxury and utilitarianism ; causeways and aqueducts ; Nature became a milch-cow and Architecture a milking-pail. Majesty of Roman buildings v. modern botches. Redemption of Architecture in the Artwork of the Future (162).

2. *Art of Sculpture.*

Objectification of nature-forces in the Forms of beast and man. Greece, and the human shape as *nothing* but the likeness of a man : the fatal ridge of Human Art. The religious garment finally cast off, revealing naked-man ; the collective artwork annihilated in the egoism of the unit (166). Sculpture and the beauty of the human body. Spartan comradeship : delight in bodily beauty, crowned by pure and unselfish sympathy. Athens' artists sought to crystallise in stone the monument of Spartan life (169). The Mummy of the Grecian world. Palaces of the Roman rich, and Sculpture sinking to a handicraft. Modern Sculpture playing the barometer to the ugliness of modern life. The Statuary's art must be annulled when actual Life is fair to see ; its redemption, as Mimetic-art, in the Artwork of the Future (173).

3. *The Painter's art.*

Grecian artwork solemnised its aftermath in Painting ; the wilful purpose to fix the vision of the fading scenes of Tragedy. Art evolving its abstract Idea ; Cultured-art (175). Painting soon won a marked advantage over Sculpture, in grouping and Landscape. Landscape-art a movement of highest importance, pointing men back to Nature. The Greek's erroneous conception of Nature, ascribing to her a self-will such as Man's (178). Philosophy, Egoism, and Judæo-oriental theory of Nature's subservience to human Use. Historical Painting flourishing in the Middle Ages ; forced into Landscape by ugliness of modern life. Man changes rôles with Landscape ; victory of Nature over man-degrading Culture. Natural-science and Landscape the only consoling outcome of modern science and art. Painting's redemption in the living Artwork (181).

IV. OUTLINES OF THE ARTWORK OF THE FUTURE.

Culture must grow up from below, not be rained down from above ; our Cultured-art like an orator speaking a strange tongue (183). Plastic-art in union with *artistic* Man, in the collective Artwork. A common urgence of every art to appeal to a common public. Architecture can have no higher task than to frame the future stage ; scenarium and auditorium (185). Scene-painting v. cabinet-pictures ; the artist has no right to pride until he is free, and he and all his tools absorbed into the artwork. Man the organ for all understanding of Nature ; the Dramatic-action ; the Sculptor and Historical-painter pass into the Mime (188). Executant artistic-man : the poet's ' Will ' embodied in the actor's ' Can.' Tone brings, in the Orchestra, the representative of *universal* feeling, to frame the *individual* feeling of the actor ; rightly placed in the " deepened foreground." An atmospheric ring of Art and Nature (191). The changeful dance of the united sister-arts in Drama. The Dramatic Aim dominating all else. One-thing is the soul of every being, its highest need; that of artist-man, to impart himself to others. In Drama he broadens to a universal-human being; the Unit expanded to the essence of the Species.—This purpose of the Drama the only true artistic purpose that ever can be fully *realised* (194).

V. THE ARTIST OF THE FUTURE.

The artist of the Future the Poet: the poet the Performer: the performer the Fellowship of all the artists. The Artwork of the Future an *associate* work, and only an associate demand can call it forth. Dramatic-action a bough from the Tree of Life (197). The last renunciation of his Egoism a man can only show us by his Death, the last fulfilment of his being; the celebration of such a death the noblest thing men can engage in; not by funeral rites, but by artistic reproduction of his deeds, therefore in Drama (199). The Love that leads hereto will always be strongest in one individual performer towards one particular Hero; he determines the *free* voices of the Fellowship to a common enterprise, and *consciously* re-enacts that which the hero did instinctively. But this poet-actor's dictatorship is only temporary, giving place to the like of others (202). Such as this, will be all the other Associations of the Future, in free alliance and under ever fresh specific Laws. Who, then, will be the Artist of the Future?—The Folk (205). Frenzied haste to regulate the Future by given present laws; eternally to-be-rivetted Property, and Five-per-cent; art-Institutes and statutes. No genuine artists because no genuine Men.—"What! the rabble to replace us in art-making?" (207). Filthy dregs of Modern Culture, state- and criminal; the rabble the 'Stuff' from which the perfume is squeezed out. Reign of absolute Egoism. But the Folk is living still, and Want will bring it back the mastery of Life. The Israelites and the Red Sea; the Land of Promise (210). The Wieland Saga.—O sole and glorious Folk, weld thou thy wings! (213).

ART AND CLIMATE.

Reply to criticisms on *Art and Revolution.* Sahara and the Northern ice-steppes; only where Earth's climate breaks up its uniformity into variety, can organic creatures exist. The tropics—Nature a too tender mother; the naked sea-plashed rocks of Attica—Hercules born and suffering amid privations (253). Nature did not *pamper* the Hellenes; vigorous Man and the Purely-human art. Creative faculty lay ever grounded on Man's *independence* of Nature's climate; it faded beneath the Asiatic sensuality of Rome, to make place for the worship of an *abstract* God. Un-Christian to appeal to Nature and Climate. Modern evolution governed not by Climate, but by alien Civilisation and Culture. Each new stock of European races grafted with a cutting from Romandom and Christendom (256). Middle Ages and strife twixt soul and body. Turks chase over to the Occident the last professors of Hellenic art. Renaissance and tombstones of Greek art; our art an abstract notion. Modern art *not* governed by Climate but by History; Pandect-civilisation; Siegfried v. "Gottlieb." Genuine Culture, which shall bear a right relation to Climate and Nature (259). From our history we must gather how the Men of Future will stand twixt Art and Nature. World's history to close of Greek era=the emanation of egoistic Unit-man from Nature; kernel of newer European history=the arising of communistic actuality of *Men.* These men will turn to Nature for *conditions* of their Art, and accent their Individuality in a common aim (262). Creed of Future. Love that issues from undistorted Human Nature, will bear works beside which the mouldering remains of Grecian art shall be as playthings for peevish children. The Universal-human ; Men, not Angels (265).

A COMMUNICATION TO MY FRIENDS.

Its object, to explain apparent contradictions between his operas and his theoretic writings ; to Friends, i.e. those who feel a desire to understand him both as Man and Artist. "Impartial critic's" notion of Friendship. Friend-ship must include Love. The Artist addresses the more or less artistically cultured Feeling, demands to be understood by *that*. The technique of Drama, unlike that of Plastic art, not solely in its maker's hands (271). When the Absolute Critic looks at the Artist he sees as good as no-thing, viz. his own likeness on the mirror of his own vanity. *Friends*, who can sympathise with the artist's aim (273). Æstheticians and their brain-spook of an "Absolute Artwork" ungoverned by time, place, or circumstance. Genuine enjoyment of art only attainable through Feeling ; the true Artwork is to the Monumental as living Man to marble Statue (276). "Universal-human" ; essence of human species consists in diverse Individuality. Annihilation of both Mode and Monumental by appeal to Life. Contents of future Drama strictly emotional ; belong to man's universal-artistic faculty, alike of utterance and reception (278). Seeming paradox in artist of Present outlining artwork of Future ; but its fashioning dependent on Life, and on the Reasonable Will and initiative of Present, no matter *who* may first tread the soil of that life of the Future. Not, however, the professional thinker or theorising critic, but the actual Artist (280). Absence of both adequate dramatic platform and sympathetic audience. *Don Giovanni* and its understanding, then and now. Time, place, surround-ings, and fellow-creating friends (283). His opera-poems and their genesis in point of Time ; tincture of Christian views ; old and new standpoints ; his art-theories ; critics killing two birds with one stone. But Friends must see the *whole* man (285).

Early efforts of an undeveloped individuality. Political v. artistic tempera-ment ; referring outer world solely to oneself, and vice versâ. Impressions from without fill the Artist to an ecstatic excess that calls for unburdening. Masculine and feminine paths of Art ; the Absolute artist, and poetic force (287). "Genius" a vapid term ; artistic-force no mere windfall, but receptivity coming to productivity, the communistic force of countless individuals brought into play by the individual force. Myth of *Wate* and the Norns; "the ne'er-contented mind that ever broods the New" (299). "Life and Art my only, quite anarchic educators." Not a "*Wunderkind*," and no mechanical dexterities drubbed in. Childish impressions, play-acting, and repugnance to going to the theatre. Imitative-impulse, musical and poetic. *Die Feen* modelled on Weber, Beethoven and Marschner ; a characteristic germ in its plot (293). "*Woman* had begun to dawn on my horizon"; *Ardinghello* and the "young-German" school. Frivolous operas. Schröder-Devrient kindles a nobler enthusiasm. *Das Liebesverbot ;* music exercised a prior sway on its subject ; contrasted with *Die Feen* (296). Conducting loose-limbed French operas ; hasty performance of *Liebesverbot ;* modern levity. Marriage and penury. Ambitious thoughts of Paris ; Scribe and draft of *Bianca und Giuseppe*. Bulwer's " Rienzi," and his own plan (298). Riga and a comic libretto. First acquaintance with "Dutchman" legend. *Rienzi*-plans resumed ; the 'stuff,' but looked at through 'opera-glasses.' Leaves Riga ; the "Dutchman" wins a psychic force ; the vision momentarily effaced by Paris (301). *Ignes fatui* of art. *Liebesverbot*, ballads, *Faust-overture*, Boulevard-vaudeville, and cornet-à-pistons. Completion of *Rienzi*, not for Paris. Farewell to the past ; revolution against Modern Art. Necessity and novelettes. Handful of true friends ; Paris ambitions buried (304). Irony and literary-poetry : beating the bundle instead of the beast. Blessed with something higher—Music, the good angel. Cannot conceive Music as aught but Love ; its influence on choice of poetic material. Origin of the opera-poems ; disclaims title "romantic" (306). The "Flying Dutchman" a myth-creation of the Folk, a blend of Ulysses and Ahasuerus, from time of voyages of discovery. The yearning for death ; the Woman of the Future. " From here begins my career as *poet*" (308).

A new path, and deeply-felt Necessity. Weakness in *Dutchman* poem, but its form dictated by 'stuff' alone. *Redeeming*-woman, not Penelope, nor exactly Senta. Home-longing and new-won pride. Preparations for *Rienzi*, and Berlin acceptance of *Dutchman* (311). " Tannhäuser" and the "Sängerkrieg," in their folk form ; Tieck's coquettish mysticism, and Hoffmann's fantastic garb. " Lohengrin " first met with ; a whole new world of poetic stuff at one blow. A mental conflict re History ; the German Home ; *Sarazenin* sketch, passed by for *Tannhäuser*, "the spirit of the Ghibellines through every age" (315). Leaves Paris ; Dresden, Rienzi-rehearsals ; Bohemia and dramatic sketch of *Tannhäuser*. *Bianca und Giuseppe* offered to Reissiger. Goodwill of singers. Fresh illusions. Becomes, "in highest spirits," a Royal Kapellmeister (318). Impatient quest for pleasure and success. Production of *Dutchman* ; its *genre* a disappointment to public. Schröder-Devrient ; never a greater-hearted woman a prey to more trivial conceptions ; her instinctive sense rejects *Sarazenin*, with its " The Prophetess can never more become a *woman*" (321). What the modern world offers to the senses ; the yearning for a nobler element, of pure and endless Love. This the mood, and not an impotently pietistic, in which *Tannhäuser*-drama conceived ; "with this work I penned my death-warrant" (323). Scores returned unopened. *Dutchman* at Cassel, and Spohr's friendly letter. D.'s second act overcoming the Berlin chill ; not a repertoire piece. *Stimmung* and 'shock' (326). "I turned no longer to the stranger Mass, but to a handful of individuals," and thus cast subjects in bolder relief. Completion of *Tannhäuser*, haunting presage of sudden death (328). Bohemian watering-place and sketch of *Meistersinger ;* Hans Sachs the last manifestation of the art-productive Folk ; plot detailed (331).

At like time sketches *Lohengrin*. Mirth, Irony, and Earnestness. Inner kernel untouched by Irony ; revolt and the Tragic mood. Lohengrin not adopted from a husbandry of gathered stores. Repugnance against painted Saints : the Folk-poem of man's yearning (333). Christian legends inherited from ' purely-human ' intuitions of earlier times. Tannhäuser, Van der Decken and Ulysses ; Zeus and Semele, sung by no god, but *man*. Love's Necessity, and longing for utmost physical reality. One primal trait runs through the Sagas of all coast-dwellers (336).

Production of *Tannhäuser ;* a week fraught with burden of a lifetime ; " to secure its understanding." Singer and Actor. A madman addressing the wind : "I now knew what I and the public were to one another." Futile attempts to get *Tannhäuser* produced at Berlin : "too epic," and "arrange some of it for military band " (339). Utter loneliness. Tannhäuser's path from Venusberg to Heaven : Lohengrin's, from dazzling heights to Earth's warm breast ; the woman who should *trust* in him, the human Heart ; there clings the tell-tale halo ; not understood, but only worshipped (341). Lohengrin the type of Tragic in modern life ; Feeling and criticism. New denouement drafted, but laid aside. The category "Christian-Romantic," and a new phenomenon (344). Only the *completion* of *Lohengrin* could demonstrate its meaning. "The subject-matter governed my every choice of form." Utmost clearness of exposition. Elsa and the heart of Woman ; Man's egoism ; "unconscious consciousness." "Woman hitherto un-understood by me, and understood at last ;" the "Spirit of the Folk, for whose redeeming hand, I too was longing" (347). Intimate communion almost solely with one friend.

Sheer solicitude for outward gain dictates promotion of *Rienzi* at Berlin ; a sludge of contradictions ; "an art-crime of my youth" and the reporters ; badly-acted rôle of diplomat (349). Unbridled ironical mirth, and the curb on a man's free heart. A more honest Christian than those who "upbraid me with my lapse from Christianity."—*Art* only left. Busying himself with formation of the organ of Stage-portrayal. The work that lay the closest ; Dresden. Theatrical institutions and their conglomerate Public ; Ennui and monetary speculation ; Opera and a "superfinely-mobbish Philistine " (352). Un-subventioned and Court theatres. The royal Intendant and second-rate speculation. Fruitless efforts to improve affairs. *Complete* reform of Stage needed ; its connexus with whole social system (354).

Politics and juristic Rights ; the inner kernel and a new physical mould. 1848 and its political movements ; his plan for reorganising the Dresden Theatre. Vaterlandsverein speech and its results. Reaction and revolution ; Above and Below ; utter solitude (356). "Siegfried" and "Barbarossa ": Myth and History. German Sagas, primal element of Home, and naked Man. Greek mythos and the human being as creator of 'relations.' "Siegfried" and the *Nibelungenlied*. "Friedrich I." (i.e. Barbarossa) conceived as drama, but abandoned because of mass of historical incidents needing *free* construction (360). History's unsuitedness to Art : *Rienzi* and the *Rothbart ;* the spoken play v. the purely-human subject and its fit dramatic form.— Artistic evolution under influence of Music ; *Feen, Liebesverbot,* and *Rienzi ;* "opera-glasses " (362). *Flying Dutchman* and a new path. "Henceforth I was in the first instance *Poet,* and only in the working-out, again, *Musician."* Music as a mother-tongue ; its enrichment. The matter that the Word-Tone poet has to utter, is *the Purely-human* freed from all historical convention (364). The Message dictated by the *spirit* of the Means of expression; "by the acquirement of facility in musical expression did I become a *poet."* A gradual growth of individual precision. Period of *conscious* artistic Will ; pressing on towards a new world (366). Reaction of his poetical procedure on his musical form. Gradual upheaval of traditional operatic forms, dictated by plastic unity of the Mythic stuff. Chief-moods in individual scenes, and tissue of thematic Motivs spread over whole drama. Senta's song, and *Dutchman* a "dramatic ballad." Thematic picture in *Tannhäuser* and *Lohengrin* (370).

'Absolute-music' period of his youth, and quest for original melodies. *Liebesverbot* and Italian cantilena; *Rienzi* and Franco-Italian melismus. *Dutchman*, folk-melody, and feeling utterance of the words. Not the *melodic* expression, per se, but the expressed *emotion*, should rouse the hearer's interest (372). Influence of operatic form still visible in *Lohengrin;* due to imperfection in our modern Verse. Rhythm of Modern Verse a mere indoc-trination. Harmonic enlivenment; the symbolic Orchestra. New rhythmic enlivenment of Form to be won from the Stuff itself (374). " Siegfried " the male embodiment of creative Instinct; unportrayable in *thought-out* verse and terminal Rhyme; requires a new speech-melody, or rather, the old *Stabreim* of Folk-Sagas.—Regret that all this must be explained in prose, instead of given in the living work of art; "so hateful to me is the scribbler's art " (377).

Public performance of *Siegfried's Tod* not dreamt of, in 1848; only an inner gratification. "Burning to write Something that might take the message of my tortured brain " and convey it to others. *Jesus of Nazareth.* The self-offering of Jesus as a disowning of the lovelessness of the world around Him. The subject abandoned as impossible to bring to public hearing, especially in present life-conditions (380). The near-approaching catastrophe, and shame-less insolence of the outlived Old. Empty writing-table; the waking Spring; Dresden rising. " I had *there* no longer any choice " (381).

Free from the world of never-granted wishes, from the world of canting Culture!—Paris again; "like a dark shadow from a hideous past." Swiss Alps and swift-won friends. Became once more a writer. Object of present group of writings. "Whoso does not even yet understand me, can never—because he *will* not " (383). Artistic sketches not yet quite given up; *Wieland the Smith* for the Grand Opéra! Still once more to Paris; bodily and mental pain; "about to rush out into God-knows-what wild unknown world." Saved by the hand of friendly love. "I believed I must openly avow the End of all my art-creation. Then rose *one Friend*, and lifted me from out my deepest discontent."—FRANZ LISZT (385).

"I have earned the reputation of being forbidding, and even malignant." First meeting with Liszt; neither knew the other's inner man. Wagner's unappreciative remarks come to the ears of Liszt, who, with "an infinitely tender misgiving," seeks to give Wagner "another opinion of him."—Con-trasted with the self-seeking of modern artists' intercourse.—Liszt's lovable and loving nature; he sets on foot a Wagner-crusade, while hardly knowing him; settles in modest little Weimar (387). The "world-wanderer" conducting *Tannhäuser* "as though he were my second self." " I won the yearned-for habitation for my art." *Lohengrin* still on death-wan paper; Liszt brings it to life at Weimar; and writes with "convincing eloquence " his views thereon. "Create for us anew a work!" The "local concept *Weimar* " (389). The Nibelungen-mythos and its huge array of correlated Sagas; most of which could only have been given as narrative, in *Siegfried's Tod. Der junge Sieg-fried* conceived, in order to give dramatic form to one part of this story; but "my myth had not as yet passed over into the sensible reality of Drama." At last, plan of whole *Ring des Nibelungen* conceived, for "a specially-appointed Festival"; to be addressed to the emotional—not critical—Understanding. The How and When of its realisation.—"Time and ease to think it out " (392).

INDEX

In consequence of the large amount of references, I have adopted the following plan of numeration — viz., the cyphers denoting specific tens and hundreds are not repeated, for one and the same *subdivision*, excepting where the indexed numbers run into a fresh line of type ; thus 14, 18, 63, 68, 103, 110, 157, 225, 227, 279 would appear as 14, 8, 63, 8, 103, 10, 57, 225, 7, 79. Economy of space must be my apology for this tax on the reader's attention.— Where the allusion is to a footnote, and so forth, of my own, the reference is given in brackets.—W. A. E.

A.

Above and Below, 143, 83, 255, 7, 263, 340, 56.

Absolute Artist, The, 287, 341 ; Artwork, 274-5 ; Critic, 272 ; Fashion, 281 ; God, 49 ; Harmony, 116 ; Melody, 372, 3 ; Music, 122, 31, 287, 303, 64, 8, 71 ; Playwright, 362 ; Poetry (vi), 140, 4, 6 ; Tonespeech, 126 ; *Vernunft*, xvii.

Abstinence, 58. See Renunciation.

Abstract Ideas, (xi), 35, 147, 75, 95, 257, 60, 82, 366 ; Speculations, xviii, 36, 264, 84, 343 ; Spirit, 38, 142 ; State, 83 ; Thought, 82, 5, 137, 79.

Achilles, 159.

Actors, see Players.

Adam (composer), 12, 393.

Admiration, 317, 9.

Æschylus, 32, 45, 46, 141 ; *Oresteia*, 52 ; *Prometheus*, 34.

Æsthetics, xvi, 7, 274-5, 8, 84, 313, 325, 60.

Agamemnon, 158.

Ahasuerus of the seas, 17, 308.

Alexander, 136, 60. .

Alexandrian poets, 175, 274.

All-faculty, 97.

Alliterative verse, see Stabreim.

Alps, The, 339, 82.

Ambition, Artistic, 12, 297, 9, 300, 302, 4, 18, 81, 6.

America, Discovery of, 128, 79, 307.

Amphitheatre, Greek, 33-4, 47, 158, 165.

Amusement, 44, 8, 351.

Anarchy, 23.

Animals, Dumb, 60, 134.

Antæus, 191.

Anthropomorphism, 70, 157, 63, 77.

Antigone, 342.

Antique, The, 87, 179, 276, 91, 352, 357.

Apel's tragedies, 4.

Aphrodite, 157.

Apollo, 32-3, 65, 157.

Apostles, The, 51.

Applause, 8, 11, 45.

Architect, The, 61, 158, 85.

Architectural art, 156-62, 73, 6, 81, 4.

Architecture, Asiatic, Greek, Medieval, Roman, 158, 60-1.

Ardinghello, Heinse's, 9, 294.

Arias, Duets, &c, 44, 119, 300, 67-68. See Opera.

Aristophanes, 35, 136.

Aristotle, 179.

Arrangements from operas, 18, 303, 311, 39.

Art, xvii, xviii, 45-6, 51, 63, 71, 252-3, 382 ; European, 31, 2, 47, 160, 251, 9 ; Greek, 32, 5, 40, 52, 90, 108, 57, 68, 74, 253, 7, 64, 75 ; Modern, 32, 42, 7, 87, 183, 205, 57, 287, 304, 5, 23 ; Public, 43, 5, 7, 62, 270, 3, 303, 18, 22, 39, 62, 83. See also Folk.

Art and art-varieties, 52, 94, 7-9, 104, 108, 49, 55, 84.

Art and Commerce, 42. See Industry.

Art and Life, xviii, 9, 24, 33-4, 58, 86, 128, 38, 44, 8, 55, 68, 74, 81-3, 195, 275, 8, 80, 7-8, 91, 320, 2, 6, 331, 78, 95.

Art and the State, 31, 63, 354, 82.
Art as a Teacher, 56, 183.
Art, masculine and feminine, 287, 376.
Art of the Future, 60, 71, 119, 26, 394.
Art's Message, 100, 84, 9, 202.
Art's Rebirth, xviii, 46, 53, 82, 7, 181, 95, 257, 61, 75.
Art-Dancer, 119 ; -Institutes, 64, 203, 206, 317, 52-4 ; -Literature, 142 ; -Music, 129 ; -Poetry, 146, 360.
Art-work, The, 24, 35, 48, 69, 73, 100, 48, 276 ; Splintering of, 52-3, 105, 36, 55, 66, 383.
Art-work of the Future, The, 53, 61, 77, 88-90, 126, 48-9, 55, 259, 79, 326, 83.
Artist, The, 24, 30, 206-7, 342, 87, 391, 5.
Artist, Creative, 29, 48, 140, 255, 61, 394 ; Procedure of, xviii, 73, 172, 287, 309, 44.
Artistic Aim, 184, 7, 200, 71-3, 302, 327, 70.
Artistic Development, or Evolution, xviii, 13, 176, 283, 5, 92, 4, 6, 309, 317, 9, 26, 44, 8, 54, 62, 6, 73, 7.
Artistic Faculties, 13, 62, 97, 116, 76, 183-4, 9, 251, 78, 394.
Artistic Illusion, 176, 87, 89.
Artistic Intercourse, 377, 87.
Artistic v. political Temperament, 286-7.
Artistic Portrayal, 101, 56-58. See Drama.
Asiatics, The, 157, 8, 62, 78, 253-4, 255, 61.
Association, 64, 96, 196, 202-4. See Fellowship.
Athene, 159.
Athens and the Athenians, 33, 46, 135-6, 144, 69, 329, 42 ; Dissolution of State, 35, 54, 166. See Art, and Greek.
Attica, 253.
Auber (composer), 12, 16, 393.
Auditorium, The, 158, 85, 352.

B.

Babel, Tower of, 104.
BACH, J. Seb., 131, 50, 284.
Ballad, The, 119. See Folk.
Ballads, His French, 15, 302.
Ballet, The, 106, 12, 51, 2, 300.
Bankers, 42, 51. See Bourse.
Barbarians, The, 50, 169.

Barbarism, Civilised, 47, 56, 9, 97, 160, 256, 395.
(*Barbarossa*, 198). See Friedrich I.
Baths and Gymnasia, 50.
(Bayreuther Taschen-Kalender, 311).
Beat, Rhythmic, 102, 111, 115.
Beauty, Physical, 38, 40, 58, 104, 57, 263 ; and Strength, 50, 6, 7, 65. See Body, and Fair, strong man.
Beauty, Sense of, 15, 84, 157, 60-1, 167, 72-3, 7, (250), 264, 78, 382.
BEETHOVEN, 7, 8, 9, 18, 46, 115, 121-6, 31, 41, 284, 93 ; *Egmont*, 5.
Beethoven's Symphonies, 10, 120, 7, 129, 292 ; in A-major 124 ; C-minor, 123 ; Ninth, 6, 9, 16, 126, 8, 30-1 ; Pastoral 123, 292.
Belief, Ye lack, 131, see 341, 9.
Bellini, 12 ; *Romeo*, 9.
Berlin, 256, 8, 81, 325 ; Theatre, 11, 19, 311, 38, 48.
BERLIOZ, 15, 393.
Bianca und Giuseppe, or *Die Franzosen vor Nizza*, 13, 298, 316, 7.
Bischoff, Prof., (269), 291.
Bodily-man, The, 91, 3, 100, 37, 66, 187.
Body, Culture of, 32, 47, 50, 8 ; Man's fair, 33, 163, 67-9, 71, 3, 263 ; Plastic motion of, 103, 4, 20, 37, 170, 395.
Bohemian baths, 10, 316, 28, 31.
Boieldieu, 16 ; *Dame Blanche*, xvi.
Bonaparte, 314.
Bookseller's counter, The, 143, 45.
Boulevard-theatre, *Vaudeville* for a, 303.
Boulogne-sur-mer, 14.
Boundaries of Art, The, 98, 108, 49-50.
Bourgeoisie, 351. See Philistines.
Bourse, The, 50, 132, 61, 282.
Brain, The, 91, 110. See Heart and Intellect.
Breitkopf und Härtel, 7, (268, 396).
Brilliancy of material, 9, 318.
(Brockhaus' *Conversations-lexikon*, 132, 312).
Brotherhood, 28, 46, 57, 136, 207, 63. See Community, and Fellowship.
"Brünnhilde," (156), 390.
(Bülow, Hans von, 376).
Bulwer's "Rienzi," 11, 298, 362.
Byzantine Empire, The, 178.

C.

Cadenza, 373, 4.

Calypso, 334.
Can and should be, 82, 183, 265. See 341, 84, and Will-and-Can.
Cancan-tunes, French, 131.
Cantilena, Italian, 371.
Caprice, 70, 3, 6, 83, 8, 94, 118, 22, 131, 78, 374. See Willkür.
Care, 57.
Carlyle, Thomas, 23-4, 9, (100, 36).
Castalian spring, 35.
Catholic music, 150. See Harmony, Christian.
Cavaignac, 46.
Chamber music, 371.
Chance, 288, 91, 350.
Change, 87, 116, 203-4, see also 290.
Chaste, 323, 39, 40.
Chief-moods, 369, 70.
Children, Training of, 32, 58, 291.
Chivalric Poetry, 39-40; Conventions, 42.
Choice, 73, 381.
Chorus, Greek, 33; Choruses, 367.
Christian, The, 39, 58, 113-4, 38, 263, 307, 35; Dogma, 38, 49, 55, 9, 74, 380; Dulness, 44; Faith, 114, 62; Legends, 333-4.
Christianity (xi), 167, 256, 60, 350, 393; and Art, 37-40, 108, 255-6, 284, 394.
Church, The, 40, 60, 259. See Roman.
Circe, 334.
Civilisation, Modern, 54, 108, 208, 255, 9.
Civilised corruption, 44. See Barbarism.
Claptrap, 48.
Climate, 89, 182, 251, 54-5.
Climax, 369.
Clothing, Greek, 50.
Coarseness and Grossness, 208.
Columbus, 115, 28.
Comedy and Comedians, 145, 7, 201, 291. See Players.
Comfort and ease, 30, 4, 319.
Comic opera planned, A, 12, 299, 328.
Commerce. See Industry.
Commonplace, 16, 46, 199.
Commonwealth, The, 75, 159. See State.
Commune, Paris, 27, 209.
Communism v. Egoism, 27, 75, 8, 84, 93-4, 9, 146, 59, 67, 97, 201, 60-1, 288. See also Egoism.
Community, The, 64, 166, 394; of Aim, 139, 84, 93, 310, 28; of

Mankind, 57, 60; Spirit of, 35, 127, 92.
Compositions, His early, 5, 6, 7, 8, 292, 96.
Comprehension, 93. See Understanding.
Comrades, Spartan, 167-8.
Conceptual faculty, 82-3. See Thought.
Concert-public, 129.
Connection, or inner coherence, of phenomena, 79, 82, 94, 139, 78, 98, 283, 354, 9, 82, 90.
Connoisseurs and Dilettantists, 182, 208, 75.
Conscience, Guilty, 45.
Conservative and Revolutionary Art, 51-2, 9, 62, 274.
Constantine, Emperor, 51.
Constructive faculty, 327.
Contents, Inner, 147, 332, 46. See Object, and Stuff.
Contradictions, apparent, 269, 78, 283-5, 344, 96.
Conventions, 35, 40, 2, 165, 364.
Corneille, 41.
Cornelius Nepos, 4.
Cornet-à-pistons, 18, 303.
Corporeal-man. See Bodily.
Cotton-mill, 49.
Counterpoint, 7, 118, 20, 9, 371.
Country-life, 123-4.
Cradle of mankind, 252.
Criminal Case, A, 355.
Critics, Art-, xvii, 143, 206, 58, 71-5, 281, 4, 305-6, 26, 40, 2-3, 5, 62, 83, 395; Wagner-, (vii), xvii, 251, 70, 309, 13, 23, 44, 9, 60, 8, 76, 94.
Crusade, Barbarossa's, 359; Liszt's, 387, 9.
Culture, xvi, 54-5, 83, 9, 174, 80, 2-3, 207-8, 52, 5, 9, 382.
Cultured-art, 175, 82, 95, 351.
Customs and costume, Popular, 40, 86, 9, 136, 65.
'Cuts,' 316.

D.

Dance, 32, 3, 168; Art of, 95, 100-110, 1, 20; Apotheosis of, 124; Modern, 106-7, 52, 3; -Tune, 120. See also Pantomime.
Dancer, The, 33, 48, 102, 19, 73, 89. See Body, and Mime.
Death, xv, 58, 96, 116, 98-9, 210, 328, 79; Yearning for, 307-8, 23, 350, 78-80.

Debts, 11. See Financial difficulties.
Deed, 80, 1, 123, 35, 91, 305, 50, 75, 392, 4.
Definition, 92, 165, 97, 276, 316, 5, 328, 46, 64, 5.
Deistic science, 77, 395.
Delphi, 32.
Democracy and Despotism, 39, 41, 158-9, 275, 382.
Desire, 112, 321, 41; Heart's, 113, 121, 260, 357, 78, 9; without an Object, 113-4, 6, 22, 53, 335.
Despair, 379, 84, 5.
Destruction, 355, 79; Self-, 378, 9, 80.
Development, natural, 34, 57. See Evolution.
Devil, The, 308.
Dialogue, xvi, 194, 345, 72, 3, 4.
Dichten and *Verdichten*, 92, 103, 15, 132, 6, 365.
(Dietsch, composer of *Vaisseau Fantôme*, 18).
(Dinger, Dr Hugo, vii, xiv).
Dionysus, 33, 158.
Disillusionment, 302, 37-9, 51, 80-1, 386.
Dodona, 157.
Drama, xviii, 43, 6, 58, 61, 95, 104, 110, 39, 48, 73, 84, 278, 80, 361, 390; of the Future, 155, 94, 6-202, 204, 360; Greek, 33, 47, 52, 90; Universal, 90, 126. See Tragedy.
Dramatic Action, The, 188, 91, 6-9.
Dramatic Aim, 44, 146, 91, 3-4, 360. See Poetic.
Dramatic Portrayal, Art of, 272, 81, 337, 50-1, 6. See Players.
Dramatic Sketches, 4, 8, 10, 12, 292, 298, 300, 13-5, 31, 57, 63, 7, 77, 383, 9.
Dramatic Surprise, 326.
Dramatic Unity, 359, 67, 9.
Dramaturgists, 136.
Drawing-lessons, 3, 292.
Dresden, 3, 11, (304), 316, 55; Kreuzschule, 3; Theatre, 16, 8, 9, 316-8, 36, 8, 51, 4.
Drum-overture, His, 6.
Dumersan (French dramatist), 14.
Dynastic interests, 203.

E.

Ear and Eye, 91, 100, 25, 34, 7, 85. See Hearing.
Earnestness in Art, 296, 324; of Life, 11, 331.

Earth, Mother, 203, 51-2, 61, 5, 341.
East, The, 314.
Ecstasy, 286.
Eddas and Christianity, 256.
Education, xvii, 47, 58, 64, 208, 9, 254, 91, 353.
Effectiveness, 349, 63, 93.
Egoism and the Egoist, 97-9, 114, 42, 145-6, 55, 8, 62, 9, 77, 9, 264, 347; Absolute, 97, 206, 9; Intellectual, 144, 207. See Communism.
Egyptians, The, 157, 62.
Elemental, or nature-forces, 78, 81, 96, 117, 21, 57, 63, 75.
"Elsa," 343, 6-7, 75.
Emotion, 91, 101, 23, 343, 72. See Feeling.
Emotional Contents, 278, 343, 63-5, 372-4.
Emotional-man, 91, 3, 191, 286, 96, 311, 44, 65, 91.
(*Encycl. Brit.*, vi, 132).
End and Endlessness, 117, 22.
English, Studying, 4.
Enjoyment, Artistic, 255, 63, 76, 8.
Ennui, 351-2.
Ensemble, 16; -Pieces, 367.
Enthusiasm, 25, 300, 14, 7, 21, 4.
Entr'acte-music, 151.
Entrance-money, 64, 352.
Envy, 146, 306, 86.
Error, 70, 2, 4.
Eternal-human, 378.
Ethical aim, 42; Man, 123; Satisfaction, 123.
Euripides, 105.
Evolution, 72, 284, 326; Human, 70, 79, 80, 9, 166, 75, 252-6, 60-2, 79; Modern, xvi, 321; Nature's, 69, 79. See Artistic.
Exclusiveness, 78, 98, 109.
Exile, 316, 81, 3, 8.
Experience, Practical, 284, 309, 17-8, 338, 51, 4, 70, 83.
Expression, Artistic, 278, 82. See Musical.

F.

Facial play, 91, 101, 6, 88.
Fair strong Man, 33, 54, 8, 63, 113, 254, 358, 75. See Beauty.
Faith, (xi), 37, 58, 114.
Fame. See Renown.
Fancy, 80, 388; Idle, 88. See Phantasy.
Fashion, 82, 4-7, 119, 44, 7, 62, 72, 9, 208, 81. See Mode.

CPSIA information can be obtained at www.ICGtesting.com
Printed in the USA
LVOW040218181212

312130LV00001B/36/A